Tradition and Change in Administrative Law

Martina Künnecke

Tradition and Change in Administrative Law

An Anglo-German Comparison

Springer

Dr. Martina Künnecke
The University of Hull
Law School
Cottingham Road
Hull HU6 7RX
United Kingdom
m.kunnecke@hull.ac.uk

Library of Congress Control Number: 2006938023

ISBN 978-3-540-48688-6 Springer Berlin Heidelberg New York

Springer is part of Springer Science+Business Media

springer.com

Production: LE-TEX Jelonek, Schmidt & Vöckler GbR, Leipzig
Cover-design: Erich Kirchner, Heidelberg

SPIN 11919414 64/3100YL - 5 4 3 2 1 0 Printed on acid-free paper

To my parents, Ingeborg and Manfred Künnecke

Preface

In writing this book, I benefited from the support of collegues, friends and family.

I would like to thank Professor Patrick Birkinshaw, Professor John Bell, Professor Karl-Peter Sommermann, Andrea Krause, *Richterin am Verwaltungsgericht Koblenz*, and Dr. John Hopkins for valuable comments on earlier drafts. I would also like to thank Zamim Dehghan, Agnes Peter and Laurenzo Arturo for their assistance with research in Germany and the UK. Finally, I am grateful to my family for their encouragement and patience.

The University of Hull, October 2006 Martina Künnecke

Contents

Chapter One Introduction

Administrative legal systems are based on national constitutional legal traditions and cultural values. English judges have for centuries applied the common law. In Germany, judges have developed administrative legal principles for the protection of the individual against state action. However, over the last few decades, administrative legal systems have become less isolated. This is the result of fundamental developments in the European legal landscape and of the increasing complexity of administrative legal problems. In the UK, the constitutional basis for judicial review, principles of judicial control and governmental liability as well as the organisation of the courts are changing. Both the English and the German administrative legal systems are increasingly faced with the question of how to balance the dynamics of change with the preserving forces of tradition. Here, the open attitude of judges and lawmakers in considering solutions offered elsewhere is a remarkable development in a field of law which has long been perceived as too nationally specific. There is a growing need for comparative analysis of these dynamics in administrative law – this book provides a valuable contribution to this field of law.

The most significant factors which have "provoked and lead the emergence of a common law for Europe"[1] are the jurisprudence of the European Court of Justice and the European Court of Human Rights. The European Court of Justice has developed the requirements of equivalence and effectiveness of domestic remedies which seek to "force national courts to view the national remedies under the prism of Community law".[2] In England, for example, the "growing extent and impact of principles of law derived from the ECJ" have recently been described as "the biggest influence in the national legal system".[3] Famously, it has been stated that Community law is a "medium and a catalyst which is starting to contribute to a convergence and approximation of administrative law in Europe and not only in a Community law context".[4] The influence is therefore twofold.[5] As a matter of fact

1 Van Gerven, W., *Ius Commune Casebook Series, Cases, Materials and Text on National, Supranational and International Tort Law*, 1999.

2 Tridimas, T. in Kilpatrick, C., Novitz, T., Skidmore, P. (eds.) *The Future of Remedies in Europe*, 2000, 35 [49].

3 Birkinshaw, P., "European Integration and United Kingdom Constitutional Law" (1997) *European Public Law* 57 [88].

4 Schwarze, J., *European Administrative Law*, revised 1st edition, 2006, 1435; see also van Gerven, W., "Bridging the Gap Between Community and National Law: towards a principle of homogeneity in the field of legal remedies", 32 *CMLR* 679.

5 Birkinshaw, P., *European Public Law*, 2003, 3.

a Europeanisation of some parts of the national legal heritage has already taken place and European law will continue to permeate national law.

It is arguable whether such further Europeanisation of national law is desirable. On the one hand it has been argued that the idea of a single "internal market" requires for its complete realisation a single system for the judicial resolution of disputes.[6] This "market" approach has been criticised for being "a thin argument to set against the deep values of heritage, legal culture and constitutional legitimacy".[7] A harmonisation on a large scale is currently not planned and would be difficult to achieve. It is important to cherish national diversity in legal tradition. However, a deeper understanding of other European legal systems might lead naturally to a dialogue and an exchange of ideas, either between national legal systems or at European level.

The further development of a common law for Europe in the field of judicial review of administrative action and governmental liability which is heavily reliant on the European Court of Justice's case law will benefit most if it draws inspiration from the concepts and principles that are *common* to the legal systems of the member states.

Another factor in the process of change is the awareness that domestic legal systems face such as striking the balance between the protection of human rights and security in the age of terrorism. Common lawyers are increasingly interested in continental jurisdictions: "... in the light of significant recent constitutional changes in this country, I can foresee our lawyers developing a great interest in the public law jurisdiction of courts elsewhere in the continent of Europe".[8] There is an increasing number of judgments by the House of Lords taking note of comparative research in the field of public law including aspects of German law.[9] Some of these developments have been supported by academic publications in the English

---

6 Jolowicz, T., Introduction in Storme, M. (ed.) *Approximation of Judiciary Law in the European Union* (the Storme Report), 1994; De Smith, *Judicial Review of Administrative Action* (1995) 897: "if Community law is to be uniformly applied, if undertakings are to benefit from comparable levels of judicial protection in different member states and if member states themselves are to be subject to comparable burdens, then there should be a more uniform approach to remedies and procedural rules governing the enforcement of Community rights".

7 Harlow, C., *Convergence and Divergence in European Public Law*, 2002, 224.

8 Lord Goff of Chieveley, "Coming Together – the Future", Clifford Chance Millennium Lectures, in Markesinis, B. (ed.) *The Coming Together of the Common Law and the Civil Law,* 2000, 249.

9 *JD (FC) v East Berkshire Community Health NHS Trust and others, Two Other Actions (FC)* 2005 WL 881875, [2005] UKHL 23, on appeal from [2003] EWCA Civ 1151, HL; *Fairchild v Glenhaven Funeral Services Ltd (t/a GH Dovener & Son)* [2002] UKHL 22; *R (Prolife Alliance) v BBC* [2004] 1 AC 185, [2002] EWCA Civ 297, [2003] UKHL 23, [2003] 2 WLR 1403, HL; *R v Ministry for Agriculture, Fisheries and Food, ex p Hamble* [1995] 2 All ER 714 at 729; for a further discussion of this case, see Chapter Three, "The principle of legitimate expectation in English administrative law".

language.[10] This trend to consider laws and institutional organisations outside one's own jurisdiction is also reflected in the legislative[11] and political processes.[12]

In Germany, where law is perceived as a scientific discipline (*Rechtswissenschaften*), English public law is of great academic interest and, as is well-known, groundbreaking comparative research cutting across the civil/common law divide in administrative law has been carried out by Professor Jürgen Schwarze.[13] English public law is seen as "extremely interesting"[14] and "providing an elucidating contrast" to German law.[15]

Comparative research into the administrative legal systems of two of the largest member states may also be of interest to the new or applicant member states. It may be of assistance in the process of institution building, providing baselines set by good European practice.

The aim of this book is to analyse by way of highlights some main strands in the English and German approaches to judicial control in administrative law. It is concerned with an understanding of the variations in the approaches taken and the complexity of the historical and constitutional backgrounds in which both systems are embedded. It seeks to identify to which extent national legal traditions produce what has been termed "path dependencies",[16] i.e. certain forms of conduct which are preset by national characteristics. Others have referred to the significance of history as "established ways of working"[17] "which might well constitute barriers

---

10 Markesinis, B., Auby, J.B., Coester-Waltjen, D. and Deakin, S.F., *Tortious Liability of Statutory Bodies, A Comparative and Economic Analysis of Five English Cases* 1999; Duncan Fairgrieve and Sarah Green, *Child Abuse Tort Claims Against Public Bodies, A Comparative Law View*, 2004.

11 A Department for Constitutional Affairs Consultation Paper "Constitutional Reform: A Supreme Court for the United Kingdom", July 2003, CP 11/03 2003. An example is the consultation process leading up to the Constitutional Reform Act 2005 establishing a Supreme Court for the United Kingdom. Here, the function of the German Federal Constitutional Court was discussed; see also Sir Andrew Leggat's report "Tribunals for Users – One System, Once Service", August 2001, in which he recommended the commissioning of research into the operation of administrative justice both in the UK and abroad.

12 David Cameron's speech on the establishment of a written bill of rights for the UK in which he refers to the German constitutional model, 26 June 2006, http://www. conservatives.com/tile.do?def=news.story.page&obj_id=130572&speeches=1. The Attorney-General Lord Goldsmith suggested a written constitution, *The Guardian*, 9. October 2006.

13 Schwarze, J., *Die gerichtliche Kontrolle der Verwaltung in England, Die Öffentliche Verwaltung*, 1998, 771; *European Administrative Law*, 2006.

14 Middeke, A., on Jochen Frowein, *Die Kontrolldichte bei der gerichtlichen Überprüfung von Handlungen der Verwaltung,* 1993, (1996) DVBl 527.

15 Brinktrine, R., *Verwaltungsermessen in Deutschland und England*, 1998, 3.

16 Großfeld, B. ,"Comparatist and language" in Legrand, A., Munday, R., *Comparative Legal Studies: Tradition and Transitions* 2006, 177.

17 David, R., *International Encyclopaedia of Comparative Law*, vol. 2, Chapter 5, 1970 cited in Bell, J., Public Law in Europe: Caught between the National, the Sub-National and the European, *Epistemology and Methodology of Comparative Law,* 2004, 265.

to convergence of legal systems".[18] A comparison of these two great legal systems is therefore significant because of the contrast in approaches taken. At the beginning of the last century it was remarked that the continental traditions of public law are "so complete an antithesis to the development of the law and constitution of England [that] the true meaning and effect ... of the latter are best shown through this antithesis".[19] It is therefore designed as an analysis of national solutions in England and Germany which may offer alternative arguments from outside one's own jurisdiction.

The comparative method in the field of public law

The comparability of administrative law has been questioned because of its extremely national character. Nevertheless first roots of comparative administrative law can be found at the end of the last century, including the work of Albert V. Dicey and his basic introduction to English constitutional law, Otto Mayer with his development of German administrative law and Edouard Lafferière, one of the founders of French administrative law. However, comparative administrative law then was mainly used to develop one's own doctrine of administrative law by investigating more developed administrative law systems.[20]

The method of comparative law has been used by legislators for their own law making by and for the international unification of law.[21] Legislative comparative law was successfully used in drafting the German Civil Code, which unified the private law of Germany from 1 January 1900. The preparation of the Code involved the careful consideration of the solutions accepted in all the systems then in force in various parts of Germany. These included the *Gemeines Recht*, Prussian law and the French Civil Code, which was in force in the Rhineland.[22] The need for national unification of the law inspired a medieval French jurist, Coquille (1523–1603), to write a commentary on the French customary law, the *Coutumes* of the County of Nevers, and an *Institution au droit français*, by using the comparative method in order to harmonise the various customs of medieval French law: "the very task which comparative law still has to perform today, with the difference that it is no longer the customs of localities but the legal systems of nations which have to be assimilated and harmonised".[23]

---

18 Bell, J., ibid.

19 Redlich, J. and Hirst, F.W., *Local Government in England*, 1903, 376–377 cited in Thomas, R., *Legitimate Expectations and Proportionality in Administrative Law*, 2000, 16.

20 Schwarze, J., *European Administrative Law*, 2006, 91.

21 van Gerven, W., "Bridging the Unbridgeable: Community and National Tort Laws after Francovich and Brasserie" (1996) 45 *International and Comparative Law Quarterly* 507.

22 Zweigert, K., Kötz, H., *An Introduction to Comparative Law*, 1987, 51.

23 Ibid 80.

Comparative law has developed from a purely academic discipline to a practical tool in the further development of a common law for Europe. As a result of the goals set in the Treaty establishing the European Community, the comparative law research method has gained momentum. As Legrand puts it, "there is now ... a prominent role for the comparatist to play – a role which is actually so meaningful that her work can help determine whether or not there will, one day, arise a common law of Europe with the obvious implications that can be imagined for every European citizen".[24] There is more awareness that comparative methods may lead the lawyer somewhere and that comparative materials may be a source of inspiration for legal decisions, "whether by legislative bodies or by the courts".[25]

In the field of administrative law, the European Treaties do not provide for legislative competences for harmonisation. The role of comparative law research in the field of administrative law is therefore less obvious than in the case of harmonisation of private law. Traditionally, comparative law is concerned with the comparison of private law.[26] The necessity of comparing national private law systems stems from the need to harmonise existing systems in order to facilitate the legal implications of the exchange of goods and services in the common market. The majority of recent articles on comparative legal issues are therefore concerned with the harmonisation of European private law.[27]

Today the role which comparative law in the field of remedies against public bodies plays in the European Community finds a clear expression in the often-quoted Art. 288, para 2 of the EEC Treaty:

"In the case of non-contractual liability, the Community shall, in accordance with the general principles common to the laws of the member states, make good any damage caused by its institutions or by its servants in the performance of their duties".

---

24 Legrand, P., "How to Compare" (1996) *Legal Studies* 232 [233].

25 See the cases mentioned above; Koopman, T., "Comparative Law and the Courts" (1996) 45 *International and Comparative Law Quarterly* 545.

26 Zweigert, K., Kötz, H., *An Introduction to Comparative Law*, 1987; Markesinis, B., *The German Law of Tort*; de Cruz, P., *Comparative Law in a Changing World,* 1995.

27 Armbrüster, C., "Braucht Europa ein umfassende Privatrechtskdifikation? Vortragsbericht Juristische Gesellschaft zu Berlin" (1998) *JR* 98; Basedow, J., "Un droit commun des contrats pour le Marché commun" (1998) *RIDC* 7; Coester-Waltjen, D., ZR: "Europäisierung des Privatrechts" (1998) *Jura* 320; Jayne, E., "Entwurf eines EU-Übereinkommens über das auf außervertragliche Schuldverhältnisse anzuwendende Recht – Tagung der Europäischen Gruppe für Internationales Privatrecht in Den Haag (998) *IPRax* 140; "Angleichung der Rechtsvorschriften der Mitgliedstaaten über die Kraftfahrzeug-haftpflichtversicherung" 13.10.1997, EWS 1998, 19; Editorial Comment, "On the Way to a European Consumer Sales Law?" (1997) 334 *CMLR* 207; Editorial, "European Private Law Between Utopia and Early Reality" (1997) *MJ* 1; Lando, O., "European Contract Law After the Year 2000" (1998) *CMLR* 821; Gamerith, H., "Das nationale Privatrecht in der Europäischen Union – Harmonisierung durch Schaffung von Gemeinschaftsprivatrecht" (1997) *ÖJZ* 165; Legrand, P., "Against a European Civil Code" (1997) *MLR* 44; Micklitz, H.W., "Ein einheitliches Kaufrecht für die Verbraucher in der EG?" (1997) *EuZW* 229; Van den Bergh, R., "Subsidiarity as an Economic Demarcation Principle and the Emergence of European Private Law" (1998) *MJ* 129.

This provision not only recognises that there *are* general principles common to the laws of the member states, but also that these principles are a source of Community law. The well-known principles of proportionality, equal protection, legal certainty, protection of legitimate expectation, etc. have been the product of the European Court of Justice's active role in further developing these two considerations in other branches of law. Here the European Court of Justice relied on Art. 220 (ex Art. 164) that it shall ensure that in the interpretation and application of the Treaty "the law is observed". In *Van Gend en Loos* the court held that Art. 220 (ex Art. 164) must mean that Community rules and the decisions, directives and regulations of Community institutions must respect general principles of law such as are common to the legal traditions of the member states.[28] Jürgen Schwarze's work on European administrative law has been groundbreaking and inspiring.[29] The focus of this book, however, remains on a detailed historical and comparative analysis of two national administrative legal traditions placing particular emphasis on judicial control of the administration and governmental liability.

Apart from disagreement amongst writers using the same language about the existence and extent of a convergence of the administrative legal systems in Europe, there remains a lack of "communication" between those writing in different languages. For example, "the continental writers find themselves ignored by those writing in the imperial language".[30] With regard to the *Francovich* decision,[31] it has been said that "each national group of scholars has examined the implications of the judgment for their own national legal order while ignoring its reception elsewhere".[32] In order to ensure an effective implementation of the Community concept it is necessary to investigate other member states' legal systems.

The significance of a comparison of the administrative legal systems of England and Germany is based on the need for reconciling the "common law" with the "civil law". This "gulf" between common law and civil law, as described by Cappeletti, has occupied many comparative lawyers.[33] The convergence of civil law and common law has been a long-term topic of discussion among comparative lawyers and has created its own "miniature Babel of terminology". Terms such as unification, harmonisation, *Angleichung* and approximation can be found in the increasing number of publications in this field.[34]

One difficulty of comparative legal analysis is that of legal concepts and their translation. The danger of translating concepts lies in the fact that the culture of the chosen language associates other or no underlying meanings to a word. Pierre Legrand in his article "The Impossibility of "Legal Transplants"" describes it like

28 *Van Gend en Loos*, C-26/62 [1963] ECR 12.

29 *European Administrative Law,* 2006.

30 "The Convergence Debate", Editorial (1996) 3 *Maastricht Journal of European and Comparative Law* 105 [106].

31 *Francovich and Bonifaci v Italy* [1991] C-6 9/90, ECR I-5357.

32 "The Convergence Debate", n. 30 at 106.

33 Cappelletti, M., *New Perspectives for a Common Law of Europe*, 1978.

34 Merryman, J.H., "Convergence of Civil Law and Common Law" in Cappelletti, M., *New Perspectives for a Common Law of Europe*, 1978, 195 [196–197]; Storme, M., *Approximation of Judiciary Law in the European Union*, 1994.

this: "... as the words cross boundaries there intervenes a different rationality and morality to underwrite and effectuate the borrowed words: the host culture continues to articulate its moral inquiry according to traditional standards of justification". Thus, the imported form of words is inevitably ascribed a different, local meaning which makes it *ipso facto* a different rule. As Benjamin wrote, "the word *Brot* means something different to a German than the word *pain* to a Frenchman"[35] or *bread* to an Englishman. In more legalistic terms, "discretion", for instance, is a term which in German law is heavily connotated by legal doctrine. As we will see, a more neutral term "area free of judicial control" has been chosen to tackle this problem. "Care must be taken to ensure that the substantive problem is formulated in terms which are wherever possible free from the specific doctrinal conceptions of the legal order in which it occurs. Only thus is it possible to recognise a rule to be found in a foreign legal order which, as a matter of doctrine, may be differently formulated or situated as a functionally equal solution."[36] The functional method has been criticised, however, for "stripping the law of all that is interesting".[37] Further, "contemporary criticism of the functional method insists on the complexity of the "law" as a phenomenon while, at the same time, stressing the importance of doing justice to such complexity when comparing laws".[38] This is particularly true when comparing administrative law because "administrative law is a combination of what is going on in the political world, combined with the reactions of the judiciary".[39]

It has been noted that administrative law traditions are more "nationally specific" than private law traditions.[40] The explanations for the structure of any one country owe as much to history and chance as they do to any deep-seated rationale.[41] It is crucial that in the field of administrative law the comparison is not restricted to rules and principles but that both the historical perspective and the constitutional context in which a legal system operates is embraced in that comparison. The origins of the administrative law traditions in both jurisdictions and the role of the courts are crucial in understanding its place in modern society. Allison has illustrated the importance of such an historical perspective even though his conclusions appear to deny the potential for change in modern English society.[42]

---

35 Legrand, P., "The Impossibility of "Legal Transplants"" (1997) 4 *Maastricht Journal of European and Comparative Law* 111 [117].

36 Schwarze, J., *European Administrative Law*, 2006, 82.

37 Graziadei, M., "The Functionalist Heritage" in Legrand, P.,Munday, R., *Comparative Legal Studies: Traditions and Transitions*, 125.

38 Ibid 114.

39 Craig, P., *Administrative Law*, 2003, 4.

40 Bell, J. in Beatson, J., Tridimas, T., *New Directions in European Public Law*, 1998, 167.

41 Ibid 166.

42 Allison, J.W.F., *A Continental Distinction in the Common Law, A Historical and Comparative Perspective in English Public Law,* 2000.

Administrative law has been referred to as "constitutional law in action"[43] and similarlyin the German legal world as "concretised constitutional law".[44] Therefore the constitutional basis for judicial review and the main constitutional concepts are essential components of a comparative study in the field of judicial review.

Further, differences in legal style and the sources of law can cause obstacles in legal comparison. The German law of judicial review and the tortious liability of public bodies, for instance, are codified in the Law on Administrative Court Procedure 1960, the Civil Code and in a constitutional provision respectively. Even though many of the codified principles are directly based on previous case law by the administrative courts, for example, the principle of substantive legitimate expectation or the most recent changes concerning the permission of in-trial curing of procedural defects (Art. 114 sentence 2 of the Law on Administrative Court Procedure 1960), case law does not play quite the same role as it does in the English administrative law tradition. Due to increased activity of the legislature to regulate judicial review it has become a highly systematised subject. Further, it is a subject concerned with complex theoretical concepts such as the unique distinction between discretionary concepts and undefined legal concepts which will be explained in detail in Chapter Three. As we will see the expansion of judicial review of administrative actions in England has been due to the active role taken on by the courts in increasingly developing the available grounds of review. However, this development has not resulted in the desire to codify and systematise the principles, neither has the incremental development of judicial supervision been accompanied by a highly theoretical approach. The reasons for this are deeply rooted in the different legal traditions and their legal reasoning.

To facilitate access to some of the detailed German law provisions and provide a clearer basis for comparison German case law examples have been chosen.

In the following chapters, four broad themes will be covered: an historical introduction to the development of administrative justice mapping out the constitutional and institutional framework , substantive judicial review, the review of procedural errors and governmental liability.

The comparison of these two administrative legal systems has been a complex and challenging undertaking and there may be many gaps to be filled in by future researchers. Despite the difficulties to be encountered, "public lawyers should not give up the struggle to make their design relevant to different times and places ... In a world of densely competing claims for cultural recognition, in which the circuits of economic power and their social ramifications extend well beyond the state, and in which, in consequence, multilevel governance is already deeply embedded, there is simply no other option".[45] As it is, practising lawyers who present

43 Mentioned by Birkinshaw, P., "European Integration and United Kingdom Constitutional Law" in Andenas, M., *English Public Law and the Common Law of Europe*, 1998.

44 Werner, F., "Verwaltungsrecht als konkretisiertes Verfassungsrecht", *DVBl* 1959, 527.

45 Walker, N., "Culture, Democracy and the Convergence of Public Law: Scepticisms" in *Convergence and Divergence in European Public Law*, 2002, 271.

arguments in court containing solutions offered in foreign jurisdictions, legal education and training of lawyers in foreign law should not be underestimated. It is hoped that comparative legal research can make a contribution.

Chapter Two The development of judicial review of administrative action

I. Historical introduction

1. The common law courts

The most striking difference between the common law and civil law system is the absence within the common law system of any separate administrative courts as they developed in Germany in the nineteenth century.[1] This institutional difference is closely linked to the lack of a clear substantive distinction between matters regarded as public law and those regarded as private law. On the contrary, the English approach to a systematisation of judicial review was based on a remedial approach, as applied to the prerogative writs. Since the thirteenth century, the common law and the courts had achieved a central legal system for England. The judges either sat in London or travelled to the localities away from the centre.[2] The writ system was a procedure of channelling individual complaints into a pre-existing system of orders from the King directed to the person who had injured the individual.[3] The writ originated in a personal request by an individual to the King to remedy a wrong suffered by another individual. They were sealed governmental documents by which the King conveyed notifications or orders.[4] These forms of personal requests developed into a set of standardised writs. Aggrieved subjects had to try and fit their complaints into one of the existing writs and submit them through the chancellor to the King. Some remains of this remedial system have survived many centuries until today. As we shall see in Chapter Four, until today claimants have to fit their claims into existing heads of tort in order to obtain compensation, for instance, for unlawful administrative action.[5] The old public law remedies of *certiorari*, *mandamus*, *prohibition* and *habeas corpus* were also called the "prerogative writs". This term stems from seventeenth century Royalist judges who encouraged the association of the remedy of *habeas corpus* with the

---

1 De Smith, S.A., *Judicial Review of Administrative Action*, 1995, 156.

2 Van Caenegem, R.C., *The Birth of the English Legal System*, 1973, 29.

3 Shapiro, M., *Courts, A Comparative and Political Analysis*, 1981, 80.

4 De Smith, S.A., *Judicial Review of Administrative Action*, 1995, 617.

5 This remedial conception has caused confusion in the context of human rights violations under Art. 6(1) in the case of *Osman v UK* (see Chapter Five).

King's beneficence.[6] *Certiorari* instructs the person or body whose decision is challenged to deliver the record of the decision to the Office of the Queen's Bench Division to be quashed. *Mandamus*, which dates back to the sixteenth century, is designed to enforce the performance by governmental bodies of their duties owed to the public.[7] *Prohibition* orders a body to refrain from illegal action. The writs of *habeas corpus* were designed to order the appearance of a person before one of the King's courts to attend judicial proceedings.[8] The writ of *certiorari* was important in controlling the decisions of inferior tribunals. The origins of the writ of *certiorari* which has been developed over centuries and which is now known under the name-quashing order dates back to the thirteenth and fourteenth century.[9] These ancestors of the writ of *certiorari* were called writs of error used to correct errors in the lower courts.

In the seventeenth century, the writ of *certiorari* developed into an order to quash administrative orders in the King's Bench beginning with the formulation: "wishing for certain reasons to be informed about a certain order, *volentes certis causis quendam ordinem de ... certiorari*".[10] *Certiorari* was therefore a writ whereby the King asked to be informed of a matter. If he did not agree with the matter at stake he would quash it. Until today the cases are reported as *R v X, ex p Y* – the King or Queen against X on the application of Y. This development was "inherently complex". De Smith summarises the main purposes served by *certiorari* between the fourteenth and middle of the seventeenth century as *inter alia*:

"To supervise the proceedings of inferior courts, for example the Commissioners of Sewers, to obtain information for administrative purposes, to bring into the Chancery or before the common law courts judicial records and other formal documents for a wide diversity of purposes".[11]

The first case in which it was certain that the writ of *certiorari* was applied is the case of *R v Commissioners of Sewers of Yorkshire* dating back to 1641. Accordingly, "all the indictments ... along with all the orders, fines and amercements presented against Thomas Stephenson before you, ""to be determined before us and not elsewhere"".[12]

These writs were collected in the Register of Writs. There were only a limited number of writs available, but the chancellor could increase the number.[13] Interesting to note is that "the development of the writ system ... has about it a hint of paradox for modern administrative law: what began as executive commands aimed at avoiding judicial proceedings became in turn the central mechanism for the ju-

6 De Smith, S.A., *Judicial Review of Administrative Action*, 1995, 618.
7 Cane, P., *An Introduction to Administrative Law*, 1996, 62.
8 De Smith, S.A., supra n. 6, 618.
9 Henderson, E., *Foundations of English Administrative Law*, 1963, 83.
10 Henderson, supra n. 9, 95.
11 De Smith, S.A., *Judicial Review of Administrative Action*, 1995, 622.
12 Controlment Roll no. 289, m. 151 as seen in Henderson, E., supra n. 9, 101.
13 Van Caenegem, R.C., *The Birth of the English Legal System*, 1973, 29.

dicial control of executive action".[14] The writs became a requirement to gain access to the jurisdiction of the common law courts.

The three first common law courts were the Court of Exchequer, the Court of Common Pleas and the Court of King's Bench.[15] The Court of Exchequer dealt with matters affecting the King's revenue. One of the stipulations in the Magna Charta in 1215 was the establishment of a permanent court seated in Westminster. The Court of Common Pleas fulfilled this function and it dealt with disputes over land, debts, detinue and covenant and trespass. The Court of King's Bench was closely connected to the King and its prime jurisdiction was in matters directly affecting the King. It could issue the prerogative writs of *mandamus*, *prohibition* and *habeas corpus*. Later the High Court of Admiralty and the Court of Exchequer Chamber were created.[16]

The law of equity attempted to fill the gaps left by the common law writ system. "If no common law writ appeared to meet the need of a prospective litigant, he might go instead to equity, which supplemented or complemented common law in a number of ways".[17] Equity developed into the provider of substantive justice in those cases which fell outside the scope of the writ sytem. Equity developed its own body of remedies. The Court of Chancery and the Court of Requests were equitable courts.[18]

The Tudor Kings had managed to withdraw matters of state from the courts of common law and had enforced their will primarily through their own prerogative courts in which substantive and procedural rules unknown to the common law were applied. As early as Edward I, the King's council exercised judicial functions. During the fourteenth century conflict broke out between the council and Parliament regarding the judicial functions of the council. Parliament tried to end the judicial function by enacting legislation. However, these statutes, which were to limit the judicial function of the council and to enforce the common law procedures as the only legal procedure, had little effect.[19] The statutes were not repealed during the Tudor reign. They were disregarded and Parliament ascribed the council some jurisdictional powers.

For the development of English administrative law the so-called bills, which were to be dealt with by the infamous Star Chamber, are of particular importance. These bills were requests from people to the King and his council, the chancellor and to Parliament by subjects who needed some form of advice or help. Many of those bills were converted into writs or legislation or direct intervention by the King. The so-called conciliar courts, which unlike the common law courts did not use writs, began to accept those bills and to issue orders. A new institution, the Star Chamber, gradually filled the gap left by the common law courts and the eq-

---

14 De Smith, S.A., *Judicial Review of Administrative Action*, 1995, 618.

15 Rudd, G.R., *The English Legal System*, 1962, 13.

16 Ibid.

17 Shapiro, M., *Courts, A Comparative and Political Analysis*, 1981, 85.

18 Ibid 89.

19 Maitland, F.W., *The Constitutional History of England: A Course of Lectures*, 1926, 217.

uity courts. The Star Chamber was from then on particularly concerned with cases concerning the state but also had jurisdiction in private law disputes and cases of religious deviation. The name Star Chamber appears to relate to the room used in the old Palace of Westminster for the meetings of the King's council. The Star Chamber court was given additional powers in the Star Chamber Statute in 1487 but had existed even before then.[20] It applied procedures unknown to the common law or equity courts including the use of torture.[21] It imposed a strict control over the organs of local government, the exercise of judicial and administrative functions.[22] It was concerned with complaints against officials or central and local government and against the justices of the peace who enjoyed wide powers in the countryside.[23] The Star Chamber therefore acted partly as an early form of administrative court. It applied the common law but followed different procedures. It exercised an inquisitorial procedure using the rack and other forms of obtaining confessions.[24] As a consequence of major criticism of the procedures and involvement in ecclesiastical decisions, the Star Chamber was eventually abolished during the seventeenth century struggles. The common lawyers joined in alliance with the parliamentarians to bring about the downfall of the Court of Star Chamber and other prerogative courts in 1641. Most of their cases were then dealt with by the King's Bench. The traditions handed down from the constitutional struggles of the seventeenth century created a prejudice against encroachments in the field of common law. Until today, the executive still enjoys a considerable degree of autonomy and immunity from judicial control.[25] After its abolition, these traumatising experiences remained in the perception of public law as an area of law which in future had to be inseparable from private law. The English tradition of judicial independence has therefore developed in a rather different form. In the early seventeenth century, some courts functioned at least partly as administrative courts. These developments 300 years ago still seem to influence the attitude of modern judicial institutions. Judicial independence was forthwith associated with the so-called "doctrine of limited judicial review".

The most distinctive characteristic of the English administrative legal system and its sources is the absence of a written constitution and the absence of an entrenched catalogue of human rights. There is also no written record of the constitutional principles of administrative law. Further, there are no separate administrative courts. Judicial review of administrative action is, in principle, exercised not by a special administrative judiciary, but by the ordinary courts. In the absence in the past of a statutory basis for the power of the courts,[26] their power to review administrative action is inherent and discretionary. The courts have developed a number of devices designed to keep them out of highly controversial areas. In par-

20 Walker, P.N., *The Courts of Law,* 1970, 181.
21 Shapiro, M., *Courts, A Comparative and Political Analysis*, 1981, 87.
22 De Smith, S.A., *Judicial Review of Administrative Action*, 1995, 226.
23 Allison, J.W.F., *A Continental Distinction in the Common Law*, 1999, 153.
24 Pollard D., Parpworth N., Hughes, D., *Constitutional and Administrative Law* (2001) 514.
25 Cane, P., *An Introduction to Administrative Law,* 1996, 13.
26 Now the Supreme Court Act 1981.

ticular, the general principle on which the exercise of discretionary powers is reviewed is that of "unreasonableness" understood in a rather strict sense which only allows judicial intervention when an administrative authority has acted so unreasonably that no reasonable authority could so act.[27] The courts are inferior to Parliament and the common law inferior as a form of law to parliamentary legislation. English constitutional history has witnessed a rigid division between law and politics and there are realms within which judges may not operate. Lawyers cannot apply the ideals of legality and constitutionality to politics and administration, certainly not in a way which is familiar to a German lawyer.[28] This judicial restraint is partly a function of the doctrine of separation of powers which will be discussed in more detail below.

The subject of judicial review of administrative action poses the question of the role which the courts fulfil in both jurisdictions of England and Germany. An area which will be dealt with in more detail in Chapter Three is the review of discretionary powers. Here, in particular, the question arises: which institutions have the responsibility to devise and apply constraints to the exercise of discretion?[29] When defining the role of the judiciary, the central issue is to investigate which forms the application of the doctrine of the separation of powers takes. The idea of a division of government powers is a common feature of western constitutional history. The doctrine of the separation of powers dates back to the seventeenth century when John Locke wrote:

> "It may be too great a temptation to human frailty, apt to grasp at power, for the same persons who have the power of making laws, to have also in their hands the power to execute them, whereby they may exempt themselves from obedience to the laws they make, and suit the law, both in its making and execution, to their own private advantage".[30]

Montesquieu developed the doctrine further and based it on the model of the British constitution. In Chapter Six of his famous *De l'Esprit de Lois*, Book XI, he emphasised that within a system of government based upon law, the judicial function should be separate from the legislature and the executive.[31] Montesquieu further saw the importance of each institution in carrying out checks and balances. However, Montesquieu saw the role of the judiciary in simply applying the law. The development of judicial review of the other branches is based on developments in American constitutional history.[32] It is important to point out that there is no one single version of the doctrine of the separation of powers. The separation of powers has been described as a fundamental principle upon which all the western democracies rest, but in none of them is it interpreted or lived in the same way. The common underlying ratio is that "power must be checked by power".[33] Therefore two positions can be identified. First, the separation of powers and, secondly,

---

27 Cane, P., *An Introduction to Administrative Law*, 1996, 356.

28 Birkinshaw, P., *Grievances, Remedies and the State* 1994, 3.

29 Galligan, D.J., *Discretionary Powers* 1986, 219.

30 Second Treatise of Civil Government, Chapter XII, para 143, quoted in Vile, M.J.C., *Constitutionalism and the Separation of Powers,* 1967.

31 Bradley, A.W., Ewing, K.D., *Constitutional and Administrative law,* 1997, 90.

32 Galligan, D.J., *Discretionary Powers* 1986, 229.

33 Mény, Y., *Government and Politics in Western Europe,* 1993, 5, 6.

the checks and balances of each power. This, however, still does not provide guidance for judicial review of administrative action. Galligan sees the problem in the application of clearly adjudicative functions to the judiciary. This would restrict the court's role to reviewing solely "matters of a preliminary or threshold kind" and exclude the courts from reviewing matters of substance of the decision. However, this has been the position of the courts particularly in the first part of this century. Galligan offers some guidance for judicial review by concluding that:

"Judicial review is most justifiable not when it is directed at substantive policy choices that occur in exercising discretion, but rather when it draws on values which form part of the constitutional framework within which discretion occurs. The justification for review lies in the assertion of certain values as sufficiently important to be constraints on the exercise of discretion".[34]

In the absence of a written constitution, such an interpretation relies on the weight given to traditional constitutional principles such as the rule of law. However, as will be shown in later chapters, the introduction of the Human Rights Act 1998 is an expression of a constitutional change as it gives the courts in England new powers.

The development of English administrative law is closely linked to the conceptions of the constitutional lawyer, A.V. Dicey, whose publication *The Law of the Constitution*[35] on the meaning of the rule of law has influenced generations of lawyers. In 1938 Frankfurter wrote:

"Few law books in modern times have had an influence comparable to that produced by the brilliant obfuscation of Dicey's *The Law of the Constitution* ... Generations of judges and lawyers were brought up in the mental climate of Dicey. Judgments, speeches in the House of Commons, letters to the Times, reflected and perpetuated Dicey's misconceptions and myopia. The persistence of the misdirection that Dicey had given to the development of administrative law strikingly proves the Elder Huxley's observation that many a theory survives long after its brains are knocked out".[36]

Dicey's conception of the rule of law embraces at least three main statements. First, he stressed the importance of the legitimacy of law in contrast to the exercise of wide discretionary powers. Secondly, every man should be subjected to the ordinary courts and therefore public officials should not enjoy any other status: "every man, whatever be his rank or condition, is subject to the ordinary law of the realm and amenable to the jurisdiction of the ordinary tribunals". Lastly, private rights do not stem from any source of higher-ranking law but are the result of judicial decisions made by ordinary courts applying the ordinary laws.[37]

In particular Dicey's second conception of the rule of law ("every man, whatever be his rank or condition, is subject to the ordinary law of the realm and ame-

34 Galligan, P. J., supra n. 32, 233.

35 Dicey, A.V., *The Law of the Constitution,* 10th edn, 1959.

36 Foreword to "Discussion of Current Developments in Administrative Law" (1938) 47 *Yale LJ* 519 as quoted in Arthurs, H.W., "Rethinking Administrative Law: A Slightly Dicey Business" (1979) *Osgoode Hall Law Journal* 1 at 4.

37 Dicey, A. V., supra n. 35, 188–203.

nable to the jurisdiction of the ordinary tribunals"[38]) has been central in the discussion concerning the establishment of a separate system of public law courts. *Droit administratif* as being "official" law enforceable in special courts and therefore being incompatible with the rule of law reaffirmed these reservations against a separate system of public law courts.[39] Dicey's view has been heavily criticised for misinterpreting *droit administratif* and for ignoring the developments in English law at the time when he was writing his thesis.

First, the end of the nineteenth century was marked by an increase in the activities of tribunals which existed alongside the ordinary courts. Secondly, Dicey ignored the extensive immunities public officials enjoyed from ordinary law.[40] For example, only since 1947 after the enactment of the Crown Immunities Act, public officials can be held liable in tort for negligent exercise of public powers in their official capacity. Before then they were immune from suit. However, they have always been subject to personal liability.

Dicey misinterpreted the fact that governments or an agency are often acting for the citizens at large and that therefore the application of the same legal principles and procedures as for a private person might not be adequate. Further, he did not realise that public law and public law remedies can be seen as a defence of the citizen against a powerful state.[41] The latter view becomes more transparent in a system with a strong tradition of constitutionally guaranteed human rights provisions like in Germany or the United States where British cases are read by the judges "with a mind dominated by the spirit of the American Constitution – stripping away the limited frame of reference of judicial review in Britain".[42] Dicey supported the idea of parliamentary control of the administration and judicial control through the ordinary courts. Dicey's understanding of judicial independence went along with the neglect of expertise in administrative matters.

H.W. Arthur discussed Dicey's belief that the ordinary courts are supreme and that ordinary law is all pervasive in detail. He questioned both whether ordinary laws are the opposite of administrative norms and whether they must be regarded as superior. First, Arthur questioned the meaning of ordinary laws. According to Dicey's definition, rules that are not enforceable by the courts cannot be considered as ordinary laws. In Dicey's view, ordinary law included the common law, judge-made law and some statutes, but certainly not all statute law.[43] Arthur raises doubts as to whether in Dicey's view administrative statutes would have fulfilled the requirements of the rule of law: "it is fair to speculate that administrative statutes would not be regarded as ordinary law by Dicey … A theory that stigmatises 20, 50, 100 years of legislation on the grounds of departure from the ordinary law

---

38 Ibid 188.

39 De Smith, S.A., *Judicial Review of Administrative Action*, 1995, 157.

40 Arthurs, H.W., "Rethinking Administrative Law: A Slightly Dicey Business" (1979) *Osgoode Hall Law Journal* 1 at 6.

41 Cane, P., *An Introduction to Administrative Law*, 1996.

42 Schwartz B., and Wade, H.W.R., *The Legal Control of Government: administrative law in Britain and the United States,* 1972.

43 Arthurs, H.W., supra n. 40 at 9.

and the ordinary courts is ... open to criticism".[44] Arthur's criticism of Dicey's views was concerned with the fact that "Dicey overestimated the extent of adjudication through judges".[45] At the time when Dicey was writing, many important issues were dealt with by tribunals. Dicey's conception that the adjudication by ordinary courts applying the ordinary law was a pillar on which the English constitution rested was incorrect. The definition of ordinary law has to include many sources, including judge-made law from judges who do not sit in the superior courts. However, despite the extensive criticism of Dicey's view:

> "To this very day, prominent jurists explicitly or by inference echo Dicey's views, legislators rely upon them as a blueprint for the design of administrative regimes, professional audiences can safely be expected to applaud them and legal scholars to derive inspiration from them. Dicey and his rule of law have acquired, within and beyond legal circles, a transcendent, a symbolic significance".[46]

2. The tribunal system

No account of administrative justice in England would be complete without a discussion of the tribunal system. The development of the tribunal system which dates back at least to the nineteenth century was accelerated after the report of the Committee on Administrative Tribunals and Enquiries chaired by Sir Oliver Franks, which became known as the Franks Report in 1957.[47] The report emphasised the importance of "openness, fairness and impartiality".[48] The committee made important recommendations which were followed in the Tribunals and Inquiries Act 1958 and consolidated Acts.[49] There are 70 tribunals with varying workloads.[50] Tribunals were established to provide less formal alternatives to the procedures in court. The largest tribunals administered by central government today are the Appeals Service, the Mental Health Review Tribunals, CICAP, SENDIST (Educational Needs and Disability Tribunal), General and Special Commissioners of Income Tax, VAT and Duties Tribunal, Social Security and Child Support Commissioners, Pension Appeals, Immigration Adjudicators and the Immigration Appeal Tribunal.[51]

The number of cases received by tribunals each year indicates their significance in the administrative justice system. The Immigration Adjudicators and the Immi-

---

44 Ibid 11.

45 Arthurs, H.W., *"Without the Law", Administrative Justice and Legal Pluralism in Nineteenth Century England*, 1985, 140.

46 Ibid 5.

47 Cmnd 218.

48 Ibid p. 10.

49 Smith, Bailey & Gunn, *Modern English Legal System* (4th edn, 2002) 46.

50 White Paper, "Transforming Public Services: Complaints, Redress and Tribunals", Cm 6243, p. 15.

51 White Paper, "Transforming Public Services: Complaints, Redress and Tribunals", Cm 6243.

gration Appeal Tribunal[52] alone for instance received more than 158,000 cases in 2004.[53] The main types of appeal dealt with are against decisions to refuse a person political asylum, refuse a person entry to, or leave to remain in, the UK for permanent settlement or to refuse a person entry to the UK for the purpose of a family visit.

The structure of tribunals and the appeal routes to other tribunals has been described as "unstructured" and in need of reform.[54] It is not entirely clear how Parliament selects certain subjects for referral to a tribunal. "Certain basic guidelines can be detected, but the choice is influenced by the interplay of various factors – the nature of the decisions, accidents of history, departmental preferences and political considerations – rather than by the application of a set of coherent principles".[55]

The institutional weakness of the tribunal system is illustrated by the parliamentary changes made in the Asylum and Immigration Act 2004. Section 81(6) replaced immigration adjudicators and tribunals and introduced a single-tier appeal tribunal as of 1 April 2005. Lord Steyn condemned the section as a limit to constitutional principle:

> "In isolation it may be unobjectionable, but the section seeks in effect to oust the jurisdiction of ordinary courts in all but limited cases. It will preclude judicial review on the grounds of lack of jurisdiction, irregularity, error of law, breach of natural justice and any other matter. These are the very areas in which the higher courts have repeatedly been called on to assert the sovereignty of the law. The section attempts to immunise manifest illegality. It is an astonishing measure. It is contrary to the rule of law".[56]

The absence of specific administrative courts is a fact closely linked to the question whether Britain possesses a distinct system of substantive administrative law. This was answered in the positive in the famous quote by Lord Denning who held that "it may truly now be said that we have a developed system of administrative law".[57] In 1981 Lord Diplock held in *R v Inland Revenue Commissioners, ex p National Federation of the Self-Employed and Small Businesses Ltd* "that progress towards a comprehensive system of administrative law … I regard as having been the greatest achievement of the English courts in my judicial lifetime".[58] Since the end of the 1960s the courts have been actively shaping England's administrative law system. However, it has been argued that the "English distinction between

52 The Immigration Adjudicators and the Immigration Appeal Tribunal merged into the Asylum and Immigration Tribunal as of 1 April 2005.

53 Judicial Statistics, 2004, 106.

54 "Tribunals for Users – One System, One Service" (Leggat Report), Stationery Office, August 2001.

55 "The Function of the Council on Tribunals", special report by the Council, Cmnd 7805, 1980, p. 1 as quoted in Smith, Bailey & Gunn, *Modern English Legal System*, 2002, 45.

56 Lord Steyn, *The Guardian*, 22 April 2006.

57 *Breen v Amalgamated Engineering* [1971] 2 QB 175 at 189 as quoted in De Smith, S.A., Judicial Review of Administrative Action, 1999, 57.

58 *R v Inland Revenue Commissioners, ex p National Federation of the Self-Employed and Small Businesses Ltd* [1982] AC 617 at 641 as quoted in De Smith S.A., *Judicial Review of Administrative Action*, 1999, 57.

public and private law procedures is proving unsatisfactory and is becoming less significant".[59] The distinction between public and private law is closely linked to the system provided by the prerogative orders which over the centuries have been reformed in order to fulfil the purposes of judicial review.

The groundbreaking case for the distinction between private and public law remedies is *O'Reilly v Mackman* (1982). In this case a prisoner challenged the decision of a disciplinary board claiming it had been taken in breach of natural justice. He brought his claim by writ as in civil cases and did not apply for judicial review under Order 53 of the Rules of the Supreme Court (now Part 54 of the 1998 Rules) enacted in the Supreme Court Act 1981. The House of Lords held that if a decision of a public body violated rights which are protected by public law, the procedure under Order 53 had to be followed. Until then it was assumed generally that the litigant had a choice between an action of summons for an injunction, a declaration or even damages or he or she could apply for judicial review.[60]

However, one of the greatest achievements of Tony Blair's Labour government has been the introduction of the Human Rights Act 1998 which incorporates the European Convention on Human Rights into the law of the United Kingdom. Even though no provision is made for the establishment of a constitutional court in order to strike down legislation which does not comply with the Convention, Sect. 3 provides that primary and subordinate legislation must be interpreted in a way which is compatible with the Convention. If this fails, there is the possibility of a declaration of incompatibility which provides for a ministerial remedial order to remove the incompatibility by amending the legislation.[61]

Three main areas of judicial review can be identified which are the grounds on which judicial review may be granted, the procedures whereby judicial review may be applied for and the requirements which the law makes of the person seeking judicial review and lastly judicial remedies and their effects.[62] However, more recent developments indicate a change of approach. An important step in the direction of judicial expertise in administrative law matters was made when the Crown Office List of the Queen's Bench Division of the High Court was created in 1977. The need for a specialist court in administrative law matters was felt in order to protect individual liberties better. All existing procedures of judicial review of administrative action were combined under a single heading called an application for judicial review. In 1981 Order 53 of the Rules of the Supreme Court was amended so that a single judge of the Queen's Bench Division could hear judicial review cases.[63] This administrative list can be compared to the commercial list. A number of Queen's Bench judges with a reputation of expertise in the field of administrative law were nominated by the Lord Chief Justice to operate the new Order 53 (now Part 54 of the Civil Procedure Rules 1998). Interesting to note is

59 Allison, J.W.F., *A Continental Distinction in the Common Law*, 2000, 135.
60 De Smith, S.A., *Judicial Review of Administrative Action*, 1995, 160.
61 Section 4.
62 Stevens, I., *Constitutional and Administrative law,* 1996, 221.
63 Supreme Court Act 1981, Sect. 6(1)(b).

that the creation of this administrative court is not based on legislation but on "administrative stealth". [64] The Bowman Report in 2000 led to further reform of the application for judicial review. The report recommended that "there is a continuing need for a specialist court as part of the High Court to deal with public and administrative law cases. To emphasise that this is the principal work of the Crown Office List, it should be renamed "the Administrative Court"". The Lord Chancellor accepted this proposal and as of 2 October 2000 the Crown Office List in the Queen's Bench Division of the High Court is known as the Administrative Court.[65] The judges hearing applications for judicial review in the Administrative Court are recruited from the Bar. They receive no special training in public administration.[66]

3. The development of separate Administrative Courts in nineteenth century Germany

The administrative courts in their current form are the result of an historical compromise which had to solve the tensions between two main competing models of administrative justice and the tensions caused by Germany's federal structure. The first forms of administrative courts exercised administrative justice (*Administrativjustiz*). Similar to the *Conseil d'Etat* they were part of the administration. The administration controlled itself and a variety of civil servants could hold office. To some extent this administrative self-control protected the interests of the citizens in that it ensured the legality of administrative action. However, its function cannot be compared with the legal protection of individual rights as provided in the modern administrative courts.[67] The administration was judge in its own cause. This was particularly true in the case of policing, where it was almost impossible for individuals to obtain favourable judgments.

In the nineteenth century the political climate changed which led to an increasing awareness for human rights protection and the development of the principle of the *Rechtsstaat*.[68] In addition, the intensity and quantity of administrative interference with individual rights had increased. Towards the middle of the nineteenth century liberal groups increasingly demanded the effective control of administrative action by independent courts. The Paulskirche constitution contained in its Art. 182 the quest for judicial control of administrative action in the ordinary courts as opposed to self-control through the administration (*Administrativjustiz*). Further, courts should no longer carry out administrative functions. However, the

---

64 Bloom-Cooper, L., "The New Face of Judicial Review: Administrative Changes in Order 53" (1982) *Public Law* 250 [259, 260].

65 Practice Direction (Administrative Establishment) Queen's Bench Division [2000] 1 *WLR* 165.

66 Bloom-Cooper, L., "Lawyers and Public Administrators: Separate and Unequal" (1984) *Public Law* 215.

67 Hufen, F., *Verwaltungsprozessrecht,* 3rd edn, 1998, 27.

68 Stolleis, M., *Geschichte des öffentlichen Rechts, Zweiter Band, Staatsrechtslehre und Verwaltungswissenschaft 1800–1914,* 1992, 241.

revolution failed in 1849 due to the refusal of Friedrich Wilhelm IV and with it reform developments came to a halt for almost two decades.

However, the quest for reform of the administrative justice in the form of independent judicial control returned and most famously found its expression in the controversial opinions of Otto Bähr (1817–1895) and Rudolf von Gneist (1816–1895). Otto Bähr supported the view that the state was part of society and should therefore be judged in the same courts as individuals. Similarly other famous liberal legal scholars such as Feuerbach, Brinkmann, Siebenpfeiffer and others supported the idea of an independent control of the administration through the ordinary courts.[69] The ordinary courts were dominated by judges stemming from the bourgeois part of society whereas the civil service still remained in aristocratic hands. Another group, partly liberals and partly conservatives, favoured the French model of the *Conseil d'Etat* and hoped to influence the procedures and the choice of judges from the perspective of the administration.

Rudolf von Gneist, on the contrary, stood for a separation of ordinary and public law courts because in his view state and society were different entities. Von Gneist was not so much concerned with the protection of individual rights but with the objective control of public authorities according to public law. Von Gneist had carried out research into the English and French legal systems which he published in his book *Der Rechtsstaat*. Accordingly, he considered the judicial control of administrative action as practiced in England as an essential element of the *Rechtsstaat*.[70] He succeeded with his reform proposals at the 12th German lawyers' convention (12. *Deutscher Juristentag*, 1875). The German model of administrative courts was therefore a compromise between control by the ordinary courts as in England and administrative justice as carried out by the French model. The creation of administrative courts can be closely connected to the failure of the 1848/49 revolution. This victory of the liberals in establishing independent courts can be interpreted as compensation for a failed revolution. It marks the beginning of a trend in Germany towards the juridification of society (with exceptions during the Nazi regime) which has steadily developed into the twentieth century.

4. The administrative law tradition in Germany

The nineteenth century was not only marked by the constitutional movement in Germany but also by the establishment of substantive administrative law (*Verwaltungsrecht*). The administrative tradition in Germany was stronger than the political confidence of society. Accordingly, German public lawyers of international reputation were mainly to be found in the field of administrative law such as Robert von Mohl, Lorenz von Stein, Rudolf von Gneist and Otto Mayer.[71] After the failed revolution the political energies of the liberal forces in society began to

---

69 Ibid.

70 Gerstner, S., *Die Drittschutzdogmatik im Spiegel des französischen und britischen Verwaltungsverfahrens,* 1995, 130.

71 Stolleis, M., supra n. 68, 229.

concentrate on the establishment of the *Rechtsstaat*. The idea of the German *Rechtsstaat* is often mistranslated as the rule of law, but it contains more than its English counterpart. The meaning of *Rechtsstaat* was synonymous with a system of administrative law which was shaped by academic experts. The relevance of the principle of the *Rechtsstaat* was seen in the fact that it eliminated the exercise of arbitrary power. In the years after the revolution the development of a substantive administrative law as a separate discipline, taught at universities and independent from constitutional law, became the central work of major academic lawyers. Due to the failure of the constitutional reforms administrative law developed independently from constitutional law. The development of the strong administrative law tradition can therefore be seen as compensation for the political and constitutional shortcomings after the revolution. The monarchy, the aristocracy, the army and the church represented the state. On the other side was the bourgeoisie who wanted to ensure that the state fulfilled its functions and at the same time kept within the legal boundaries. The development of a system, a theory of substantive administrative law, became the passion of famous lawyers. Administrative law was separated from the difficult question of constitutional law and after 1850 it developed into its own science. There was opposition from Robert von Mohl and Lorenz von Stein, for instance, who argued administrative law could not be seen in isolation from constitutional law. However, the independent development of an administrative law system could not be prevented[72] and it seemed to be the best compromise in securing the *Rechtsstat* at the time. In 1865 Carl Friedrich von Gerber argued that the discipline of public law would suffer as a scientific subject if there was no separate category for the rights of the *Landstände* (body of representatives of various classes) and the provisions against foot and mouth disease.[73] As a result, the administrative law of the nineteenth century developed into an academic playing field, which was somewhat distant from the field of constitutional law. What remained was an area lacking practical and political associations and the task to categorise it in abstract and dogmatic terms.[74] Due to this lack of political or substantive content, the concept of the *Rechtsstaat* was merely of a formal nature. Otto Mayer defined the *Rechtsstaat* in 1895 as follows:

> "The word [*Rechtsstaat*] appeared after the thing was already under way. It seeks to describe something that does not yet exist, at least not in a finished state, but has yet to come about. That is why the concept varies so greatly, because everyone is inclined to invest it with his own juridical ideals".[75]

---

72 Ibid 383.

73 Gerber, C.F., *Grundzüge eines Systems des deutschen Staatrechts,* 1865, 233: "die Reinheit und Selbständigkeit des Staatsrechts würde leiden, wenn man dasselbe wissenschaftliche system für den Platz der Darstellung der Rechte der Landstände und der Bestimmungen über Vorkehrungen gegen die Rinderpest ansehen wollte ... So würden wir es gewiss in diesem Sinne als einen Fortschritt begrüssen, wenn endlich auch das Verwaltungsrecht in seiner Selbständigkeit erkannt und von der Verbindung mit dem Staatsrecht gelöst wird".

74 Stolleis, M., supra n. 68, 383.

75 Cited in Böckenförde, E.W., *State, Society and Libert,y* 1992 47.

Mayer's idea of the *Rechtsstaat* entailed the progressive legislative shaping of the material and organisational administrative law for the protection of civil liberties and development of a system of effective, judicial legal protection against administrative authorities.[76]

Forerunners of this realisation of the idea of the *Rechtsstaat* were a variety of early developments at state level of which the introduction of the first Administrative Court (*Verwaltungsgerichtshof*) in Baden in 1863 and Preussen (*Oberverwaltungsgericht*) in 1875 were the beginning of independent specialised courts dealing with administrative matters.[77] Baden had started reorganising its administration earlier than other states and reacted to the industrialisation and increase in the population as well as to the liberal quest for an independent judiciary in administrative matters.[78] A recent study has described the Administrative Courts as a late child of the (failed) revolution in 1848/49.[79] Sydow's article identifies the direct origin of the Administrative Courts in the discussions on the *Paulskirche* constitution. In particular in Baden, first legislative drafts dated back to 1848 which contained the establishment of first instance Administrative Courts and higher Administrative Courts (*Verwaltungsgerichtshof*). These proposals were based on a compromise drafted in 1835 by Ludwig von Minnigerode, the president of the highest court in *Hessen*.[80] In order to find a compromise between the position of the government which was opposed to the introduction of judicial review in the ordinary courts and those who favoured the idea of independent judicial control, he suggested the introduction of an independent institution which would not act as an ordinary court, but which would be staffed with lawyers not civil servants. This reform proposal formed the basis for those first attempts in Baden to establish an independent Administrative Court as early as 1848. However, the constitution of 1848 did not opt for an independent administrative judicial review system but opted for control through the ordinary courts.

The separation of the three powers became a dominant feature of government. Similar to the French system of administrative courts with the *Conseil d'État* at the top of the hierarchy, the first lower Prussian Administrative Courts that were established between 1872 and 1875 maintained links with the administration. This was a system of Administrative Courts with county committees (*Kreisausschüsse*) at the lowest level, regional committees (*Bezirksausschüsse*) in the middle and the

---

76 Mayer, O., *Deutsches Verwaltungsrecht*, 1895, 61–65.

77 Hufen, F., *Verwaltungsprozessrecht*, 1998, 27.

78 Stolleis, M., supra n. 68, 293.

79 Sydow, G., "Die Revolution von 1848/49: Ursprung der modernen Verwaltungsgerichtsbarkeit" (2001) *Verwaltungs Archiv 2001* 389.

80 Von Minnigerode, L., *Beitrag zur Beantwortung der Frage: Was ist Justiz – und was ist Administrativezache*?,1835, 74 in Sydow, supra n. 79 at 934: "wenn aber der Staatsregierung so viel daran gelegen ware, das die sogenannten Administrativ-Justiz-Sachen von einer besonderen Behörde [statt von den ordentlichen Gerichten] entschieden wurden, so müsste dieselbe doch als wahrhaftige Justiz-Behörde con-stituiert, also von der Administration ganz getrennt, ganz unabhangig und nur mit Rechtsgelehrten – keineswegs aber mit Individuen besetzt seyn, welche zugleich in der Administration zu functionieren hatten".

Prussian Supreme Administrative Court (*Preußisches Obervewaltungsgericht*) at the top. Only the Supreme Administrative Court was totally separated from the administrative authorities. As a consequence the scope of review in the lower Administrative Courts included the power to review the expediency or policy (*Zweckmäßigeit*) of administrative decisions. The model of the separation of powers was therefore not strictly applied. Other states except for *Württemberg* copied the Prussian model. The lower Administrative Courts were abolished during the reign of the Nazi government.[81]

II. The constitutional role of the courts

1. The constitutional basis for the role of the courts in judicial review in England

In the UK the constitutional basis for the jurisdiction of the courts in their supervisory function has recently been vigorously debated.[82] This search for a new constitutional foundation for the supervisory function of the courts might be due to the "increasing prominence of judicial review".[83] The main principle which provided the legal basis for the courts' jurisdiction has been the *ultra vires* rule. This notion of *ultra vires*, however, as the basis for judicial review has come under increasing criticism. The *ultra vires* theory contains the idea that "judicial review was legitimated on the ground that the courts were applying the intent of the legislature. The courts' function was to police the boundaries stipulated by Parliament".[84] This meant that the justification for the development of the grounds of review had to derive from the notion that it was Parliament's intent that they would apply in a particular statutory context.[85] The competing model is the so-called common law model of illegality. The supporters of this theory argue that the development of the grounds of review has been due to the courts. The principles of judicial review are based on the common law.[86] The main criticism centred on the question of how the *ultra vires* theory would be able to explain the role of the courts in reviewing non-statutory powers. Further, the *ultra vires* theory was unable to provide an explanation for the development and expansion of the grounds of review:

---

81 Singh, M.P., *German Administrative Law,* 1985 10–11.

82 For a collection of articles on this subject, see Forsyth, C., *Judicial Review and the Constitution*, 2000.

83 Elliott, M., "The Ultra Vires Doctrine in a Constitutional Setting" in Forsyth, *Judicial Review and the Constitution*, 2000, 85.

84 Craig, P., "Competing Models of Judicial Review" in Forsyth, *Judicial Review and the Constitution*, 373.

85 Ibid 374.

86 See De Smith, S.A., *Judicial Review of Administrative Action* 1995; Craig, P., "Ultra Vires and the Foundations of Judicial Review" (1998) *CLJ* 63; Jowell, J., "Of Vires and Vacuums: the Constitutional Context of Judicial Review" (1999) *PL* 448.

"The constraints which exist on the exercise of discretionary power are not static. Existing constraints evolve and new types of control are added to the judicial armoury. Changes in judicial attitudes towards fundamental rights, the acceptance of legitimate expectations and the possible inclusion of proportionality as a head of review in its own right are but three examples of this process. These developments cannot plausibly be explained by reference to legislative intent".[87]

The modified *ultra vires* theory therefore acknowledges now that the courts may impose the judicial review mechanism on non-statutory bodies.[88] Secondly, the modified *ultra vires* theory does not try to establish a direct link between the formulation of the grounds of review and the legislative intention. It takes a modified view in that "it is possible to understand the development of administrative law within an analytical model which ascribes relevance to legislative intention, but without resorting to the strained proposition that changes in judicial control correspond directly to the will of Parliament".[89] In this comparative thesis the debate is of interest with respect to the way in which either version of the theories might influence the jurisprudence of British courts in human rights issues under the Human Right Act 1998. The Act appears in itself a compromise between competing models of democracy, i.e. systems which either operate on the basis that the will of the majority is paramount or on the basis that the values of the community, i.e. higher ranking principles and rights, are of supreme meaning. The difference between these conceptions has been described by Allan as an "inescapable tension"[90] However, the question remains to what extent the Human Rights Act 1998 has solved this tension. According to Sect. 6(1) of the Act it is unlawful for a public authority to act in a way which is incompatible with a Convention right. The *ultra vires* theory appears sufficient to guide the courts in the application of more substantive review under the Human Rights Act which is "either expressly or impliedly" authorised by Parliament.[91] Elliott argues further that the existence of the Human Rights Act 1998 proves that the common law theory or the "rule-based approach" as he calls it is insufficient as it is inconsistent with the Act. In his view the rule-based approach would lead to an entrenchment of the Act, whereas the *ultra vires* theory would be consistent with the Act and the constitutional order.[92]

---

87 Craig, P., supra n. 86, 63.

88 Forsyth, C., "Of Fig Leaves and Fairy Tales: the Ultra Vires Doctrine, the Soveignty of Parliament and Judicial Review" (1996) *CLJ* 122; Elliott, M., "The Demise of Parliamentary Sovereignty? The Implications for Justifying Judicial Review" (1999) *LQR* 115, 119.

89 Elliott, M., "The Ultra Vires Doctrine in a Constitutional Setting: Still the Central Principle of Administrative Law" in Forsyth, *Judicial Review and the Constitution*, 2000.

89 Allan, T.R.S., "Fairness, Equality, Rationality" in Forsyth, C. and Hare, I., *The Golden Metwand and the Crooked Cord*, 1998.

90 Ibid 15.

91 Feldman, D., "Convention Rights and Substantive Ultra Vires" in Forsyth, *Judicial Review and the Constitution* 2000, 266.

92 Craig, P., Review Article, "Constitutional Analysis, Constitutional Principle and Judicial Review" (2001) *Public Law* 763 [766].

Whichever view one may take, the debate indicates a change in the climate. There appears to be an increasing desire to lay the foundations for judicial review in a theoretical, highly scholarly manner. The development of judicial review in England in the courts on the other hand displays an extremely pragmatic approach. Harden and Lewis observe that "despite the theoretical basis of *ultra vires* in statutory interpretation, the courts have in fact developed a number of principles for the control of discretion, for limiting the sphere of public autonomy created by statute ... for the most part they are judge-made law".[93] Therefore without explicitly identifying their role the courts have expanded judicial review beyond the traditional *ultra vires* model. However, the "lack of a clear understanding of the nature and purpose of judicial review, the courts have vacillated between a helpless quietism and an active interventionism which has too often appeared to depend on the judges' views of the merits of particular policies rather than upon a view of their role in the constitutional order of things".[94]

In the absence of a written constitution, however, which sets out the overall value order in terms of a clear entrenchment of human rights and a constitutional mandate to protect those values imposed on all three powers, it appears difficult to reach consensus on a single theoretical foundation. It has been suggested that consensus is not even necessary as different justification for different principles as applied by the courts may be employed.[95] This appears to have happened in practice anyway as witnessed by, for instance, the revival of the common law rules of natural justice. Finally, Sir John Laws' view of the constitutional position of the courts is even more pragmatic:

> "For every body other than the courts, legal power depends upon an imprimatur from an external source; but this is not true of the High Court and its appellate hierarchy. In point of theory, there exists no higher order of law for them. It follows that any analysis of their jurisdiction, if it is not to be confined to the simplest statement that the court reviews what it chooses to review, must consist in a description of the nature and extent of judicial review in practice ... The ultimate freedom of movement which on my own analysis the judges enjoy needs to be understood in order to appreciate that the court, if it decides in effect to push out the boundaries of judicial review in the particular case, is not guilty of any constitutional solecism".[96]

However, a decision concerned with the protection of the right to free speech under the Human Rights Act 1998 illustrates that the judges are expressing their constitutional role directly. In *R (ProLife Alliance) v BBC* citing extensive case law, Laws LJ held that:

---

93 Harden, I. and Lewis, N., *The Noble Lie*, 1988, 202.

94 Ibid 203.

95 Sir Robert Carnwath, "No Need for a Single Foundation" in Forsyth, *Judicial Review and the Constitution*, 2000.

96 "Illegality: the Problem of Jurisdiction" in Supperstone, M. and Goudie, J., *Judicial Review,* 1991, 69.

"As a matter of domestic law the courts owe a special responsibility to the public as the constitutional guardian of the freedom of political debate. The responsibility is most acute at the time and in the context of a public election. It has its origin in a deeper truth, which is that the courts are ultimately the trustees of our democracy's framework".[97]

In conclusion, the debate concerning the constitutional foundation of the supervisory role of the courts in judicial review proceedings cannot be fully analysed in this book. However, it can at least be regarded as an indicator that there is a strong trend towards the more explicit articulation of constitutional foundations both in court decisions and at an academic level based on a broader understanding of the rule of law and the increasing human rights culture in this country.

2. The Basic Law and the Administrative Courts

The crowning principle of German constitutionalism after 1949 became the principle of the substantive *Rechtstaat.* Article 20 III Basic Law clearly expresses that law and justice bind all three powers. This constitutional order is based on values and all acts of the legislature, the executive and the judiciary must be carried out in the light of these values. Böckenförde defines this substantive content of the *Rechtsstaat* as follows:

"The logic of thinking about values and justice demands that the constitution conceived along the lines of the material *Rechtsstaat* should lay claim to an absolute validity extending to all spheres of social life. It thus sanctions certain basic politico-ethnic convictions, giving them general legal validity, and discriminates against others that run counter to them. It no longer guarantees liberty unconditionally by way of formal legal demarcation; it does so only within the fundamental system of values embodied in the constitution".[98]

This change from a formal to a substantive concept of the *Rechtsstaat* has its roots in the abandonment of juridical positivism as a response to the abuse of law during Germany's years of Nazi dictatorship. As a result the substantive *Rechtsstaat* protects the basic rights as "overriding principles of justice which claim "validity for all spheres of law"".[99]

The principle of the *Rechtsstaat*[100] as applied today contains the guarantee to effective judicial protection (Art. 19 IV Basic Law), the independence of the judici-

---

97 [2002] 2 All ER 756 at 773.

98 Böckenförde, *State, Society and Liberty*, 1992, 67.

99 Ibid 66–67.

100 As contained in Arts. 20 and 28 of the Basic Law. Article 20:
(1) The Federal Republic of Germany shall be a democratic and social federal state.
(2) All public authority emanates from the people. It shall be exercised by the people through elections and referenda and by specific legislative, executive and judicial bodies.
(3) The legislature shall be bound by the constitutional order, the executive and the judiciary by law and justice.
Article 28:

ary (Arts. 92 and 97 Basic Law), the guarantee of the jurisdiction by a lawful judge (Art. 101 Basic Law), the right to a court hearing (Art. 103 Basic Law), the principle of equality (Art. 3 Basic Law) and the principle of proportionality and legitimate expectation (see Arts. 48 and 49 Law on Administrative Procedure).[101]

In 1960 the Federal Law on Administrative Courts established a uniform system of Administrative Courts in Germany. The modern form of Administrative Courts maintains no more links with the administration and as a reaction to historical developments now embodies the stricter form of the doctrine of the separation of powers. Like English courts, German Administrative Courts do not review questions of policy (*Zweckmäßigkeit*). This would be regarded a violation of the principle of the separation of powers. The Law on Administrative Courts provides for this stricter application of the doctrine by providing for a separate review procedure within the administration (*Widerspruchsverfahren*) which is compulsory for suits for the invalidity of an administrative act (*Anfechtungsklage*) or mandatory suits (*Verpflichtungsklage*). Within this procedure questions of policy can be reviewed by the administration.

Article 19 IV of the Basic Law is of particular importance as it is the cornerstone of the *Rechtsstaat*. It guarantees judicial protection against infringements committed by public authorities. Under the general clause of Sect. 40 of the Statute relating to Administrative Courts (*Verwaltungsgerichtsordnung – VwGO*) all public law disputes which are not constitutional in nature fall within the jurisdiction of the Administrative Courts. The power of the courts is therefore not discretionary but clearly laid down in statute law. The inherent power of the English judiciary to adjudicate is strictly rejected by civil law systems. So at this early stage of evaluation one can observe fundamental differences between the common law system and the continental legal system, which have been described as "irreducible".[102] The modern basis for judicial review of administrative action is the Statute on Administrative Courts 1960 which itself is based on the relatively modern constitution of 1949. Therefore legislation supported by the constitution is the immediate basis of judicial review of administrative powers in Germany. The central norm is Art. 19 IV of the Basic Law, which guarantees judicial protection to the individual. Further it has been expressed in the Basic Law itself that the basic rights bind the executive in the same measure as the legislature and the judiciary and are directly enforceable law. Besides, the Basic Law expressly subordinates the executive to legislation by a clear provision that law and justice shall bind the executive (Arts. 1(3) and 20). It also treats this provision as a basic principle which cannot be changed even by an amendment of the Basic Law. It falls under the so-called "eternity" clause in Art. 79(3) which makes it impossible to alter Arts. 1(3) and 20 of the Basic Law. Certainly the comparatively weak position of

(1) The constitutional order in the *Länder* shall conform to the principles of the republican, democratic and social state governed by the rule of law within the meaning of the Basic Law.

101 Hufen, F., *Verwaltungsprozeßrecht*, 1998, 4; see Chapter Three for a more detailed discussion of these principles.

102 Legrand, P., "European Legal Systems are not Converging" (1996) *ICLQ* 52 [74].

the executive and the strong protection of the individual in Germany are a direct consequence from the experiences during the Nazi regime. Even though the modern German constitution had famous predecessors which influenced its drafting, the current model has proven to be the most successful with a population who have great faith in the rights guaranteed in it through judicial protection.

Judges are recruited from amongst all applicants who have passed their second state exam and therefore are automatically eligible for any position in the judiciary. No special expertise in administrative law is required. However, before taking the second state exam, German lawyers train within the civil service and some general training (up to six months) within the administration is provided. However, this is not very much so most Administrative Court judges have little experience within the administration. It can be argued that they are highly qualified but maybe sometimes too theoretical and dogmatic in their approach.

However, by comparison with English courts, the scope of review of the German Administrative Courts is wider. Indicators of this wider review is the fact that German Administrative Courts apply the inquisitorial principle which enables the court to collect and demand evidence as it wishes. It prepares its own records and takes a very active role in the proceedings. Further, no distinction is drawn between illegality within its jurisdiction and the court fully reviews the fact-finding procedure of the administration. The basis for this approach is laid down in the constitution itself which provides in Art. 1 III that "the following fundamental rights shall bind the legislature, the executive and the judiciary as directly enforceable law". This rule imposes the duty on the courts to enforce such rights against the executive and the legislature. The German constitution does not embody the principle of parliamentary sovereignty but provides for constitutional review of all legislation.

However, the intense scrutiny approach of the German Administrative Courts has been the focus of criticism for a long time. The strict control of the administration is a feature of the interpretation of the doctrine of the separation of powers. The idea of checks and balances in its present form is clearly applied in favour of the judiciary. This is particularly true in cases which involve a strong basic rights element. However, it is generally recognised that the clear separation of powers should not be violated. The Constitutional Court has expressed that no organ of the state is permitted to have superiority over another and no organ can be deprived of its competence necessary to fulfil its constitutional obligations. Any violation of the core sphere of any of the three powers will violate the separation of powers. However, the position of the Constitutional Court in this matter is not very clear. In a recent decision, the court established that the principle of separation of powers does not constitute an obstacle to the power of the legislature to enact planning permission. The grant of planning permission is traditionally within the sphere of the executive. The court found a loophole in Art. 14 III of the Basic Law which allows for expropriations to be carried out by way of legislation. The planning permission at stake required an expropriation; therefore a legislative act for the planning permission was justified in the view of the court.[103]

---

[103] BVerfGE 95, 1.

III. The grounds of review

1. The grounds of review for administrative action in England

In England judicial review of administrative action has become an important protection of the individual. This has not always been so. The role of the courts in relation to the administration of government has undergone major changes within the last 30 years.[104] To appreciate the development in judicial review proceedings fully, I shall first define judicial review by contrasting it with appellate proceedings and, secondly, briefly describe the constitutional framework in which light judicial review in England has to be seen. Thirdly, I will introduce the main features of judicial review, which will be examined in the comparative context in the following chapters.

Judicial review has to be distinguished from appellate powers which are provided by Parliament against an administrative decision. Judicial review can be described as an exercise of a residual supervisory jurisdiction by the superior courts.[105] There are two differences between judicial review procedures and appellate powers. First, an appeal court can adjust the decision of an administrative body, whereas in judicial review proceedings it can only refer the matter back to the original body. Secondly, judicial review proceedings differ from appellate powers with regard to the court's jurisdiction. The appellate court has the power to review the merits of the decision contested, whereas in judicial review proceedings the scope of review is limited to the legality of the decision.[106] The difficulties arising out of this not always clear distinction will be discussed shortly. Thirdly, it is important to discuss the relationship between the courts of law and administrative action.

The modern form of judicial review is a result of a gradual development. Judicial review now is the procedure by which the Administrative Court exercises a supervisory jurisdiction over inferior courts, tribunals or other public bodies. It is governed by the Supreme Court Act 1981, Sect. 31 and the Civil Proceedings Rules, Part 54. It can be described as a public law remedy.[107]

Lord Diplock identified three grounds of judicial review in *Council of Civil Service Unions v Minister for the Civil Service* (1984)[108]: illegality, irrationality and procedural impropriety. In this case staff employed at the Government Communications Headquarters were no longer permitted to be members of national trade unions even though they had been permitted to do so since 1947. Before the instruction of the Minister for the Civil Service was issued there had been no con-

---

104 Jowell, J. and Birkinshaw, P., "Tendencies Towards European Standards in National Administrative Law: England, Wales and Northern Ireland" in Schwarze, *Das Verwaltungsrecht unter europäischem Einfluß: zur Konvergenz der mitgliedstaatlichen Verwaltungsrechtsordnungen in der Europäischen Union*, 1996.

105 Craig, P., *Administrative Law*, 2003, 7.

106 Cane, P., *An Introduction to Administrative Law*, 1996, 35.

107 Gordon, R., *Judicial Review and the Crown Office Practice* 1996, 3.

108 [1984] 3 All ER 935, HL.

sultation of the trade unions or the employees. The House of Lords held that the government's action was reviewable, that the applicants would have had a legitimate expectation to be consulted before the instruction, but that national security issues outweighed the legitimate expectation of the applicants.

Lord Diplock's trilogy draws important distinctions between the various more traditional grounds of review.[109] A far less traditional ground of review is the principle of proportionality, which was suggested by Lord Diplock in this decision, and could become the fourth established ground of review. Even if the court in *Brind*[110] stated that proportionality, as a general rule, could not be inserted into the substantive law of judicial review, there appears to be a chance for the principle to be applied on a case-by-case basis.[111] Proportionality will be discussed in some detail in Chapter Three.

The first ground for judicial review is illegality. Here, the courts are concerned with the review for error of law. This area of judicial review has been notoriously difficult centred upon the accommodation of jurisdiction within the *ultra vires* principle and the exclusion of judicial review in ouster clauses.[112] The most famous case to illustrate the complexity of English administrative law is probably *Anisminic Ltd v Foreign Compensation Commission*.[113] Here a tribunal denied the applicant compensation for the nationalisation of its property by the Egyptian government because the applicant's successor in title was not a British national. The error consisted in the fact that the right to compensation in law did not depend on the nationality of the successor in title. The legal issues involved are complex and a few points require an introductory explanation. The doctrine of *ultra vires* permits the courts to quash decisions made by administrative bodies which they have no power to make. Traditionally, before the decision in *Anisminic*, an administrative tribunal or an administrative body could make a wrong decision as long as it acted within jurisdiction which was not reviewable by way of judicial review, but it was not permitted to exceed its statutory vires, i.e. act *ultra vires*.[114] Traditionally, the term "vires" is used in the context of administrative decisions and "jurisdiction" in the context of judicial decisions.[115] Before 1969 the division between reviewable decisions of the administration, i.e. those that were clearly *ultra vires* and those which were not reviewable, i.e. which contained an error within jurisdiction, was clear. The only exception to that clear rule was that those errors which were patent "on the face of the record", even though within jurisdiction,

---

109 See Bailey, S.H., Jones, B.L. and Mowbray, A.R., *Cases and Materials on Administrative Law,* 1992 193 et seq, where a distinction is being made between simple *ultra vires*, failure to retain discretion as to exercise of power, abuse of discretion, procedural irregularity and error of law on the face of the record.

110 *R v Secretary of State for the Home Department, ex p Bugdaycay* [1987] AC 514.

111 Jowell, J., and Birkinshaw, P., supra n. 104, 12; Gordon, R., *Judicial Review and Crown Office Practice*, 1996, 193.

112 See Hare, I., "Separation of Powers and Error of Law" in Forsyth and Hare, *The Golden Metwand and the Crooked Cord*, 1998, 113.

113 [1969] 2 AC 147.

114 De Smith, S.A., *Judicial Review of Administrative Action*, 1995, 223.

115 Ibid 229.

were reviewable as well.[116] The reason for this distinction is deeply rooted in constitutional law. For once, it is the rule of law which imposes restrictions on administrative bodies to determine their own powers and therefore opens the court to review such decisions which are taken *ultra vires*. On the other hand, it is the principle of sovereignty of Parliament which restricts courts to review the legality of actions of the executive in particular in case of ouster clauses, i.e. parliamentary legislation to restrict the courts' jurisdiction.[117] However, the distinction between these two errors is rather difficult to achieve. Just as difficult can be the distinction between law and fact. Generally speaking only legal errors can be reviewed. The administrative body is entitled to decide over facts and no judicial review takes place into the merits of a case. The distinction between law, fact and policy can cause particular difficulties. In a case about two decisions by the immigration authorities, it was held that the question whether immigrants should be granted asylum in the UK because they were political refugees constituted a so-called question on a "legislative fact" dealing with policy issues and therefore was not reviewable. The second question was whether an immigrant would be in danger of persecution in his country of origin. This was held to be a question of "jurisdictional fact" and therefore reviewable.

After the decision in *Anisminic* in 1969 the distinction between errors within or without jurisdiction became rather blurred.[118] However *Anisminic* did not fully answer all the questions. For instance it remained unclear whether all errors in law resulted in illegality, whether within or without jurisdiction. In the following years some judges took the view that all errors of law should go to jurisdiction and that there remained nothing of the traditional distinction as held before *Anisminic*.

In *Pearlman v Keepers and Governors of Harrow School*[119] a county court judge had to determine whether the installation of central heating in a dwelling house amounted to structural alteration, extension or addition. Without proffering a definition of the statutory words, the judge held that the work under consideration did not fall within them. The appellant sought an order of *certiorari* to quash the judge's decision on the ground that it depended on an error of law and accordingly was beyond jurisdiction. It was held by majority that the judge's decision on the issue was such that he must be taken to have made an error of law in the interpretation of the statutory words. Lord Denning held that the distinction between an error which entails absence of jurisdiction "is fine. So fine indeed that it is rapidly being eroded ... I would suggest that this distinction should now be discarded ..." The way to get things right is to hold thus: no court or tribunal has any jurisdiction to make an error of law on which the decision of the case depends. If it makes such an error, it goes outside its jurisdiction and *certiorari* will lie to correct it.

However, the doctrine of error of law remains complex and has been described as "hopelessly confused".[120] In *R v Hull University Visitor, ex p Page*[121] it was

---

116 Ibid 223.
117 Ibid 223, 224.
118 Cane, P., *An Introduction to Administrative Law*, 1996, 122.
119 [1979] QB 56.
120 Hare, I., supra n. 112 at 120.

held that the distinction between jurisdictional and non-jurisdictional errors of law should still be relevant. However, this related to decisions of university visitors only because there the distinction between domestic laws of the university as distinct from the general law of the land was drawn.[122] It appears that after the decision in *Anisminic* every error of law is a jurisdictional error which is reviewable by the courts as it amounts to an *ultra vires* action which cannot be protected by an ouster clause. There is very little room for non-jurisdictional errors which might be protected by an ouster clause. In *Racal Communications* Lord Diplock suggested that a tribunal could make an error when the matter involves as many inter-related questions of law, fact and degree.[123] However, "the distinction between jurisdictional and non-jurisdictional error is ultimately based upon foundations of sand".[124] It is interesting to note that the development of the grounds of review is closely connected to the availability of remedies in the courts. Early cases dating back to the seventeenth and early eighteenth century show that the prerogative writ of *certiorari*, now the quashing order, was originally aimed at errors within jurisdiction.

The three remaining grounds of review will be discussed in some detail in the following chapter. They are irrationality, procedural impropriety and possibly proportionality.

2. The grounds of review for administrative action in Germany

Judicial review of administrative action in Germany falls within the category of *Verwaltungsprozeßrecht* (Administrative Procedural Law) as opposed to the *Allgemeines* and *Besonderes Verwaltungsrecht* (General and Special Administrative Law). The constitutional basis for judicial review of administrative action is Art. 19 IV of the Basic Law which is of great importance in administrative law and reads as follows: "should any person's rights be violated by public authority, recourse to the court shall be open to him ..." Article 19 IV not only guarantees access to justice but also the scope of judicial review (*Kontrolldichte*). The scope of judicial review is closely connected with the relationship between the executive, the legislature and the judiciary and constitutes not only an issue of administrative law but also a constitutional one.[125]

The relationship between constitutional law and adminstrative law has been described as "administrative law as concrete constitutional law".[126] In Germany, the Basic Law is the highest form of law, so one could speak of constitutional rather than parliamentary sovereignty. As a result, the basic rights bind all three powers in the state. By contrast to the British Parliament , the German legislature is bound

---

121 [1993] AC 682.

122 Cane, P., *An Introduction to Administrative Law*, 1996, 124.

123 *Re Racal Communications* [1981] AC 374 at 390–391.

124 De Smith, S.A., *Principles of Judicial Review,* 1999, 120.

125 Schwarze, J., *Verwaltungsrecht unter europäischem Einfluß*, 1996, 197.

126 Werner, F. "Verwaltungsrecht als konkretisiertes Verfassungsrecht" (1959) *DVBl* 527.

to observe these basic rights and some provisions contain specific guidance as to the required legislation.[127]

Further, according to Art. 20 III, the executive is under a duty to observe the law. This principle is of great importance when reviewing the legality of administrative action. Both beneficial administrative acts and those which impose a duty on the citizen may not contradict the law (*Vorrang des Gesetzes*) and those administrative acts which impose a duty on the citizen require a statute which empowers the authorities to issue such an act (*Vorbehalt des Gesetzes*). The exemption of beneficial administrative acts from the requirement of a statute has been abandoned by the Constitutional Court, which extended this requirement to all relevant areas.[128] However, most statutes confer discretion on the authorities which guarantee a certain amount of liberty to the administration. Further, Art. 1 Sect. 3 of the Basic Law binds the executive directly to observe the human rights provisions in Arts. 1 to 19. This provision cannot be altered, which is laid down in Art. 79 III of the Basic Law. Article 79 III is sometimes referred to as the "eternity clause", i.e. a clause which guarantees the rights contained in Arts. 1 and 20 for an unlimited period of time. Article 1 III is a direct consequence of the weaknesses the Weimar constitution suffered from in so far as it binds all three powers in the state to protect the provisions of the Basic Law, particularly the first 20 human rights provisions. Under the Weimar constitution, the human rights provisions had a mere declaratory function. The danger that the administrative authorities violate human rights provisions is larger than within the legislative sphere because of time pressures in reaching decisions. These human rights provisions play an important role in two ways. First, when reviewing the administrative acts, review if relevant the constitutionality of the enabling acts, i.e. the statute on which the administrative act is based. Here the administration is bound by constitutional principles in a more indirect way. Secondly, the activity of the authorities in exercising their discretion will be bound directly by constitutional principles. The principle of equality, proportionality and legitimate expectation play a major role in the review of discretionary powers.[129] According to Art. 114 of the Law on Administrative Courts, the courts examine whether the administrative act or its refusal or omission is illegal because the statutory limits of the discretion have been exceeded or because the discretion has not been exercised for the purpose of the authorisation. Article 114 was amended in 1996 and it is now permissible for the authority to complete its discretionary decision during the judicial review proceedings. The question whether the exercise of discretion was carried out in an illegal manner is further defined in statute, this time in Art. 40 of the Law on Administrative Procedure 1976, which lays down that if an administrative authority is authorised to act at its discretion, it has to exercise its discretion in consonance with the purpose of the authorisation and the legal limits of the discretion to be observed.

---

127 See, for instance, Art. 14 Sect. 2 of the Basic Law; Ehlers, D., "Verwaltung und Verfassungsrecht" in *Allgemeines Verwaltungsrecht*, 2002, 130.

128 BVerfGE 49, 89, 126.

129 For a detailed discussion, see Chapter Three.

One of the major differences between the common law and civil law approach is the fact that judicial action under the civil law must be based on statutory grant of power. Common law courts, on the other hand, "reason instructively, ascribing much importance to facts and past decisions. In this they differ from the civil law courts which, because their power of adjudication is derivative, must operate within a predetermined, legislated, conceptualised system".[130] In Germany, the legal basis is now laid down in the modern Law on Administrative Courts 1960 (*Verwaltungsgerichtsordnung*) which consists of 195 articles. The Law on Administrative Courts covers both the judicial review of administrative action as well as the non-judicial complaints procedure within the administration, which is a prerequisite for some of the lawsuits discussed below[131]. This is a federal statute which is further supplemented by state legislation on minor issues such as name and seat of the Administrative Courts, review of delegated legislation, etc. and some regional peculiarities (for instance the non-judicial committee for complaints procedures within the administration – *Widerspruchsausschüsse* – in Hessen) which will be dealt with later on. Article 173 contains a general reference clause to provisions in the Law on Courts (*Gerichtsverfassungsgesetz*) and the Civil Procedure Act (*Zivilprozeßordnung*) which shall apply accordingly in cases of gaps in the Law on Administrative Courts. Since 1990 the Law on Administrative Courts, including some extra temporary regulations, applies to the five new *Länder* from the former German Democratic Republic as well.[132] A consequence of the statutory basis of the power of the court is that the courts do not exercise any discretion when granting or refusing a remedy. Therefore the courts cannot deny a remedy if all conditions for the grant of a remedy are satisfied. Common law remedies in public law on the contrary are discretionary remedies and the public interest, as well as the support of a functioning administration, plays an important role in the courts' exercise of discretion.[133]

Under the first heading of formal legality of the administrative action the courts review questions of competence, procedure and form. Competence describes the substantive, functional and territorial jurisdiction of the administrative authority. The substantive competence refers to the choice of the responsible authority, i.e. a federal or state authority, municipal authority or other administrative body. The functional competence refers to the hierarchical structure of the authorities. The local competence regulates the local borders of the authorities. Questions of competence can be very difficult due to a variety of statutes and delegated legislation and the federal structure of the German authorities.[134] One of the most important procedural principles, as in English law, under the German Law on Administrative Procedure 1976 is the right to a hearing.[135] Another procedural defect could be the

130 Legrand, P., supra n. 102, 52.

131 See Art. 68 et seq Law on Administrative Courts 1960.

132 Articles 8 and 45 of the Treaty of Union and annexe I, chapter III, part A III, no.1 lit. t and u, no. 6, part IV, no. 2c.

133 De Smith, S.A., *Judicial Review of Administrative Action*, 1995.

134 Erichsen H.U., Martens, W., *Allgemeines Verwaltungsrecht,* 8th edn, 1988, 228.

135 See Art. 28 et seq Law on Administrative Procedure 1976 and exceptions in Sects. 2 and 3.

non-compliance with a statute, which requires the participation of another authority.[136] Formal requirements are to be found in provisions, which require the administrative decision to be precise, and further administrative acts have to include reasons.[137] However, not all illegal administrative acts are void or voidable. Article 44 of the Administrative Procedure Act now contains a catalogue of those administrative acts which are to be considered void.[138] This catalogue contains formal and material defects. Only under these circumstances is an administrative act rendered void, otherwise it is possible for the authorities to remedy a defective administrative act under Art. 45 of the Law on Administrative Procedure. Number 3 of that article deals with the issue of a hearing which can be remedied after the decision of the administration by granting a hearing to the applicant. An administrative act is only voidable if the illegality has a consequence and the act cannot be interpreted. Generally speaking, administrative acts suffer from material rather than procedural defects which lead to an annulment.[139]

Three forms of illegality can be found in German administrative law: excess of discretion, failure to exercise discretion and abuse of discretion. Excess of discretion in German administrative law is comparable with the principle of *ultra vires* in English law. However, abuse of discretion is an illegality within the granted powers. Excess of discretion and a failure to exercise discretion where the authority assumed that it was bound to decide in a particular way are treated as similar. More important is the abuse of discretion. The administration is obliged to be guided only by rational considerations. It is not permissible to take personal motives into account and only use such considerations for the statutory grant of discretion.

German administrative law has developed a further limitation of the exercise of discretion by recognising the concept of "reduction of discretion to zero". According to this concept there are cases in which, despite the discretion granted to the authorities, only one course of action will be legal. In these cases the discretionary freedom is seen to develop into a duty to act in a particular way. The groundbreaking decision was delivered by the *Bundesverwaltungsgericht* in 1960[140]. Here the builder of a house was misusing it so that it caused harm to legally-protected interests of the neighbours. Even though the intervention by building inspectors was discretionary, the court held that in cases of high levels of disturbance or danger the only legal measure was the exercise of the authorities' power to intervene.

---

136 See Art. 36 Law on Planning.

137 See Arts. 37 and 39 (exceptions in Sect. 2) Law on Administrative Procedure 1976.

138 See Art. 44 Administrative Procedure Act 1976: "an administrative act is void: 1. if it is in writing, but the issuing authority cannot be identified; 2. if its issue does not comply with the statutory requirement of the form of a certificate; 3. non-compliance with Art. 3 no. 1 (local competence for questions regarding immovable property or legal relationships attached to a place); 4. if for factual reasons no one could exercise it; 5. if it requires the performance of a criminal act; 6. if it is against good morals".

139 Erichsen, H.U., Martens, W., *Allgemeines Verwaltungsrecht*, 1988, 238.

140 BVerwGE 11, 95, 97.

German administrative law has recently undergone changes in order to accelerate court procedures[141] and basic foundations of German administrative law have been questioned.[142] In environmental law, administrative authorities have gained more discretionary powers.[143] The doctrine of discretion in German administrative law contains a peculiarity not known in any other member state or European Community law: undefined legal concepts which are determined within the facts in a decision. Only in clearly defined circumstances has the Federal Administrative Court granted some subjective area of evaluation to the authorities which are not fully reviewable.[144]

However, a decision by the *Bundesverfassungsgericht* in 1990[145] has revived a long-standing debate about these concepts within the elaborate doctrine of discretion and sparked off a discussion about a closer orientation on European models.[146] The decision concerned the publication of a pornographic novel entitled *Josefine Mutzenbacher* telling the life story of a prostitute in Vienna around the turn of the century. According to the law on the distribution of publications considered to be dangerous to minors, the Federal Scrutiny Agency included the book on a list which sets out certain limitations regarding the dissemination of such books. An exception is provided for books considered to be art. The applicant considered the book to be a work of art protected under Art. 5 of the Basic Law and asked the authorities to delete its name from the list. The relevant issue for the area of administrative law is the way in which the Constitutional Court dealt with the sensitive area of undefined legal concepts, here the question whether the book fell within the category of "dangerous to minors" and the connected question of whether the Scrutiny Agency had any subjective area of evaluation. As a result the court held that there was no area of subjective evaluation and widened the scope of judicial review in this case in order to protect constitutional rights.

---

141 See the reform of the Law on Administrative Courts 1960 in the statute of 1.11.1996.

142 Sendler, H., "Über richterliche Kontrolldichte in Deutschland und anderswo" (1994) *NJW* 1511 [1520]; Ipsen, H.P., von Dannwitz, T., "Verwaltungsrechtliches System und Europäische Integration" (1996) *DVBl* 627.

143 Schwarze, J., *Das Verwaltungsrecht unter europäischem Einfluß*, 1996, 793.

144 Decisions in examinations, assessment of personnel in the Civil Service, decisions of valuation by experts, for instance the Federal Scrutiny Agency under the Law of the Distribution of Publications Dangerous to Minors, and policy decisions of the administration.

145 BverfGE 83, 130 – *Josefine Mutzenbacher*. The Constitutional Court held that the prohibition of a publication needs to be balanced with the freedom of art and that the administration has no subjective element of evaluation (*Beurteilungsspielraum*) and that therefore the decision is fully reviewable.

146 Schwarze, J., *Das Verwaltungsrecht unter europäschem Einfluß*, 1996, 794; Sieckmann, J.R.,"Beurteilungsspielräume und richterliche Kontrollkompetenzen" (1997) *DVBl* 101; Sendler, H., "Über richterliche Kontrolldichte in Deutschland und anderswo"(1994) *NJW* 1511 [1520].

IV. Administrative law remedies for unlawful government action

1. Remedies in English courts

Until today English administrative law is organised around remedies and causes of action. Administrative law distinguishes two categories of remedies: private law remedies and public law remedies. The former includes damages, the remedy of injunction and declaration. The old order of *mandamus* is now called mandatory order, an order of *prohibition* is now referred to as a prohibiting order and the order of *certiorari* is now called a quashing order. These changes in the language are interesting but merely cosmetic.[147] The application procedure of judicial review is now contained in the Civil Procedure Rules, Part 8, as modified by Part 54. This is the result of the Bowman Report on proceedings in the Crown Office published in March 2000. These new rules govern all applications filed on or after 2 October 2000. Part 54 displays similar features to the previous Order 53 of the Rules of the Supreme Court. Changes have been made to the requirement of standing, discovery and cross-examination.[148]

As we shall see in later chapters, overlaps between private and public law occur in other jurisdictions as well, for example, in the field of state liability in German administrative law, which is dealt with by the ordinary, i.e., civil courts.[149] The reason why state liability in Germany is dealt with by the civil courts lies in the fact that a claim against a civil servant was originally a civil law matter until the introduction of vicarious liability of the state for its servants. This is an example in German law where a public law right is dealt with by the civil courts, which are separate from the administrative courts, i.e. the procedural side is a purely private law matter. Private law remedies in English law were originally only used in private law matters but were later transposed into public law remedies.[150] German administrative law on the other hand is centred on rights (*Rechtsansprüche*) and causes of action. However, by comparing the two systems it is important to understand that the English legal system has never provided a clear distinction between substantive and procedural administrative law.[151] English law is concerned with remedies rather than rights: *ubi remedium, ibi ius*. In Germany, on the contrary, an individual right against a public authority to an act or omission of that authority is always accompanied by a procedural means to effectuate the act or omission directly: *ubi ius ibi remedium*. Further, in German law some topics dealt with by the English courts under the heading of "remedies" would not be considered as proce-

---

147 Civil Proceedings Rules (Sect. 31(1); rules 54.1(2), 54.2); Cornford, T., "The New Rules of Procedure for Judicial Review" (2000) 5 *Web JCLI*; Fordham, M., "Judicial Review: the New Rules" (2001) *Public Law* 4.

148 With regard to the right to cross-examine, see below under "The adversarial procedure".

149 See Art. 34(2) Basic Law.

150 Cane, P., *An Introduction to Administrative Law*, 1996, 66.

151 Schwarze, J., *European Administrative Law*, 2006, 148.

dural topics. In German law, damages are dealt with in "substantive" rather than "procedural" provisions.[152] The term "rights" is used in English law, however, it is said "that it does not reveal any rational adherence to a legal philosophy that would locate in the legal subject a legally authoritative form of sovereignty so that he would be invested with the power to frame a legal claim in the language of "individual prerogatives"".[153] In Germany the focus on rights rather than remedies dates back to the nineteenth century. German criticism of the European Court of Justice's jurisprudence on direct effect is based on these conceptual difficulties between rights and remedies because the ECJ seems to follow the common law model.[154]

Since the Administration of Justice (Miscellaneous Provisions) Act 1938 *certiorari*, *mandamus* and *prohibition* are also referred to as the prerogative orders. The writ of *habeas corpus* remained unchanged until the Administration of Justice Act 1960 which provided a new procedure. It is now mainly used in connection with immigration and deportation cases.[155] The private law remedies are injunctions, declaration and damages. An injunction can be granted either to forbid a person from a certain action or to require him to do something. Interim relief also falls under the heading "injunction". The main function of interim relief is to prevent a challenged governmental decision from being enforced, i.e. to achieve a "stay of proceedings".[156] The traditional position that injunctions could not be awarded against the Crown has been reversed in the aftermath of the famous *Factortame* litigation.[157] The new rule 54.10 states that "where leave to apply for judicial review is granted, then if the relief sought is an order of *prohibition* or *certiorari* and the court so directs, the grant shall operate as a stay of proceedings to which the application relates until the determination of the application or until the court otherwise orders".

The declaration is a non-coercive remedy and failure to comply with it does not amount to contempt of court. The declaration merely states the legal position of the parties but does not change their legal position or rights.[158] Damages are a purely private law remedy. They cannot be awarded in order to compensate an authority's illegal activity unless a private law cause of action can be shown, for example, damages for breach of contract or tort.

The availability of these remedies, which are appropriate to judicial review, underlay certain restrictions. These are: the court's discretion, *locus standi* provisions, exclusions of remedies, time limits and the exhaustion of remedies. Under an application for judicial review, the English High Court enjoys a considerable amount of flexibility because of the discretion it is granted in exercising its pow-

---

[152] See Art. 34 Basic Law in connection with Art. 839 Civil Code.

[153] Legrand, P., "European Legal Systems are not Converging" (1996) *ICLQ* 52 [70] and further references.

[154] Ruffert, M., "Rights and Remedies in European Community Law: A Comparative View" (1997) *CMLR* 309 [333].

[155] Stevens, I., *Constitutional and Administrative Law* ,1996, 259.

[156] Cane, P., *An Introduction to Administrative Law*, 1996, 66.

[157] *M v Home Office* [1994] 1 AC 377.

[158] Gordon, R., Supra n. 107, 69.

ers. The court has discretion on deciding whether to grant leave to apply for judicial review, when deciding about the nature of the preparation and the procedure for the hearing, when deciding whether the application succeeds on its merits and when deciding the relief.[159] However, it is important to distinguish between different remedies. The remedy of damages, for instance, is not discretionary and will only be awarded if this would have been the case in a private law action. Further, the remedy of declaration is a non-coercive remedy, which means the legal position of the applicant does not change with the granting of a declaration. They are granted when no other order succeeds. When exercising its discretion the court has taken the "*prima facie* approach", which consists of the rule that where an applicant can successfully show that the administrative action is unlawful, he is entitled to a remedy. However, in exceptional cases, the court can have "reasons to depart from it" if the non-granting of a remedy is in the public interest.[160]

The drafting of the new rules in Part 54 has raised hopes that the rules regarding the release of evidence and disclosure of documents would be changed in favour of the defendants. "Hitherto, perhaps the single greatest source of inequality between claimant and defendant in judicial review has been their differing positions with respect to information".[161] As we shall see in Chapter Three, English law does not recognise a general duty to give reasons. Therefore, traditionally the defendant authority, as opposed to the claimant, has always had the advantage of having access to the information on which a decision was based. Even though discovery was introduced in 1977 into the Rules of the Supreme Court, it was rarely ordered. Orders of discovery required that the court had to be of the opinion that discovery would enable the court to dispose of the case fairly or for the purpose of saving costs.[162] The so-called Protocols Practice Direction has created some hope, which is clearly supportive of the idea that parties should exchange information before initiating proceedings:

> "In cases not covered by any approved protocol, the court will expect the parties, in accordance with the overriding objective and the matters referred to in the Civil Procedure Rules 1.1(2)(a), (b) and (c), to act reasonably in exchanging information and documents relevant to the claim and generally in trying to avoid the necessity for the start of proceedings".[163]

However, it is unlikely that this will increase the numbers of orders made for discovery as the intention of the new Civil Procedure Rules is to save time and speed up litigation. Further, judicial review is supposed to remain a "special jurisdiction unlikely to involve a substantial dispute of fact".[164]

159 De Smith, S.A., *Judicial Review of Administrative Actio*n, 1995, 805.
160 Ibid 808.
161 Cornford, M., "The New Rules of Procedure for Judicial Review" (2000) 5 *Web JCLI* 7.
162 Order 24 rules 8 and 13(1) of the Rules of the Supreme Court.
163 As cited in Cornford, supra n. 161, 8.
164 Ibid 9.

2. Remedies in German Administrative Courts

Before describing the standard procedures available to the aggrieved citizen in the German Administrative Courts, it is necessary to point out that the division of remedies and procedures cannot simply be applied to the German system. Again, conceptual differences require some explanation. Unlike the English legal system, the German system draws a clear distinction between substantive and procedural administrative law (*Allgemeines Verwaltungsrecht und Verwaltungsprozessrecht*). As pointed out before, the rules on state liability[165] for instance and those concerning the restitution of levies[166] are dealt with in substantive provisions rather than under a procedural heading, therefore belonging to the "rights side" of the issue.[167] The other side will be purely procedural. The somehow separate level remedies, also found in Community law, finds no equivalent in German law. Again, this conceptual difference is deeply rooted within the concept of a *right* and the constitutional protection of the individual under Art. 19 IV of the Basic Law which guarantees recourse to the courts. This principle finds its clear expression in administrative law and what is known as the doctrine of the *Schutznorm*, which is of great relevance at the standing stage. This subjective public law right enables the citizen to pursue his or her own interests with the help of the legal order.[168] At the same time the doctrine of the *Schutznorm* constitutes a hurdle with the result that a norm can only confer rights on the individual under certain circumstances. Its roots go back to the beginning of the century. The concept is applied by the Administrative Courts and has found wide acceptance amongst academic writers.[169] The concept is concerned with the question whether the legislator has intended to confer individual rights on the citizen. To detect such subjective rights within a legal statute the provision in question has to be interpreted. Three conditions have been developed according to which a statute confers a subjective right on the individual. First, a public law statute has to contain a particular duty to act on the side of the administration. Secondly, the statute must have been partly enacted at least to satisfy some individual interest. Thirdly, the applicant must be granted the legal power to exercise such rights. Naturally, compliance with these conditions has caused the courts some difficulties. Further, with a view to the requirements of Community law and the concept of direct effect, clashes have been unavoidable[170] and this position in German law will have to adapt.

Depending on the type of grievance there are six different types of action in German administrative law, which are governed by Arts 42 and 43 of the Law on

---

[165] Article 34 Basic Law in connection with Art. 839 Civil Code.

[166] Articles 48, 49 Law on Administrative Procedure.

[167] Ruffert, M., "Rights and Remedies in European Community Law: A Comparative View" (1997) *CMLR* 307.

[168] Erichsen, H.U., in Erichsen, H.U., Ehlers, D., *Allgemeines Verwaltungsrecht*, 2002, 250.

[169] Ibid 155 with further references.

[170] Case C-431/92, *Commission v Germany* [1995] ECR I-2189, para 43 (Environmental Impact Assessment Directive); Case C-433/93, *Commission v Germany* [1995] ECR I-2305, para 18.

Administrative Courts. The *Anfechtungsklage* is an action to annul an administrative act and roughly equivalent to the prerogative order of *certiorari*, the quashing order. The most important prerequisite for the availability of that action is the existence of an administrative act. Article 35 of the Law on Administrative Procedure governs the latter. It is defined as "every order, decision or other sovereign measure taken by an authority for the regulation of a particular case in the sphere of public law and directed at immediate external legal consequence". The concept of the administrative act first appeared in the early nineteenth century German public law literature and was a direct translation of the French term *acte administratif*, which in French law covered both the activities of the administration whether in the field of private or public law. In Germany, however, the term was only used in pure public law matters. The concept of the administrative act was originally of great importance with regard to the availability of remedies in the Administrative Courts. Only if the activity of the administration could be classified as an administrative act was a remedy available to the applicant. This concept was laid down in the Weimar constitution as well as in the Regulation on the Administrative Jurisdiction in the British Occupation Zone after the Second World War.[171] However, the relevance of the concept was reduced by the introduction of the Law on Administrative Courts 1960 which provides for judicial review proceedings in all non-constitutional public law disputes regardless of whether an administrative act is at stake.[172] The administrative act still has a special position within the forms of administrative action. Three of the six causes of action are designed for legal disputes relating to administrative acts.

In addition to the act of annulment (*Anfechtungsklage*), the Law on Administrative Courts provides for an action to compel the authorities to grant an administrative act (*Verpflichtungsklage*). This means that the courts may direct the authorities to enact a certain decision. Both actions require the applicant to apply for the non-judicial complaints procedure within the administration (*Widerspruchsverfahren*) and obtain a reply (*Widerspruchsbescheid*).[173] The third type of action provided for the challenge of an administrative act is a declaration that the administrative act, which no longer exists, was illegal (*Fortsetzungsfeststellungsklage*).[174]

For other forms of administrative action other than administrative acts, an action for a declaration (*Feststellungsklage*) is provided for by the Law on Administrative Courts which is subsidiary to the general action (*Leistungsklage*). Another form of action is the norm control regarding local byelaws as provided in Art. 47 of the Law on Administrative Courts. This action is only available in the Higher Administrative Courts (*Oberverwaltungsgericht*).

Finally, an individual may bring an individual complaint with regard to a judgment to the Federal Constitutional Court (*Bundesverfassungsgericht*).

---

171 Article 107 of the Weimar Constitution; Art. 25 Regulation no. 165 of the British Military Government on the Administrative Jurisdiction in the British Zone.

172 Erichsen/Martens, *Allgemeines Verwaltungsrecht*, 1998, 171.

173 See Art. 68 et seq Law on Administrative Courts.

174 See Art. 113 Sect. 4 Law on Administrative Courts.

An important effect of a non-judicial complaint and an action for annulment is the automatic suspending effect governed by Art. 80 of the Law on Administrative Courts. As a result of the suspending effect, the administrative act cannot be enforced. However, there are exceptions to that general rule and in particular cases there is no automatic suspending effect. The protection under Art. 19 IV of the Basic Law however had direct influence on the provisions in Art. 80 and provides for the restoration of the suspending effect if the interests of the applicant justify it. This rather intense judicial protection however collided with the jurisprudence of the European Court of Justice in its interim relief rulings.[175]

V. Procedural aspects

1. The adversarial procedure

In England the adversarial procedure applies to judicial review cases as well as to private law disputes. More specifically, when deciding on questions of fact or public policy in the course of an application for judicial review, the underlying facts on which an application is based are set out by the applicant and then are agreed by the parties.[176] Generally speaking the available forms of evidence are affidavit, cross-examination and interrogatories and discovery. Affidavits are sworn written statements and are usually the sole form of evidence for decisions in public law procedures. In order to speed up the proceedings under the Civil Procedure Rules, Part 54, no pleadings are allowed for the purpose of clarifying disputes relating to questions of fact. Further, cross-examination of the party which produced an affidavit no longer appears to be contained in Part 54 (which has superseded the former Order 53 of the Rules of the Supreme Court). However, a recent decision by the Administrative Court[177] seems to suggest that the court could still receive oral evidence and order the cross-examination of witnesses in judicial review proceedings. Another decision emphasises that "in some judicial review cases cross-examination is regarded not only as appropriate but also essential".[178]

Discovery of documents is a procedure to ensure that documents in the possession or custody of a party are disclosed. In actions begun by writ, discovery is automatic and mutual and all parties must make discovery without having been ordered to do so by the court. Discovery consists of serving a list of documents on the other party. However, in applications for judicial review under Part 54, these so-called interlocutory procedures are only available following a court order. In

175 *Zuckerfabrik Süderdiethmarschen AG v Hauptzollamt Itzehoe and Zuckerfabrik Soest GmbH v Hauptzollamt Paderborn* [1991] ECR I-415 C-143 and C-92/89.

176 De Smith, S.A., *Judicial Review of Administrative Action*, 1995, 15–085.

177 *R (G) v Ealing London Borough Council and others* (2002) *The Times*, 18 March.

178 *R (Wilkinson) v Broadmoor Special Hospital Authority* (2001) *The Times*, 2 November, [2002] 1 WLR 419.

practice the courts have only rarely used this procedure.[179] The reasoning behind this rather restrictive use of fact-finding procedures is to reduce the length of judicial review procedures and also to "minimise the pressure to disclose government documents".[180] Further, English law does not contain a general duty to give reasons for administrative decisions. Despite exceptions, i.e. in statutes which contain the duty to give reasons for a decision made (for instance in the Homeless Persons Act, Sect. 8(4) and the Housing Act 1980, Sect. 5), this constitutes another obstacle to applicants in judicial review applications.

The burden of proof generally lies with the applicant. The maxim *omnia praesumuntur rite esse acta* comprises the presumption that the authority's action was legal.[181] Therefore it is the applicant's duty to present such facts to challenge this presumption. Because of the above-mentioned restrictions of interlocutory procedures, "any conflict between an applicant's and respondent's evidence normally has to be resolved in the respondent public body's favour, on the grounds that the applicant has failed to discharge the onus which he is required to satisfy to show that the respondent has acted unlawfully".[182]

These shortcomings in the fact-finding procedure at trial stage have been critised widely. In Griffith's view, the English have "an interventionist judiciary but a judiciary which is limited by procedures and practices designed to exclude certain sources of information and factual investigation without which the policy choices made by the courts – that is, their decisions – are inevitably less good than they could be".[183] In an article concerned with the work by L.L. Fuller on polycentric disputes,[184] Allison argues, "the judge who responds only to the proofs and arguments of the parties cannot ensure that relevant repercussions are considered or that affected parties other than the litigating parties participate in proceedings".[185] These criticisms all result in a call for reform of the adversarial procedure which would involve a movement from the adversarial towards the inquisitorial system. The most famous proposal in this context stems from Lord Woolf:

"... I have been concerned as to whether our adversarial procedure, which applies to judicial review in the same way as it applies to an ordinary action, sufficiently safeguards the public. It has been suggested again recently that there is a need for a Minister of Justice. If this is too dramatic a constitutional innovation, I would suggest consideration should be given to the introduction into civil procedure of an independent body that can represent the public. For the want of a better title, I should like to see established a Director of Civil Proceed-

---

179 De Smith, S.A., supra n. 176, 15–086; Cane, supra n. 156, 96; *A Concise Dictionary of Law*, 1990, 131.

180 Cane, P., supra n. 156, 93.

181 Wade, H.W.R., and Forsyth, C.F.,*Administrative Law*, 1994, 333.

182 De Smith, S.A., supra n. 176, 15–086.

183 Griffith, J.A.G., "Judicial Decision Making in Public Law" (1985) *Public Law* 564 [580].

184 Fuller, L.L., "Adjudication and the Rule of Law" (1960) 54 *American Society for International Law Proceedings* 1; "The Forms and Limits of Adjudication" (1978) 92 *Harvard Law Review* 353; for further references, see Allison, J., "The Procedural Reason for Judicial Restraint" (1994) *Public Law* 452.

185 Allison, J.W.F., supra n. 184, 467.

ings who at least in administrative law proceedings would have a status similar to that of the Director of Public Prosecutions in criminal proceedings".[186]

The Director of Civil Proceedings would be empowered to initiate proceedings in the public interest, be of help to applicants and present evidence of the public interest to the court. However, this proposal has not yet been put into practice and "such a development seems unlikely for the foreseeable future".[187]

2. The inquisitorial procedure

In judicial review procedures of administrative decisions the inquisitorial procedure applies (*Inquisitionsmaxime*). Article 86 of the Law on Administrative Courts lays down that the court examines the facts of a case *suo moto*; the participants are called upon to co-operate. It is not bound by the pleadings and evidence of the participants to the dispute. Similar to criminal proceedings or in proceedings in the finance or social courts and others the public interest in a correct decision requires an objectively correct and complete establishment of the facts which underlie the decision. This stands in contrast to the civil procedure where the parties are required to present their versions of the facts to the court. The main emphasis of the inquisitorial process is completeness, openness and neutrality of the establishment of the facts. However, as mentioned above, the participants are called upon to co-operate. The participants have to contribute to the fact-finding process, in particular in questions of fact to which they have easy access because they lie within their sphere. The procedure is flawed if the court does not comply with its duty to investigate the facts properly. The court may not request data or facts which are not within the sphere of knowledge or access of that particular party. Forms of evidence which can be taken by the court are documents, witnesses, experts and even direct evidence taken at the location (*Augenschein*). The court has to use all these methods of taking evidence fully. However, limits to the use of evidence are set by the principle of proportionality. It is, for instance, not necessary to call an official from abroad as witness in a trial concerning the granting of asylum.[188] According to Art. 99 of the Law on Administrative Courts, the court may order that the authorities disclose documents, files and information to the court. However, limitations exist, for instance, if the disclosure of such documents or files would be harmful to the federation or one of the states.[189]

The investigation into the facts which underlie an administrative decision, in particular the question of how the authorities have exercised their discretion, is facilitated by the provision in Art. 39 of the Law on Administrative Procedure which states:

186 Woolf, H., "Public Law–Private Law: Why the Divide? A Personal View" (1986) *Public Law* 220 [235–236]; *Protection of the Public, A New Challenge,* 1990, 109.

187 Birkinshaw, P., *Grievances, Remedies and the State*, 1994, 259.

188 BVerwG, NJW 1989, 678.

189 Hufen, F., *Verwaltungsprozessrecht*, 1998, 594.

"A written administrative act or an act confirmed in writing must carry written reasons. In the reasons important factual and legal grounds, which the authority has taken into consideration in arriving at its decision, have to be communicated. Reasons for discretionary decisions must also state the viewpoints on which the authority has exercised its discretion".

According to the general rule of proof which applies in civil procedure, the burden of proof rests upon that party for which the proof of a fact is beneficial. However, this principle can only be applied destructively in judicial review procedures. Here, the burden of proof rests upon that party which has more access to the relevant facts and information. This approach is referred to as *Sphährenverantwortung* (responsibility for one's sphere). The aggrieved citizen has to present all facts truthfully and name sources of evidence which are in his sphere and which are accessible to him. The court has to ensure that the authorities disclose all facts and produce evidence within their sphere.

VI. Constitutional adjudication - the institutional dimension

1. Introduction

The rule of law and the principle of the *Rechtsstaat* are of fundamental importance to the development of the principles of judicial review, both in England and Germany respectively. The quote of the former president of the German Federal Administrative Court remains valid: Administrative law can be understood as "concrete Constitutional law".[190] The German Federal Constitutional Court has played a crucial role in upholding the principle of the *Rechtsstaat.* In many decisions it has confirmed the protection of individual rights and articulated constitutional standards for procedural and substantive Administrative law.[191]
Constitutional reform has been accorded high priority on the British government's agenda. When "New Labour" came to power in 1997 it initiated legislative reform of the composition of the House of Lords, devolution for Scotland, Wales and Northern Ireland, the incorporation of the European Convention on Human Rights into English law and freedom of information. The Constitutional Reform Act 2005 provides for the establishment of a new "Supreme Court". Further, it contains reforms of the selection process for judges by establishing a Judicial Appointments Commission and changes to the ancient office of Lord Chancellor.

Germany's constitutional history is clearly very different from the British experience. In a country that experienced several unsuccessful attempts to establish the rule of law and then its total denial, the setting up of a Constitutional Court in

190 Werner, F., „Verwaltungsrecht als konkretisiertes Verfassungsrecht", *DVBl* 1959, 527.

191 BVerfGE 33, 1, 10 (prisoner's rights); BVerfGE 73, 280, 296 (advertisement of public service employment); BVerfGE 1, 97, 104 (*Sozialstaatsprinzip*); BverfGE 84, 34 (Intensity of judicial review, law state exam case II, see below chapter 3); for further references see Erichsen, H.U., Ehlers, D., *Allgemeines Verwaltungsrecht,* 2002, 119 ff.

1951 was the "crowning jewel on the constitution", the guarantor to secure basic constitutional principles. Germany's history explains why many eastern European states have found the German court influential as a model.

The wave of constitutional reform in the UK stops short of drafting a written constitution establishing a framework of entrenched legal principles and fundamental rights. As is well known, the UK's constitution is a functional self-referential constitution built on custom and practice, laws and principles and not one enshrined in a superior status document. According to Lord Falconer, the new Secretary of State for Constitutional Affairs, a written constitution is currently clearly not envisaged – not even in the light of a proposed new constitution for the European Union. Lord Woolf, the Lord Chief Justice of England and Wales, suggested such a step in a lecture in 2004 to protect the British constitution, which, he feared, was subject to change at such an alarming pace.[192] Even though a written constitution is not an option, recent commentators on the Constitutional Reform Bill (now the Constitutional Reform Act 2005) argued that a move towards a constitution which is more law-based rather than a constitution based on politics is under way.[193] This transformation is interesting but also problematic as "the British traditionally prefer experience to principle".[194] One of the Law Lords, Lord Hoffmann, declared that the proposal to establish a Supreme Court was the "abandonment of constitutional pragmatism".[195] Another Law Lord, Lord Hope, opined: "the reality is that no doubt due to one of the many accidents of our history we have built up a system here that has advantages that simply cannot be reproduced anywhere else".[196]

The Constitutional Reform Act 2005 has to be seen in this context of change towards a more principled approach to governance. The coming into force in the UK of the Human Rights Act 1998, which introduced much of the ECHR into UK laws, had been described as a "quantum leap into a new legal culture of fundamental rights and freedoms".[197] It clearly emphasised this change in the legal culture. Nevertheless, changes in British constitutional law seem to be most palatable if they are made gradually and with careful consideration of Britain's constitutional legacy. The structure of the Human Rights Act 1998, for instance, which does not give judges the power to strike down legislation, merely to declare it in-

---

192 Lord Woolf, the Lord Chief Justice of England and Wales, "The Rule of Law and a Change in the Constitution", Squire Centenary Lecture, Cambridge University, 3 March 2004, www.dca.gov.uk/judicial/speeches/lcj030304.htm.

193 Hale, B., "A Supreme Court for the United Kingdom?" (2004) *Legal Studies*, vol. 24, Issue 1 and 2; Constitutional Innovations: the Creation of a Supreme Court for the UK; Domestic, Comparative and International Reflections, A Special Issue, 36; Woodhouse, D., "The Constitutional and Political Implications of a UK Supreme Court" (2004) *Legal Studies* 134.

194 Stevens, R., "Judicial Independence in England, A Loss of Innocence" in Russell, P., O'Brien, D., *Judicial Independence in the Age of Democracy: Critical Perspective from Around the World*, 2001, 171.

195 *The Guardian*, 5 March 2004.

196 *The Guardian*, 5 March 2004.

197 Wade, W., "Human Rights and the Judiciary" (1998) *EHRL Rev* 520, 532.

compatible with Convention rights, has been praised for revealing "an elegant balance between respect for Parliament's legislative supremacy and the legal security of the Convention rights".[198] Finding this balance between the past and the present to provide for continuity has been described as a particularly British virtue. While the endurance of British constitutional law has been admired by continental academics, constitutional reform has to be seen increasingly within a European context where exigencies may quicken the pace for change.

Admittedly, other European legal systems have taken very different paths. Germany's constitution, for instance, radically changed the balance of powers in the state and entrusted a Constitutional Court with the protection of constitutional values half a century ago. It is worth noting that, however, 55 years after the drafting of a new constitution for Germany, the process of selecting the German judiciary is on the political agenda again. There is a variety of selection processes in Germany. It should be noted that the selection at federal level has been criticised for a lack of input by the judiciary. At state level an overemphasis of executive decision-making through the ministries of justice is controversial. Unlike many other European countries, there is no independent judicial council to oversee judicial appointments.[199] This trend to more autonomy is afforded general support by a recommendation of the Committee of Ministers of the Council of Europe on the independence, efficiency and role of judges. Accordingly, "the authority taking the decision on the selection and career of judges should be independent of the government and the administration. In order to safeguard its independence, rules should ensure that, for instance, its members are selected by the judiciary ..."[200] Where the constitutional or legal provisions and traditions allow judges to be appointed by the government, there should be guarantees to ensure that the procedures to appoint judges are transparent and independent. Assisted by comparative reflections on Germany, this section assesses the complexities of the issues raised by the UK's Constitutional Reform Act 2005.

2. The ancient office of Lord Chancellor

For several years arguments for modernising the English judiciary, including the re-evaluation of the role of the Lord Chancellor, have been discussed in great de-

---

198 *International Transport Roth GmbH and others v Secretary of State for the Home Department* [2002] EWCA Civ 158, [2002] 3 WLR 344 per Laws LJ, para 71.

199 See Teetzmann, H., "Selbstverwaltung der Justiz; Rechtsvergleichender Überblick" in *Deutsche Richterzeitung*, 2003, 44.

200 "Council of Europe Committee of Ministers Recommendation Number R (94) 12 of the Committee of Ministers to Member States on the Independence, Efficiency and Role of Judges" (adopted by the Committee of Ministers on 13 October 1994 at the 518th meeting of the Ministers' Deputies).

tail.[201] One commentator distinguished between "pressure towards a constitution based on law rather than on politics" as coming from the European Court of Human Rights as well as stemming from internal changes.[202] The office of the Lord Chancellor, which dates back before the Norman Conquest, has most often been criticised for its violation of the separation of powers. He is the head of the judiciary and may sit as a judge and until recently did so. He is the President of the Supreme Court, which comprises the Court of Appeal, the High Court and Crown Courts which deal with the more important criminal cases. He is also a member of the executive as a senior member of the Cabinet and a member of the House of Lords as well as being the Keeper of the King's conscience – which must of necessity be a Protestant one, a matter itself of some controversy today. As a political office holder, he is subject to dismissal at will. The protean nature of the Lord Chancellor's roles are most conspicuous when he is speaking in the House of Lords taking the position of the government. To indicate the change of role from Speaker, he emerges from the Woolsack, which represents his seat in the upper chamber, and addresses the Lords from a spot originally designated by Henry VIII in 1539.[203]

This anomalous confusion of roles has been described as "flying in the face of Art. 6" of the European Convention on Human Rights.[204] Two decisions by the European Court of Human Rights underline this concern. In *McGonnell v UK*[205] the European Court of Human Rights held that it was incompatible with Art. 6 that the Deputy Bailiff of Guernsey was both the sole judge in the case before him and President of the Parliament, which enacted the law in question. In *Starrs v Ruxton*[206] the Scottish High Court of Justiciary decided that the position of Temporary Sheriff (a judicial office in Scotland subject for re-appointment by the executive) lacked sufficient independence required by Art. 6.

Despite the anomaly of the constitutional position of the Lord Chancellor, the role has been defended by previous office holders. The Lord Chancellor's office has been justified as one representative of "each branch of our constitution to the other".[207] Some senior members of the judiciary maintain that the Lord Chancellor embodies a "guardian of constitutional propriety".[208] This traditional institutional framework has been defended for working well in practice because the Lord

201 See, for instance, Lord Bingham, "A New Supreme Court for the United Kingdom", the Constitution Unit Spring Lecture 2002, 1 May 2002; Department for Constitutional Affairs, Consultation Paper, "Constitutional Reform: A New Way of Appointing Judges"; Consultation Paper 10/03, July 2003, "Constitutional Reform: A Supreme Court for the United Kingdom".

202 Oliver, D., *Constitutional Reform*, 2003, 331.

203 Barnett, H., *Constitutional and Administrative Law*, 2002, 109 et seq.

204 Lord Patten, Motion on Judicial Appointments, Hansard HL Debates, vol. 597, col. 1441 (1 March 1999) quoted in Stevens, R., *The English Judges*, 2002, 105.

205 8 BHRC 56, (2000) Times, 22 February.

206 2000 JC 208.

207 Stevens, R., *The English Judges*, 2002, with further references, 126.

208 Lord Bingham, Select Committee on the Constitutional Reform Bill [HL], vol. I, HL paper no. 125-I, para 22.9, 2 July 2004.

Chancellor acted as a "buffer" between the executive and the judiciary. His responsibility was to achieve both the protection of the judiciary's interests and to ensure that the position of the executive is fully understood by the judges. Those worried about the lack of a clear separation of powers were assured that convention (the custom and practice of the UK constitution) guaranteed that the Lord Chancellor selected candidates for judicial office on a non-partisan basis.[209] Not all were assuaged by such assurances.

It became increasingly difficult to retain a system which is not readily capable of rational justification within modern conceptions of governance. One commentator summarised the central theme of the process of constitutional reform since 1997 as "the need to refashion our political system so that it no longer depends on tacit understandings, but is based upon clear public principles for organising and controlling power".[210]

3. The new Supreme Court

The Constitutional Reform Act 2005 establishes a new Supreme Court for the United Kingdom, which will combine the jurisdiction of the Appellate Committee of the House of Lords and the Judicial Committee of the Privy Council. The present position is deeply confusing. The Appellate Committee of the House of Lords currently hears appeals from the courts in England and Wales and Northern Ireland and in civil cases *alone* from Scotland. The Judicial Committee of the Privy Council, a legacy of Royal Prerogative, has overseas and ecclesiastical jurisdiction and hears devolution cases amongst other matters. To secure a "distinct constitutional separation between the legislature and the judiciary" the new Supreme Court will be separate from the House of Lords and the Act disqualifies judges in the new Supreme Court to sit and vote in the legislative chamber of the House of Lords.[211]

The need for reform has been related to the absence of a complete separation of powers in the UK constitution which, in theory, allows the judges in the highest court in the country, the Appellate Committee of the House of Lords, to take part in the work of the legislature. Subsequently, they may then interpret legislation in which they had been involved in Bill stages and which could be seen by litigants as less than impartial. The consultation paper announced that the new Supreme Court "will reflect and enhance the independence of the judiciary from both the legislature and the executive". Several commentators of the proposal supported this view.[212] However, Lord Norton of Louth, an academic and Chair of the influ-

---

209 Malleson, K.E., "Modernising the Constitution: Completing the Unfinished Business" (2004) *Legal Studies* 119 [124].

210 Bogdanor, V., written evidence to the Select Committee on the Constitutional Reform Bill [HL], vol. I, HL paper no. 125-I, p. 325 (2 July 2004).

211 Part 6 Nr 137 of the Constitutional Reform Act 2005

212 See, for instance, Woodhouse, D., "Constitutional and Political Implications of a UK Supreme Court" (2004) *Legal Studies* 134 [139].

ential Lords Select Committee on the Constitution, expressed unease with the logic of the proposals.

Lord Norton referred to the government's assurance that the changes should not be understood as the expression of dissatisfaction with the *performance* of the House of Lords in its judicial capacity at present. Therefore, in his view "the argument is one of perception". It follows, he believes, that it does not make sense to remove the Law Lords from the House of Lords if in fact they are exercising their judicial role properly. Therefore the debate is not one on independence but on "how people see independence". He then suggests two alternative ways of dealing with this misconception; either to introduce changes or to "correct the misperception".[213] In his view the government has not yet made the case for the introduction of radical change.

Increasingly, most judges, lawyers and politicians want to be seen as a model of good practice in a growing European Union as well as in a wider Europe and Lord Falconer hopes that the new Supreme Court will be "a real flagship for the British legal system which would improve its standing both domestically and abroad".[214] The current constitutional arrangements may not lend themselves as a model for weaker democracies in, for example, eastern Europe. This present position in the UK reflects the practice and theory of a powerful sovereign Parliament. Many eastern European states have adopted the Austro-German model of constitutional adjudication which "compensates for the weaknesses of the emerging political culture with its special institutional strengths".[215] If the need for change is mainly based on the misperception of the public and other European member states, does it not lead to a risk of further confusion or even damage to a highly regarded British institution, it is asked? Is the damage not increased if that institution is named after a court which in the USA protects the values of a written constitution and which set the template for a remarkable growth of constitutional courts in Europe in the twentieth century?

Amongst the senior judiciary, there is little evidence for support, let alone enthusiasm, for the new Supreme Court. Several of the Law Lords were openly opposed to the proposal regarding it as "harmful", "unnecessary" and whose costs are disproportionate to its benefit.[216] The former Lord Chancellor and the current Lord Chief Justice have criticised the proposal for being mainly architectural[217]

[213] Lord Norton, 652, HL Official Report (5th series), cols 122 and 123, 8 September 2003.

[214] Malleson, K.E., "Modernising the Constitution: Completing the Unfinished Business" (2004) *Legal Studies* 119 [130–131].

[215] Hoffmann-Riem, W. (judge at the Federal Constitutional Court), "Two Hundred Years of *Marbury v Madison*: The Struggle for Judicial Review of Constitutional Questions in the United States and Europe" in *German Law Journal*, vol. 5, no. 6, 1 June 2004, p. 11, www/germanlawjournal.com.

[216] Stevens, R., "Reform in Haste and Repent at Leisure" (2004) *Legal Studies* 1 [30] with further references. For the views of the Law Lords, see "Law Lords' Response to a Government Consultation on a Supreme Court", Consultation Paper 11/03, July 2003, www.parliament.uk/judicial_work/judicial_work.cfm.

[217] Lord Irvine and Lord Woolf cited in Stevens, R., "Reform in Haste and Repent at Leisure" (2004) *Legal Studies* 1 [30].

and indeed the physical separation of powers, the search for separate accommodation for the new court, appear to be more important to the government than a more serious reflection on refining its jurisdiction. The Law Lords and senior judges have also been extremely sensitive about the proposals for the location of the new court. Whilst divergent in their views on the desirability of a Supreme Court in principle, the Law Lords agree that the originally suggested site, the Middlesex Guildhall in Westminster, is unsuitable without further major structural changes.[218]

The new Supreme Court will, in the absence of any plans for a written constitution, have no new powers and will not strike down legislation. So far, judgments of the Appellate Committee and Privy Council are in the form *de lege* of a *report* to the House of Lords and *advice* to the Crown respectively. They are always accepted *de facto* and are binding legal authority on lower courts. Without clearer and newly defined powers therefore, the new court is in danger of simply being viewed as an empty shell or a "second class Supreme Court". Lord Woolf, the present Lord Chief Justice, warned that among the "Supreme Courts of the world, our Supreme Court will, because of its more limited role, be a poor relation. We will be exchanging a first class final court of appeal for a second class Supreme Court".[219] The complexity of the reforms is illustrated by the conclusions from the report of the House of Lords Select Committee on the Bill referred to above and published on 2 July 2004. It could not reach agreement on the question of whether or not to establish a Supreme Court. Oddly perhaps, it did manage to agree that if the reforms were successful, the new court should be named "The Supreme Court of the United Kingdom" and the judges were to have the title of "Justices of the Supreme Court".[220]

During the legislative process critics complained of a lack of basic principle in the reforms. "The government's proposals enter far more complex territory than is acknowledged in the consultation papers, perhaps reflecting the haste in which the proposals were generated".[221] Some commentators, on the contrary, described the proposals as principled. "Principled" is however a relative term. In some ways, it may well appear principled to sit down and draft legislation on constitutional reform. Some hastily drafted arguments, however, do not change a political culture in a principled way. The most radical suggestion for reform stems from Lord Woolf who, in a lecture at Cambridge University in March 2004, called for a written constitution to secure the position of the judiciary: "a virtue [of our constitution] … is that our constitution has always been capable of evolving as the needs of society change, but flexibility comes at a price. We have never had the protec-

---

218 See conflicting reports in the Times, 17 May 2004, reporting that Lord Falconer allegedly announced to put plans for a Supreme Court on "ice cold storage" for up to 10 years. Lord Falconer denied this statement a day later, see the Daily Telegraph, 19 May 2004.

219 Lord Woolf, the Lord Chief Justice of England and Wales, "The Rule of Law and a Change in the Constitution", Squire Centenary Lecture, Cambridge University, 3 March 2004, p. 8, www.dca.gov.uk/judicial/speeches/lcj030304.htm.

220 Select Committee on the Constitutional Reform Bill, HL 125-I (2 July 2004) para 442.

221 Lord Norton, Hansard HL Debate, vol. 652, cols 122 and 123 (8 September 2003).

tion that a written constitution can provide for institutions that have a fundamental role to play in society". This suggestion was made in the context of previous reforms in the government's 2004 Asylum and Immigration Bill, which proposed the removal of rights of judicial review against Home Office decisions in asylum and immigration matters.[222] The judges see judicial review as a constitutional guarantee of the rule of law – they were apoplectic!

Lord Woolf's lecture pays tribute to the "national culture" which has not required a written document setting out Britain's constitutional arrangements: "our ability to cope without a written constitution has depended on our tradition of mutual respect, restraint and co-operation".[223] In his view, both the protection of the independence of the judiciary as well as the protection of an individual's access to the courts in cases concerning "basic human rights" could, however, now be a catalyst for a campaign for a written constitution.[224] Unsurprisingly, Lord Woolf's remarks made dramatic headlines in the media although the minister, Lord Falconer, swiftly rejected such a prospect. Lord Woolf's approach, though radical, is logical. The government has, consciously or not, stirred up deeply rooted cultural anxieties. As with the reforms involving the Lord Chancellor, the reform was badly managed by the government.

The court will take on the role of an adjudicator in constitutional matters such as devolution and human rights issues. It will not, however, have the power to strike down legislation; it will interpret legislation. The Consultation Paper stated: "the establishment of a new court accordingly gives us the opportunity to restore a single apex to the UK's judicial system where all the constitutional issues can be considered".[225] The Consultation Paper then clearly distinguishes the jurisdiction of the new court from other models such as the US Supreme Court or the German Constitutional Court. It is undoubtedly the case that the competence attributed to the new court "is recognised elsewhere as constitutional".[226] However, the government's retreat into "the UK's constitutional traditions", i.e. the maintenance of parliamentary supremacy, only serves to produce a dilemma.[227] Great changes will be hindered by an element of loyalty to the past. In countries with more "modern constitutions" a more rational approach can perhaps be found. According to the views of a distinguished German Constitutional Court judge, the logical step before setting up a Constitutional Court is the acceptance of a written constitution, of a higher order law.[228] The German constitutional model is less modern than gener-

---

222 Lord Woolf, supra n. 219, pp. 2, 9 and 11.

223 Lord Woolf, supra n. 219, p. 2.

224 Lord Woolf, supra n. 219, p. 11.

225 Constitutional Reform: "A Supreme Court for the United Kingdom", Consultation Paper 11/03 (July 2003), para 20, Lord Chancellor's Department.

226 Bell, J., "Reflections on Continental European Supreme Courts" (2004) *Legal Studies* 157 [165].

227 Constitutional Reform: "A Supreme Court for the United Kingdom", Consultation Paper 11/03 (July 2003), para 23.

228 Hoffmann-Riem, W. (judge at the Federal Constitutional Court), "Two Hundred Years of *Marbury v Madison*: The Struggle for Judicial Review of Constitutional Questions in

ally perceived. Its first roots can be traced back to the middle of the nineteenth century.

4. The long path to Germany's Constitutional Court

The historical roots of the German Federal Constitutional Court date back to the debates surrounding the draft constitution of the St. Paul's Church Assembly in Frankfurt in 1848. The jurisdiction of the German Supreme Court (*Reichsgericht*) included features such as the constitutional complaint[229] and review of the legality of laws and the constitution enumerated a catalogue of human rights. Some parts of this draft were clearly influenced by the US Supreme Court and its decision in *Marbury v Madison*.[230] The 1848 revolution failed and with it the proposal to introduce jurisdiction over constitutional questions. In the late nineteenth century, Germany lacked the "readiness for political change" that had grasped the country before 1848. The "monarchical constitution" in the years after 1871 did not allow for a "neutral and higher ranking institution" such as a Supreme Court.

After the defeat of the Reich in 1919, the idea of setting up a Constitutional Court was revived with the establishment of the *Staatsgerichtshof des Deutschen Reiches* in the Weimar constitution. However, "in post World War I Germany there was not even a glimmering of the readiness to change which the successful struggle against British colonial [rule] might have engendered in the United States – drawing its strength from the ideas of popular sovereignty, the immutable right to liberty and the separation of powers".[231] The Weimar constitution suffered from several weaknesses and the Supreme Court decision in 1932[232] failed to exercise its control over measures which allowed for the removal of the politically inconvenient state government in Prussia.[233] The decision was criticised both for being either anti-republican or entirely politically naïve.[234] After the collapse of the Third Reich in 1945, Germany's 1949 written constitution, the Basic Law, provided for a system based on the idea of the *Rechtsstaat* commencing with 19 human rights. Following lengthy debates, an independent institution was established to secure the values of the constitution: the Federal Constitutional Court.

the United States and Europe" in *German Law Journal*, vol. 5, no. 6, 1 June 2004, p. 9, www/germanlawjournal.com.

229 Complaint of an individual to the Federal Constitutional Court against any act of the state infringing basic rights.

230 Frotscher, W. and Pieroth, B., *Verfassungsgeschichte*, 1997, 23, 169.

231 Hoffmann-Riem, W. (judge at the Federal Constitutional Court), "Two Hundred Years of *Marbury v Madison*: The Struggle for Judicial Review of Constitutional Questions in the United States and Europe" in *German Law Journal*, vol. 5, no. 6, 1 June 2004, p. 9, www/germanlawjournal.com.

232 RGZ 138, Anhang Sect. 1.

233 Frotscher, W. and Pieroth, B., *Verfassungsgeschichte*, 1997, 280.

234 Ibid, 282 with further references.

In contrast to Germany's history, "the growth of the English constitution has been organic, the rate of change glacial" and steeped in tradition.[235] The UK will have to make its own path. In the absence of great constitutional upheavals or revolutions, reform will have to be gradual. Lady Brenda Hale, former academic and now the only female Law Lord (sic) in the House of Lords, has argued that the jurisdiction of the House of Lords should be refined and limited to "cases of real constitutional importance … These would include the ground-breaking human rights cases, cases about our relationship with Europe or the rest of the world, including important cases interpreting international treaties or concepts such as sovereign immunity, and devolution cases".[236] A more refined role in the adjudication of cases, which deal with Britain's relationship to the European Union, is to be welcomed in a time "where national Constitutional Courts have become part of a network of courts in and for Europe".[237] Strengthening this role of the current House of Lords within Europe could be achieved by a diversification of the selection process for judicial office in a Supreme Court. In Brenda Hale's view, the new court could benefit from selecting candidates from amongst the lower judiciary, the Chief Prosecutor's or Attorney General's Office, other public services, the universities or private practice.[238] In accepting the constitutional role of the new court and by further refining it, the Bill could have taken a step further. This could have been reflected in the appointment process. However, the potential pool of candidates for the government's proposed judicial office in the Supreme Court does not reflect a significant change in legal culture. Appointments to the highest court remain within the field of highly qualified (i.e. remunerated) legal practitioners. The qualifications for appointment are tailored to suit candidates in high judicial office for two years or qualifying practitioners of 15 years' experience. The case for academics in the Supreme Court has been made by the academic body, the Society of Legal Scholars. In its view academics can contribute through their "knowledge and expertise, which outweighs their lack of judicial experience".[239] Such a view is largely rejected by the existing professional legal culture.

5. The Supreme Court Appointments Commission

The appointment process for new judges to the Supreme Court includes the setting up of an appointments commission. This ad hoc Supreme Court Appointments Commission, appointed by Lord Falconer, will only convene if a vacancy for the

[235] Stevens, R., *The English Judges*, 2002.

[236] Hale, B., "A Supreme Court for the United Kingdom?" (2002) *Legal Studies* 36 [43].

[237] Wahl, R., "Das Bundesverfassungsgericht im europäischen und internationalen Umfeld" in *Aus Politik und Zeitgeschichte* (B 37–38, 2001) 45 at 52; J. Dutheil de la Rochère and I. Pernice in Lord Slynn of Hadley and M. Andenas (eds.) *FIDE XX Congress* (2002) vol.1, chapter 2, pp. 47–105.

[238] Hale, B., "A Supreme Court for the United Kingdom?" (2002) *Legal Studies* 36 [44].

[239] Response to Consultation Paper 11/03 on a Supreme Court for the United Kingdom, *The Reporter, the Newsletter of the Society of Legal Scholars*, Spring 2004, pp. 9 and 10.

Supreme Court arises. It will consist of five members, the proposed President and Deputy President of the Supreme Court and one member of each of the judicial appointing bodies of England and Wales (established by the Bill), Scotland and Northern Ireland. Initially it was to provide the Secretary of State for Constitutional Affairs with two to five suitable candidates (for each new post) and for him to choose the most suitable name.[240]

The changes to the judicial system also include a reform of the current selection process for judicial offices other than the Supreme Court.[241] The 15 member strong Appointments Commission will be appointed by Her Majesty the Queen on the recommendation of the minister. The controversy over other aspects of the independence of the judges, i.e. questions relating to their background and the selection process, are partly the consequence of internal developments, in particular the coming into force of the Human Rights Act 1998. The existing non-statutory Commission for Judicial Appointments which has been in existence for several years and which is headed by Sir Colin Campbell, Vice Chancellor of Nottingham University and an academic lawyer, has just presented the findings of the first independent audit of the judicial selection process to the Lord Chancellor. Unsurprisingly, the existing selection procedure was described as lacking transparency and consistency. The process which the Lord Chancellor followed in the appointments process was criticised for being unclear to the Commission.[242]

So far the selection for the appointment of judges in England and Wales was within the responsibility of the Lord Chancellor. The process of appointments varied according to the type of judicial office. Appointment to the offices of Lord of Appeal in Ordinary (Law Lords), the Heads of Division of the Supreme Court (Queen's Bench Division, Chancery Division and Family Division) and Lord Justice of Appeal (Judges of the Appeal Court) were made by the Queen on the recommendation of the Prime Minister as her principal adviser. According to tradition the Prime Minister seeks advice from the Lord Chancellor on such appointments. Appointment to the offices of High Court Judge, Circuit Judge, Recorder, District Judge (Magistrates Courts), Magistrates, Social Security Commissioners, the Judge Advocate General and the Judge Advocate of Her Majesty's Fleet are made by the Queen on the recommendation of the Lord Chancellor. The Lord Chancellor was personally responsible for making a wide range of full-time and part-time appointments to the judiciary, including appointment to the offices of District Judge (Civil and Deputy District Judge) and to a wide range of tribunals.[243]

240 Part 3 and Schedule 8 of the Constitutional Reform Act 2005..

241 Part 4 and Schedule 12 of the Constitutional Reform Act 2005.

242 "Her Majesty's Commissioners for Judicial Appointments: Review of the 2003 High Court Competition", July 2004, available from http://www.cja.gov.uk.

243 Explanatory Notes to the Constitutional Reform Bill 2004, Part 3, Background, Sect. 132.

6. Diversity in the appointments process

The rationale for the reform has been summarised as one that "will guarantee the independence of the system from inappropriate politicisation, strengthen the quality of the appointments made, enhance the fairness of the selection process, promote diversity in the composition of the judiciary and so rebuild public confidence in the system".[244] One of the most "immediate and pressing rationales for change is the need to tackle the lack of diversity in the composition of the judiciary".[245] This concern includes the "conspicuous absence of women among the Law Lords" and all ranks of the judiciary, the lack of expertise in particular areas of law, such as criminal law, and the imbalance between judges from different parts of the country.[246] Of the 12 Lords of Appeal in Ordinary there is only one woman who currently will be able to sit in the proposed Supreme Court. There is only one female amongst the five Heads of Division and women make up only 7.9 per cent of Lord Justices of Appeal and 5.7 per cent of High Court Judges. Further, it is seen as increasingly problematic in a multi-racial country that there are no ethnic minority judges sitting in the High Court, Court of Appeal or the House of Lords.[247]

The Consultation Paper acknowledged that the present judiciary is "overwhelmingly white, male and from a narrow social and educational background". The aim of the government therefore was to "open the system of appointments, both to attract suitably qualified candidates from a wider range of social backgrounds and from a wider range of legal practice".[248]

The Act, however, stipulates that the selection shall be made on merit only. The minister may issue guidance to be taken into account by the Commission in assessing merit and "the Commission and any selection panel must have regard to the guidance in matters to which it relates."".[249] The definition of merit will remain a controversial point.. It has been argued, "there is real tension between diversifying the composition of the judiciary on the one hand and appointing on merit on the other – at least on merit as we have hitherto understood it".[250] The current appointment procedure is based on professional merit, "but the concept of merit is more fluid that might at first appear". Success in practice, particularly in

244 Malleson, K., "Creating a Judicial Appointments Commission: Which Model Works Best?" (2004) *Public Law* 102 [103].

245 Ibid 105.

246 Le Sueur, A., Cornes, R, "The Future of the United Kingdom's Highest Courts", The Constitution Unit, 2001, at p. 110.

247 House of Commons, Select Committee on Constitutional Affairs, First Report (2003–04), HC 48 vol. I, chapter 3, Judicial Appointments, para 134 with further reference to the Department of Constitutional Affairs Statistics, as of 1 September 2003. See also from the same Committee HC 628 (2003–04) and HC 746 (2003–04).

248 "Constitutional Reform: a New Way of Appointing Judges", Consultation Paper 10/03, July 2003, paras 27–29.

249 Part IV, sect. 63 - 65 of the Constitutional Reform Act 2005.

250 Sir Thomas Legg, "Brave New World – Supreme Court and Judicial Appointments" (2004) *Legal Studies* 45 [50].

advocacy, evidenced crucially by high earnings, "is taken to guarantee independence, status and incorruptibility".[251]

In its response to the consultation exercise, the Association of Women Judges stated that:

"The current system of appointing to the High Court by invitation is discriminatory to women, who are likely to be less visible [i.e. prominent] than men. Further, it is an approach which places undue emphasis on advocacy and on seniority of barristers. That approach is unlikely to identify others, e.g. members of the junior bar, academics and solicitors (the so-called junior branch of the legal profession) who might be suitable to hold office. All those who aspire to judicial office should be prepared to make an application and submit to assessment and interview".[252]

Lady Brenda Hale, the first woman likely to be appointed as one of 12 judges in the new Supreme Court, stated that this approach has disadvantaged women who may have had career breaks due to family commitments.[253] She argues forcefully that the quality of judges can be enhanced by promoting diversity:

"I prefer to regard the present judiciary as disadvantaged. They mean well. Few if any of its members are actively misogynist or racist, but they have a lamentable lack of experience of having female or ethnic minority colleagues of equal status. They often simply do not know what to do with us [females] or how to interpret what we say. Giving them a greater diversity of colleagues would do them no end of good. So what I am really saying is let's have some affirmative action to rid them of their disadvantages".[254]

She distinguishes between the merit criteria in its old sense, i.e. based purely on professional success evidenced by high earnings, and the objective of promoting diversity: "I am a supporter of confronting the merit principle head on and saying that there are many more very able, capable, independently minded people of integrity who could make a contribution as judges than the ones who are currently regarded as the obvious candidates under the present system".[255]

However, JUSTICE, an all-party law reform and human rights organisation, is of the view that there is no potential conflict between the two criteria of merit and diversity. JUSTICE said in evidence to the Select Committee that:

"There should be no conflict between appointment criteria that include a requirement of merit with an objective of diversity, though this is sometimes erroneously argued. There must be no diminution of the quality of our bench and, in particular, its independence of government. An independent and courageous spirit must remain a major criterion for senior judicial appointments".[256]

---

251 Jowell, J., "The Judiciary" in Oliver, D., *Constitutional Reform*, 2003, 340.

252 House of Commons, Select Committee on Constitutional Affairs, supra n. 247, para 150.

253 Supra n. 238.

254 House of Commons, Select Committee on Constitutional Affairs, supra n. 247, para 144.

255 Ibid.

256 Ibid para 145.

Other aspects of diversity concern the inclusion of a "wider range of legal practice" in the government's plans, other than simply concentrating, as traditionally, on being a senior advocate.[257] This aim, which the government expressed in its Consultation Paper, has been criticised as "changing the character and skills of the English Bench, especially at first-instance level":[258]

> "This close and long-standing connection with advocacy, and more recently litigation, has given the English judges their characteristic strengths, especially in trial handling. Their mastery of the adversarial process, learned and lived [experienced] over years of courtroom warfare, their personal self-reliance and their ability and readiness to give rulings and judgments on the spot, have been a staple asset of our legal system".[259]

The inclusion of both social and professional diversification envisaged by the reforms touches upon deeply rooted cultural perceptions about the English judiciary.

The involvement of Parliament in the selection process is not envisaged by the Act. There are those who would argue, however, that as in other continental countries, Parliament should play a role in the appointment process.[260] Democratic accountability of the judiciary, at least at the highest level, is one of the main features of the German selection process. The judges of the Federal Constitutional Court are elected by both the *Bundestag* and the *Bundesrat*. The German Judicial Selection Committee responsible for the selection of judges to the higher courts merges the influence of the executive and Parliament. The involvement of Parliament in the selection of candidates could result in a politicised process as seen in Germany.

The lack of parliamentary influence over judicial appointments in the Constitutional Reform Bill was controversial. The more powerful role given to judges under the UK Human Rights Act 1998 in controlling executive action and declaring legislation as incompatible with Convention rights has been seen by some commentators as something requiring a more democratically accountable judiciary. The Commission will be within the jurisdiction of the House of Commons Select Committee on Constitutional Affairs in its general scrutiny role over the executive. However, despite all criticism, the new statutory Judicial Appointments Commission is a step in the right direction.

7. Judicial independence under the Basic Law[261]

The relationship between accountability and the independence of the judiciary raises basic constitutional questions. A change in the legal culture of a nation im-

---

[257] "Constitutional Reform: a New Way of Appointing Judges", Consultation Paper 10/03, July 2003, para 27.

[258] Sir Thomas Legg, "Brave New World – Supreme Court and Judicial Appointments" (2004) *Legal Studies* 45 [51].

[259] Ibid 51.

[260] Le Sueur, A., Cornes, R., "The Future of the United Kingdom's Highest Courts", 2001, available online on the Constitution Unit's website, 126 et seq; Sir Thomas Legg, supra n. 258, 46 and Stevens, R., *The English Judges*, 2002, 30.

[261] This section is based on a chapter published in *The Independence and Accountability of the Judiciary,* 2006, 217.

pacts on this delicate balance. In Britain, the coming into force of the Human Rights Act 1998 has been described as a "quantum leap into a new legal culture of fundamental rights and freedoms"[262] and most clearly confirmed this change in the legal culture. Commentators on the Constitutional Reform Bill have argued that a move towards a more law based rather than a constitution based on politics is under way.[263] Nevertheless, changes in British constitutional law seem to be most acceptable if they are made gradually and with careful consideration of Britain's constitutional legacy. The structure of the Human Rights Act 1998, for instance, has been praised for revealing "an elegant balance between respect for Parliament's legislative supremacy and the legal security of the Convention rights".[264] Finding this balance between the past and the present is a particularly British quality. While the continuity of British constitutional law has been admired by continental academics, constitutional reform has to be seen increasingly within a European context. Admittedly, other European legal systems have taken very different paths. Germany's constitution radically changed the balance of powers in the state and entrusted a Constitutional Court with the protection of its values half a century ago. It is worth noting that, however, 55 years after the drafting of a new constitution for Germany, the process of selecting the German judiciary is on the political agenda again. There are a variety of selection processes in Germany. However, the selection at federal level has been criticised for a lack of input by the judiciary. At state level an overemphasis of executive decision making through the ministries of justice is controversial. Unlike in many other European countries, there is no judicial council to oversee judicial appointments.[265] The trend to more autonomy is supported by a recommendation of the Council of Europe Committee of Ministers on the independence, efficiency and role of judges. Accordingly:

"The authority taking the decision on the selection and career of judges should be independent of the government and the administration. In order to safeguard its independence, rules should ensure that, for instance, its members are selected by the judiciary ... However, where the constitutional or legal provisions and traditions allow judges to be appointed by the government, there should be guarantees to ensure that the procedures to appoint judges are transparent and independent".[266]

---

262 Wade, W., "Human Rights and the Judiciary" (1998) *EHRLR* 520 [532].

263 Hale, B., "A Supreme Court for the United Kingdom" (2004) *Legal Studies* vol. 24 Issue 1 and 2; Constitutional Innovations: the Creation of a Supreme Court for the UK; Domestic, Comparative and International Reflections, A Special Issue, 36; Woodhouse, D., "The Constitutional and Political Implications of a UK Supreme Court" (2004) *Legal Studies* 134.

264 *International Transport Roth GmbH and others v Secretary of State for the Home Department* [2002] EWCA Civ 158, [2002] 3 WLR 344 per Laws LJ, para 71.

265 Not in Germany, see Teetzmann, H., "Selbstverwaltung der Justiz; Rechtsvergleichender Überblick" in *Deutsche Richterzeitung*, 2003, 44.

266 Council of Europe Committee of Ministers Recommendation Number R (94) 12 of the Committee of Ministers to Member States on the Independence, Efficiency and Role of Judges (adopted by the Committee of Ministers on 13 October 1994 at the 518th meeting of the Ministers' Deputies).

In Germany's written constitution, the Basic Law of 1949, Art. 20(2) underscores the judiciary's organisational independence by requiring that "all public authority ... shall be exercised by specific legislative, executive and judicial bodies". This results in the judges being barred from exercising non-judicial functions. Further, Art. 97 of the Basic Law provides that "judges shall be independent and subject only to the law". The role of the courts in upholding individual rights is a fundamental feature of modern Germany. This *Rechtsstaat* principle, guarded by a powerful constitutional organ, the Federal Constitutional Court (*Bundesverfassungsgericht*), serves as a justification for a high level of review in administrative law matters.[267] Litigation rates are amongst the highest in the world.[268] However, the question of judicial accountability creates an inevitable tension within the powerful role occupied by the German judiciary. Despite several provisions in the Basic Law, the German Judiciary Act and the Civil and Criminal Codes, the issue is as complex as in other legal traditions and requires an initial analysis of the training and selection process.

8. Qualification for judicial office in Germany

There are almost 21,000 judges in the Federal Republic of Germany, a quarter of which are female, and only 495 at federal level, the remaining number spread across the state courts.[269] There are currently 53 Administrative Courts, 16 Higher Administrative Courts and the Federal Administrative Court.[270] In addition there are 19 Finance Courts, the Federal Finance Court, 69 Social Courts, 15 Higher Social Courts and the Federal Social Court. The Administrative Courts employ 2316 judges (59 at federal level), the Finance Courts 661 judges and the Social Courts 1274 judges.[271]

According to a questionnaire of the international association of judges, launched in 2001,[272] German judges in first time positions belong to the medium income category, as compared with English judges who lead in this comparison. This difference is due to the fact that German judges are comparatively young when they take up their posts. They can be as young as 25 after having obtained a law degree at university and undergone their training. Legal education in Germany is designed to produce standardised lawyers who meet the qualifications for judicial office. The first examination is administered by the state justice ministries, as-

---

267 Article 19 IV Basic Law: where rights are violated by public authority, the person affected shall have recourse to the law.

268 Erhard Blankenberg, "Changes in Political Regimes and Continuity of the Rule of Law in Germany" in Herbert Jacobs, *Courts, Law and Politics in Comparative Perspective,* 1996, 249.

269 Statistisches Bundesamt Deutschland 2002, Personal der Rechtspflege, http://www.destatis.de/cgi-bin/printview.pl.

270 http://www.bmj.bund.de/media/archive/1161.pdf, 1 January 2006.

271 http://www.bmj.bund.de/media/archive/192.pdf, 1 November 2002.

272 Richtereinkommen im Europäischen Vergleich, Eine Umfrage der Europäischen Richtervereinigung, 2001.

sisted by law faculties. The second state examination is at the end of the preparatory phase, which lasts for two years. The second state exam is prepared and administered by judges, senior civil servants and law professors. Currently, every law student wishing to enter the legal profession has to undergo comprehensive training. German legal education is heavily based on its historic legacy, where legal education in the universities and the standardised training period served as a unifying factor in geographically and politically splintered legal systems. Other than in common law countries where the training of young lawyers was firmly in the hands of confident legal practitioners, in Germany law had been perceived as a science to be taught by scholars. This approach is still reflected, for instance, by the high level of review of administrative discretion where German doctrine operates the obscure principle of undefined legal concepts which may be fully reviewed by the courts. University professors enjoy a high status in Germany and they hold positions in the Federal Constitution Court. According to Sect. 7 of the German Judiciary Act 1972, every professor of law at a university within the meaning of the statute is qualified to hold judicial office. Of the 16 judges in the Federal Constitutional Court, nine currently hold offices as professors in law schools and four are female.[273]

German legal education has been criticised for its length and narrow emphasis on codes and statutes. Changes in legal education have been discussed intensely but reforming legal education requires the taking of small steps. Recent reforms by the *Justizministerkonferenz* in November 2004 include proposals to change the career path of judges. The reform proposals include the abolition of the preparatory phase in its current form and the specialisation of training for judges. Further, it includes plans to allow other legal professionals to enter the judiciary.[274]

Democratic accountability of the judiciary, at least at the highest level, is one of the main features of the German selection process. The German Judicial Selection Committee responsible for the selection of judges to the higher courts merges the influence of the executive and Parliament. However, the involvement of Parliament in the selection of candidates can result in a politicised process.

a) The selection process - federal level

Until 1945 judges were promoted by high ministerial officials. "The post war procedure attempts to maintain a delicate balance among judicial, legislative and executive interests and influence".[275] Due to the often highly political subject matters and the high degree of intensity of review in German higher courts, this system of selection is more democratically accountable, even though the involvement of politics in the election process has been fiercely criticised.

Article 95 Sect. 2 of the Basic Law sets out the process of selection:

---

273 http://www.bundesverfassungsgericht.de/texte.deutsch/richter/richter.html.

274 BDVR-Rundschreiben 06/2004, p 202, http://www.bdvr.de.

275 Clark, D.S., "The Selection and Accountability of Judges in West Germany: Implementation of a Rechtsstaat" (1988) *Southern Californian Law Review* 1797 [1823].

(1) For the purposes of ordinary, administrative, financial, labour and social jurisdiction, the federation shall establish as supreme courts the Federal Court of Justice, the Federal Administrative Court, the Federal Finance Court, the Federal Labour Court and the Federal Social Court.

(2) The judges of each of these courts shall be selected jointly by the appropriate federal minister and a selection committee composed of the appropriate *Land* ministers and an equal number of members elected by the *Bundestag*.

(3) In order to ensure uniformity in the administration of justice, a joint panel of the courts … shall be formed. Details shall be subject to a federal law. Further details on the selection of judges in the federation and the states are governed by the German Judiciary Act.[276]

For the highest courts, judges are selected jointly by the appropriate federal minister and a selection committee composed of the appropriate *Land* ministries and an equal number of members elected by the *Bundestag*. The selection committee (*Richterwahlausschuss*) is composed of the 16 state justice ministers and an equal number of parliamentary representatives, whose partisan colouring would be proportionate to the numerical strength of each political party in the *Bundestag*. The federal minister of justice chairs the committee but does not vote. "The committee of 32 voting members at this point meets to vote on a final list of one nominee for each vacancy. Decisions are made by a simple majority. Three factors seem to influence the committee's voting on a candidate: professional qualifications, geographical origin and political party affiliation or sympathy".[277] The latter factor in particular has often led to controversy. Judges ae permitted to be members of political parties and to utter their own opinions in political matters. They may even serve on local councils. However, in the exercise of their judicial function, they are required to remain neutral. In Germany, the political activity of judges is perceived as an important exercise of their rights under the constitution. It has been suggested that this involvement in political questions is an important counterweight to the highly theoretical and formal education: "permitting them to join political parties may help to expose career judges to the values, needs and problems of the community as a whole, perhaps producing as a consequence a better balance between autonomy and accountability."[278]

Due to Germany's federal structure situations may arise where one party dominates the selection committee. This situation arose in 1995 when 15 new federal judges were elected, nine of which belonged to the SPD, even though Germany was governed by a CDU/FDP coalition. This was due to the strong position of the SPD as the opposition party at a *Länder* level (18 members). The conservative media (*Frankfurter Allgemeine Zeitung*) commented on this with the headline,

---

[276] In the version published on 19 April 1972 (Bundesgesetzblatt, part I, p.713) as last amended by Art. 1 of the Law of 11 July 2002 (Bundesgesetzblatt, part I, p. 2592).

[277] Clark, D.S., "The Selection and Accountability of Judges in West Germany: Implementation of a Rechtsstaat" (1988) *Southern Californian Law Review* 1797 [1825].

[278] Kommers, D.P., "The German Judiciary" in Peter H. Russell, David O'Brien, Judicial Independence in the Age of Democracy: Critical Perspective from Around the World, 2001, 138.

"SPD judicial selection self-service". Currently there is a majority of committee members belonging to the CDU and FDP (10 in total) because 10 state justice ministries are held by these two parties, whereas the SPD and the Greens are in the minority at a state level (five SPD, one Green). This situation reflects the political trends in the states rather than the federal government. This phenomenon has attracted criticism for years. The main criticism was therefore focused on the political criteria for selection. After intense discussions and media coverage the selection committee agreed in April 2003 that in the future less emphasis should be laid on the political affiliation or sympathy of a candidate. To reach a broad consensus in the committee only a few other small changes were introduced. However, one member of the committee commented that nothing much had in fact changed.[279]

The judiciary itself plays a rather small role in the selection process. There are no judges in the selection committee. Candidates are reviewed by a committee of judges sitting in the final appeal court in criminal and civil matters, the BGH, the so-called *Präsidialrat* (Presiding Council). However, its recommendations are not binding and in 2001 the selection of two candidates lacking the Council's support led to controversy and legal action.[280] This lack of judicial input in the selection process has more recently led to a new debate on the selection process. Unsurprisingly, this debate is mainly led by members of the highest courts in the country. According to the president of the BGH (the highest court for federal and civil matters), judges should be permitted to sit in the selection committee in order to prevent the politicisation of the process and safeguard the interests of the courts.[281] This lack of participation of the judiciary itself has been described as a violation of the constitution and Parliament and the Constitutional Court should consider the constitutionality of the provision which lays down the procedure.[282] At the annual meeting of judges (*Deutscher Richtertag*), calls for radical reforms have recently been made. One of Germany's highest judges, Renate Jaeger,[283] described the structure of the German judiciary as outdated and as a relic from a pre-democratic era. She expressed that the quality and autonomy of the judiciary correspond with responsibility and independence of the judges and require institutional safeguards.[284] This "polarisation of the appointment process has invited strong criti-

279 *Frankfurter Allgemeine Zeitung*, 11 April 2003, no. 86, p.2.

280 "Judicial Selection Controversy at the Federal Court of Justice", Legal Culture, *German Law Journal*, vol. 2, no. 8, 1 May 2001.

281 Edinger, T., "Die Justiz muss eine Stimme bekommen", ein DriZ-Gespräch mit dem Präsidenten des Bundesgerichtshofs Professor Dr. Günter Hirsch zu Qualität und mehr Selbstverwaltung der Justiz (2003) *Deutsche Richterzeitung* 188.

282 Weber-Grellet, H.W., judge at the BFH (Federal Finance Court), "Eigenständigkeit und Demokratisierung der Justiz" (2003) *Deutsche Richterzeitung* 303 [308]; Bertram, G., "Ergänzung des Wahlausschusses um eine Richterbank" (2001) *NJW* 1838 [1839].

283 Judge at the Federal Constitutional Court since 1994.

284 "Richter müssen Verantwortung übernehmen, radikale Reformen sind notwendig", *Frankfurter Rundschau*, 18 September 2003.

cism from commentators troubled by its implications for judicial independence".[285]

b) The selection process at the Federal Constitutional Court

The Federal Constitutional Court is a constitutional organ and is not subject to supervision by a ministry. It has a variety of competences, most famously the power to invalidate legislation. The court consists of 16 judges. Germany's constitutional history is clearly very different from the British experience and a brief excursion into the history of this court explains its central role in modern Germany. In a country which experienced several unsuccessful attempts to establish the rule of law, the setting up of a Supreme Court in 1951 was the "crowning jewel on the constitution" and the guarantor to secure the constitutional principles. Germany's history explains why many eastern European states use the German court as a model.

The selection of the judges in the Federal Constitutional Court (*Bundesverfassungsgericht*) differs from the selection process described above as, according to Art. 94 of the Basic Law, half of its members are selected by the *Bundestag* and half by the *Bundesrat*. Here, a two-thirds majority is required for the selection so the two parties need to agree on a candidate. Judges are elected for a limited tenure of 12 years only. It has been argued that the procedure lacks transparency that the party headquarters choose the candidates in the forefield. This is due to the fact that not the whole of the *Bundestag* elects the judges, but a group of 12 delegates (so-called *Wahlmänner*). The path to Karlsruhe (seat of the *Bundesverfassungsgericht*) has been described as "mysterious". The selection is highly confidential, the candidates' biographies are often entirely unknown to the public and their selection is discussed in small circles of two to three people.[286] Therefore, despite its international reputation as a court with democratically elected judges, many critics in Germany are less enthusiastic about its democratic legitimisation.[287] However, it is difficult to think of a procedure which is democratic but entirely separate from political convictions.[288] Further, the decisions of the Federal Constitutional Court enjoy a high degree of acceptance by the population. The rulings are praised as comprehensible and well balanced and the work of the court is perceived as accessible and trustworthy.[289] Discussions concerning the selection of the constitutional judges tend to be re-ignited whenever a decision of high political significance has been taken. One highly controversial decision in 1995 was concerned with the statement that "soldiers are murderers" and the question whether

[285] Kommers, D.P., "The German Judiciary" in Peter H. Russell, David O'Brien, *Judicial Independence in the Age of Democracy: Critical Perspective from Around the World*, 2001, 149.

[286] Lamprecht, R., *Vom Mythos der Unabhängigkeit: Über das Dasein und Sosein der deutschen Richter*, 1995, 72.

[287] Ibid 72–74.

[288] Grimm, D., "Nicht den Parteien, sondern der Verfassung dienstbar", *Frankfurter Allgemeine Zeitung*, 19 February 2000, no. 42, p. 11.

[289] Lamprecht, R., supra n. 286, 71.

this was defamatory under the Criminal Code. The court ruled on the extent of protection given to freedom of speech and held that the statement was protected under the Basic Law.[290] The Constitutional Court faced criticism from the major political parties, the media and the general public because the statement was detrimental to the reputation of the German *Bundeswehr*. The former president of the Federal Constitutional Court, Jutta Limbach, admitted that criticism was necessary to protect the court from becoming narrow-minded and self-righteous and that it was one of the court's own early rulings which upheld freedom of expression.[291]

c) The selection process at state level

The selection of the majority of judges in Germany (more than 20,000) takes place at state and local level. A different procedure provided for by Art. 98 Sect. 4 of the Basic Law applies. Accordingly, the states may provide that the state ministry of justice, together with a selection committee, shall decide on the appointment of state judges. The Basic Law guarantees a large margin of appreciation in the organisation of the states' judicial system. Therefore different arrangements can be found. Despite the fact that the state laws provide for selection committees, the state justice ministries remain the final decision maker in the selection process. This has been confirmed by the Federal Constitutional Court in May 1998.[292] Currently, judges at state level are selected by the relevant ministries unless a selection committee has been established.[293] Party membership is of no relevance in the staffing of the lower courts. At a lower level, candidates usually file an application with the ministry of justice in a given state. At this level, the selection is largely based on qualifications and performance. Only the very best will be eligible for the office of a judge; the vast majority enter the civil service or private practice. Reformers demand an increased role for the judiciary itself in the selection process, a strengthening of democratic accountability through parliamentary approval and a reduced role for the ministries of justice. Other proposals for change to the recruitment process includes features which are more familiar to the English appointment system such as admitting successful senior practising lawyers (*Rechtsanwälte*) to the bar.[294]

In conclusion, it is interesting to note that despite the differences in constitutional backgrounds, both England and Germany are tackling a common problem. The question which both legal systems have to answer is how institutional independence of judges is best achieved. The strong position of the executive in selecting members of the judiciary does not square easily with the increased intensity of

290 BVerfGE 93, 266–312 ("soldiers are murderers") and BVerfGE 93, 1 ("classroom crucifix case"). For a translation, see http://www.ucl.ac.uk/laws/global_law/german-cases/cases_bverg.shtml?16may1995.

291 Limbach, J., *Im Namen des Volkes*, 1999, 200.

292 Weber-Grellet, H.W., judge at the BFH (Federal Finance Court), "Eigenständigkeit und Demokratisierung der Justiz" (2003) *Deutsche Richterzeitung* 303 [308].

293 Voßkuhle, A., Sydow, G., "Die demokratische Legitimation des Richters" (2002) *Juristen Zeitung* 673 [676].

294 *Frankfurter Allgemeine Zeitung*, 18 September 2003.

control granted by the Basic Law and the provisions in the Human Rights Act 1998. One can detect an element of convergence in the debate over the development of the courts in England and Germany. There is a general trend towards more autonomy of the judiciary, a loosening of ties to the executive and more openness towards the inclusion of other legal professions to judicial office.[295]
The Constitutional Reform Act 2005 has made some fundamental changes to British and English constitutional arrangements. We have seen that the government clearly has withdrawn from introducing a full constitutional court model. Germany's experience illustrated the long and difficult route to setting up its Constitutional Court, which was the end product of great political changes taking place over more than one and a half centuries. The speed at which the legislative plans have been produced and the unavoidable and rushed modifications which they required have been damaging to the government's case for important and necessary reforms affecting the "judicial branch". The Secretary of State for Constitutional Affairs had reluctantly to maintain his title as Lord Chancellor: demission of that office required parliamentary legislation. The new Supreme Court is not going to be a Constitutional Court interpreting a written constitution. A more refined jurisdiction and a diversification of its personnel may enhance the role of the highest court as an equal player in comparison to European Constitutional Courts and the court will have to develop the jurisdiction and jurisprudence under the human rights and devolution legislation. There is no doubt that the proposals significantly change the "dignified part" of the UK constitution by abolishing the office of Lord Chancellor (the government is likely to re-insert the relevant clause in the Bill on its introduction into the House of Commons and in the event of a clash between the House of Commons and the Lords, the Commons has the final say[296]) and by removing the highest appeal court from its status as a committee of the House of Lords into an institutionally separate body. The proposed changes to judicial appointments could be profound in their impact on this, although the inherent conservatism of the legal profession and its ability to influence events should not be overlooked.

The changes proposed to the judicial selection process are to be welcomed. The reduction of the role of the Lord Chancellor/Secretary of State for Constitutional Affairs in the selection process is to be applauded. That role in the past has often been a barrier to true judicial independence, but a strong Lord Chancellor could act as a champion for judicial independence. That role will now have to fall to the Lord Chief Justice and senior judges and the new more open processes for making judicial appointments. However, Parliament should not miss the opportunity to define the criteria for selection more clearly. The success of the new Judicial Appointments Commission will depend on the quality, experience and perceived strengths of that body's composition. To achieve more democratic legitimacy, it could be argued that an involvement of Parliament in the selection process should be considered more carefully. The German experience has shown that it is difficult

[295] See above with further references.

[296] Though procedurally this may be very time consuming and cumbersome under the Parliament Acts 1911 and 1949.

to achieve a balance of involvement that pleases everyone. Parliamentary groupings may well have their own agenda which could diminish independence and perhaps direct parliamentary involvement in the UK is not the answer. However, the increasingly powerful role of the British judiciary in controlling executive decisions requires a change in focus when it comes to judicial appointments and greater safeguards in those appointments to ensure independence. The success of the Constitutional Reform Act in establishing workable and beneficial changes in judicial appointments hinges on this fundamental point. Existing arrangements cannot be entrusted with this task. The Constitutional Reform Act 2005 does at least have the framework of statute and new independent safeguards. In that respect it is to be welcomed. It is regrettable that the Prime Minister's intemperate rush for change may jeopardise essential and long over-due reforms to bring the judiciary and their top court into the twenty-first century.

VII. Conclusion

The most striking difference between the English and German judicial review system is the development of a separate system of German Administrative Courts in the middle of the nineteenth century. The separation of public and private law matters was encouraged by the influence of the French revolution. The southern German states in particular adopted the French model of a separation of private and public law matters. Unlike his English colleague, the influential A.V. Dicey, the leading German administrative lawyer, Otto Mayer, clearly expressed his admiration for the French separation of private and public law. The following two quotes illustrate these different approaches well:

"If there is something that should be recommended, then it is the spirit of it all, the great form of respect paid to the nature of the activity of the state, which is concerned with the development of the [public] law. Here [in Germany] the state has mainly been treated like a private citizen ..."[297]

"*Droit administratif*, as it exists in France, is not the sum of the powers possessed or of the functions discharged by the administration; it is rather the sum of the principles which govern the relation between French citizens, as individuals, and the administration as the representatives of the state. Here, we touch upon the fundamental difference between the English and the French ideas. In England, the powers of the Crown and its servants may from time to time be increased as they may also be diminished, but these powers, whatever they are,

[297] Mayer, O., *Theorie des französischen Verwaltungsrechts,* 1886, p. VIII, translation (by the author) of the original : "Wenn aber etwas zur Nachahmung empfohlen werden konnte, so ware es viel mehr noch der Geist des Ganzen, jener grossartiger Zug von Achtung vor der hoheitlichen Natur der Thatigkeit des Staates, der in der kräftigen Ausbildung jenes Rechtes sich bezeugt. Bei uns überwiegt von jeher die Neigung, den Staat im Verhältnis zu seinen Bürgern einfach wie ein Rechtssubjekt des Civilrechts zu behandeln".

must be exercised in accordance with the ordinary common law principles which govern the relation of one Englishman to another".[298]

The systematic development and categorisation of administrative law in Germany raised the issue of which court or body should be responsible for the review of public law matters. In England, on the other hand, no such systematisation took place. Therefore there was no need to take cases of a public law nature away from the ordinary courts or to create a separate system of administrative courts. The English remedial approach centred on the question of which remedies should be available for disputes of a public law nature. However, these prerogative writs as they existed did not require the establishment of a new court.

With regard to the position of citizens in English and German administrative law disputes, it can be observed that the applicant in an English court faces the shortcomings of the adversarial procedure, which makes it harder to establish the objective facts which underlay the original decision. This is partly due to a limitation of forms of evidence such as cross-examination and discovery. Further it is due to the onus of proof, which generally rests with the applicant. The court will assume that the authority acted properly unless otherwise proven. In Germany, on the contrary, the inquisitorial procedure assures that the facts are examined in depth on behalf of the court applying a variety of means of evidence including appearing on site. The onus of proof not necessarily rests upon the applicant as it is acknowledged that certain facts are not within the sphere of knowledge of the citizen. In addition to some of the conceptual differences, these procedural differences make it harder for an applicant in an English judicial review procedure to be successful with his claim.

The historical introduction into the development of the Administrative Courts in Germany as the expression of libertarian developments after the 1848/49 revolution explain the strong role of the Administrative Courts which display both independence and expertise in the area of administrative law. This process was accelerated after the Second World War when the general mistrust in the executive found expression in the newly drafted Art. 19 IV of the Basic Law, according to which aggrieved citizens have guaranteed legal protection against unlawful official action. Article 19 IV, however, does not guarantee the establishment of the administrative courts. The *Bundesverfassungsgericht*, established in 1959, complements this system of effective judicial protection of basic rights and enables individuals to complain about the violation of individual rights. The *Bundesverfassungsgericht*'s power to strike down any kind of legislation is also a distinctive feature of Germany's perception of the separation of powers.

By contrast no separate system of administrative courts has been developed in England. Since the abolition of the prerogative Star Chamber, the idea of a separate system of public law courts applying public law as distinct from private law has never found favour. However, it can now be said that England has a system of administrative law including both a substantive body of law containing grounds of review. In addition, a large number of administrative tribunals deal with statutory appeals from decisions of public bodies. The Queen's Bench of the High Court is

[298] Dicey, A.V., *Law of the Constitution*, 1952, 387.

now named the Administrative Court and has acquired a high level of expertise in dealing with administrative cases. The new Supreme Court for the UK is not going to be a constitutional court with powers comparable to the German Constitutional Court. However, English law displays flexibility and the potential for further development. Since the 1960s the courts have begun to shift the balance of power in their favour. By extending the doctrine of *ultra vires* and establishing the grounds of review and reviving the rules of natural justice, they have begun to shape a system of administrative law. The following chapters will assess these developments of the grounds of review in more detail.

Chapter Three Judicial review of discretionary powers

I. Introduction

This chapter will deal with "one of the most important areas of European administrative law in the future": the scope of judicial review of administrative discretionary powers.[1] It is an area which most clearly displays the role of the courts in controlling the acts of public authorities. This area of judicial review goes to the heart of both systems' approaches to judicial review and the relationship between public authorities and individual citizens. Both in English and German administrative law discretionary powers are an important feature of the administration. In England, review of discretionary powers is traditionally more limited than in Germany. However, the Human Rights Act 1998 poses new questions. As will be shown the Human Rights Act 1998 has made British constitutional discourse more "nuanced and more complicated".[2] In Germany, where the position of the administration has been weakened by being subject to an over-intensive judicial scrutiny, basic foundations of the concept of discretion and its review by the Administrative Courts have been questioned.[3]

This part will provide an overview over forms of discretion and the main grounds of review. Cases have been carefully selected to illustrate the English and German approach. As far as possible cases with similar factual backgrounds have been chosen to enable the reader to draw direct comparisons. However, this has not always been possible. The cases represent the main areas of review in each jurisdiction respectively. As will be shown, the focus of the courts on particular issues may vary.

---

1 Redeker, K/., von Oertzen, H.J., *Verwaltungsgerichtsordnung*, 1997, Vorwort, p. V.

2 "Cases, *A. v Secretary of State for the Home Department, Introduction*" (2005) *MLR*, 654

3 Sendler, H., "Über richterliche Kontrolldichte in Deutschland und anderswo" (1994) *NJW* 1511 [1520]; Ipsen, H.P., von Dannwitz, T., "Verwaltungsrechtliches System und Europäische Integration" (1996) *DVBl* 627.

1. The concept of discretion and the constitutional basis for judicial review of discretionary powers in England

In the administrative decision-making process the concept of discretion is an important tool to reach just decisions. It offers an important degree of flexibility. The concept of discretion in English law does not distinguish between different forms of discretion. However, three different sources which contain the authorisation of discretionary powers can be identified. First, express statutory provisions can be found within the areas of education, social welfare, planning and immigration law which confer discretionary powers on the authorities. They are contained in phrases such as "if the minister has reasonable grounds to believe that ...", "if there is evidence that ..." or "if he thinks that ..."[4] A second form of discretionary power is that of implied discretionary power. Such powers can be found in concepts such as "public interest". These open concepts require the administration to make choices as to their meaning. There is, however, no conceptual difference between express and implied forms of discretionary powers. A third group of discretionary powers is the royal prerogative. When defining the meaning of prerogative powers, no express written list of powers can be found within the British constitution. They are entrenched by practice and example. Prerogative powers are all those powers which were traditionally exercised by the monarch and which have not been regulated by statute. When referring to prerogative powers, any common law power of government is understood as such.[5] Prerogative powers are no longer free from judicial control. However, some exercises of prerogative power are still exempted from any form of control. Some examples were cited in the *GCHQ* case.[6] Examples of the unreviewable powers under the royal prerogative can be found in connection with foreign relations, the conduct of war and peace, the regulation and disposition of the armed forces, the appointment and dismissal of ministers and the dissolution of Parliament. Another form of discretionary powers is classified as common law discretionary powers. These are neither statutory nor prerogative in nature. The power to contract has been identified as such a type of common law discretionary power. However, the existence of such powers is controversial.[7] The majority of discretionary powers are based on statutory authorisation, be it express or implied. K.C. Davis famously stated that "where law ends, discretion begins, and the exercise of discretion may mean either beneficence or tyranny, either justice or injustice, either reasonableness or arbitrariness".[8] The important question is therefore how discretion can be controlled.

English courts have generally been ill-equipped to review the merits of the exercise of a discretionary administrative power. "The courts have repeatedly af-

4 Craig, P. in Bullinger, M., Starck, C., *Verwaltungsermessen im modernen Staat*, "Discretionary power in modern administration", Rechtsvergleichender Generalbericht (1986) 79.

5 Pollard, P., "Judicial Review of Prerogative Power in the United Kingdom and France" in Peter Leyland and Terry Woods, *Administrative Law Facing the Future*, 1997, 300.

6 *Council of Civil Service Unions v Minister for the Civil Service* [1985] AC 374 at 418.

7 Craig, P, *Administrative Law*, 1999, 539.

8 Davis, K.C., *Discretionary Justice* ,1971, 34.

firmed their incapacity to substitute their own discretion for that of an authority in which the discretion has been confided". However, the principle that discretion must be exercised "according to law" is indeed deeply entrenched in the common law.[9] As discussed earlier in Chapter Two, this was clearly expressed by A.V. Dicey in his famous *Law of the Constitution*: "it means, in the first place, the absolute supremacy or predominance of regular law as opposed to the influence of arbitrary power and excludes the existence of arbitrariness of prerogative or even of wide discretionary authority on the part of the government".[10] As pointed out in Chapter Two, the justification for judicial control of the exercise of administrative powers has been the protection of the intention of Parliament. Traditionally, English courts have not been equipped to deal with a comprehensive control of administrative decisions. The most important distinction between the administrative legal system in England and those in France and Germany is still the absence of a separate court system for public law matters.[11] The *Conseil d'Etat* and *tribunaux administratifs* in France and the *Verwaltungsgerichte* in Germany institutionalise this division. This different position in England has been explained by the constitutional history of the relationship between Parliament and the courts and the rule of law. A particularly crucial time was the period of the Tudors and Stuarts in the sixteenth and seventeenth centuries when the conflict between Parliament and the English kings broke out. During this time the Star Chamber was created, a superior court which dealt with crimes of political significance.[12] It imposed a strict control over the organs of local government and the exercise of judicial and administrative functions.[13] After its abolition, these traumatising experiences remained in the perception of public law as an area of law which in future had to be inseparable from private law.

A.V. Dicey's interpretation of *droit administratif* in 1885 as being "official" law enforceable in special courts and therefore being incompatible with the rule of law reaffirmed the reservations against a separate system of public law courts.[14] The rule of law has a number of meanings. According to Dicey, the second meaning is that "every man, whatever be his rank or condition, is subject to the ordinary law of the realm and amenable to the jurisdiction of the ordinary tribunals".[15] Dicey's view has been heavily criticised for misinterpreting the *droit administratif.* Two arguments against his theory are that the government or an agency is often acting for the citizens at large and that therefore the application of the same legal principles and procedures which would apply to a private person might not be adequate. On the other hand, public law and public law remedies can be seen as a defence of the citizen against a powerful state.[16] The latter view becomes more transparent in a system with a strong tradition of constitutionally guaranteed hu-

9 De Smith, S.A., *Judicial Review of Administrative Action*, 1995, 297.
10 Dicey, A.V., *Introduction to the Study of the Law of the Constitution*, 1927, 198.
11 De Smith, S.A., *Judicial Review of Administrative Action*, 1995, 156.
12 Zweigert, K., Kötz, H., *An Introduction to Comparative Law*, 1992, 202.
13 De Smith, S.A., *Judicial Review of Administrative Action*, 1995, 226.
14 Ibid at 157.
15 Foulkes, D., *Administrative Law* ,7th edn, 1990, 8.
16 Cane, P., *An Introduction to Administrative Law*, 1996.

man rights provisions like in Germany or the United States where British cases are read by the judges "with a mind dominated by the spirit of the American Constitution – stripping away the limited frame of reference of judicial review in Britain".[17]

However, the constitutional justification for an expansion of judicial review has been found in a more substantive interpretation of the rule of law and an increase in the protection of personal liberty and dignity.[18] We will see that the methods of control applied by the courts have undergone a gradual development which has been accelerated by the influence of legal principles employed by the European Court of Human Rights and the European Court of Justice. Principles such as proportionality and the protection of substantive legitimate expectation have found their way into English legal reasoning and have enriched the traditional judicial review mechanisms. The Human Rights Act 1998 will change the legal landscape of judicial review fundamentally. Section 6 of the Human Rights Act 1998 provides that "it is unlawful for a public authority to act in a way which is incompatible with one or more of the Convention rights (unless primary legislation leaves the public body with no choice other than to breach the Convention)". Under Sect. 7, a victim or potential victim who claims that a public authority has acted (or proposes to act) in a way contrary to Art. 6(1) of the ECHR may bring proceedings against that authority or rely on the Convention rights in any legal proceedings. The Convention rights thereby form a new ground of review. Section 6(1) "creates a new statutory head of illegality for breach of a Convention right. It is a free-standing statutory ground of challenge".[19]

The standard of review to be applied by domestic courts will in the near future be one of the most exciting issues. In Sect. 2, the Human Rights Act explicitly empowers the courts to take the European Convention and a judgment of the European Court of Human Rights, an opinion of the European Commission on Human Rights or a decision of the Committee of Ministers into account. With regard to judicial review of administrative action, this could mean an increased application of the principle of proportionality:

> "Though the Act itself does not explicitly enjoin the courts to apply a test of proportionality, it is arguable that it implicitly does so, and there are eminent voices, including the Lord Chancellor, who argue for judicial recognition and application of the test of proportionality, at least for cases that fall within the scope of the Act".[20]

By requiring the courts to interpret the Convention, they will have to decide whether a restriction of a Convention right is "necessary in a democratic society". This will clearly invoke the test of proportionality. Therefore objections of the House of Lords to the introduction of the principle of proportionality as a ground

---

17 Schwartz, B. in Schwartz, B. and Wade, H.W.R., *The Legal Control of Government*, 1972.

18 See Chapter Two:.

19 Craig, P., *Administrative Law*, 1999, 556–557.

20 Wong, G., "Towards the Nutcracker Principle, Reconsidering the Objections to Proportionality" (2000) *Public Law* 92 [95].

of review in *R v Secretary of State for the Home Department, ex p Brind*[21] will not be valid any longer. In the comparative cases section below, most recent case law on the development of the principle of proportionality will be discussed.

2. The concept of discretion and the constitutional basis for judicial review of discretionary powers in Germany

In Germany, discretionary powers require an express statutory authorisation by Parliament. Discretion is an area of free exercise of power granted by the legislature. The *Bundesverfassungsgericht* has clearly recognised the granting of discretionary powers as constitutional.[22] Accordingly, the exercise of discretionary powers is compatible with the principle of the rule of law if they are granted by the legislature. In 1959 the Constitutional Court held that the granting of discretionary powers does not contravene the principle of the rule of law. The court arrived at this ruling making three important statements. First, the court emphasised the constitutional limitations to the exercise of discretion, the compliance of which is open to judicial review. Secondly, it stated discretionary powers guarantee the protection of personal freedom by enabling the authorities to make just decisions within their discretion. Thirdly, the court held that:

> "The rule of law requires that the administration can interfere with the rights of an individual only with the authority of law and that the authorisation is clearly limited in its contents, subject matter, purpose and extent so that the interference is measurable and to a certain extent is foreseeable and calculable by the citizen".[23]

However, the basic rights can set clear limits to the authorisation of such discretionary powers. The right to artistic freedom guaranteed in Art. 5(3)[24] of the Basic Law, for instance, requires that the composition of the agency for the protection of minors is based on a statute and that it does not exercise any powers which cannot be reviewed by the courts.[25] The authorities have to exercise their discretion within the limits set by the provisions in the Administrative Court Procedure Act (Sect. 114 *VwGO*)[26] and the Administrative Procedure Act (Sect. 40 *VwVfG*).[27]

---

21 [1991] 1 AC 696.

22 BVerfGE 8, 274; BVerfGE 9, 137.

23 BVerfGE 80, 274, 326; translation by Singh, M.P., *German Administrative Law*, 1985, 84.

24 Art and scholarship, research and teaching shall be free.

25 Jarass, H.D., Pieroth B., *Grundgesetz* ,1995, Art. 5 Rn 74.

26 Article 114 Administrative Court Procedure Act (as amended in 1996): "if an administrative authority is authorised to act at its discretion, the court has to review whether the administrative act or the refusal or omission to enact an administrative act was illegal on the grounds that the authority acted beyond its authorisation or that the authority has exercised its discretion in a way which was not intended by the authorisation. The administrative authority may complement its reasons for the discretionary administrative act as late as during the judicial review proceedings".

The legal basis for the review of discretionary powers can be found in Art. 114 of the Law on Administrative Courts. According to this article, the courts examine whether the administrative act or its refusal or omission is illegal because the statutory limits of the discretion have been exceeded or because the discretion has not been exercised for the purpose of the authorisation. Article 114 was amended in 1996 and it is now permissible for the authority to complete its discretionary decision during the judicial review proceedings. This is the only norm which contains criteria for the review of discretionary powers.

However, this provision has been described as insufficient and therefore requires to be complemented by general principles of the doctrine of discretion.[28] In numerous decisions by the Federal Administrative Court and the Constitutional Courts and in legal writings the attempt has been made to clarify the exact scope of review. However, the controversy has not reached clarification yet. The question whether the exercise of discretion was carried out in an illegal manner is further defined in statute, this time in Art. 40 of the Law on Administrative Procedure 1976 which lays down that if an administrative authority is authorised to act at its discretion, it has to exercise its discretion in consonance with the purpose of the authorisation and the legal limits of the discretion to be observed. The issues involved were mainly dealt with by the Administrative Courts and legal writing. In recent decisions the Constitutional Court has given some constitutional guidelines with regard to the scope of jurisdiction in the area of review of discretionary decisions of the administration. The court has derived its guiding principles from the basic rights and Art. 19 IV of the Basic Law. Article 19 IV, which guarantees full legal protection to everyone, serves as a legal basis for the duty of the courts to review fully the legality and the facts of an administrative decision.[29] This constitutional basis has led to a very intensive control of decisions of the administration which has been described as a second "administrative procedure with better means".[30] There are, however, restrictions upon the courts when reviewing purely discretionary decisions of an administrative body.

German administrative law contains a highly abstract theory of the concept of discretion. The concept of discretion is not a uniform one. Rather, it contains three different forms of discretion which require some explanation. These forms of discretion can be localised in different parts of authorising statutes. First, there is *einfaches Ermessen* (ordinary discretion). This can be identified in so-called "conditional norms" which contain a *Tatbestand* (constituent elements of a provision) and a *Rechtsfolge* (legal effect).

---

27 Section 40 Administrative Procedure Act: "if an administrative authority is authorised to act at its discretion, it has to exercise its discretion in consonance with the purpose of the authorisation and has to observe the legal limits of the discretion".

28 Redeker, K., von Oertzen, H.-.J., *Verwaltungsgerichtsordnung*, 1997, Art. 114 Rn 1 with further references.

29 Jarass, H.D., Pieroth, B., *Grundgesetz*, 1995, Art. 19 Rn 35; BVerfGE 61, 81 (111).

30 Lerche, C., "Die Kontrolldichte hinsichtlich der Tatsachenfeststellung" in Frowein, J.A., *Die Kontrolldichte bei der gerichtlichen Überprüfung von Handlungen der Verwaltung*, 1993, 249.

Secondly, elements of discretion can be found in the *Beurteilungsspielraum* (margin of appreciation) granted to authorities in the determination of undefined legal concepts on the constituent elements of a provision. The concept of undefined legal concepts and margin of appreciation is a peculiarity not known in any other member state or in European Community law.[31] The undefined legal concepts are those such as "public welfare", "public need", "public safety", etc. which are quite commonly used in statutes conferring powers on the administrative authorities. Such legal concepts can only be interpreted in a correct way. As a consequence its application is fully reviewable by the courts. The German concept of discretion has to be seen in the context of the German method of statutory structure. Statutes are seen to consist of two parts: a distinction is drawn between those elements which constitute the facts (*Tatbestand*) and those parts which deal with the legal consequence. Both parts of a statute under this concept can contain elements of discretion. On the constituent part of the norm, undefined legal concepts (*unbestimmte Rechtsbegriffe*) which govern the application of the law can be found such as the public weal, public interest, public order, road safety, danger or the reliability or ability of people. The other part of the norm might include real discretion (*Ermessen*) which is the freedom to decide which of a number of possible legal consequences will be adopted by the decision maker.[32] Not only the common lawyer will have difficulties understanding this division. There is no equivalence to undefined legal concepts in common law or European law and amongst German legal scholars and the courts this concept has been the focus of controversy which exists to this day. The distinction between the two concepts is based on legal reasoning in German law which dates back to the post-war period. The ordinary structure of a norm is regarded as conditional. If certain requirements are given, a particular legal consequence follows. If only one particular consequence is laid down in the statute, then the decision maker has no choice. In case the decision maker is given a choice between one or more legal consequences, he has discretion. However, with regard to the fulfilment of the elements of fact, the decision maker is never given a choice. Under this legal reasoning there is only one right decision possible even when confronted with an undefined legal concept which is not always clear in its meaning. However, this distinction between *Tatbestand* and legal consequence has been relaxed by the granting of a margin of appreciation (*Beurteilungsspielraum*) in deciding on undefined legal concepts.[33] Only in clearly defined circumstances has the Federal Administrative Court granted some subjective area of evaluation to the authorities which is not fully reviewable.[34] However, a decision by the *Bundesverfassungsgericht* in 1990[35]

---

31 Strictly speaking, undefined legal concepts are not seen to be part of the doctrine of discretion in Germany; however, in this chapter for ease of reference undefined legal concepts are covered under the heading of discretion.

32 Schwarze, J., *European Administrative Law*, 2006, 270 ff. .

33 Arai-Takahashi, Y., "Discretion in German Administrative Law: Doctrinal Discourse Revisited" (2000) *European Public Law* 69 [75].

34 Decisions in examinations, assessment of personnel in the Civil Service, decisions of valuation by experts, for instance, the Federal Scrutiny Agency under the law on the distribution of books dangerous to minors and policy decisions of the administration.

has revived a long-standing debate about these concepts within the elaborate doctrine of discretion and sparked off a discussion about a closer orientation on European models.[36] The decision concerned the publication of a pornographic novel entitled *Josefine Mutzenbacher* telling the life story of a prostitute in Vienna around the turn of the century. According to the law on the distribution of books dangerous to minors, the Federal Scrutiny Agency included the book on a list which sets out certain limitations regarding the dissemination of such books. An exception is provided for books considered to be art. The applicant considered the book to be a piece of art protected under Art. 5 of the Basic Law and required the authorities to delete its name from the list. The Constitutional Court's view on the sensitive area of undefined legal concepts, here the question whether the book falls within the category of "dangerous to minors", and the question whether the Scrutiny Agency had any subjective area of evaluation is of great importance for administrative law. As a result the court held that there was no area of subjective evaluation and widened the scope of judicial review in this case in order to protect the constitutional right in Art. 5 of the Basic Law.

Finally, discretionary powers can be found in statutes on planning, so-called *Planungsermessen* (discretion in the planning process). These provisions are described as *Finalnorm*; they do not contain *Tatbestand* und *Rechtsfolge* in the sense described above. Planning decisions are based on provisions containing programmes with predispositioned aims and objectives. They require the balancing of interests rather than the determination of legal concepts.[37] Therefore the standards of review applied for ordinary discretionary powers are not equally applied for planning decisions. Planning authorities enjoy comparably greater freedom. The courts, however, review in particular the balancing process of competing interests. In contrast to the generally high intensity of review of discretionary decisions, the courts have illustrated an increasing willingness to reduce the intensity of control of planning decisions. The reasons for a reduction of the standard of review are due to the nature of planning decisions, which often entail highly technical issues.[38] An important decision in this context is the decision of the Federal Administrative Court in *Wyhl*.[39] The applicants lived in the close neighbourhood (between three and seven km) of a planned nuclear power station in Wyhl. In 1975 the defendants were granted building permission for the power station including ancillary buildings. The applicants challenged the building permission on the

---

35 BVerfGE 83, 130 – *Josefine Mutzenbacher*. The Constitutional Court held that the prohibition of a publication needs to be balanced with the freedom of art and that the administration has no subjective element of evaluation (*Beurteilungsspielraum*) and that therefore the decision is fully reviewable.

36 Schwarze, J., *Das Verwaltungsrecht unter europäischem Einfluß*, 1996, 794; Sieckmann, J.R., "Beurteilungsspielräume und richterliche Kontrollkompetenzen" (1997) *DVBl* 101; Sendler, H., "Über richterliche Kontrolldichte in Deutschland und anderswo" (1994) *NJW* 1511 [1520].

37 Maurer, M., *Allgemeines Verwaltungsrecht,* 1999, 149.

38 Schwarze, J., "Europäische Rahmenbedingungen für die Verwaltungsgerichtsbarkeit" (2000) *NVwZ* 241 [249].

39 BVerwGE 72, 300, 312.

grounds that the erection of the power station would put their lives and health at risk and that the power station would harm the growth of tobacco, wine and fruit which was planted in the region. The Lower Administrative Court quashed the building permit. However, the applicants were subsequently unsuccessful in the Higher Administrative Court and the Federal Adminstrative Court. The Federal Administrative Court held that judicial review has to be restricted to a legality review and that judges may not substitute the decision of the authority with their own value judgment. It held that it is not the task of judges retrospectively to substitute the opinion of the executive whose task it is to decide matters of a highly scientific nature. It is for the authorities to decide on the risks of such a project. The court is entitled to quash the decision if it is shown clear deficits concerning the gathering of facts or the investigation of the technical issues concerned. According to Sect. 7 para 2 of the *Atomgesetz*, the executive is responsible for the investigation of the risks involved and the decision concerning the running of the power station. Accordingly, the courts have to respect this division of power intended by the legislator. Similarly, the courts have applied a reduced intensity of control and accepted a margin of appreciation in decisions concerning the planning of railways[40] and motorways.[41]

A brief look at the historical development of judicial control of discretionary powers reveals that it reflects the changes in Germany's constitutional history. During the second half of the nineteenth century when Administrative Courts were established, judges and academics respected that the administration had to be permitted an area free of judicial control in reaching their decisions. Germany's system of constitutional monarchy allowed for discretionary powers to remain an area of unlimited exercise of sovereign powers by the monarch: "in a constitutional monarchy the *pouvoir administratif* is the area of sovereign power where Parliament and the courts have no role to play".[42] Intrusions into the rights and freedoms of citizens could only be justified if based on law, but such laws only had to be of a very general nature and did not have to contain the right to appeal. Often the courts were expressly barred from judicial control of discretionary powers. In case a law provided a framework laying out the purpose of discretion, the courts were merely empowered to review whether discretion was exercised within the boundaries of the set purpose. A limited control of the merits of a discretionary decision only developed slowly. The central issue was the identification of discretionary powers. As opposed to theories developed in Austria, in Germany this question was closely linked to whether or not the legislator had made the exercise of a statutory discretion subject to appeal.[43] The absence of a statutory right to appeal was interpreted as the intention of Parliament to leave areas of discretionary pow-

40 BVerwG *NVwZ* 1998, 513.

41 BVerwG, *NVwZ* 1997, 914; BVerwG *NVwZ* 1998, 961.

42 Laband, P., *Das Staatsrecht des Deutschen Reiches*, Bd. II ,5th edn, 1911, 175 cited in Bullinger, M., *Das Verwaltungsermessen im modernen Staat*, 132.

43 In Germany, the difference between appeal and judicial review is unknown, which means if there were no provisions of appeal, no other form of judicial control would be available.

ers free from judicial scrutiny. Accordingly, all concepts contained in statutes without provision of appeal such as "public interest" were regarded as concepts of discretion. On the other hand, similar concepts such as "public order" were regarded as questions of law if the statute in question provided for judicial review.

A decisive shift in the interpretation of discretion occurred in 1945. This was a direct response to the experiences during the Nazi dictatorship during which government and administration possessed all powers and Administrative Courts were deprived of their functions. Discretionary powers were no longer regarded as an area of free exercise of administrative power but as a tool to grant a limited area of flexibility in the enforcement of the law. This development was the necessary consequence of history and the effect that the establishment of the *Rechtsstaat* had on German administrative law. The *Rechtstaat* principle includes elements such as "a state, which founded on and subject to the rule of law, a state respecting and conforming to the rule of law, a state governed by the rule of law".[44] Therefore "judicial review is ... a key element of the *Rechtsstaat* under the Basic Law".[45] In Art. 19 IV, the Basic Law[46] now requires effective judicial protection against decisions by public authorities. Article 19(4) of the Basic Law provides the constitutional justification for the strong position of the courts in reviewing the decision-making process of public authorities. This constitutional guarantee of judicial review plays a pivotal role with regard to the standard of review and to any reforms of the concept of discretion. Article 19 IV is part of the principle of the *Rechtsstaat.* It has developed into a constitutional justification for the doctrine that there is only one right answer,[47] an idea that goes back to German idealism.[48] Accordingly, the protection of substantive rights is more important than the protection of procedural safeguards. This approach has most recently found clear legislative expression in the new laws on Administrative Court procedure which will be discussed in detail in Chapter Four. As will be shown in case examples below, three important constitutional principles – the principle of equality (Art. 3 Basic Law), the principle of the protection of substantive legitimate expectation and the principle of proportionality – set limits to the exercise of discretionary powers.

German commentators have suggested giving up the division within the doctrine of discretion and adapting a uniform concept of discretion which other member states in the European Union have.[49] The other demand is concerned with a reduction of the intensity of judicial control which ironically has led to immense delays in litigation and as a result violates Art. 19(4) of the Basic Law and Art. 6 of the European Convention on Human Rights.

---

44 Foster, N., *German Legal System and Laws*, 1993, 149.

45 Kommers, D. P., *The Constitutional Jurisprudence of the Federal Republic of Germany* ,2nd edn, 1997.

46 Article 19(4) Basic Law: "where rights are violated by public authorities the person affected shall have recourse to law. In so far as no other jurisdiction has been established such recourse shall be to the ordinary courts".

47 Brinktrine, R., *Verwaltungsermessen in Deutschland und England*, 1998, 459.

48 Hufen, F., *Verwaltungsprozessrecht* ,1998, 18 with further references.

49 Sendler, H.,"Über richterliche Kontrolldichte in Deutschland und anderswo" (1994) *NJW* 1511 [1520].

3. Evaluation

In comparing the concept of discretionary powers one can observe that both legal systems grant discretionary powers to their administrative authorities and accept that they are an important feature of modern administration. Both in England and Germany, the exercise of discretionary powers has to comply with the principles of the rule of law or the concept of the *Rechtsstaat*. Discretionary powers have to be granted on the basis of statutory authorisation. Nevertheless, in England, prerogative discretionary powers, which are not based on statute, may provide the basis for the exercise of discretionary powers. The German concept of discretion is based on a highly abstract theory of the structure of statutory provisions. It identifies three different forms of discretion: *Einfaches Ermessen* (ordinary discretion), *Beurteilungsspielraum* (margin of appreciation) in the determination of undefined legal concepts and *Planungsermessen* (discretion in the planning process). Each of these three concepts of discretion requires a different intensity of review. The intensity of the review of discretionary powers in the planning process is the least intensive form of review. An increasing number of cases illustrates that the courts have reduced the intensity of control of planning decisions. English law does not distinguish between these forms of discretion, even though the notion of the undefined legal concept is similar to a question of fact and degree.

Both legal systems provide for mechanisms of reviewing the decisions of public authorities. The main justification of judicial control of administrative action in England has long been the protection of the will of Parliament. In Germany, on the other hand, the historical development after 1945, in particular, has placed the courts in a position which requires them to uphold individual rights against actions by public authorities.

The next part will deal with the grounds of review of discretionary powers. It illustrates the way in which courts apply standards of review which define the border between the role of the courts and the decision-making bodies and thereby define the concept of discretion.

II. Comparative cases

1. Failure to exercise discretion under English law

The law dealing with the control of discretionary powers shows a gradual development. The wealth of case law in the field of judicial review of discretionary powers has prompted numerous legal writers to collect cases under specific headings. Generally speaking, two areas of review of the exercise of discretionary powers can be identified. The courts are concerned with the question whether an authority has "failed properly to retain that degree of free and unfettered power of judgment" or whether it "has exercised its power in a way which the reviewing court may categorise as an abuse of power".[50] Craig has chosen similar categories such as the "failure to exercise discretion" and the "abuse of discretionary power".[51] Under the first heading, five groups of cases can be identified, such as the review of self-created rules which structure discretion, unauthorised delegation of power, acting under dictation, fettering discretion by contractual or similar undertakings, fettering discretion by estoppel and error of law. Under the heading of abuse of power, the courts judge on the question whether discretionary powers have been used for an improper purpose, whether irrelevant considerations have been taken into account and whether the exercise of power was unreasonable and irrational. The famous *Wednesbury* unreasonableness test is of major importance in deciding whether authorities have abused their powers. The application of the unreasonableness test raises questions of major constitutional importance. It has led to a major discussion of how far the courts should engage in the substantive review of administrative decisions. In this context, the application of the principle of proportionality as a possible fourth ground of review as suggested in the *GCHQ* case has enriched the discussion.

a) Review of self-created rules

Administrative discretionary powers give the authorities the choice between alternative forms of decision in each case. It is a common practice to structure discretion by formulating rules or guidelines "to bridge the gap between the general power and the particular case".[52] "The central issue in the legal control of policies is now clear: it is the resolution of the apparent conflict between the interest of the decisions maker in developing policies which determine particular decisions and the interest of the individual in obtaining discretionary decisions which take proper account of the special features of his claim".[53] However, often self-created rules have restricting effect on the original discretionary power. There are a number of relevant cases which illustrate well how the courts have developed principles of review of such policy decisions.

The earliest case is that of *R v Port of London Authority, ex p Kynoch Ltd.*[54] Here, the Port of London Authority was given discretionary power to grant licences for the construction of private wharfs. The applicant was refused the grant of a licence on the grounds that an existing policy contained the rule that in case the Authority was planning to build the same type of wharf itself an application for the construction of a private wharf would be unsuccessful. Even though the Court of Appeal upheld the refusal of the grant, Bankes LJ established an important principle. Accordingly, "an administrative body may have a substantive gen-

50 Bailey, S.H, Jones B.L & Mowbray A.R , *Cases and Materials on Administrative Law*, 1997, 235.
51 Craig, P., *Administrative Law*, 1994, 384.
52 Galligan, D.G., "The Nature and Function of Policies within Discretionary Power" (1976) *Public Law* 332 [333].
53 Ibid 335.
54 [1919] 1 KB 176.

eral policy, but, secondly, it may apply its policy only after considering the merits of each situation".[55]

In *Lavender v MHLG*[56] the applicant was refused permission to extract sand, gravel and ballast from part of Rivernook Farm in Walton-on-Thames. The official in charge refused permission and the applicant appealed to the Ministry of Housing. The latter refused permission too on the ground that the Ministry of Agriculture had not given his permission. The decision was based on the policy of the Ministry of Agriculture that generally "land in the reservations should not be released for mineral working unless the Minister of Agriculture, Fisheries and Food is not opposed to working". The decision was held to be invalid because the Minister of Housing did not exercise his discretion but delegated it to another ministry. So in one way this is a case of "improper delegation of discretion but it may also be regarded as the equally improper rigid application of a policy".[57]

Once again Bankes LJ's principle was applied in the case of *British Oxygen v Board of Trade*.[58] Here, the applicants applied for an investment grant under the Industrial Development Act 1966. The Board of Trade had discretion to award these grants and had established a policy according to which grants could not be awarded for expenditure on items which each cost less than £25. However, the company had spent more than £4 million on gas cylinders, each at a price of £20. According to the above-stated rule and the Board of Trade having taken the merits of the case into account, the company was refused the grant. The House of Lords applied the Bankes LJ principle and upheld the Board's decision. Even though Lord Reid confirmed that "the general rule is that anyone who has to exercise a statutory discretion must not "shut his ears to an application"", he said: "if the minister thinks that policy or good administration requires the operation of some limiting rule, I find nothing to stop him". In this case, the court applied the Bankes rules and considered the individual circumstances of the case. Lord Reid held that there is no great difference between a policy and a rule whereas Viscount Dilhorne thought it was difficult to distinguish the two, but he admitted that the applicant in the case had to be allowed to bring arguments against the policy forward. However, as a consequence it was held that the policy did not restrict the Board's discretionary power.

In the case of *R v Secretary of State for Transport, ex p Sheriff*[59] the company Sheriff & Sons Ltd had been granted the sum of £250,000 according to Sect. 8 of the Railway Act for the provision of rail freight facilities. However, the so-called Memorandum of Explanation which was issued by the Department of Transport stipulated that any "commitment to a project for the provision of rail freight facilities in advance of a decision to make a grant would render the project ineligible for a grant". This guidance, which was also referred to as "rules, conditions and procedures", left no room for an exception or a waiver. The Department's reason-

[55] Galligan, D.G., supra n. 52, 346.
[56] [1970] 1 WLR 1231.
[57] Galligan, D.G., supra n. 52, 338.
[58] [1971] AC 610.
[59] *The Times*, 18 December 1986.

ing was that if "works had begun, it could not be satisfied that a grant was needed". The court ruled that the decision was unlawful because the Memorandum was a rule which fettered the Secretary's discretion to award grants under the Railways Act.

b) Unauthorised delegation of power

The principle against delegation, which is also referred to as the maxim *delegatus non potest delegare*, is designed to protect the exercise of discretionary power so that it can only be exercised by the person who is expressly given that power. However, in order to ensure the functioning of the administration, there are legislative and judicial limitations to that principle.

In *Carltona*[60] the appellants owned a food factory which was requisitioned in 1942 by the Commissioners of Work. The appellants claimed that the notice to requisition was invalid because the persons constituting the authority had not been involved in the process. The Commissioners of Work had never met and the Minister of Works and Planning had carried out its functions. The assistant secretary had signed the notice. Lord Greene held that:

> "In the administration of government in this country the functions which are given to ministers and constitutionally properly given to ministers because they are constitutionally responsible are functions so multifarious that no minister could ever personally attend to them ... Constitutionally, the decision of such an official is of course, the decision of the minister. The minister is responsible".

The *Carltona* principle was confirmed in *R v Secretary of State for the Home Department, ex p Oladehinde.*[61] Here, the minister had delegated his power to deport to senior immigration officers. Lord Griffiths held that this was permissible provided that the delegations to officials "do not conflict with or embarrass them in the discharge of their specific statutory duties under the Act and that the decisions are suitable to their grading and experience".

c) Acting under dictation

When exercising a given discretionary power an authority is not allowed to act under the dictation of another body. This clear rule that one must not simply act under the dictation of others was well illustrated in the case of *Lavender and Son Ltd v Minister of Housing and Local Government.*[62] The applicants had applied for planning permission to extract sand and other substances from a site of high agricultural quality. The permission was refused. The applicants argued that the Minister for Housing and Local Government had fettered his discretion by dismissing the application on the grounds that it was his policy not to release land for mineral working unless there was no objection from the Minister of Agriculture. The court

---

60 *Carltona v Commissioner of Works* [1943] 2 All ER 560, CA.
61 [1991] 1 AC 254.
62 [1970] 1 WLR 1231.

held that the decision of the Minister of Housing and Local Government had to be quashed because he had allowed for the final decision to be made by the Minister of Agriculture.

d) Fettering discretion by contractual undertaking

Another series of cases deals with the restrictions of discretionary powers through contractual or similar commitments on decision makers. The difficulty in these cases arises out of the necessity of modern administration to enter into contractual relationships with private parties. At the same time, the authorities have to preserve their public law functions and exercise their discretionary administrative powers. Clashes between these two issues have been the content of various judgments.[63] DeSmith suggests three general solutions. Generally, "a public authority cannot effectively disable itself by contractual or other undertaking from making or enforcing a byelaw, refusing or revoking a grant of planning permission, or exercising any other statutory power of primary importance such as a power of compulsory purchase, nor can it effectively bind itself to exercise such a power in any particular way". Thirdly, contracts entered into by the Crown cannot exclude the exercise of discretionary powers for the public weal.[64]

The case of *Steeples v Derbyshire County Council*[65] is a good example for this group of cases. The county council owned an area of parkland which they proposed to develop as a leisure centre with recreational facilities. An agreement was entered into between the council and a company whereby the company were appointed as consultants and managers of the development. The agreement provided that the council would take all reasonable steps to obtain such outline planning permission and other outline consents as were necessary to enable the proposed development to proceed. The agreement also provided that if the council failed, *inter alia*, to use their best endeavours to obtain such permission or consents, they would pay the company £116,875 liquidated damages. Notices were given by an officer of the council that they proposed to seek planning permission.

On a claim by the plaintiff, who was the owner of land adjoining the proposed development and a local ratepayer, against the council, *inter alia*, for declarations that the grant of planning permission was void on the grounds, *inter alia*, that the decision to grant planning permission was in breach of the rules of natural justice because the terms of the council's agreement with the company might lead a reasonable person to suspect that they were likely to be biased in favour of granting the applications for permission, the court held that, although the decision of the planning committee had been fairly and properly made, natural justice required

---

63 In *Birkdale* for instance it was held that "if a person or public body is entrusted by the legislature with certain powers and duties expressly or impliedly for public purposes, those persons or bodies cannot divest themselves of these powers and duties. They cannot enter into any contract or take any action incompatible with the due exercise of their powers or duties". However, this should not be understood as a strict rule.

64 De Smith, S.A., *Judicial Review of Administrative Action*, 1995, 516, 517.

65 [1985] 1 WLR 256.

that the decision to grant planning permission should be seen to have been fairly made. In deciding whether the decision was seen to have been fairly made, the court had to ask whether a reasonable man, who was not present when the decision was made and was unaware that it had in fact been fairly made, but who was aware of all the terms of the council's agreement with the company, would think that there was a real likelihood that the agreement had had a material and significant effect on the planning committee's decision was not seen to have been fairly made and was either void or voidable as being in breach of natural justice.

The question was whether there was a failure to comply with any of the requirements of natural justice. The plaintiff contended that the decision of 10 December 1970 failed to comply with the requirement of natural justice in one respect only, namely that, primarily because of the terms of the contract made with K.L.F., it was not seen to have been fairly made in that the public had reason to suspect that the decision was a mere formality, to suspect at the very least that when the decision was made there was a strong bias in favour of the decision which was in fact made and to suspect accordingly that it was not a proper decision at all. The plaintiff did not contend that the decision was in fact not fairly made. He did not seriously challenge the evidence of Mr Crowther, the chairman of the planning committee, which was to the effect that the meeting at which the decision was made was open to the public and that about 50 members of the public attended it, that his committee had considered the objections received, that in the morning before debating the matter they visited the site and spoke to people there, that Mr Crowther thought that the contract with K.L.F. was subject to the obtaining of planning permission, that the committee looked at the matter only from the planning point of view and that the committee could have turned down the county council's application. The court accepted the evidence of Mr Crowther and was satisfied that the decision was in fact fairly and properly made.

The court held that to satisfy the requirements of natural justice, it must not only have been properly made, it must also be seen to have been fairly made, but that, on the contrary, it was seen or was seen by the public at large to have been pre-judged because having agreed with K.L.F. to use their best endeavours and generally by reason of the terms of the contract they had given the appearance of having imposed upon themselves and upon the planning committee a fetter or restraint on their freedom to discharge that duty in the way prescribed by the Regulations and the 1971 Act.

Finally, the court asked what amounts to a fetter upon the discretion in question. The court reached the conclusion "that anything constitutes a fetter for this purpose at the very least if a reasonable man would regard it as being likely to have a material and significant effect one way or another on the outcome of the decision in question". The court held that:

"In conclusion, it is probable that a reasonable man, not having been present at the meeting when the decision was made, and not knowing of my conclusion as to the actual fairness of it, knowing of the existence and of all the terms of the contract ... would think that there was a real likelihood that those provisions in the contract which require the county council, and for that matter the joint venture committee, to use their best endeavours to obtain planning permission, and the contract as a whole in the light of its provisions to which I have referred, had had a material and significant effect on the planning committee's decision to grant the permission, and accordingly, on that ground, I hold that that decision was either voidable or void".

Other High Court decisions, however, did not follow *Steeples*.[66] In *R v St Edmundsbury BC, ex p Investors in Industry Commercial Properties Ltd* it was held that "the reasonable man test has no application in the case of an administrative decision", as opposed to a decision "of a judicial nature".[67]

2. Failure to exercise discretion in German administrative law

Three forms of illegality can be found in German administrative law: failure to exercise discretion, abuse of discretion and excess of discretion (dealt with below). There is some debate in Germany whether excess of discretion should be considered as part as the category of abuse of discretion which illustrates the desire to conceptualise the grounds of review. The courts differentiate between two main types of error, the first being errors occurring within the decision-making process and the second errors with regard to the result of the decision as such in its substance.

a) Review of self-created rules

This is a classic case in which the decision maker errs in believing that he has to apply a self-created rule. The decision maker believes that he is bound by a standard practice and that according to the principle of equality (as discussed below) he has to conform to the standard practice. An illegal standard practice, for instance, does not require the decision maker to be bound by it.[68]

b) Unauthorised delegation of power

This category is not particularly important in Germany. This is due to the nature of the provisions at stake. Violations of provisions which deal with the jurisdiction of an official or an authority usually have no direct connection to the exercise of discretionary powers. These provisions are usually only internally relevant. Internal delegation is therefore only problematic if the provision was designed to be binding externally.[69]

---

66 See *R v Sevenoaks District Council, ex p Terry* [1985] 3 All ER 226; *R v St Edmundsbury BC, ex p Investors in Industry Commercial Properties Ltd* [1985] 1 WLR 1168.

67 [1985] 1 WLR 1168 at 1193, 1194.

68 BverwGE 92, 153, 154.

69 Maurer, H., *Allgemeines Verwaltungsrecht*, 1999, 508.

c) Fettering discretion by contractual undertaking

The failure to exercise discretion was considered in the *Floatglass* case (BVerwGE 45, 309).

In 1970, a permit for the building of a factory producing floatglass was granted to the D-Corporation on a piece of land. The applicant's house and 26 other private properties were located on a directly adjoining piece of land. To the north and east of the land in question were extensive residential areas. The Federal Law on Building (*Bundesbaugesetz*)[70] is the law governing the establishment of development plans and the granting of building permits. According to Art. 1 para 4 sentence 2 (now Art. 1 para 6) of the Federal Law on Building, a development plan shall only be established after thorough comparative examination (*Abwägung*) of the competing interests. These competing interests are the public and private protective interests (*Belange*). In winter 1970, the major and a local councillor decided to offer the D-Corporation a large piece of land for sale for the erection of a factory. A few days later the local council approved this. The programme for the development of the region (*Gebietsentwicklungsplan*) had designated the land in question as a residential area. The land development plan (*Flächennutzungsplan*) designated the area as landscape or an area for the erection of small buildings. The plans were altered in order to accommodate the envisaged project and the area in question was designated for industrial development. Afterwards, the D-Corporation applied formally for building permission. It was granted a building permit in October 1970. Only afterwards did the supervisory authority approve of the changes to the building scheme (*Bebauungsplan*).

It was held that the comparative examination is incomplete if the authority entered into either legal or factual commitments before exercising its discretion. This contravenes Art. 1 para 4 sentence 2 of the Federal Law on Building. However, such a deficit can be remedied if the prejudgment is justified, the division of competences has been complied with and if the decision is materially correct. However, this demands that the result complies with the requirement of comparative examination as set out in Art. 1 para 4 sentence 2 of the Federal Law on Building. Industrial and residential areas should be built a sufficient distance from each other. The appeal was allowed.

The court held that the administrative authority has to carry out a comparative examination of the contradicting interests. If such examination does not take place at all the authority has violated its duty. The authority has acted against its duty to carry out a comparative examination if it does not consider those questions which should be considered within the given situation. Further, if the significance of the private protective interests has not been recognised and if the balance between the public interests and the private interests is disproportionate. These requirements refer both to the process of examination and the result of the examination. Regarding the process of examination, the *Bundesverwaltungsgericht* agreed with the appellate court in so far as the initial decisions during the planning stage had shortened the process and therefore no proper examination had taken place at all. It is

[70] Now called *Baugesetzbuch*.

indisputable that in particular the planning of larger projects often requires the authorities to make decisions before the final examination stage. Discussions, agreements, representations and contracts which take place before the formal planning stage may be essential for good planning and in order to guarantee an effective realisation of the plan. It would be unrealistic to consider all these above-mentioned commitments during a planning decision as illegal.

Therefore, prejudgments which are directed towards a comparative examination can be in the interests of an effective planning procedure. Planning deficits, which are based on previous decisions, which influence the course of procedure can therefore be remedied if three cumulative conditions are met. The prejudgment must be materially justified, it has to be taken in accordance with the required procedural rules, i.e. if the planning is within the council's authority, any prejudgment has to take the council's view into account and the decision has to be materially correct. However, this demands that the result complies with the requirement of comparative examination as set out in Art. 1 para 4 sentence 2 of the Federal Law on Building.

The court had no doubt that residential and industrial areas should not be situated in the same neighbourhood. The positioning of residential and industrial areas bears the potential for conflict and cannot be dealt with by imposing restrictions on industrial projects, but should be avoided in the first place. Therefore, the building permit was illegal and it violated the rights of the applicant based on Art. 14 of the Basic Law.[71]

3. Evaluation

The comparison shows that there is a certain amount of resemblance in the category of abuse of discretion. Both the English and German systems have developed grounds of review to control that discretion is exercised unfettered. The German decision in the *Floatglass* case and the English decision in *Steeples* v *Derbyshire County Council*[72] both reach the same result by quashing the building permission on the ground that the planning authorities' decision was illegal. Both courts apply the ground of review of fettering of discretion and the similarity of the courts' approaches is striking. The High Court's decision is based on the reasoning that the contract which preceded the planning permission had had a material and significant effect on the planning committee's decision to grant the permission and, accordingly, on that ground, held that that decision was either voidable or void. The *Bundesverwaltungsgericht* states that the prejudgments, i.e. the offer of the piece of land in question, had shortened the required process of examining competing interests during the planning stage and a correct examination of competing interests could not be carried out at all. However, the *Bundesverwaltungsgericht* would have been prepared to remedy the deficit in the exercise of the authorities' powers

[71] Article 14 I Basic Law provides: "property and the right of inheritance shall be guaranteed. Their content and limits shall be determined by law".

[72] [1985] 1 WLR 256.

if the result in its substance had been correct and the prejudgment had been made with the involvement of the council. The *Bundesverwaltungsgericht* was not satisfied with the planning decision in its substance and allowed the application. The High Court on the other hand was more concerned with issues of natural justice such as bias and applies the so-called "reasonable man" test. Accordingly, the decision must not only have been properly made, it must also be seen to have been fairly made.

4. Abuse of discretion in English law

a) Use of power for an improper purpose

There is no absolute discretion in public law. Statutory power conferred for public purposes is conferred as it were upon trust, not absolutely, i.e. it can only validly be used in the right and proper way which Parliament is presumed to have intended when conferring it.

The groundbreaking decision was *Padfield v Minister of Agriculture, Fisheries and Food.*[73]

The Agricultural Marketing Act 1958 provided for a committee of investigation which had to consider certain kind of reports "if the minister in any case so directs". Producers in the southeast of England complained that the differential element in the price fixed for their milk by the Milk Marketing Board was not sufficient. The minister had the discretion of referring such complaints to a committee of investigation. He did not do so, giving the reasons that the complaint was unsuitable for investigation because it raised wide issues and the producers were presented on the board and should be content with "the normal democratic machinery". However, in *Padfield*, the minister gave bad reasons which showed that he was not exercising his discretion in accordance with the intentions of the Act. The whole aim of the minister's overriding power, however, was to correct the "normal democratic machinery" if necessary. It was further held that there is no general requirement that the authority should give reasons for its decisions. The minister could have refused properly to act on a complaint without any reasons and that in such a case a complainant would have no remedy unless other known facts and circumstances appear to point overwhelmingly in favour of a different decision. The court held that where there was a relevant and substantial complaint, the minister had a duty, as well as a power, to act. Otherwise he would deprive the producers of a remedy which Parliament provided for them, i.e. defeat statutory intent and purpose.[74]

---

73 [1968] AC 997.
74 [1968] AC 997.

b) Unreasonableness

The ground of review of unreasonableness is more controversial than the previously discussed categories of review. The law relating to the principle of unreasonableness has undergone a considerable development recently. The *locus classicus* for the ground of review of unreasonableness is the case of *Associated Provincial Picture Houses Ltd v Wednesbury Corporation.*[75] Sir John Laws describes the *Wednesbury* case as the "legal equivalent of Beethoven's Fifth Symphony: it has been hackneyed through no fault of its own".[76] In keeping with the analogies of the musical world, one could also describe it as the legal equivalent of Schubert's Unfinished Symphony as it leaves scope for its development into a richer test. Under the Sunday Entertainments Act 1932, the corporation gave permission to the appellants to run their cinema on Sundays. However, children under the age of 15 were not admitted. The appellants argued that this restriction was unreasonable. It was held that the subject matter of the condition was to be decided by the corporation. Lord Greene held: "it is true to say that if a decision on a competent matter is so unreasonable that no reasonable authority could ever have come to it, then the courts can interfere. That, I think, is quite right; but to prove a case of that kind would require something overwhelming and, in this case, the facts do not come anywhere near anything of that kind".

Lord Greene distinguishes between two forms of *Wednesbury* unreasonableness. First, he identifies the test for irrelevant considerations as follows: "the court is entitled to investigate the action of the local authority with a view to seeing whether they have taken into account matters which they ought not to take into account or, conversely, have refused to take into account or neglected to take into account matters which they ought to take into account". This first limb of the *Wednesbury* test is more concerned with the process of the decision making itself.

The second limb of Lord Greene's test, however, is concerned with the substantive conclusion of the decision. Under this test Lord Greene, however, is very eager to describe the limited role of the courts in reviewing the exercise of discretionary powers: "once that question is answered in favour of the local authority, it may still be possible to say that, although the local authority kept within the four corners of the matter which they ought to consider, they have nevertheless come to a conclusion so unreasonable that no reasonable authority could ever have come to it". He is clear in his point that a merits-based review has to be avoided. "The power of the court to interfere in each case is not as an appellate authority to override a decision of the local authority, but as a judicial authority which is concerned, and concerned only, to see whether the local authority has contravened the law by acting in excess of powers which Parliament has confided in them". The meaning of "unreasonable" is sometimes described as extreme behaviour, such as acting in bad faith, taking inappropriate considerations into account or strictly act-

---

75 [1984] 1 KB 223.

76 Forsyth, C., and Hare,I., *The Golden Metwand and the Crooked Cord*, 1998, 185.

ing irrationally. Less technically, it has been described as a decision which evokes the remark: "my goodness, that is certainly wrong!"[77]

The *Wednesbury* principle has developed into one of the "bedrocks" of modern administrative law in England.[78] This principle has served as a test to be applied in many other cases[79] and has undergone a development which is not completed yet. The courts have shaped the test in that they have adopted different standards of review depending on the subject matter. First, the courts have applied the rather strict form in its original meaning into a softer *Wednesbury* test. In the *ITF*[80] case, Lord Cooke formulated the *Wednesbury* test in a way which lowered the high hurdle as imposed by Lord Greene in the *Wednesbury* decision. He asked whether the decision was one which a reasonable authority could reach. The case was concerned with protests against the export of livestock. The Chief Constable of Sussex deployed manpower to control the protests. However, due to limited resources he had to reduce the police presence to two days a week. ITF claimed that this decision was unreasonable. The House of Lords held that the decision was a proportionate measure. However, the test applied by Lord Cooke is a refreshingly new phrasing of the old *Wednesbury* principle. The fact that the courts have begun to shape the traditional unreasonableness principle into a flexible tool, which applies different standards of review, raises the question whether the introduction of the principle of proportionality into English law is desirable and which form this should take.[81]

Craig identifies three options open to the courts in dealing with this question. First, the "retention of traditional *Wednesbury* alongside proportionality". Accordingly, the courts could apply the traditional *Wednesbury* test outside those areas where they are obliged to apply the proportionality test such as under the Human Rights Act 1998 or in cases with EC law context. However, this solution appears to be too theoretical as the courts have already started to modify the *Wednesbury* test.[82]

Secondly, the courts could develop *Wednesbury* in the way suggested by Lord Cooke in the *ITF* case. Accordingly, the traditional *Wednesbury* test would be retained in a modified version alongside proportionality. Sir John Laws describes the common law as containing the quality "which above all else allows it to harness old principles to new conditions without offence to the democratic arms of government". He justifies the varying standards of the *Wednesbury* test with the nature of the common law. The principle of *Wednesbury* is not engraved in statute

---

77 De Smith, S.A., *Judicial Review of Administrative Action*, 1995, 550; May LJ in *Neale v Hereford & Worcester CC* [1986] ICR 471 at 483.

78 Sir John Laws in Forsyth and Hare, *The Golden Metwand and the Crooked Cord*, 1998, 186.

79 See *Council of Civil Service Unions v Minister for the Civil Service* [1985] AC 374.

80 *R v Chief Constable of Sussex, ex p International Trader's Ferry Ltd* [1999] 1 All ER 129.

81 Craig, P., *Administrative Law*, 1999, 586; Fordham M. and de la Mare, T. in Jowell, J. and Cooper, J., *Understanding Human Rights Principles*, 2001, 27; Sir John Laws in Forsyth, C.and Hare, I., *The Golden Metwand and the Crooked Cord*, 1998, 185.

82 Craig, P., *Administrative Law*, 1999, 598.

and is therefore able to be applied flexibly. He supports the idea that the *Wednesbury* principle is "alive and well" and that the concept of proportionality can be embraced by adapting the existing modes of review.[83]

Finally, proportionality could become the general criteria for review. Advantages of such an approach are seen in the streamlining of tests applied with an EC law context and actions under the Human Rights Act 1998. Further, the test applied under the proportionality test is more detailed and structured than the traditional *Wednesbury* test. Finally, this test could be applied with varying standards of review to take account of decisions which might not be suited for full judicial scrutiny.[84]

However, whatever route is chosen the crucial point in the application of the principle of modified unreasonableness or proportionality is the standard of review which is applied in a particular context. This issue is closely linked to questions such as burden of proof, investigation into facts by applying different modes of inquiry, be it inquisitorial or adversarial, and the application of procedural guarantees such as the duty to give reasons.

c) The principle of proportionality in English administrative law

Lord Diplock suggested the introduction of the principle of proportionality as a potential fourth ground of review in the case of *CCSU v Minister for the Civil Service*.[85] Inevitably such a transplantation of a European principle of German origin meant a challenge to the traditional common law approach. More precisely the *Wednesbury* principle of unreasonableness and the relationship to the principle of proportionality has since been at the centre of the discussion whether the European concept has been successfully integrated into English law.[86] The *Wednesbury* principle as established in *Associated Provincial Picture Houses Ltd v Wednesbury Corporation*[87] contains the rule that a discretionary decision of a public body is illegal if it is so unreasonable that no reasonable authority could ever come to it. The principle of proportionality in its European formulation, however, embraces the test of whether the challenged act is suitable and necessary for the achievement of its objective and one which does not impose excessive burdens on the individual.[88] The proportionality test clearly requires "the express articulation and explicit weighing of the specific aims of a measure in relation to its impact on a right or interest invoked by the applicant".[89] This test poses two difficulties for a smooth accommodation into the existing system of judicial review of administra-

83 Sir John Laws in Forsyth, C., and Hare, I., *The Golden Metwand and the Crooked Cord*, 1998, 201.
84 Craig, P., *Administrative Law*, 1999, 602.
85 [1985] AC 374.
86 See de Búrca, G., "Proportionality and Wednesbury Unreasonableness: The Influence of European Legal Concepts on UK Law" (1997) *European Public Law* 561.
87 [1948] 1 KB 223.
88 Craig, P., de Burca, G., *EU Law*, 1998, 350.
89 See de Burca, G., supra n. 87.

tive action in English courts. The first difficulty is the degree of review of an original decision which such a test would require. The weighing of public and private interests amounts to a form of review, which is closer to that of an appellate jurisdiction and goes beyond the traditional supervisory function of judicial review proceedings.

The second possible obstacle was seen in "the absence of a fundamental law" in the UK. Both concerns were clearly expressed in the case of *Brind v Secretary of State for the Home Department*,[90] however, at the same time this decision marked the era of development of the recognition of human rights in judicial review. In 1988 the Home Secretary issued a directive under the Broadcasting Act 1981 prohibiting the broadcasting of "words spoken" by any person representing or purporting to represent certain organisations including Sinn Féin and the Ulster Defence Association. *Brind* raised two issues. First, the question whether human rights law had any room in judicial review and, secondly, whether the principle of proportionality should be used as a separate ground of review as suggested in the *GCHQ* case. In *Brind* the proportionality test was discussed intensively.

Having stressed that the Convention is not part of domestic law and that the courts have no power to enforce human rights directly, Lord Bridge added that ambiguous domestic legislation was intended to conform with the Convention by Parliament:

"It is accepted, of course, by the appellants that, like any other treaty obligations which have not been embodied in the law by statute, the Convention is not part of the domestic law, that the courts accordingly have no power to enforce Convention rights directly and that, if domestic legislation conflicts with the Convention, the courts must nevertheless enforce it. But it is already well settled that, in construing any provision in domestic legislation which is ambiguous in the sense that it is capable of a meaning which either conforms to or conflicts with the Convention, the courts will presume that Parliament intended to legislate in conformity with the Convention, not in conflict with it".

Lord Templeman stressed that "in terms of the Convention, as construed by the European Court of Human Rights, the interference with freedom of expression must be necessary and proportionate to the damage which the restriction is designed to prevent". Lord Templeman was therefore the only one who suggested applying the proportionality test in general even though in this case he held it was not appropriate. Lord Ackner argued that the principle was incompatible with the judicial review approach, which does not review the merits of a case, and also described it as "the forbidden appellate approach". Secondly, he held that in the absence of a "fundamental law" there was no room for the principle. Lord Roskill and Lord Bridge concluded with Lord Ackner, however, preserving the possible future incorporation of the ground of proportionality as a separate ground of review. Lord Roskill said:

"I am clearly of the view that the present is not a case in which the first step can be taken for the reason that to apply the principle in the present case would be for the court to substitute its own judgment of what was needed to achieve a particular objective for the judgment of the Secretary of State upon whom that duty has been laid by Parliament. But so to hold

[90] R *v Secretary of State for the Home Department, ex p Brind* [1991] AC 696.

in the present case is not to exclude the possible future development of the law in this respect ..."

Murray Hunt describes the decision as a "double-edged sword" by establishing that unincorporated law is irrelevant and at the same time favouring a refinement of the traditional approach in fundamental rights cases by lowering the *Wednesbury* threshold.[91]

In a recent article, Sir John Laws is concerned with the meaning and dangers of rights, which in his view have not been paid enough attention.[92] This is probably true, as the common law world does not possess a culture of rights in the way countries like Italy and Germany have developed it. Both Italy and Germany see in their constitutions and the judicial review of the constitutionality of legislation a protection against "the return of the evil – the horrors of dictatorship and the consequent trampling on fundamental human rights by legislators subservient to oppressive regimes".[93] Therefore continental legal systems are aware of the rights that a written constitution actually ascribes to them. Due to this rights-based background a different attitude of continental scholars in analysing the legal development of the European Union can be witnessed. Politicians and academic writers on the continent are deeply concerned with the question of the legal basis for member state liability and the *Schutznormtheorie* (theory of the protective norm), which requires that the rule infringed by the member state must be for the protection of the individual.[94] In Alan Ryan's words, "the British tradition cannot say anything convincing about our rights ..."[95] This "national accusation", as Ryan puts it, is an exaggeration and used by Legrand to illustrate the importance of recognising the socio-historical and socio-cultural background of the common law legal culture when comparing it with the civil law tradition.[96]

The protection of human rights has, however, progressed significantly in the United Kingdom. The explicit protection of human rights has found clear expression in the Human Rights Act 1998. The Act is merely a step in a process of development which can be described as a change in the legal climate. The Act has incorporated a number of the rights contained in the European Convention on Human Rights into English domestic law. It "should produce huge changes in the way our public authorities, including the courts and tribunals, approach all aspects

---

91 Hunt, M., *Human Rights Law in English Courts*, 1997, 208.

92 Sir John Laws, "The Limitations of Human Rights" (1998) *Public Law* 254.

93 Cappelletti, M., *The Judicial Process in Comparative Perspective*, 1989, 161.

94 von Dannwitz, T., "Die gemeinschaftsrechtliche Staatshaftung der Mitgliedstaaten" (1997) *DVBl* 1; see the submission of the German government in judgment in joined cases C-46/93 and C-48/93, *Brasserie du Pécheur* and *Factortame*, I-1143; Ruffert, M., "Rights and Remedies in European Community Law: A Comparative View" (1997) *CMLR* 309.

95 Ryan, A., "The British, The Americans, and Rights" in Lacey, M.J., Haakonssen, K., *A Culture of Rights: the Bill of Rights in Philosophy, Politics, and Law – 1791 and 1991* ,1991, 39.

96 Legrand, P., "How to Compare" (1996) *Legal Studies* 232 [237].

of the law".[97] Section 2(1) of the Act requires them to take into account any "judgment, decision, declaration or advisory opinion of the European Court of Human Rights". This means that UK courts must have regard to the case law of the European Court of Human Rights, which applies the principle of proportionality. However, the UK courts are under no duty to adopt exactly the same test.[98] It has been noted: "the most difficult and important problem facing British courts will be to develop (or rather invent) a coherent and defensible doctrine of proportionality".[99] It is most likely that the existing public law principles will influence the way in which proportionality is going to be applied in the future.[100]

However, the following cases illustrate that there are a significant number of cases which apply the language of proportionality and which have recognised the principle in cases decided even before the coming into force of the Human Rights Act.

The case of *R v Secretary of State for the Home Department, ex p Simms*[101] was concerned with two prisoners serving life sentences for murder having their separate applications for leave to appeal against conviction refused by the Court of Appeal (Criminal Division). The men continued to protest their innocence. In order to obtain the reopening of their cases, they wished to have oral interviews with journalists who had taken an interest in their cases. Relying on the policy of the Home Secretary, the governors of the prisons were only prepared to allow the oral interviews to take place if the journalists signed written undertakings not to publish any part of the interviews. The journalists refused to sign the undertakings. The prisoners sought judicial review of the decision denying them the right to have oral interviews. They relied on the right to free speech not in a general way, but restricted to a very specific context. They argued that only if they are allowed to have oral interviews in prison with the journalists will they be able to have the safety of their convictions further investigated and to put forward a case in the media for the consideration of their convictions. They seeked to enlist the investigative services of journalists as a means to gaining access to justice by way of the reference of their cases to the Court of Appeal (Criminal Division).

The House of Lords allowed both appeals and held that declarations should be granted in both cases to the effect that the Home Secretary's current policy is unlawful and that the governors' administrative decisions pursuant to that policy were also unlawful.

The case is a good example of the high intensity of judicial control applied in cases with a strong human rights context. The House of Lords emphasised the need for the protection of the right to freedom of expression:

---

97 Feldman, D., "Proportionality and the Human Rights Act 1998" in Ellis, E., *The Principle of Proportionality in the Laws of Europe* ,1999, 117.

98 Ibid 121.

99 Kentridge, S., "The Incorporation of the European Convention on Human Rights" in the University of Cambridge Centre for Public Law, *Constitutional Reform in the United Kingdom* ,1998, 70.

100 Feldman, D., supra n. 97, 143.

101 [1999] 3 WLR 328.

"In a democracy it is the primary right: without it an effective rule of law is not possible. Nevertheless, freedom of expression is not an absolute right. Sometimes it must yield to other cogent social interests. Article 10 of the European Convention for the Protection of Human Rights and Fundamental Freedoms (1953) is in the following terms".

The court went on to describe the content of this fundamental right: "everyone has the right to freedom of expression. This right shall include freedom to hold opinions and to receive and impart information and ideas without interference by public authority and regardless of frontiers". However, the court made clear that this right may not be exercised in isolation of other rights, but is subject to limitations:

"The exercise of these freedoms, since it carries with it duties and responsibilities, may be subject to such formalities, conditions, restrictions or penalties as are prescribed by law and are necessary in a democratic society, in the interests of national security, territorial integrity or public safety, for the prevention of disorder or crime, for the protection of health or morals, for the protection of the reputation or rights of others, for preventing the disclosure of information received in confidence, or for maintaining the authority and impartiality of the judiciary".

The court further referred to the case of *Derbyshire County Council v Times Newspapers Ltd*[102] in which the requirements of necessary restrictions in a democratic society were defined as follows:

"As regards the words "necessary in a democratic society" in connection with the restrictions on the right to freedom of expression which may properly be prescribed by law, the jurisprudence of the European Court of Human Rights has established that "necessary" requires the existence of a pressing social need and that the restrictions should be no more than is proportionate to the legitimate aim pursued".

In that context Lord Keith observed that he reached his conclusion on the issue before the House without any need to rely on the Convention, but he expressed agreement with the observation of Lord Goff of Chieveley in the *Guardian Newspapers* case and added "that I find it satisfactory to be able to conclude that the common law of England is consistent with the obligations assumed by the Crown under the treaty in this particular field".

Lord Steyn went on to interpret the wide enabling power by referring to the principle of legality:

"Literally construed there is force in the extensive construction put forward, but one cannot lose sight that there is at stake a fundamental or basic right, namely the right of a prisoner to seek through oral interviews to persuade a journalist to investigate the safety of the prisoner's conviction and to publicise his findings in an effort to gain access to justice for the prisoner. In these circumstances, even in the absence of an ambiguity, there comes into play a presumption of general application operating as a constitutional principle as Sir Rupert Cross explained in successive editions of his classic work *Statutory Interpretations* (3rd edn, 1995) pp. 165–6. This is called "the principle of legality" ... Applying this principle I would hold that the standing orders leave untouched the fundamental and basic rights asserted by the applicants in the present case".

---

102 [1993] AC 534.

Similarly, Lord Hoffmann also referred to the importance of the principle of legality in a constitution which "acknowledges the sovereignty of Parliament":

"Parliamentary sovereignty means that Parliament can, if it chooses, legislate contrary to fundamental principles of human rights. The Human Rights Act 1998 will not detract from this power. The constraints upon its exercise by Parliament are ultimately political, not legal, but the principle of legality means that Parliament must squarely confront what it is doing and accept the political cost. Fundamental rights cannot be overridden by general or ambiguous words. This is because there is too great a risk that the full implications of their unqualified meaning may have passed unnoticed in the democratic process. In the absence of express language or necessary implications to the contrary, the courts must therefore presume that even the most general words were intended to be subject to the basic rights of the individual. In this way the courts of the United Kingdom, though acknowledging the sovereignty of Parliament, apply principles of constitutionality little different from those which exist in countries where the power of the legislature is expressly limited by a constitutional document".[103]

Lord Hoffmann's speech is significant as it tackles the difficult question of parliamentary sovereignty and the protection of basic rights. He acknowledges that in other countries the legislature is often directly bound by the constitutional mandate to observe the protection of individual rights. In the absence of such a constitutional requirement, the principle of legality serves as a legal tool to justify the role of the courts in protecting individual rights by way of controlling the exercise of public powers.

Lord Hobhouse of Woodborough expressly referred to the principle of proportionality. However, he used the word "disproportionate" as equivalent to unreasonable in the negative meaning of the word: He held that:

"In this extreme policy is both unreasonable and disproportionate and cannot be justified as a permissible restraint upon the rights of the prisoner. In certain situations a face-to-face visit by a journalist is appropriate as a necessary supplement to the other means of communication. The evidence shows that a prisoner has legitimate interest in seeking to obtain a reference back of his case to the Court of Appeal. He does not have the benefit of Legal Aid for this purpose. In practical terms the reference back will normally have to be on the basis of fresh evidence not previously available. Someone has to unearth that evidence if it exists. I would also agree with the concluding words of Latham J. Respect must be had for those who have the responsibility of running penal establishments. If basic rights are being asserted, the relevant criterion to apply in evaluating any conduct alleged to interfere with those rights is that adopted by the Court of Appeal in *R v Ministry of Defence, ex p Smith* [1996] QB 517 at 554. The court must be satisfied that the relevant decision is unreasonable in the sense that it is beyond the range of responses open to a reasonable decision maker: the more substantial the interference with human rights, the more the court will require by way of justification before it is satisfied that the decision is not unreasonable".

In conclusion, the case of *Simms* is a good example for the development of the common law in the absence of a written constitutional document which might impose a duty for the legislator to act in accordance with human rights. Having said that, Sect. 19 of the Human Rights Act 1998 requires a minister of the Crown in charge of a Bill in either House of Parliament to make a statement of compatibility

[103] [1999] 3 WLR 328 at 341f–h.

with the Convention rights before the second reading of a Bill. *Simms* illustrates how English judges have embraced the protection of human rights, apply the principle of proportionality by referring to the requirement of a pressing social need to restrict a basic right and therefore applying an intensive control to administrative power. Lord Hoffmann engages the traditional principle of legality to justify the role of the courts in protecting individual rights without encroaching upon the principle of parliamentary sovereignty.

The case of *Simms* applies the proportionality test in cases with a human rights context. It is an interesting example of the development of substantive review in English law as it uses the principle of legality as a justification for the increased intensity of control. The use of such a traditional principle appears to be a very effective way of justifying the increased standard of substantive review. However, the high standard of review in *Simms* and the express use of the principle of proportionality are due to its strong human rights context and it is important to note that the intensity of review of discretionary decisions still varies greatly according to the subject matter. The principle of proportionality is clearly applied in cases with a human rights consideration, under the Human Rights Act 1998 or in the context of EC law. However, Lord Slynn made an important statement in the case of *R v Secretary of State for the Environment, Transport and the Regions, ex p Holding and Barnes and others* (referred to as *Alconbury*) concerning the spill-over effect into domestic law:

"I consider that even without references to the Human Rights Act the time has come to recognise that this principle [of proportionality] is part of English administrative law, not only when judges are dealing with Community acts but also when they are dealing with acts subject to domestic law. Trying to keep the *Wednesbury* principle and proportionality in separate compartments seems to me to be unnecessary and confusing".[104]

R v Secretary of State for the Home Department, ex p Daly[105] is another important example of the change in climate that can be observed in some recent decisions by the House of Lords concerning the application of the test of proportionality in the context of human rights violations. Lord Steyn's speech is important as he makes very clear observations regarding the application of the principle of proportionality in English law.

The case concerned a prisoner, Mr Daly, who challenged the lawfulness of a policy under the Prison Act which contained the requirement that a prisoner may not be present when his legally privileged correspondence is examined by prison officers. He submitted that this policy contravenes human rights under the European Convention on Human Rights.

The judicial review test to be applied, as described by Lord Steyn, was as follows:

"When anxiously scrutinising an executive decision that interferes with human rights, the court will ask the question, applying an objective test, whether the decision maker could reasonably have concluded that the interference was necessary to achieve one or more of

104 [2001] EWHL 23, para 51.
105 [2001] 2 WLR 1622.

the legitimate aims recognised by the Convention. When considering the test of necessity in the relevant context, the court must take into account the European jurisprudence in accordance with Sect. 2 of the 1998 Act".

Lord Steyn further distinguished clearly the traditional *Wednesbury* test from the more "precise and sophisticated" test of proportionality:

"The contours of the principle of proportionality are familiar. In *de Freitas v Permanent Secretary of Ministry of Agriculture, Fisheries, Lands and Housing*[106] the Privy Council adopted a three-stage test. Lord Clyde observed, at p. 80, that in determining whether a limitation (by an act, rule or decision) is arbitrary or excessive the court should ask itself: "whether: (i) the legislative objective is sufficiently important to justify limiting a fundamental right; (ii) the measures designed to meet the legislative objective are rationally connected to it; and (iii) the means used to impair the right or freedom are no more than is necessary to accomplish the objective"".

Lord Steyn further held that there are overlaps between the *Wednesbury* test and the latter test, however, he stated that the intensity of review under the proportionality test is more intensive. He held that the proportionality test involves the assessment of the balance which the decision maker had to strike, rather than just judging on the rationality or reasonableness of the decision. Secondly, he stated that this test would have to pay attention to the weight given to interests and considerations and is therefore wider than the traditional approach. Finally, he referred to the heightened scrutiny test in *R v Ministry of Defence, ex p Smith*[107] which "is not necessarily appropriate to the protection of human rights. The "anxious scrutiny test" applied in this case imposed a high threshold test on which the challenge based on Art. 8 of the ECHR failed (the right to respect for private and family life)".[108]

Lord Steyn concluded that "the intensity of the review, in similar cases, is guaranteed by the twin requirements that the limitation of the right was necessary in a democratic society, in the sense of meeting a pressing social need, and the question whether the interference was really proportionate to the legitimate aim being pursued". The application of this test may produce different results. He emphasised therefore that cases based on Convention rights must "be analysed in the correct way". However, referring to Professor Jowell's article, he held that this would not amount to a merits review.[109] Finally, he referred to Laws LJ who emphasised in *Mahmood* "that the intensity of review in a public law case will depend on the subject matter in hand. That is so even in cases involving Convention rights. In law, context is everything".[110]

---

106 [1999] 1 AC 69.

107 [1996] QB 517 at 554.

108 The European Court of Human Rights came to the opposite conclusion: *Smith and Grady v United Kingdom* (1999) 29 EHRR 493.

109 "Beyond the Rule of Law, Towards Constitutional Judicial Review" (2000) *Public Law* 671 [681].

110 [2001] 1 WLR 840 at 847, para 18.

The case of *Secretary of State for the Home Department v Rehman*[111] illustrates this point clearly. Lord Hoffmann stated that:

"The need for restraint in second guessing policy decisions of the Home Secretary flows from a common sense recognition of the nature of the issue and the differences in the decision-making process of the Home Secretary and the Commission ... This seems to me to underline the need for the judicial arm of government to respect the decisions of ministers of the Crown on the question of whether support for terrorist activities in a foreign country constitutes a threat to national security ... It is also that such decisions, with serious potential results for the community, require a legitimacy which can be conferred only by entrusting them to persons responsible to the community through the democratic process".[112]

The principle of proportionality under the Human Rights Act 1998 was discussed in March 2002 in the case of *R (on the application of ProLife Alliance) v BBC.*[113] The case was concerned with the banning of a video which was part of the party election broadcast of a registered political party which was opposed to abortion. The video was planned to be used in the 2001 General Election. The video showed clear images of aborted foetuses in a "mangled and mutilated state". The broadcasters refused transmission on the grounds of taste and decency (on the basis of Sect. 6(1) of the Broadcasting Act 1990). The applicants submitted that the ban was in violation of their right to freedom of expression under Art. 10 of the European Convention on Human Rights and that the ban was not "necessary in a democratic society" under Art. 10(2).

The Court of Appeal held that the broadcasters had failed to "give sufficient weight to the pressing imperative of free political expression" and allowed the appeal.[114] The court held that the "English court is not a Strasbourg surrogate", but that under the Human Rights Act 1998 there was a duty "to develop by the common law's incremental method a coherent and principled domestic law of human rights". This followed from Sect. 6 and in particular Sect. 2 of the Human Rights Act. Accordingly, the court had to "take account of the Strasbourg cases".[115] The court emphasised the importance of freedom of speech: "freedom of speech is always the first casualty under a totalitarian regime"[116] and phrased the essential question to the case as "was the ban necessary in a democratic society under Art. 10(2)?"[117]

In pointing out the heightened objections against prior restraint in the context of a party election broadcast, the court cited a decision by the German Federal Constitutional Court dating from 1978 when the Communist Party (KPD) was banned:

---

111 [2002] 1 All ER 122.

112 Ibid, also see the decision of *R (on the application of Saadi and others) v Secretary of State for the Home Department* [2001] 4 All ER 961.

113 [2003] UKHL 23

114 Ibid 757.

115 Ibid 771.

116 Ibid 772.

117 Ibid 776.

"... it must not be forgotten that it is impossible to compensate for the serious legal disadvantages that arise where an election broadcast is rejected after a summary consideration and this is subsequently proved wrong ... owing to the proximity of the broadcasting slots in time to the election date, the latter will usually have passed".[118]

The court defined the role of the English courts as "owing a special responsibility to the public as the constitutional guardian of the freedom of political debate". As to the test to be applied, the court referred to the decision in *R v Secretary of State for the Home Department, ex p Daly* which has been discussed above and held that the bare test of rationality or reasonableness is no longer sufficient in cases concerning the interference with fundamental rights.[119]

The main criticism to the adoption of the principle of proportionality has been the difficulty of accommodating this invasive test into a system of judicial review which emphasises the supervisory function of the courts. Therefore the question has been asked whether the introduction of the principle of proportionality "amount to a merits-based form of review".[120] The most recent decision illustrates this concern when stating the opinion of the lower court that "even today, in cases such [as] the present, the court's role remains supervisory. Great care must be taken to ensure that the Administrative Court does not assume the mantle of decision taker".[121] Commentators indicate that a more substantive test will not lead to a merits-based review:

"The court will not ask itself whether the decision is one that it would have made (a merits-based approach), nor will it ask itself whether the decision was so unreasonable that it cannot be sustained (*Wednesbury*). Rather the court will require the decision which interferes with the human right of any individual is one that is for a permissible reason and one that is necessary in a democratic society".[122]

At the root of the tension felt in applying the proportionality principle as a more searching test lie fundamental constitutional considerations as to the appropriate role of the courts. No recent case could illustrate this better than the case of *A v Secretary of State for the Home Department*.[123] The case concerned the detention of suspected international terrorists who could not be deported from the UK. The decisions of the Home Secretary were based on s. 23 of the Anti-Terrorism, Crime and Security 2001. The House of Lords held that this section was incompatible with Article 5 of the European Convention of Human Rights. Lord Bingham set out in his leading speech that the detention powers were disproportionate and discriminatory. In defending the court's role he held that "the 1998 Act gives the

118 Kommunistische Partei/Marxisten (1978) 2 BvR 523/75.

119 [2002] 2 All ER 773.

120 Plowden, P. and Kerrigan, K., "Judicial Review – a New Test?" (2001) *New Law Journal* 1291 [1292]; Jeffrey Jowell, "Beyond the Rule of Law: Towards Constitutional Judicial Review" (2000) *Public Law* 671 [681].

121 Scott Baker J in *R (on the application of ProLife Alliance) v BBC* [2002] 2 All ER 756 at 766.

122 Plowden, P., and Kerrigan, K., "Judicial Review – a New Test?" (2001) *New Law Journal* 1291 [1292].

123 [2004] UKHL 56.

courts a very specific, wholly democratic, mandate." Citing Professor Jowell he went on to say: "The courts are charged by Parliament with delineating the boundaries of a rights-based democracy" ("Judicial Deference: servility, civility or institutional capacity?" [2003] PL 592, 597)".[124] Lord Bingham's speech is an important building block in the development of UK constitutionalism[125]: "The greater intensity of review now required in determining questions of proportionality, and the duty of the courts to protect Convention rights, would in my view be emasculated if a judgment at first instance on such a question were conclusively to preclude any further review. So would excessive deference, in a field involving indefinite detention without charge or trial, to ministerial decision. In my opinion, SIAC erred in law and the Court of Appeal erred in failing to correct its error."[126]

d) The principle of legitimate expectation in English administrative law

In more recent years, another important principle has gained recognition English administrative law: the principle of legitimate expectation.[127] The development of the principle in modern English administrative law has been influenced by the principle as applied in European law.[128] In the 1990s, De Smith described it as still being:

> "In the process of evolution. It is founded upon a basic principle of fairness that legitimate expectations ought not be thwarted. The protection of legitimate expectations is at the root of the constitutional principle of the rule of law, which requires regularity, predictability and certainty in government's dealings with the public".[129]

An increasing number of cases dealing both with procedural and substantive legitimate expectation have shaped this concept into an important principle of English administrative law. The concept of procedural legitimate expectations is used to describe the "right which the applicant claims to possess as the result of behaviour by the public body which generates the expectation".[130] The concept of substantive legitimate expectations "refers to the situation in which the applicant seeks a particular benefit or commodity, such as a welfare benefit or a licence".[131] In cases in which the public body wants to deviate from an existing policy such as

---

124 *A v Secretary of State for the Home Department* [UKHL] 2004, 56, Nr 42.

125 Hickman, T.R., "Between Human Rights and the Rule of Law: Indefinite Detention and the Derogation Model of Constitutionalism," (2005) *MLR*, 655 [668].

126 *A v Secretary of State for the Home Department* [UKHL] 2004, 56, Nr 44.

127 Robert, T., Legitimate Expectations and Proportionality in Administrative Law, 2000, 46.

128 Ibid 49.

129 De Smith, S.A., *Judicial Review of Administrative Action*, 1995, 417.

130 Craig, P., *Administrative Law*, 1999, 611.

131 Ibid 611.

in *R v Secretary of State for the Home Department, ex p Asif Mahmood Khan*[132] overlaps between these two concepts can be detected:

"It is also clear from cases commonly categorised as being about procedural expectations that the test laid down in such decisions has a substantive dimension. This is exemplified by *Khan*[133], *Liverpool Taxis*[134] and other cases. If some undertaking had been given which was relied on by the individual then the public body was not able to resile from it through a change in policy without giving an opportunity for a hearing and then only if the public interest demanded that this should be so".

In *R v Secretary of State for the Home Department, ex p Asif Mahmood Khan*[135] a Home Office circular letter stated that although the Immigration Rules did not permit a foreign child subject to immigration control to enter the United Kingdom for the purposes of adoption, the Secretary of State would permit such entry provided certain specified criteria were met. The criteria involved the adoption being genuine and not merely a device for obtaining entry, that the child's welfare in this country be assured, that the courts here would be likely to grant an adoption order and that one of the intending adopters be domiciled in the United Kingdom. The letter then stated the procedure to be followed by would-be adopters. This was to obtain an entry clearance from an entry clearance officer abroad. That officer would have to be satisfied of the child's wishes and the wishes of the natural parents. The applicant and his wife wished to adopt a relative's child living with its natural mother in Pakistan. An application for an entry clearance was made in Islamabad. All the various criteria listed above appeared to have been satisfied. However, in due course, following referral of the matter to the Home Office, entry clearance was refused. This was on the ground that there were no "serious and compelling family and other considerations" such as would make refusal of permission to enter undesirable. The entry clearance officer's report to the Home Office had made clear the fact that the child in question was living in good conditions with his natural mother.

The court held that:

"There is not a word [in the circular letter] to suggest that in exercising his discretion the Secretary of State requires to be satisfied that the natural parents are incapable of looking after the prospective adoptee, or even that their ability or inability to do so was considered relevant ... The whole tenor of the letter is that, if the application was genuine, if the child's welfare was assured, if a court would be likely to grant an order and if the natural parents gave a real consent, the child would be let in and its ultimate fate left to the court here ... Here, it is contended that the applicant, by virtue of the terms of the Home Office letter, had a legitimate expectation that the procedures set out in the letter would be followed and that such legitimate expectation gave him sufficient interest to challenge the admitted failure of the Secretary of State to observe such procedures".

---

132 [1984] 1 WLR 1337.
133 [1984] 1 WLR 1337.
134 [1972] 2 QB 299.
135 [1984] 1 WLR 1337.

(1) "“Legitimate expectations” in this context are capable of concluding expectations which go beyond enforceable legal rights, provided they have some reasonable basis".

(2) "The expectations may be based on some statement or undertaking by, or on behalf of, the public authority which has the duty of making the decision if the authority which has the duty of making the decision has, through his officers, acted in a way that would make it unfair or inconsistent with good administration for him to be denied such an inquiry".

(3) "... The justification for it is primarily that when a public authority has promised to follow a certain procedure, it is in the interest of good administration that it should act fairly and should implement its promise so long as implementation does not interfere with its statutory duty ... I have no doubt that the Home Office letter afforded the applicant a reasonable expectation of the procedures it set out".

The development of possible justifications for recognising the existence of substantive legitimate expectation can be illustrated by a variety of more recent cases. Sedley J stated his reasons for recognising the existence of substantive legitimate expectation in the case of *R v Ministry for Agriculture, Fisheries and Food, ex p Hamble*:[136] "the real question is one of fairness in public administration. It is difficult to see why it is any less unfair to frustrate a legitimate expectation that the applicant will be listened to before the decision maker decides to take a particular step". Sedley J defined the principle of legitimate expectations by referring to case law of the European Court of Justice and Jürgen Schwarze's research as follows:

> "Legitimacy in this sense is not an absolute. It is a function of expectations induced by government and policy considerations, which militate against their fulfillment. The balance must in the first instance be for the policy maker to strike, but if the outcome is challenged by way of judicial review, I do not consider that the court's criterion is the bare rationality of the policy maker's conclusion. While policy is for the policy maker alone, the fairness of his or her decision not to accommodate reasonable expectations which the policy will thwart remains the court's concern".[137]

Craig places much on the idea of legal certainty. This is an important part of legitimate expectation, as it aims to preserve expectations that an individual might have acted upon in certain cases. The main argument against the existence of substantive legitimate expectations is that it has an undesirable effect of fettering governmental policy choices. If there is to be effective government, then it is argued by some that they must have total discretion to alter policies at any time. As Craig notes, however, any argument about the fettering of governmental policy is countered fairly effectively by the realisation that the fetter on policy is only temporal.[138] The strongest claim for substantive legitimate expectation arises from a clear and unambiguous claim. Another way of showing that there are substantive

---

136 [1995] 2 All ER 714 at 729.

137 [1995] 2 All ER 714 at 731.

138 Craig, P., *Administrative Law*, 1999, 617–618.

legitimate expectations is through a course of dealing where there is consistent conduct over a long period of time.[139]

The concept of substantive legitimate expectation has been confirmed in the decision of *R v North and East Devon Health Authority, ex p Coughlan*.[140] Ms Coughlin had been the victim of a road traffic accident and as a consequence had been physically disabled. In 1993 the applicant was moved to a purpose built facility and was assured by the health authority that this would be her home for life. However, the health authority decided to close the house. The applicant challenged the decision, *inter alia*, that on the grounds of the promise made the applicant had a substantive legitimate expectation to stay in the house. It was held that the closure was not justified by overriding public interest and that the applicant had a substantive legitimate expectation. Since the decision in *Coughlan* it appears to be more likely to establish substantive legitimate expectation if the representation was made in a direct manner, if the expectation arises within a limited class of people and if the individual relied to their detriment on the expectation.

However, even if substantive legitimate expectations are identified, there is the need for the individual to prove that the departure from the legitimate expectation was unreasonable. The question therefore is which test should be applied in determining the unreasonableness of the departure? Should it be the traditional *Wednesbury* test, a modified version of it or the test of proportionality? Both cases *Hamble* and *Coughlan* seem to direct towards a test based on fairness and proportionality. Accordingly, the breach of a legitimate expectation is an abuse of power and that is unlawful. Lord Woolf said in *Coughlan*: "for our part, in relation to this category of legitimate expectation, we do not consider it necessary to explain the modern doctrine in *Wednesbury* terms ..."[141]

In the case of *R v Secretary of State for Education and Employment, ex p Begbie*[142] the existence of the principle was confirmed. Peter Gibson LJ said:

> "Mr Beloff submits that the rule that a public authority should not defeat a person's legitimate expectations is an aspect of the rule that it must act fairly and reasonably, that the rule operates in the field of substantive as well as procedural rights. He cites authority in support of all these submissions and for my part I am prepared to accept them as correct, as far as they go".[143]

The further development and establishment of the principle in English public law will depend on the clarification of outstanding issues: the question whether it may be based on policies which are unknown to the person claiming the expectation and *ultra vires* representations.

In *R (Rashid) v Secretary of State for the Home Department*[144] the question arose whether a legitimate expectation may be based on a policy which the claim-

---

139 See *R v Inland Revenue Commissioners, ex p Unilever plc* [1996] STC 681.

140 [1999] LGR 703.

141 [1999] LGR 703.

142 [2001] 1 WLR 1115. The case concerned the claim for legitimate expectation stemming from a pre-election statement with regard to assistance with independent school fees.

143 [2001] 1 WLR 1115.

144 [2005] EWCA Civ 744, (2005) *The Times*, 12 July.

ant was not aware of at the relevant time. The claimant was refused asylum in the United Kingdom and was unsuccessful before the adjudicator and Immigration Appeal Tribunal. The reasons given were that he could seek refuge in the Kurdish Autonomous Zone where he would be safe. One issue in the case was that the claimant was unaware of a policy in the Home Office on internal relocation which was in place at the time of the proceedings. Accordingly:

> "The internal relocation to the former [Kurdish Autonomous Zone] from government controlled Iraq would not be advanced as a reason to refuse a claim for refugee status. This was based on the stance of the Kurdish authorities of not admitting to their territory those who were not previously resident in that area because of a lack of infrastructure and resources".[145]

The Court of Appeal held that the Secretary of State had breached the claimant's legitimate expectation. However, it has been questioned, on a more theoretical level, whether "it makes sense to use legitimate expectation as the doctrinal vehicle to secure compliance with policy in circumstances such as these".[146] It has been suggested that the principle of consistency would be the more appropriate avenue to justice. This has been defined as "the idea that administrative bodies should not arbitrarily decline to apply the same, self-proclaimed norms to all relevant cases which come before them so long as the policy remains in force. This is without prejudice to the capacity of the public body to change its policy".[147]

This view displays a remarkable similarity with the operation of the German general principle of equality as enshrined in Art. 3 para 1 of the Basic Law as developed by the majority of academic opinion.[148] The advantages of this approach are the limitation of the principle of legitimate expectation to cases where there is actual knowledge of the policy or representation which could then refine a distinction between legal and *ultra vires* representations. In cases of *ultra vires* policies falling outside the scope of legitimate expectations, the German courts have emphasised that there is no right to the consistent application of an *ultra vires* policy (*kein Recht im Unrecht*). The position is different in the context of legitimate expectation where the subjective element, i.e. the knowledge of an *ultra vires* act, is a crucial factor in the protection or denial of legitimate expectation.

The principle of legitimate expectations has taken root in English Administrative law. However, some questions remain to be addressed in future decision. One of those remaining issues is the problem of *ultra vires* representation and the question whether a legitimate expectation can arise from it and is worthy of protection. The traditional approach is based on the premise that a public authority is restricted by its statutory duties.[149] However, in a recent case involving the potential interference with Art. 1 of the First Protocol of the Convention the courts had

---

145 Home Office letter, 16 January 2004, as set out in Pill LJ's judgment: see [2005] EWCA Civ 744 at [4]–[5] cited in Elliot, M., "Legitimate Expectation, Consistency and Abuse of Power: The Rashid Case" (2005) *JR* 281.

146 Elliot, M., ibid 282.

147 Ibid 286.

148 Maurer, H., *Allgemeines Verwaltungsrecht*, 1999, 608.

149 *Attorney-General of Hong Kong v Ng Yuen Shiu* [1983] 2 AC 629.

to tackle the question once more. *Rowland v The Environment Agency*[150] was concerned with the question whether the *ultra vires* representations of several navigation authorities that a stretch of water was private was able to give rise to a legitimate expectation. Mrs Rowland claimed that she was entitled to continue to use the stretch of water as private and that it constituted a possession within Art. 1 of the First Protocol of the Convention. The Court of Appeal held that her expectation was protected by Art. 1 but that departing from the representations was not disproportionate. Despite the fact that Mrs Rowland's claim was unsuccessful the decision marks an important step forward in the recognition of legitimate expectations on the basis of *ultra vires* representations as long as interference with Art. 1 of the Convention can be shown. Mance LJ acknowledged the development of the principle and acknowledged that the *ultra vires* doctrine was not an "automatic answer" to this question any more.[151]

5. Abuse of discretion in German law

a) The principle of proportionality in German administrative law

Compared to all other legal systems "under German law, the proportionality principle has found its clearest expression both in case law and in the available literature".[152] The principle of proportionality plays a very important role in reviewing the legality of discretionary decisions in the Administrative Courts.[153] Dating back to a decision by the Prussian *Oberverwaltungsgericht* in 1882, the *Bundesverfassungsgericht* has based it on the principle of the *Rechtsstaat* and basic rights.[154] There are three requirements which have to be complied with in the application of the principle:

> "First, the state measure concerned must be suitable for the purpose of facilitating or achieving the pursued objective. Secondly, the suitable measure must also be necessary, in the sense that the authority concerned has no other mechanism at its disposal which is less restrictive of freedom ... Finally, the measure concerned may not be disproportionate to the restrictions which it involves".[155]

The principle enjoys constitutional status[156] and has to be applied by all public authorities in the exercise of their powers.[157] Because of its importance when exercising public powers, it is contained expressly in some statutes such as the law regulating the police. The following case is one of the numerous decisions by the *Bundesverwaltungsgericht* which held an administrative decision unlawful on the

---

150 [2003] EWCA Civ 1885.
151 Blundell, D., "Ultra Vires Legitimate Expectations", [2005] *JR*, 147 [154].
152 Schwarze, J. ,*European Administrative Law*, 2006, 685.
153 Brinktrine, R., *Verwaltungsermessen in Deutschland und England*, 1998, 129.
154 BVerfGE 23, 127 (133); BverfGE 69, 1 (35).
155 Schwarze, J., *European Administrative Law*, 2006, 687.
156 BVerfGE 61, 126 (134).
157 BVerfGE 23,127 (133).

grounds of a violation of the principle of proportionality.[158] It is an uncontroversial case which, however, illustrates well the rational approach by the German court.

However, three cases decided in the 1990s illustrate that the standard of review applied by Administrative Courts and the Constitutional Court is in a state of flux and not always uncontroversial. As will be illustrated in cases below, the standard of review applied by the Federal Administrative Court has varied depending on the subject matter. Another case will illustrate the strict application of the principle of proportionality in the Federal Constitutional Court which has led to controversy within the panel. Finally, the *Bundesverwaltungsgericht* has applied a reduced intensity of review in a case concerning the exercise of the German airforce. More recently the strict operation of proportionality in the context of balancing individual rights and security in the fight against terror has been called into question.

In *Bundesverwaltungsgericht* (BverwG, *NJW* 1995, 3334) the appellant was a bus driver with 18 years' work experience. In 1992 the relevant authority refused his application for an extension of his licence. The reason for the refusal was the fact that he had reached the age of 50 and had failed to submit a medical and psychological certificate containing details about his personality. Instead the applicant had submitted an undetailed certificate by a doctor specialising in occupational medicine confirming his fitness for the driving of a bus. The *Straßenverkehrszulassungsordnung* (Law on Admission to the Highways) is the basic text governing licences for buses and other vehicles. According to Sect. 15, the applicant for an extension of a bus driving licence has to submit either a certificate by a specialised doctor or a certificate issued by an institution specialising in medical and psychological reports. Further regulations by the Ministry of the Interior lay down that a more detailed report is required for applicants who have reached the age of 50. The concrete content, which such a report should have, is not laid down by the regulations. The authority considered the short medical certificate, which was submitted by the applicant alone, insufficient and required the applicant to submit a medical and psychological certificate issued by a recognised institution. The applicant refused any further examinations claiming that the requirement of such a certificate was disproportional and was refused the extension of his driving licence. The Lower and Higher Administrative Courts dismissed his application and he then appealed to the *Bundesverwaltungsgericht* on a point of law.

The *Bundesverwaltungsgericht* held that the requirement of a detailed medical and psychological report violated the principles of legal certainty and proportionality. A medical report should concentrate on particular issues concerning the age-related abilities such as attention span and stamina. The court further held that the requirement that such a certificate had to be issued by a recognised institution rather than a specialised doctor was disproportionate.

Generally, a medical certificate is sufficient as proof for the fitness of an applicant. However, the authority is empowered to request a more detailed medical report. The law does not contain any specifications as to when one or the other is required. However, the order in which both proofs appear within the law implies

158 See Brinktrine, R., *Verwaltungsermessen in Deutschland und England*, 1998, 129 with further references.

that a certificate is required in general, whereas a report will be required if specific circumstances such as age may give particular reason for a more detailed medical and psychological examination. However, if the authority decides that a full medical report is necessary the principle of legal certainty and proportionality require the authority to specify which particular issues are to be covered by the medical expert. In this case, the examination would have to be restricted to the abilities of a driver which with an increase of age tend to be affected such as attention span, stamina, the ability to react quickly and to concentrate. The authorities though failed to specify the content of the required detailed examination and therefore violated the principle of proportionality. The requirement to submit a report issued by a recognised institution rather than a single specialised doctor also violates the principle of proportionality.

This case illustrates the stringent approach by the *Bundesverwaltungsgericht* in applying the principle of proportionality to the authority's decision. The court identified the purpose of the law as protecting the public from danger stemming from bus drivers who do not have the physical ability to drive a bus safely, i.e. the court identified qualities such as attention span and stamina. However, in reviewing the discretion which was given to the authority in deciding whether they required a full medical report, the court balanced the interests of the general public against the interests of the individual bus driver. Without referring to human rights or basic rights, the court held that no full medical report, including a psychological assessment, was required. In order to comply with the principles of legal certainty and proportionality, the authority was under a duty to specify which tests should have been carried out. This would have been a less restrictive measure. The case illustrates the emphasis on the analysis of the purpose of the enabling statute in asking whether the request of a full medical report was necessary to achieve the objective of the Law on Admission to the Highways. It carried out tests which required the balancing of the competing public and private interests at stake and reached the conclusion that the authority could have reached an alternative course of action, i.e. the request of a *detailed* report concerning specific qualities which are vital to the fitness of the applicant in order to drive a bus as opposed to a full medical report.

That the principle of proportionality is applied too often has been criticised and the judge who decides that the decision is not suitable, unnecessary or disproportionate is likely to replace the decision of the authorities with his or her own view.[159] With regard to the separation of powers between the legislature and the court, this point has been raised in 1995 in the dissenting speeches by three of the judges in Germany's highest court, the Federal Constitutional Court.

In the *East German Spies* case (BVerfGE *NJW* 1995, 1811) the decision by the Federal Constitutional Court is interesting in this context as it illustrates an extensive use of the principle of proportionality which has been described as embarking "on a problematic course of striking down federal legislation on the basis of mere policy arguments".[160] The decision concerned the conviction of East German spies

159 Schwerdtfeger, G., *Öffentliches Recht in der Fallbearbeitung,* 10th edn, 1993, para 99.
160 Nolte, G., Rädler, P., "Rapports: Germany" (1995) *European Public Law* 494 [501].

under the West German Criminal Code for espionage before reunification. They had not acted from the territory of the Federal Republic.[161] The applicants challenged their convictions on the basis that they were in contravention to the equality principle as their West German counterparts were not liable in the absence of any East German criminal law after reunification. The Constitutional Court did not find a violation of the equality principle as East and West German spies did not belong to the same category of persons. The Constitutional Court held, however, that different from the convictions of spies having acted on West German territory, the convictions were disproportionate. It held that:

> "in the light of the "unique situation", i.e. that the protecting and supporting state had ceased to exist ... the prosecution of espionage activities which were conducted strictly from East German territory was disproportionate having regard to the purposes which could legitimately be pursued through criminal law".[162]

The three dissenting judges[163] criticised the majority for having overextended the principle of proportionality as they had in effect granted amnesty for East German spies. The court, however, did not have the power to act like a legislator. An amnesty for espionage activity had at no point been agreed upon by the partners of the Treaty of Unification. The dissenting judges further stated that the majority had used the principle of proportionality in order to disguise considerations of policy, which cannot be dealt with in correctly applying the principle. The guiding principles should have been the principle of legal certainty and the protection of legitimate expectation. The expectation of the spies was, however, not to be protected as they relied on the fact that German reunification would not take place in the foreseeable future. Such an expectation was not to be worthy of protection under the federal constitution. The judges pointed out that the principle of proportionality is in danger of being overstretched into a wide constitutional principle (*verfassungsrechtliche Generalklausel*). The competing interests at stake cannot be decided by the court alone, but have to be defined in accordance with existing values, here the criminal law.

Academics and to an extent the Administrative Courts in opposition to the Constitutional Court have always been concerned with a strengthening of the administration. It is interesting to note that there appear to be varying standards of review depending on the subject matter. A more recent decision by the Federal Administrative Court illustrates the application of a lower standard of review than the standard applied by the Federal Constitutional Court in the context of low-level flights carried out by the German airforce.[164]

In the *Low Level Flights* case (BverwG *JZ* 1995, 510) the Federal Administrative Court refrained from an intensive review of the decision of the Federal Ministry of Defence to allow flights below the regular flight level. The governing statute authorises such flights if they are necessary to fulfil compelling state interests. The Federal Administrative Court restricted its review on the question whether the

[161] (1995) *NJW* 1811; see a short summary in Nolte and Rädler, supra n. 160, 503.
[162] Nolte and Rädler, supra n. 160, 501.
[163] Judges Klein, Kirchhof and Winter.
[164] (1995) *JZ* 510; see a short summary in Nolte and Rädler, supra n. 160, 153.

Ministry had taken into account all relevant circumstances and whether they had adequately considered the interests of the affected local communities and citizens. It thereby granted the Ministry a margin of appreciation which is usually confined to planning decisions.

The contrast between the approaches taken by the Federal Administrative Court and the Constitutional Court was well illustrated by a controversial case which was concerned with the margin of appreciation of examination bodies. What is taking place in an increasing juridification of the exercise of administrative discretion is, however, mainly due to the intensive protection of basic rights.[165] An important case of the Federal Constitutional Court decided in 1991 emphasised that the protection of individual rights plays a vital role in the review of discretionary powers. Therefore a change in the application of the principle of proportionality, which is based on the protection of basic rights and the principle of the *Rechtsstaat*, is unlikely. The position of the Federal Constitutional Court in this case differs significantly from the Administrative Courts. It is a decision by the Federal Constitutional Court concerning constitutional complaints by candidates in the state law exam who alleged a potential violation of their right to choose a profession freely (Art. 12 Basic Law).

b) Human rights protection and discretion in Germany

Basic rights may set clear limitations on the exercise of administrative discretion. The following case illustrates the approach taken by the Federal Administrative Court in reviewing the exercise of discretionary powers based on a statute which limits the right to freedom of assembly as contained in Art. 8 of the Basic Law.[166]

In the *Assembly* case (BVerwGE 26, 135) the applicant was a member of the "international association of conscientious dissenters". About eight members met in May 1962 to demonstrate against nuclear tests which were planned by the United States. They met in front of the American Consulate General to express their views. Half an hour later the police appeared and dissolved the demonstration. The applicant's complaint against the dissolution was unsuccessful. The police argued that the demonstration had not been registered and that no leader was identifiable. The law governing the organisation of demonstrations and their dissolution is the Law on Assembly (*Versammlungsgesetz*). According to Sect. 14, demonstrations in the open air have to be registered with the relevant authorities. According to Sect. 15, the police may dissolve a demonstration if it is not registered. This law constitutes a restriction on the right to freedom of assembly protected under Art. 8 of the Basic Law. Therefore the Federal Administrative Court was concerned with the constitutionality of the authorising statute. German law poses restrictions on these enabling statutes if they potentially interfere with basic rights (*Schranken*). Accordingly, the legislator has to respect other constitutional rights such as the right to equality and the constitutional principle enshrined in

---

165 Maurer, H., *Allgemeines Verwaltungsrecht*, 1999, 144.

166 Article 8 Basic Law: "(1) All Germans have the right to assemble peacefully and unarmed without prior notification or permission".

Art. 19(2) that in no case may the essence of a basic right be encroached upon. The proportionality principle plays an important role in that the legislator has to balance the individual freedom carefully against the protection of the public interest. The court held that the provisions concerning the registration and the dissolution of a demonstration contained in the Law on Assembly complied with these requirements. The court held that the nature of demonstrations in the open air carries potential risks for public order and security. Accordingly, the authorities need to be informed in advance in order to take appropriate measures for the protection of public order. Further, the court held that the decision to dissolve the demonstration was the lawful exercise of a police officer's discretion under the statute. According to Sect. 15, the police may dissolve a demonstration if it is not registered. The exercise of discretion would be unlawful if it were exercised in a way which would contravene the intention of the statute, for example, it would be unlawful if the officer had dissolved the demonstration in order to prevent the expression of particular political or philosophical views. The discretion has to be exercised according to the purpose of the statute. The decision was also proportionate because the police were concerned that the demonstration could expand to a degree which would jeopardise public order. Further, the demonstrators were able to register another demonstration to be held in the next few days which would give the police the chance to be prepared. For the same reasons, there was no violation of the right to equal treatment.

One of the controversial areas of judicial review of undefined legal concepts for the German courts has been the appeal against examination results. The Administrative Courts clearly have jurisdiction over these cases because in some subjects such as medicine, teaching and the legal profession the universities do not carry out the final exams, but the state does in so-called state exams. The results in these exams are classified as administrative acts which are open for appeal to the Administrative Courts. The jurisprudence developed by the Administrative Courts in these cases was marked by a restrictive approach. In the review of examination results, the Administrative Courts recognised a highly sensitive issue which could not easily be reviewed by a court and which would have no expertise in the matter unless the examination at stake was a law exam. In the Administrative Court's view, pedagogic-scientific value judgments of examiners were only subject to limited review. The courts restricted their scrutiny to the questions whether the examiner based his or her decision on incorrect facts, erred in general principles of assessment or took irrelevant considerations into account. However, the Federal Constitutional Court ruled in 1991 that Administrative Courts may fully review the decisions by examination boards.

In *Law State Exam* case II (BVerfGE 84, 34) the applicants for the constitutional complaint were both candidates in the state exams for lawyers. The first applicant had unsuccessfully appealed against the exam result awarded in the second state exam. In his view the marks he had been given for his oral presentation were too low. In the candidate's view the examiners had based the assessment on the fact that the candidate had followed a legal opinion other than that contained in the leading case law and academic opinion. He also appealed against the result of his oral examination.

The second applicant had failed his first state exam for the second time. He appealed against the result given for his dissertation. The Administrative Courts held that neither of the decisions could be annulled because the examiners had acted within their margin of evaluation (*Beurteilungsspielraum*). According to the Administrative Courts the content of the decision could not be subject to judicial review. The constitutional complaints were admissible, but unsuccessful on their merits. According to Art. 12 of the Basic Law, examinations which lead to a profession or occupation have to be designed in compliance with the basic right to choose a profession or occupation. Article 12 provides that: "(1) All Germans have the right freely to choose their occupation or profession, their place of work, study or training. The practice of an occupation or profession may be regulated by or pursuant to a law". Therefore, candidates should have the right to appeal against the final examination results. However, the decision by the higher court may not amount to a second guessing of the original decision.

The case law developed by the Administrative Courts on the margin of evaluation for the administrative authorities sufficiently protects the right under Art. 19(4) of the Basic Law to the extent that it is granted for decisions regarding evaluations specific to exam situations. However, the courts may review disputes between the examiner and the candidate relating to questions on the subject matter. Article 19(4) provides that: "where public authority violates rights the person affected shall have recourse to law ..."

Article 12(1) of the Basic Law contains the principle that an answer in an exam which leads to a profession or occupation which contains an acceptable solution (*vertretbar*) based on logical arguments may not be considered a wrong answer. The *Bundesverfassungsgericht* held that laws which regulate the training for an occupation and which contain provisions on required assessments and examinations interfere with the right freely to choose an occupation or a profession guaranteed in Art. 12(1) of the Basic Law. This applies to the first and second state exam for lawyers.

The state exams interfere with the right to choose a profession because the result in the exam is decisive concerning the choices a candidate can make over his professional development. However, judicial review of such examination decisions is limited by the fact that the assessment procedure is marked by a number of difficulties which can hardly be tackled in a court proceeding. The marking process is influenced by subjective impressions and the coincidental preference of an examiner for a specific subject. The internal appeal body (*Widerspruchsbehörde*) merely reviewed whether any substantial errors were made in the assessment of the candidates.

The applicants take the view that the Administrative Courts should have reviewed the exam results more intensely. The case law of the Administrative Courts regarding the granting of a margin of evaluation does not fully comply with the guarantees contained in Art. 19 IV of the Basic Law. Article 19 IV provides that: "where public authority violates rights the person affected shall have recourse to law ... Hereby not only access to justice but also efficient judicial protection is safeguarded. The citizen has the right to efficient judicial protection".

Generally the courts are under a duty fully to review both facts and legal questions underlying an administrative decision. If part of the decision is concerned with the application of an undefined legal concept such intensive retrospective judicial review will also be carried out. Restrictions on the intensity of judicial review generally only apply to the review of discretionary decisions. The decision whether or not a candidate is entitled to be rewarded a pass in a state exam involves the application of an undefined legal concept. This has to be distinguished from a discretionary power. However, exams which restrict access to certain professions require difficult evaluations which have to be carried out within the context of the whole examination. This requirement flows from the equality principle contained in Art. 3 of the Basic Law. As a result, the decision maker should be granted a margin of evaluation which is free from judicial control.

However, this margin of appreciation only covers questions concerning the examiner's evaluation. Purely academic questions regarding the content of an answer, however, can be fully reviewed. The review of such questions will normally require an expert to assist the judges. However, such practical obstacles are no reason to restrict the effective judicial protection guaranteed in Art. 19 IV of the Basic Law.

Here, the legal limits to discretion imposed on the legislator by the constitution in the Constitutional Court's jurisprudence and the mechanisms of judicial review through the Administrative Courts, as well as the final jurisdiction of the Constitutional Court, leave the authorities with a rather limited area of discretionary power. It is questionable whether this approach is feasible. It may lead to an overburdening of Administrative Court judges who in the light of this decision will have to review decisions of a highly technical and subject-specific nature requiring the support of expert witnesses.

The traditional protection of Basic rights and the proportionality principle has become under new pressures as a result of the developments since 11 September 2001. The fight against terror has become a common problem for different legal systems in Europe. There are no indications that terror attacks are to be expected within Germany.[167] However, Germany had been host to some of the attackers of 9/11. In response the German Parliament swiftly enacted counter-terrorism legislation. The Security Packages I and II contain amendments to 19 different statutes and six statutory orders. Amongst these are eavesdropping and phone tapping, the extension of powers of the security authorities, banning of extremist religious associations, measures affecting asylum seekers and grid search (*Rasterfahndung*).[168] Grid search involves the compilation of records from various sources used for statistical profiling of potential terror suspects. These legislative changes involved striking the difficult balance between the "the protection of in-

167 Gross, T., "Terrorbekämpfung und Grundrechte, Zur Operationalisierung des Verhältnismäßigkeitsgrundsatzes" (2002) *Kritische Justiz* 1.

168 BR – Drucksache 1059/01, 14 December 2001; for a good discussion of these legislative changes in English, see Zöller, V., "Liberty Dies by Inches: German Counter-Terrorism Measures and Human Rights", 5 *German Law Journal* no. 5 (1 May 2004) – Special Edition; Martin Nolte, "Die Anti-Terror-Pakete im Lichte des Verfassungsrechts" (2002) *DVBl* 573.

dividual rights and collective security".[169] It has been argued that this is not a new challenge posed to German law. The threat by German terrorists in the 1970s and the consequences of the Schengen agreement posed questions that required a careful weighing of individual rights and the need for security.[170] The challenge has, however, changed in that the 1970s anti-terrorism legislation was tackling threats from individual terrorists or smaller circles. In this current political climate, the question of whether the cornerstone of German constitutional law, the principle of proportionality, could survive has been widely discussed:

> "The danger is no longer regarded as emanating from individual culprits, rather from a diffuse level of threat that has to be dealt with by way of preventive measures. The weighing ratio has shifted away from the weighing of individual, subjective legal positions to a weighing of objective legal perspectives".[171]

This shift in constitutional law has been described as follows:

> "Security concerns tend to override civil liberties. The weighing of freedom and security tends to work in favour of the latter because individual civil liberties no longer constitute a relevant legal position within the balancing process, can be levelled with "protection duties" and find themselves in a situation of disproportionality where factual (empirical) evidence overrides normative validity".

Lepsius sees the danger in the ill-definition of "security" and "danger", terms which are replaced by a "diffuse scenario of threat, risk and networks" resulting in a "loss of legal rationality". It has been suggested that this could mean a shift away from a legal to a political constitution: "constitutional law is then limited to the restating of political thinking for which it can no longer maintain safeguards. As a consequence, the protection of individual civil liberties can no longer be achieved through legal means, but only through political means". [172]

However, in its decision of 4 April 2006, the Federal Constitutional Court set limits to the grid search practice in upholding the principle of proportionality.[173] The decision was concerned with the constitutional complaint of a Moroccan student who claimed that his right to informational self-determination had been breached by data screening *in Nordrhein-Westfalien*. This was part of a national grid search for Islamic terrorists. State officials searched data from universities, registration offices and the Central Register of Foreigners. The data was then evaluated applying criteria such as sex, age (18–40), student status, Islamic religion and land of origin. The court held that the principle of proportionality required that the legislator can only breach human rights if a concrete danger is present or for higher values – a general danger or threat is insufficient. Concrete facts point to the preparation and execution of further terrorist attacks. The court held that such facts had not been established. The decision was welcomed by elec-

[169] Lepsius, O., "Liberty, Security, and Terrorism: The Legal Position in Germany", 5 *German Law Journal* no. 5 (1 May 2004) – Special Edition.

[170] Ibid.

[171] Ibid.

[172] Ibid 459.

[173] 1 BvR 518/02.

tronic/data privacy lawyers and politicians from the Greens, *FDP* and the Left Party; the Bavarian Interior Minister Beckstein referred to the ruling as a black day for the war on terror.[174] In conclusion, the doubts as to the appropriate role of legal means in securing civil libterties remain purely academic since the role of the Federal Constitutional Court in upholding individual rights cannot be reduced that easily.

c) Undefined legal concepts

The following case has been chosen to illustrate the high intensity of judicial control in reviewing so-called undefined legal concepts. The scrutiny of judicial control of the two related concepts (undefined legal concepts and discretion) differs. Generally speaking, the interpretation of undefined legal concepts is reviewed fully by the courts. This scrutiny even includes the correct application of law to the facts of the case. This often requires that the courts take fresh evidence, for example, by hearing expert witnesses.[175]

This general principle, which is still applied by the Administrative Courts, however, has been widely criticised in academic writing since 1955.[176] Bachof has developed the doctrine of margin of appreciation (*Beurteilungsspielraum*). As a consequence, this doctrine has led to a restriction of the full scrutiny approach of the courts when reviewing undefined legal concepts. The current discussion focuses on the question whether the concept of the norm in its form as described above should be given up in order to conform to European standards. The distinction between undefined legal concepts such as public weal or danger to minors and discretionary powers merely covering the legal consequences of a norm where there is a choice of action is not known in English or European law. In clearly defined circumstances the Federal Administrative Court has granted some subjective area of evaluation with regard to undefined legal concepts to the authorities which are not fully reviewable.[177]

To name a few examples, the Federal Administrative Court has held that those decisions which are based on circumstances which are not comprehensible or cannot be repeated are not fully reviewable. Under this heading fall decisions about personal abilities such as the suitability of a civil servant for a post. Highly controversial still is the area of decisions in examination situations and a variety of cases can be found. Other main groups in which the power to review decisions is restricted are decisions based on scientific or artistic considerations and for which the legislator has provided for the decision to be made by a specially qualified person within the administration. Examples would be the decision on the admissibil-

---

174 http://www.heute.de/ZDFheute/inhalt/18/0,3672,3936690,00.html.

175 Redeker, K.von Oertzen, H.J. *Verwaltungsgerichtsordnung*, 1997, 708; Nolte, G., Rädler, P., "Judicial Review in Germany" (1996) *European Public Law* 26 [28].

176 Redeker, K., von Oertzen, H.J., *Verwaltungsgerichtsordnung*, 1997, 694 with further references.

177 Decisions in examinations, assessment of personnel in the Civil Service, decisions of valuation by experts, for instance, the Federal Scrutiny Agency under the law on the distribution of books dangerous to minors and policy decisions of the administration.

ity of a child to a special needs school or the requirements needed to become an architect. A margin of appreciation is further recognised for decisions which are taken by specially designated agencies such as the Federal Scrutiny Agency (*Bundesprüfstelle*) on the question whether publications represent a danger to minors. However, as we will see below, in a controversial decision in 1983 the Constitutional Court has reversed the position of the administration and ordered more judicial scrutiny in cases of constitutional relevance.[178] Other groups of decisions for which a margin of appreciation was granted include those which involve a prognosis regarding political, economic, social or cultural developments or decisions regarding highly technical issues or planning considerations.[179]

The remaining question is to what extent is judicial scrutiny limited in these cases in which a margin of appreciation is granted? A general standard for the limitation of judicial scrutiny appears to be difficult and the case law seems to have developed independent rules in each group of cases. The finding of facts remains fully reviewable. Furthermore, procedural issues are reviewable, in particular, the right to a hearing. However, procedural defects can be cured under Art. 45 of the Law on Administrative Procedure or considered irrelevant under Art. 46.[180] The power to review the decision is restricted to a review of its legality.

The following example is a decision by the *Bundesverwaltungsgericht*, dated 10 November 1988.[181]

---

178 BVerfGE 83, 130.

179 Redeker, K., von Oertzen, H.J., *Verwaltungsgerichtsordnung*, 1997, Art. 114, 703.

180 Article 45 Law of Administrative Procedure 1976 (*Verwaltungsverfahrensgesetz*) Curing of Defects of Procedure and Form:
"(1) Unless it makes an administrative act void under Art. 44, a violation of the provisions relating to form or procedure is inconsequential if:
1. an application required for the taking of an administrative act is made after the act;
2. the required reasons are given after the act was issued;
3. the required hearing to a participant is given after the act was issued;
4. the decision of a committee whose participation in the taking of the administrative act is required has considered it afterwards;
5. the required participation of another authority takes place afterwards.
(2) Actions under clause (1) nos. 2 to 5 may only take place before the conclusion of the procedure and in case no procedure takes place before the filing of a suit in an Administrative Court".
Article 46 Consequences of Defects of Procedure and Form (old version before 1996):
"Quashing of an administrative act which is not void under Art. 44 cannot be claimed on the ground that it has been taken in violation of the provision on procedure, form or territorial competence if no other decision could have been taken in the matter".
Note the change in the wording in Art. 46 after the reforms in 1996. See Chapter Four for more details.
Consequences of Defects of Procedure and Form (new version from 1996):
"Annulment of an administrative act which is not void according to the provision in Art. 44 cannot be sought if the flaw only relates to either the procedure, the formal aspects or local administrative competence if it is obvious that the breach had no influence on the decision on its merits".

181 (1988) 81 BVerwGE 12.

The case was concerned with the refusal of a licence for pesticides. The applicant was engaged in the production and marketing of pesticides. The Federal Licensing Authority refused the application for a renewal of existing licences and a new licence for a new pesticide. The reason for refusing the applications was that research had shown pesticides of that kind had unacceptable harmful effects according to scientific knowledge. The Lower Administrative Court (*Verwaltungsgericht*) allowed the claim in part and instructed the Licensing Authority to renew part of the licences for two years and ten months. The court held that during this time no harmful effects on nature were to be expected. The revision was allowed in part. The interesting part of the decision concerns the interpretation of the legal basis for granting licences of such kind. The *Pflanzenschutzgesetz* (Law on the Protection of Plants) as amended in 1986 is the basic law governing licences for pesticides in Germany. It sets out the requirements for the award of a licence in Art. 15 Sect. 1. Accordingly, the following requirements have to be met:

"(1) the pesticide has to meet the requirement of efficacy
(2) it should not jeopardise public health
(3)(a) it should not have any harmful effects on human health, the well being of animals or on fresh water resources
(b) it should not have any "other effects", in particular, "on the ecological system which according to scientific knowledge are unacceptable"".

The requirement at stake was that contained in Sect. 3b, according to which pesticides should not have any "other effects", in particular, "on the ecological system" which according to scientific knowledge are unacceptable.

The Lower Administrative Court erred in the interpretation of that requirement by assuming that a licence should only be refused if, with a high degree of probability, the pesticide has harmful effects on the ecological system. However, what is meant is that harmful effects with a high degree of probability should by excluded. As a result it reached a judgment partly in favour of the applicant.

The defendant authority submitted that the question of whether the pesticide has any "other effects on the ecological system" is an undefined legal concept (*unbestimmter Rechtsbegriff*) and subject to only a restricted review by the courts. The authority argued that deciding such a question is a value judgment which depends on the choice between alternative points and that the Authority had discretionary powers to decide the matter (*Beurteilungsspielraum*). As a result, judicial review was restricted to particular errors being made in the exercise of the discretionary powers.

However, the *Bundesverwaltungsgericht* did not share the view of the Licensing Authority and the Lower Administrative Court and held that the courts are required to review fully the value judgment involving an undefined legal concept. This means their review is not restricted as in the case of discretionary powers. The Lower Administrative Court was under a duty to review the balancing of competing issues and the value judgment in full which includes a full review of the underlying facts of the case. At this point the *Bundesverwaltungsgericht* refers to its earlier decisions regarding the full review of concepts such as "danger" and "probability". Therefore the question of whether the pesticide would have "any other effects" had to be decided afresh by the administrative authority. The court is required to review the correct application of the law to the facts, which can include the taking of fresh evidence and the questioning of expert witnesses on complex issues of a scientific or technical nature.

d) European standards for the intensity of review

The previous section has illustrated the different standards of judicial review of discretionary powers in both jurisdictions. This part is concerned with the guidelines given by the European Court of Justice in setting standards for judicial control. The first case is a decision by the European Court of Justice which had been addressed by the English High Court with a question regarding the scope of judicial review required by Community law. The ruling makes interesting reading because it deals with two alternative forms of review. The ruling shows that European law does not require any standards of review which go further than the approach taken by English courts. The more intensive review approach taken by German courts therefore goes beyond what is required by European standards and places itself in splendid isolation.

In *Upjohn Ltd v The Licensing Authority Established by the Medicines Act 1968 and others*[182] the European Court of Justice had to deal with the question whether national courts (here the Court of Appeal) were under an obligation to substitute their assessment of the facts for that of the competent national authorities. The case was concerned with the question to which effect the standard of review in domestic courts should be guided by the European Court of Justice's view. It was concerned with the review of discretionary powers of the Licensing Authority regarding the revocation of a marketing licence of medicines. The applicant was Upjohn Ltd which is the United Kingdom operating company of the Upjohn Company of Kalamazoo, Michigan, United States of America, a research-based worldwide pharmaceutical undertaking which produced a drug called Triazolam, a prescription drug for the treatment of insomnia. As a consequence of a case in the United States in which a woman killed her mother while under the influence of Triazolam, the Licensing Authority had decided to suspend the Triazolam marketing licences for three months. This decision was renewed every three months. The revocation was based on the Medicines Act 1968 in connection with Council Directives 65/65/EEC, 75/318 and 75/319, as amended by Council Directive 83/570/EEC. Accordingly, an administrative phase is instituted when the Licensing Authority is considering the revocation or marketing of a licence and the holder of the marketing licence may argue his case and, in particular, submit any relevant documentation and be assisted by experts of his choosing in order to establish that the medicinal product which the authorities are investigating possesses the characteristics of safety, therapeutic efficacy and quality. The Licensing Authority informed Upjohn that all marketing licences for Triazolam were going to be revoked with immediate effect as conclusions made by the "persons appointed"

[182] (Case C-120/97) 21 January 1999.

were rejected on the issues of dose equivalence and safety margins. Upjohn commenced proceedings for judicial review and took the view:

"That the judicial procedure in force in the United kingdom is contrary to Community law, which, in its opinion, requires member states to institute a procedure for judicial review of decisions taken by national authorities enabling national courts to verify the reliability of the scientific evidence on which the administration bases its decisions to revoke marketing licences, and thus to assess afresh the issues of fact and law and to rule, in particular, on whether the decision taken is "correct" and complies with the principle of proportionality. In other words, the national court ought to verify that the decision taken by the authority is the proper decision and, if necessary, substitute its own decision for that of the authority".[183]

However, the European Court of Justice held that Community law did not require national courts to substitute their assessment of the facts for that of the competent national authorities. The court made clear that in cases:

"Where a Community authority is called upon, in the performance of its duties, to make complex assessments, it enjoys a wide measure of discretion, the exercise of which is subject to a limited judicial review in the course of which the Community judicature may not substitute its assessment of the facts for the assessment made by the authority concerned. Thus, in such cases, the Community judicature must restrict itself to examining the accuracy of the findings of fact and law made by the authority concerned and to verifying, in particular, that the action taken by that authority is not vitiated by a manifest error or a misuse of powers and that it did not clearly exceed the bounds of its discretion".[184]

This case illustrates that the standard of review as applied by English courts with regard to the characteristics of safety, therapeutic efficacy and quality is in line with the standards applied by the European Court of Justice. The European Court of Justice did not require a test that would go further than the review of discretionary decisions as to whether they were flawed by a "manifest error", a "misuse of power" or an "excess of power". As opposed to the findings by the European Court of Justice, the view taken by Upjohn regarding closer scrutiny of the reliability of the scientific evidence on which the original decision by the Licensing Authority was based would have found strong support in German courts as the next example will show. The European Court of Justice categorised the questions above as discretionary whereas the German courts would have considered them as undefined legal concepts with the consequence of a full review. It has been suggested that the consequence for the German courts might be that the interpretation of the substantive law as contained in the implementing legislation in Germany will have to conform to the content of the Directive.[185] Accordingly, the German courts might have to refrain from full control of these concepts. In this context,

---

183 *Upjohn Ltd v The Licensing Authority Established by the Medicines Act* 1968 and others, Case C-120/97 [1999] 1 CMLR 825 at 834.

184 Ibid 847.

185 Götz, V., "Europarechtliche Vorgaben für das Verwaltungsprozeßrecht" (2002) *DVBl* 1 [5].

Schwarze, however, argues that the European Court of Justice does not require the German courts to reduce their standards of review.[186]

The case of *Upjohn Ltd v The Licensing Authority Established by the Medicines Act 1968 and others*[187] which we dealt with above was concerned with the question to what extent the effectiveness of European Community law requires the application of a particular standard in national judicial review systems. The decision illustrates that the European Court of Justice does not require a stricter standard of review than it would apply itself. It held that the standard of review applied by the English court was sufficient. The German case has illustrated the higher standard of review in the context of undefined legal concepts, which in English and European law would be considered as questions falling within the discretion of the authorities. The concept of undefined legal concepts and their full judicial review is not known in English or European law. The case of *Upjohn* has illustrated that the European Court of Justice refers to its own standards of review, which in this case were similar to the standards applied by the English court. As a consequence, interference with the German standard of review is not to be expected.[188]

e) The principle of legitimate expectations (Vertrauensschutz) in German law

The principles of legal certainty and substantive legitimate expectation, equality and proportionality are well established in Germany to exercise control over administrative discretionary powers. The principles of legal certainty and substantive legitimate expectation are based on the constitutional provisions in Arts. 20[189] and 28[190] of the Basic Law.[191] They form the basis for the principle of the *Rechtsstaat.* The constitutional status of these principles has the effect that they enjoy status equal to legislation. As a result, in cases of conflict between the principle of administrative compliance with statute law and the principles, a balancing process of

---

186 Schwarze, J., "Europäische Rahmenbedingungen für die Verwaltungsgerichtsbarkeit" (2000) *NVwZ* 241 [249].

187 (Case C-120/97) 21 January 1999.

188 Schwarze, J., "Europäische Rahmenbedingungen für die Verwaltungsgerichtsbarkeit" (2000) *NVwZ* 241 [249].

189 Article 20 Political and Social Structure, Defence of the Constitutional Order:
"(1) The Federal Republic of Germany shall be a democratic and social federal state.
(2) All public authority emanates from the people. It shall be exercised by the people through elections and referenda and by specific legislative, executive and judicial bodies.
(3) The legislature shall be bound by the constitutional order, the executive and the judiciary by law and justice.
(4) [...]"

190 Article 28 Federal Guarantee of *Land* Constitutions and Local Government:
"(1) The constitutional order in the *Länder* shall conform to the principles of the republican, democratic and social state governed by the rule of law within the meaning of this Basic Law ..."

191 Schwarze, J., *European Administrative Law*, 2006, 886.

weighing the competing interests has to be carried out.[192] Court decisions and academic literature have provided detailed criteria concerning the fair balancing of competing public interests and the right to the protection of legitimate expectation for both cases of revocation of unlawful administrative decisions and the withdrawal of lawful administrative decisions. A further distinction is drawn within both categories between those decisions by which benefits are conferred and those which impose burdens on the individual citizen. In 1976 these criteria were codified in some detail in the Law on Administrative Procedure (*Verwaltungsverfahrensgesetz*).

The following case decided before the enactment of the Law on Administrative Procedure concerned the question whether the applicant could rely on the principle of legitimate expectation after an unlawful benefit had been revoked by the authorities.

The Widow case[193] concerned the revocation of welfare benefits which had been paid to a widow between 1953 and 1954 after she had moved from East to West Germany. The payments were revoked on the basis that the payments had been made unlawfully and the widow was required to repay the overpaid sums. The court upheld the widow's legitimate expectation that the payments were made lawfully. The decision by the Federal Administrative Court in 1959 was a major breakthrough for the acceptance of the principle of legitimate expectation and led to the inclusion of a provision in Art. 48(2) of the Law on Administrative Procedure:[194]

"(1) An unlawful administrative act may, even after it has become non-appealable, be withdrawn wholly or in part either retrospectively or with effect for the future. An administrative act which gives rise to a right or an advantage relevant in legal proceedings or confirms such a right or advantage (beneficial administrative act) may only be withdrawn subject to the restrictions of paragraphs 2 to 4.

(2) An unlawful administrative act which provides for a one-tier or continuing payment of money or a divisible material benefit, or which is a prerequisite for these, may not be withdrawn so far as the beneficiary has relied upon the continued existence of the administrative act and his reliance deserves protection relative to the public interest in a withdrawal. Reliance is in general deserving of protection when the beneficiary has utilised the contributions made or has made financial arrangements which he can no longer cancel or can cancel only by suffering a disadvantage which cannot reasonably be asked of him. The beneficiary cannot claim reliance when:

1. he obtained the administrative act by false pretences, threat or bribery;
2. he obtained the administrative act by giving information which was substantially incorrect or incomplete;
3. he was aware of the illegality of the administrative act or was unaware thereof due to gross negligence.

In the case provided for in sentence 3, the administrative act shall in general be withdrawn with retrospective effect.

(3) If an unlawful administrative act not covered by paragraph 2 is withdrawn, the authority shall upon application make good the disadvantage to the person affected deriving

---

192 Ibid 887.

193 9 BVerwGE 251.

194 Richter, I., Schuppert, G.F., *Casebook Verwaltungsrecht* ,2nd edn, 1995, 194.

from his reliance on the existence of the act to the extent that his reliance merits protection having regard to the public interest. Paragraph 2, third sentence shall apply. However, the disadvantage in financial terms shall be made good to an amount not to exceed the interest which the person affected has in the continuance of the administrative act. The financial disadvantage to be made good shall be determined by the authority. A claim may only be made within a year, which period shall commence as soon as the authority has informed the person affected thereof.

(4) If the authority learns of facts which justify the withdrawal of an unlawful administrative act, the withdrawal may only be made within one year from the date of gaining such knowledge. This shall not apply in the case of paragraph 2, third sentence, no.1.

(5) Once the administrative act has become non-appealable, the decision concerning withdrawal shall be taken by the authority competent under section 3. This shall also apply when the administrative act to be withdrawn has been issued by another authority".[195]

The revocation of a lawful administrative act is dealt with in an equally detailed fashion in Art. 49 of the Administrative Procedure Act. The special feature of this article is the provision of compensation to make good the disadvantage to the person who relied on the existence of the act to his or her own detriment.[196]

---

195 Translation from http://www.bmi.bund.de/cln_012/nn_174390/Internet/Content/Common/Anlagen/Gesetze/VwVfg__englisch,templateId=raw,roperty=publicationFile.pdf/VwVfg_englisch.

196 http://www.bmi.bund.de/cln_012/nn_174390/Internet/Content/Common/Anlagen/Gsetze/VwVfg__englisch,templateId=raw,property=publicationFile.pdf/VwVfg_englisch:

Article 49 Revocation of a Lawful Administrative Act:

"(1) A lawful, non-beneficial administrative act may, even after it has become non-appealable, be revoked wholly or in part with effect for the future, except when an administrative act of like content would have to be issued or when revocation is not allowable for other reasons.

(2) A lawful, beneficial administrative act may, even when it has become non-appealable, be revoked in whole or in part with effect for the future only when:

1. revocation is permitted by law or the right of revocation is reserved in the administrative act itself;
2. the administrative act is combined with an obligation which the beneficiary has not complied with fully or not within the time limit set;
3. the authority would be entitled, as a result of a subsequent change in circumstances, not to issue the administrative act and if failure to revoke it would be contrary to the public interest;
4. the authority would be entitled, as a result of an amendment to a legal provision, not to issue the administrative act where the beneficiary has not availed himself of the benefit or has not received any benefits derived from the administrative act and when failure to revoke would be contrary to the public interest; or
5. in order to prevent or eliminate serious harm to the common good.

Section 48 para 4 applies *mutatis mutandis*.

(3) A lawful administrative act which provides for a one-off or a continuing payment of money or a divisible material benefit for a particular purpose, or which is a prerequisite for these, may be revoked even after such time as it has become non-appealable, either wholly or in part and with retrospective effect:

f) The Europeanisation of the principle of legitimate expectations in German law

The protection of substantive legitimate expectation is therefore highly protected even if the original administrative act was unlawful. However, this generous approach has had to be adapted in the context of European provisions concerning the regulation of state aid. If the granting of state aid on the basis of EC legislation is in contravention of EC law, the rules on revocation of such an unlawful decision are applied. According to the German provisions the revocation would be at the discretion of the authorities. The European Court of Justice's decision in *Land Rheinland-Pfalz/Alcan Deutschland GmbH*[197] concerned the recovery of unlawfully paid state aid as it had been granted in breach of Art. 93(3) of the EC Treaty which requires that the European Commission be informed before state is granted. Subsequently the European Commission requested that the state aid should be revoked. In the application of the rules on the recovery of unlawfully granted payments as contained in Art. 48 of the Law on Administrative Procedure (see above) the federal government informed the Commission "that there were substantial political and legal obstacles to the recovery". The Federal Administrative Court then referred three questions concerning the interpretation of the German provisions to the European Court of Justice. First, it submitted the concern that the time limit of one year for the recovery as laid out in Art. 48(4) of the Law on Administrative Procedure had elapsed and that therefore under German law revocation was not possible. Secondly, it referred the question whether the state aid could be revoked despite the substantive legitimate expectation of the beneficiary, Alcan (Art. 48(2) above). Finally, it asked whether the German authority was obliged to revoke the decision despite the fact that under German law "such demand was excluded because the gain no longer existed in the absence of bad faith on the part of the recipient of the aid" (Art. 48(3) above). The European Court of Justice held that the authority had to revoke the decision regardless of the time limit as set out in Art.

---

1. if, once this payment is rendered, it is not put to use, or is not put to use either without undue delay or for the purpose for which it was intended in the administrative act;
2. if the administrative act had an obligation attached to it which the beneficiary either fails to satisfy or does not satisfy within the stipulated period.

Section 48 para 4 applies *mutatis mutandis*.

(4) The revoked administrative act shall become null and void with the coming into force of the revocation, except where the authority fixes some other date.

(5) Once the administrative act has become non-appealable, decisions as to revocation shall be taken by the authority competent under section 3. This shall also apply when the administrative act to be revoked has been issued by another authority.

(6) In the event of a beneficial administrative act being revoked in cases covered by para 2, nos. 3 to 5, the authority shall upon application make good the disadvantage to the person affected deriving from his reliance on the continued existence of the act to the extent that his reliance merits protection. Section 48, para 3, third to fifth sentences shall apply as appropriate. Disputes concerning compensation shall be settled by the ordinary court".

[197] Case C-24/95.

48 of the Law on Administrative Procedure. Secondly, the court held that Alcan had no substantive legitimate expectation as it should have been aware of the requirements of EC law under Art. 93 of the EC Treaty. Finally, it held that the beneficiary could not claim that the gain no longer existed, even if it was not in bad faith.

The decision triggered off a "lively discussion" concerning the effects of EC law on established principles such as the protection of legitimate expectation.[198] It was argued that the court acted *ultra vires* concerning the establishment of new rules for the recovery of state aid. However, the Federal Administrative Court followed the ECJ's decision and accepted that in the context of recovery of state aid the highly protective provisions of German law have to yield to the interests of the Community in controlling the equal treatment of member states. However, it is unlikely that this reduction in protection will spill over to other areas where substantive legitimate expectation requires protection under the existing provisions.

g) The principle of equality

Further, there are direct limitations stemming from the basic rights such as the principle of equality in Art. 3 para 1 of the Basic Law which reads: "all people are equal before the law".[199] The general principle of equality requires that the authorities exercise their discretion equally. Where, for instance, the authorities have developed a regular pattern of dealing with particular matters, the equality principle will bind the decision maker to conform to that practice in subsequent cases. The authorities are bound by their own practice and may only deviate from it where there is a reason in substance to do so. The following case illustrates the Federal Administrative Court's reasoning concerning the question whether an individual may rely on the context of internal administrative instructions (*Verwaltungsvorschriften*). It may be uncontroversial that an internal administrative instruction has a factual effect (*faktische Außenwirkung*) on the position of the individual citizen who is adversely affected by it. However, whether an individual may rely on the internal administrative instruction to reach a more favourable decision relies on the question whether the internal administrative instruction has a legal effect on the individual (*rechtliche Außenwirkung*). It is now generally accepted that the factual effect of an administrative instruction also results in a legal effect on the individual.[200] The following case illustrates that there is some controversy over the legal basis for this effect as well as concerning the distinction between different types of administrative instruction.

In the *Army Service* case (BVerwGE 34, 278) the applicant was in full-time education at a state school for mechanical studies. The army authorities decided

---

[198] Schwarze, J., "Europäische Rahmenbedingungen für die Verwaltungsgerichtsbarkeit" (2000) *NVwZ* 241 [251]; for a detailed discussion on the recovery of state aid and the German principle of substantive legitimate expectation, see Schwarze, J., *Das Verwaltungsrecht unter Europäischem Einfluss*, 1996, German report.

[199] Alle Menschen sind vor dem Gesetz gleich.

[200] Maurer, H., *Allgemeines Verwaltungsrecht*, 1999, 608.

not to recruit him before 31 March 1969 in order to enable him to complete his course. In early March 1969 he commenced a degree in engineering which he expected to complete in March 1972. In April 1969 the applicant was recruited to the army. The applicant appealed against this decision. The law governing the recruitment of men to compulsory army service is the *Wehrpflichtgesetz*. According to Art. 12 para 4 sentence 1, a national serviceman can apply for a postponement of service if it would impose a burden of a personal, in particular domestic, economic or professional nature. Accordingly, the completion of large parts of a degree is considered as a burden. This was clearly not the case here as the applicant had only just begun his degree. The Lower Administrative Court, however, decided in favour of the applicant. It based its decision on an administrative instruction (*Verwaltungsvorschriften für die Musterung und Einberufung ungedienter Wehrpflichtiger*) issued by the Ministry of Defence which stated that national servicemen who take a course in engineering or building cannot be compelled to join the service even if they have only just started the course.

The *Bundesverwaltungsgericht* has repeatedly decided that administrative instructions, in addition to their merely internal effects, can have external effects which create rights for the citizen. Such effect is referred to as a self-imposed limitation of public bodies (*Selbstbindung*). Administrative instructions can only lead to a self-imposed limitation in such cases in which discretionary powers have been vested upon a public body by law. Here, administrative instructions serve the purpose of confining discretion in order to guarantee a consistent exercise of such a power. The legal basis for the self-imposed limitation is not of a generally binding nature of administrative instructions, but rather based on the principle of equality enshrined in Art. 3 of the Basic Law. This principle requires the equal exercise of discretionary powers. The court held that if a public body applies administrative instructions regularly in the exercise of discretion then it violates the principle of equality if it does not apply the same in similar cases. The citizen has the right to challenge a decision in which the public body has deviated from its standard practice without sufficient grounds.

However, the administrative instructions in this case are not designed to confine the authorities' discretionary powers, they are designed to interpret the statute (*Wehrpflichtgesetz*). The instructions can be regarded as a tool for the construction of the statutory requirements (*norminterpretierende Verwaltusvorschrift*), but not as a confinement of the exercise of the discretionary power (*Ermessensrichtlinie*). The instruction is not binding and does not have any external legal effects, therefore it does not create any self-imposed limitations. There is no room for the application of the principle of equality.

This case has illustrated the importance of the principle of equality in Germany which operates as a legal basis for the fair and consistent exercise of discretionary powers. The German courts, however, draw a distinction between different forms of administrative instructions: those which are able to bind a public body because they are concerned with the confinement of discretionary powers and those which are designed to aid the interpretation of the objective elements of a statute. The latter form of administrative instruction does not create any external legal effects because it is the role of the judge to interpret the law.[201] Therefore these aids to interpretation do not bind judges in the interpretation of the law and therefore do not create legal effects for the citizen. The *Bundesverwaltungsgericht* does not regard the principle of legitimate expectation as a legal basis for the external effect of administrative instructions. Administrative instructions are only directed to administrative authorities internally so that no legitimate expectations are created which could result in a self-imposed limitation on the authorities. The principle of legitimate expectation is only applicable if an internal instruction can be qualified as a direct representation to a limited class of people.[202]

However, those instructions which are designed to confine discretionary powers may be binding and the citizen has a right derived from the equality principle to challenge a decision which deviates from the standard practice of the public body. This requires the establishment of a continuity of practice in dealing with similar cases. The application of the equality principle has therefore been criticised for being incapable of explaining the external legal effect of administrative instructions which have never been applied before. For these cases, the courts have developed the fiction of anticipated administrative practice (*antizipierte Verwaltungspraxis*) which assumes a violation against the equality principle in similar future cases.[203] The principle of equality, however, does not give rise to equal treatment on the basis of an *ultra vires* instruction or practice (*keine Gleichheit im Unrecht*).[204] Some commentators have argued these cases fall under the doctrine of legitimate expectation. Accordingly, the citizen can legitimately expect that the authorities are applying administrative instructions properly.[205]

Finally, it has been argued that internal administrative instructions can be relied on without having to depend on the equality principle or the principle of legitimate expectation.[206] This view, however, is controversial and has been denied by the European Court of Justice in which it held that German administrative instructions concerning the implementation of the Air Pollution Directive (*TA Luft* – the Technical Instruction on Clean Air Maintenance) were insufficient.[207]

---

201 BVerwGE 94, 307 [309]; Erichsen, Hans-Uwe, Ehlers, Dirk, *Allgemeines Verwaltungsrecht*, 2002, 163.

202 Maurer, H., *Allgemeines Verwaltungsrecht* ,1999, 609, 610 with further references.

203 Erichsen, H.-U., Ehlers, D., *Allgemeines Verwaltungsrecht*, 2002, 161.

204 BverfG *NVwZ* 1994, 475; Wolff, H. J., Bachof, Ot., Stober, R, *Verwaltungsrecht Band 1*, 1999, 516.

205 Maurer, H., *Allgemeines Verwaltungsrecht*, 609 citing Klein, *Festgabe für Forsthoff*, 179.

206 Maurer, H., *Allgemeines Verwaltungsrecht*, 610 with further references on 611.

207 EUGH, *NVwZ* 1991, 866 [868]; see a criticism of this judgment in Rupp, H., J.Z., 1991, 1034; v Dannwitz , T., *VerwARchiv*, 1993, 73.

III. Conclusion

This chapter has illustrated the standards of review engaged by English and German courts in reviewing the exercise of discretionary powers. Both legal systems have developed grounds which are applied to review the substance of the decision, i.e. the principles of unreasonableness, legitimate expectation, equality and proportionality. The development of these principles in England is due to a fairly recent trend of the courts to embrace principles as applied in the European courts. However, the rigour with which these principles are applied varies between the two legal systems.

The principle of substantive legitimate expectation in Germany is well established and codified in detail. Equally well established is the principle of proportionality in Germany. It consists of three limbs and in short requires that means or measures must be suitable and necessary for achieving an aspired result and that the means and end stand in a reasonable proportion. The three limbs of the principle are interconnected and overlap, but they are still exclusive in the sense that each of them must be satisfied for the validity of the administrative action. The principle requires a proper balancing between the injury to an individual and the gain to the community caused by an administrative measure and prohibits those measures whose disadvantages to the individual outweigh the advantages to the community.

In English law, proportionality is not often explicitly adopted as a ground of review, but it was suggested that it appears under the guise of *Wednesbury* unreasonableness. This is said to occur, first, where decisions have been struck down because of improper balance of material considerations and, secondly, in cases of unreasonably oppressive decisions.[208] In *R v Home Secretary, ex p Brind*[209] the broadcasting ban imposed by directives made by the Home Secretary were challenged. In this case, two of the judges indicated that it might be applied in the future. For once, it was argued that the principle was incompatible with the judicial review approach with does not review the merits of a case, also described as "the forbidden appellate approach". Secondly, it was held that in the absence of a "fundamental law" there was no room for the principle. The difficulties in importing the principle of proportionality are of a conceptual nature. The German approach concentrates on the review of the actual result of an administrative decision using a stringent balancing formula with equal weight to individual rights and the common interest. The traditional *Wednesbury* unreasonableness test is more concerned with the negative formulation of what is unreasonable focusing more on the solution-finding process rather than on the review of the result. The proportionality test is by contrast concerned with the legitimacy of the interference with rights. The German approach is marked by the application of a detailed test, asking

208 Jowell, J., Birkinshaw, P., "Tendencies Towards European Standards in National Administrative Law" in Schwarze J., *Das Verwaltungsrecht unter Europäischem Einfluß*, 1996, English report.

209 [1991] 1 AC 696.

whether the interference was suitable, necessary and overall proportionate. It is also the vigour with which this test is answered which is crucial.

However, the cases of *Simms* and *Daly* have illustrated a remarkable development in English law. Here, the House of Lords applied a test, similar to the one applied in Germany, by asking whether the interference with the right to freedom of expression was necessary, requiring the existence of a pressing social need and that the restrictions should be no more than is proportionate to the legitimate aim pursued.[210]

In Germany, on the other hand, a reduction of some of the standards of review has either been required by the European Court of Justice, as witnessed in the *Alcan* decision, or criticism has been uttered as to how the principle of proportionality is applied. The dissenting judges in the *East German Spies* case criticised the application of the principle as an excuse to exercise quasi-legislative functions. The *Low Level Flight* decision indicates that the standard of the application of the principle may vary depending on the context. However, with regard to the standard of review of undefined legal concepts, the Federal Constitutional Court has indicated a high level of review on the basis of human rights protection (*Law State Exam* case). In sum, the emphasis on the protection of individual rights has shaped the development of German administrative legal principles such as the principle of legitimate expectation, equality and proportionality. It has been argued that this has lead to a individualisation of administrative legal thinking and that this bears dangers.[211] Academic commentators warn that the principle of equality might lead to a reduction in the binding force of the law. Further, the courts are increasingly concentrating on the individual interest of the claimant which does not take account of the greater context in which an administrative decision has to be taken.[212] Further, the reconstruction of the context in which the decision was taken in the court process tends to be more beneficial to the enforcement of individual interests. This tendency is said to be underlined by the principle of full judicial control of the material decision.[213]

In England, the constitutional framework is characterised by the principle of parliamentary sovereignty which in traditional terms limited the reviewing powers of the judges to the protection of the legislative intent. It is not for the judges to second-guess the authorities' decisions, the judges' function lies in the assurance that Parliament's will has been carried out. This principle is the basis for judicial restraint which has traditionally been applied. Unlike the German administrative judges, English judges do not carry out a mandate enshrined in a constitutional provision to provide effective judicial protection for the rights of individuals. Even though this traditional judicial restraint has changed enormously over the last decades which have witnessed an increasing creativity by judges to expand judicial review, more recent decisions under the new powers in the Human Rights Act

210 [1999] 3 WLR 328 at 338g–h.

211 Schmidt-Assmann, E., *Das allgemeine Verwaltungsrecht als Ordnungsidee, Grundlagen und Aufgaben der verwaltungsrechtlichen Systembildung*, 2nd edn, 2006, 78–79.

212 Ibid.

213 Ibid 222–223.

1998 indicate a careful use of the new judicial review "tools". In Germany, on the other hand, the control of discretionary powers is driven by the protection of an individual's rights which might potentially have been abused by the public authorities. The principle of judicial protection against unlawful acts of the public authorities is laid down in the constitutional provision of Art. 19(4) of the Basic Law. German courts do not only review the decision itself, but also carry out a detailed review of the constitutionality of the enabling statute. The principles of proportionality and equality are frequently applied tools engaged in this process.

Further, limitations to a convergence are clearly set by the different procedures applied by the courts. The differences between the adversarial and the inquisitorial procedure have already been discussed in some detail in Chapter Two. The grounds of review such as irrationality and proportionality in English law are harder to prove in a system which lays the onus of proof on the applicant. Further, the difficulties in obtaining an order for discovery of documentation make it hard for applicants in English courts to obtain information about the authorities' reasoning. German administrative courts, on the other hand, inquire into the facts applying a variety of means of evidence. The onus of proof does not necessarily rest upon the applicant because it is accepted that some facts may not lie within the sphere of the citizen.

The comparison of judicial review of discretionary powers in England and Germany has shown that both systems recognise the existence of an area of administrative activity which cannot be fully reviewed by the courts. In both systems discretionary powers are a product of the conflict between modern administration and the rule of law. The freedom of the administration requires both legal boundaries and judicial control. Discretion has been described as a hinge which brings together legislation, the execution of laws and judicial control. This applies equally to both countries. Similar developments can be traced which at least led to the common form of modern type of state based on the rule of law with judicial control of the administration.[214]

However, in Germany, the discretionary administrative powers are required to be expressly authorised by law. As shown in the demonstration case, the legislature must clearly delimit the scope of interference with fundamental rights. The authorisation of discretionary powers is therefore rather detailed. In England, on the other hand, wide discretionary powers are given to the administration. They are mainly based on statute, but discretionary powers can also be based on prerogative powers or the common law. In Germany, the concept of discretion is characterised by a highly abstract theory of the localisation of discretionary powers in a norm. Discretion found on the *Tatbestand* of a provision has been distinguished from discretion on the *Rechtsfolgenseite* of a provision. The former has been described as undefined legal concepts and only in a limited number of cases have the courts allowed a margin of appreciation (*Beurteilungsspielraum*) to be applied in the determination of these concepts. As a result these undefined legal concepts are usually fully reviewable by the courts. This flows from the principle

[214] Oeter, S. in Frowein, J.A. (Hrsg.), *Die Kontrolldichte bei der gerichtlichen Überprüfung von Handlungen der Verwaltung*, 1993, 267.

of effective judicial protection as enshrined in Art. 19(4) of the Basic Law. This article plays a pivotal role in the modern theory of discretion and it sets the constitutional limits to any changes in the theory of discretion. Another category of discretion is in planning decisions (*Planungsermessen*) which has been classified as a *Finalnorm*. Here, the authority has wider powers with regard to the overall balancing of interests. English law, on the other hand, does not contain an abstract theory of the structure of the norm. In comparison, the concept of discretion is narrower in German law due to the restrictions imposed by the requirements as described above, the complex theory of the structure of the norm and where discretionary powers should be located.

On the surface the grounds of review bear some resemblance. However, even if some overlaps can be observed such as the cases mentioned concerned with fettering of discretion, one can observe major differences with regard to the conceptual approach of discretion. The undefined legal concepts in German administrative law narrow the scope of discretionary powers as illustrated by the comparison of the *Upjohn Ltd v The Licensing Authority* and *Licence for Pesticides* cases. Even though harshly criticised in German academia, the recent decision of the *Bundesverfassungsgericht* in the *State Exam* case indicates a trend to more scrutiny rather than liberalisation of the German conceptual approach. At the centre of the discussion in Germany stands Art. 19(4) of the Basic Law which requires the effective judicial protection of individuals. English law, on the other hand, contains no constitutional principle which requires full judicial control. Here, the protection of the intention of Parliament is the traditional basis for the review of discretionary powers.

The grounds of review and the questions asked display some similarities on the surface. Both jurisdictions apply numerous grounds of review and some are identical in name such as fettering of discretion and the proportionality test. However, the rigour with which the questions posed are answered differs in English and German courts. The comparison has identified the reasons for the different judicial approaches. First, English and German judges in administrative law cases find themselves in different constitutional frameworks when asked to review an executive decision. Secondly, the inquisitorial procedure applied in the German Administrative Courts enables German judges to carry out a much more thorough reconstruction and review of the case in front of them.

However, the cases discussed under abuse of discretionary powers and proportionality in both jurisdictions illustrate highly interesting developments. The English cases display an enormous willingness by English judges, inspired by European principles, to expand the intensity of review beyond what might be justified as carrying out Parliament's intention. They have developed English law to embrace the principle of proportionality and substantive legitimate expectation. It might be unclear at the moment whether the traditional *Wednesbury* unreasonableness test will cease to be applied or whether it will be amended to embrace the proportionality test eventually. This is one of the qualities of English administrative law. It has shown enormous flexibility in developing itself further and the study of case law can be delightful. The courts apply varying standards of review depending on the context. Clearly, in cases with a strong human rights context, the review will be more intensive than in other areas. The justifications for the intensity of judicial control appear to vary as well. The cases of *Simms* has illustrated the use of the principle of legality, for instance, which has been applied to interpret the source of the administrative power in a way that does not restrict fundamental rights in an unjustified way. The application of the Human Rights Act 1998, however, will lead to further changes in the approaches the courts take in reviewing discretionary decisions. The courts will have to engage in a more detailed legality review of enabling statutes and apply stricter standards in the review of substantive questions more evenly. The cases of *Daly* and *ProLife* indicate clearly that the principle of proportionality is accepted as a standard of review in human rights cases.

Particularly in England, a change in the legal climate can be noted with regard to applying more substantive standards of review. In Germany, less intensive review of administrative decisions and varying standards of review are being discussed. The reasons for the need for change is the fact that the position of the administration in Germany has been weakened and the constitutional right to judicial protection has been transformed into an over-intense controlling mechanism with overworked courts and delayed procedures. The principles of equality, substantive legitimate expectation and proportionality are well established in German administrative law. A fine distinction is drawn between the application of the equality principle and the principle of substantive legitimate expectation in cases where internal rules of the administration are applied differently or change. The decision by the European Court of Justice in *Alcan* indicates that the protection of substantive legitimate expectation goes further than the standards set by the European Court of Justice. In the interest of protecting the objectives of Community law, German law had to adapt and lower the standard of review in these cases. No effect on other cases, where substantive legitimate expectations are protected under German law, will, however, be expected. On the contrary, in cases with a basic rights context, the German Constitutional Court has increased the scope of judicial review. The latter is therefore a trend to be witnessed both in England and Germany. Particularly in the context of human rights protection in England, one can witness movements towards bridging the gap between the English and German administrative legal systems. Further, the quest for an increase in power for the German administration can be interpreted as a move towards reducing the difference to countries like England where the administration has traditionally enjoyed greater powers.

In Germany, the quest for less intensive review and a move away from legal to political protection of civil liberties is unlikely to become reality. An erosion of traditional principles such as the concepts of free evaluation is likely to be hindered by constitutional safeguards enshrined in Germany's written constitution (Art. 19(4). The case law of the European Court of Justice indicates that there is no obligation to reduce the standard of review in Germany concerning the review of undefined legal concepts. Nevertheless, it may serve as an impulse for a revision of the German complex concept of discretion. It is concerning that due to this unique concept judges are getting involved in highly technical decisions which can often only be taken with the help of expert witnesses. With regard to the principle of substantive legitimate expectation in the context of the recovery of unlawfully granted state aid, it is clear that German law has to accept a reduction in the standard of protection it offers. The stringent application of the principles of substantive legitimate expectations, equality and proportionality is an expression of the purpose of administrative law in Germany. Günter Frankenberg noted that the transformation of relationships of power between the state and the citizen into a relationship of law is at the heart of German administrative law.[215]

Similarly, in England, the development of clear principles and standards to intensify a more substantive review of the actions of the administration will have to overcome the difficulties of combining the new principles of substantive review with the traditional supervisory function of judicial review. The fear of engaging in a merits-based review has been expressed widely and commentators in favour of substantive review seem convinced that the courts will acknowledge the limitations in competence of their own role.[216] The comparison has shown though that the introduction of these new principles, inspired by European laws, will not amount to a mere transplant of "foreign" concepts. Rather, these principles will "take a different shape in English soil".[217] A form of "cross-fertilisation"[218] is taking place according to which the British style is europeanised, however, it will not surrender its national characteristics.

Only time will tell to which extent the increasing protection of human rights strengthens the role of the courts. The comparison with the German judicial review system might lead to the conclusion that this will not be without a price to pay, i.e. that the development of a rights-based culture might encroach upon the freedom of the executive.

215 Frankenberg, G., "Remarks on the Philosophy and Politics of Public Law" (1998) *Legal Studies*, vol. 18, 177 [179].

216 Jowell, J., "Beyond the Rule of Law: Towards Constitutional Judicial Review" (2000) *Public Law* 671 [681]; see Lord Steyn in *Daly* [2001] 2 WLR 1622.

217 Jowell, J., Birkinshaw, P. in Schwarze J., *Das Verwaltungsrecht unter Europäischem Einfluß* ,1996, English report.

218 Bell, J. in Beatson, J., Tridimas, T., *New Directions in European Public Law*, 1998, 147.

Chapter Four Procedural errors in the administrative procedure

I. Introduction

Both in England and Germany the proper performance of procedures in the decision-making process of public authorities is recognised as an expression of the rule of law or the *Rechtsstaatsprinzip* respectively. In England, procedural safeguards are increasingly important as a means of controlling, confining and structuring discretion. The notion of administrative procedural protection has therefore become an important topic in the laws of the two member states. The importance of procedural protection in complex decision-making processes is increasing in both countries, not least because of European impulses, particularly in the field of environmental protection. However, in Germany, despite a relatively modern Law on Administrative Procedure (1976) the status of administrative procedural law is in a state of flux. The codified principles of a right to a hearing and the duty to give reasons have an important role to play in the administrative decision-making process. However, the relevance of these procedural safeguards is slowly eroding. This process has been accelerated by the so-called *Standortdiskussion* which has partly put the blame on the complex and lengthy German administrative procedures for the lack of foreign investment. The term *Standort Deutschland* (location Germany) has become a keyword in post-unification Germany which is still struggling with the economic burdens of the political success. In the hope of accelerating the administrative process, the *Bundestag* introduced reforms in 1996, the so-called *Beschleunigungsgesetze*,[1] which legalise the curing of procedural defects up to the end of the trial in the last instance. Accordingly, for example, the denial of the right to a hearing may be cured at trail. This will inevitably lead to extra burdens for the Administrative Courts. Further, the quality of administrative decisions will suffer from the more relaxed attitude of administrators who will rely on the "in-trial curing" (*Heilung im Prozeß*).[2] It is not yet clear to what extent the Administrative Courts will apply these reforms. In particular, in the indirect implementation of European law such as the application of the *Umweltverträglichkeitsprüfung*, conflicts between German law and the jurisprudence of the Euro-

1 Genehmigungsbeschleunigungsgesetz – GenBeschlG, dated 12 September 1996 BGBl. I, 1354.

2 Hufen, F., *Fehler im Verwaltungsverfahren* ,3rd edn, 1998, 7; Goller, B. and Schmid, A., "Reform of the German Administrative Courts Act" (1998) *European Public Law* 31 [35].

pean Court of Justice are likely.[3] The comparison with the English principles of natural justice and fairness will illustrate that procedural protection enjoys a higher status in English law. Even though the principles are not codified, English courts are more willing to strike down a procedurally flawed decision as *ultra vires*. More recently, the ground of review of unfairness has been applied in cases which did not fit into the traditional categories of procedural impropriety. This indicates that the division between procedure and substance of a decision is beginning to blur. This chapter will analyse the reasons for the traditional difference in the attitudes to procedural protection. Particular attention will be paid to the right to a hearing and the duty to give reasons and the consequences for non-compliance with these procedural safeguards.

1. The rules of natural justice in English law

In English law questions of procedure have traditionally played an important role. This is not only evident in the sophisticated rules of evidence in the adversarial court procedure, but also a characteristic feature of today's English administrative procedure. However, the rules of administrative procedure which the third ground of review of procedural impropriety embraces and which were spelt out by Lord Diplock in his famous *GCHQ*[4] ruling are the product of a more recent development in English administrative law. Rules of procedure may be contained in statutes or delegated legislation or in the rules of natural justice or procedural fairness as it is more commonly referred to today. The rules of natural justice which have been formulated by the courts contain two main principles: the principle of *audi alteram partem* and the rule against bias. These are two very old principles which are associated with the Old Testament and which have been the content of many cases since the seventeenth century.[5] The earliest reports go back to a case in 1615 which concerned the reinstatement of James Bagg who had lost his office without having been given notice or the chance of a hearing.[6] Another case was that of Dr Bentley in 1723 who was successful in having his academic degrees from the University of Cambridge restored after they had been taken away from him without notice.[7] As a matter of principle, offices could not be removed without complying with the principle that the officer had to be given notice and had to be heard before removal. This related to offices which were freehold or which could only be forfeited for cause. It did not relate to a discretionary power to remove the office holder at pleasure. However, the importance of these principles decreased. In the nineteenth century, the *audi alteram partem* principle regained some of its

3 Hufen, F., supra n. 2, 385 with further references; Ehlers, D., "Die Europäisierung des Verwaltungsprozessrechts" (2004) *DVBl* 1441 [1449].

4 *Council of Civil Service Unions v Minister for the Civil Service* [1985] AC 374.

5 De Smith, S.A., *Judicial Review of Administrative Action*, 1995, 7-010.

6 *Bagg's Case* (1615) 11 Co Rep 93b, cited in De Smith, *Judicial Review of Administrative Action*, 1995, 7-011.

7 *R v Chancellor of the University of Cambridge* (1723) 1 Str 557 cited in De Smith, S.A., *Judicial Review of Administrative Action*, 1995, 7-011.

relevance when it was decided that it should apply to the conduct of arbitrators and tribunals which were concerned with decisions having civil consequences to individuals.[8] The attitude of the courts was then to require that judicial or quasi-judicial bodies must observe the principle. Consequently natural justice was not to be observed in purely administrative decisions.

The case of *Cooper v Wandsworth Board of Works*[9] illustrates how unreliable the distinction between administrative and judicial decisions is. In that case clearly administrative decisions were classified as judicial. The case concerned a house which was demolished because it was not built in accordance with the Metropolis Local Management Act 1855. The owner of the house had not been given any notice of the demolition. Section 76 contained a provision that before building a foundation for a new house, the owner of the new house had to give seven days' notice to the board. This provision ensured that the board could take the necessary steps with regard to the drains. Under the Act the authorities were entitled to demolish a house if no such notice had been given to the board. The plaintiff admitted that he had not waited for seven days after he had sent the notice and that he nevertheless had started digging. The Court of Common Pleas held that the plaintiff had been deprived of a right to a hearing. Even though the statute did not mention such a right, the court considered a hearing in this case to be recognised: "no man is to be deprived of his property without his having an opportunity of being heard ..." The court held that the district board exercised functions which are similar to the nature of judicial proceedings "because, certainly when they are appealed from, the appellant and the respondent are to be heard as parties and the matter is to be decided at least according to judicial forms".

However, the principle of *audi alteram partem* gradually declined. This was particularly due to the necessity of emergency decisions during wartime. Secondly, the development of wide discretionary powers to make policy decisions equally did not allow judicial review of the merits of a decision and the imposition of procedural standards to be observed by the decision maker.[10] Even though some statutes contained the common law requirement of a right to a hearing, it nevertheless lost its former meaning. The Prevention of Terrorism Act 1989, for instance, on exclusion orders contains in Schedule 2 Sect. 3 the right to make representations:

> "If after being served with notice of the making of an exclusion order the person against whom it is made objects to the order he may – (a) make representations in writing to the Secretary of State setting out the grounds of his objections; and (b) include in those representations a request for a personal interview with the person or persons nominated by the Secretary of State ..."

Case law further limited the principle in the first half of the twentieth century.

In 1915 the case of *Local Government Board v Arlidge*[11] clearly illustrated that the right to a fair hearing did not apply in circumstances where the authority did

---

8 De Smith, S.A., supra n. 5, 7-011.

9 (1863) 14 CBNS 180.

10 De Smith, S.A., supra n. 5, 7-19.

11 [1915] AC 120.

not act in a judicial capacity. In this case a closing order according to the Housing and Town Planning Act 1909 was served on the property of Arlidge which had followed the report of a housing inspector. According to this report the house was unfit for habitation. Arlidge was denied access to the report and was not given the right to a hearing before the board. The Act did not contain any provisions regarding a right to a hearing. The House of Lords held that the board was entitled to apply such a procedure. The Act contained the right of appeal to the Local Government Board which could not dismiss an appeal without holding a public inquiry. The House of Lords held that "such a body as the Local Government Board has the duty of enforcing obligations on the individual which are imposed in the interests of the community. Its character is that of an organisation with executive functions". Therefore the House of Lords saw no need to impose a duty on the authority to hear the applicant orally.

In 1964 the decision in *Ridge v Baldwin*[12] marked a turning point in the attitudes of the courts towards the application of the rules of natural justice. It "removed some restrictions on the rule's application that had developed since 1914 in lower courts and led to an "explosion" of natural justice cases".[13] The case concerned the dismissal of Charles Ridge who was appointed Chief Constable of the County Borough of Brighton. Ridge and two of his colleagues were indicted for conspiracy to obstruct the course of justice, but Ridge was acquitted. Nevertheless, in the following months the Watch Committee decided to discharge Ridge of duties as Chief Constable because they held him to be unfit for office following the evidence heard at the trial. Accordingly, the trial judge, Donovan J, described the Chief Constable as someone who "had been shown not to possess a sense of probity or of responsibility sufficient for the office which he held and so had been unable to provide the essential leadership and example to the police force under his control which his office properly required". He was given no notice and no opportunity to a hearing. The case reached the House of Lords and it was held that the decision had been made in breach of the rules of natural justice. In this case "the House of Lords revived the principles of natural justice".[14] First, it revived the nineteenth century jurisprudence and, secondly, the House of Lords disapproved with "some of the impediments which had been created in the twentieth century: the requirements of lies *inter partes* and a superadded duty to act judicially were said to be false constraints".[15] The decision of *Ridge v Baldwin* is mainly important because of the explicit revival of the concept of natural justice and the inspiration it has offered for consequent decisions. However, the decision itself does not define the boundaries of the rules of natural justice sufficiently.

In *Lloyd and others v McMahon*[16] Lord Bridge explained the flexibility of the rules of natural justice as follows:

---

[12] [1964] AC 40.

[13] Bailey, Jones & Mowbray, *Cases and Materials on Administrative Law*, 1997, 419.

[14] Craig, P., *Administrative Law*, 1999, 406.

[15] Ibid.

[16] [1987] 1 AC 625.

"My Lords, the so-called rules of natural justice are not engraved on tablets of stone. To use the phrase which better expresses the underlying concept, what the requirements of fairness demand when any body, domestic, administrative or judicial, has to make a decision which will affect the rights of individuals depends on the character of the decision-making body, the kind of decision it has to make and the statutory or other framework in which it operates. In particular, it is well established that when a statute has conferred on any body the power to make decisions affecting individuals, the courts will not only require the procedure prescribed by the statute to be followed, but will readily imply so much and no more to be introduced by way of additional procedural safeguards as will ensure the attainment of fairness".

The content of the right to a hearing has been discussed in *Bushell v Secretary of State for the Environment*[17] which was concerned with the question of whether the applicant had a right to cross-examine the opponents of the case. The case dealt with complaints by local residents against the building of two stretches of motorway. According to the Highways Act 1959, the Secretary of State held a local public inquiry. In this inquiry the respondents were not allowed to cross-examine the representatives of the department to challenge statistical methods used to predict future traffic needs. Lord Lane held that there may be situations in which the right to cross-examine might be important, for instance, in cases where the accuracy of a witness statement is questionable. However, he held that in the case of a local inquiry such as the present case no such right existed. Dicta about the right to cross-examine should not be taken out of context. This would be misleading. It depends on the circumstances of the case, the purpose of the hearing, the issue involved and the nature of the evidence.

Another case that dealt with the quality of the right to a hearing was that *of R v Board of Visitors of HM Prison, The Maze, ex p Hone.*[18] The appellant served a life prison sentence in Northern Ireland. He was in breach of the Prison Rules (Northern Ireland) 1982 and charged with an offence against discipline. The Board of Visitors confirmed the charge and the appellant were sentenced to 30 days' confinement to a cell and a loss of privileges for a further 60 days. The appellant filed the case for judicial review arguing that he had been denied the right to legal representation before the board. The House of Lords held that there was no such right except in circumstances where the prisoner is charged with a criminal offence or the equivalent. The House held that the rules of natural justice may give rise to a right to legal representation before the board of visitors, but that this would depend on the circumstances in the particular case.

A variety of exceptions to the right to a hearing exist. DeSmith summarises them as:

"1. Express statutory exclusion of a fair hearing;
2. Where the legislation expressly requires notice and hearing for certain purposes but imposes no procedural requirement for other purposes;
3. Where an obligation to give notice and opportunity to be heard would obstruct the taking of prompt action;

---

17 [1981] AC 75.

18 [1988] 1 AC 379.

4. Where for other reasons it is impracticable to give prior notice or opportunity to be heard;
5. Where a procedurally flawed decision has been followed by an *ex post facto* hearing or by an appeal which complies with the requirements of fairness;
6. Where the decision complained of is only a preliminary to a decision subject to procedural fairness;
7. Where the defect of natural justice has made no difference to the result;
8. Where to require fairness or natural justice would be futile;
9. Where no prejudice has been caused to the applicant".[19]

With regard to no. 5, an "increased willingness" by the courts can be seen to be satisfied with the "curing of defective decisions in the form of a subsequent hearing in an appeal".[20] In *Calvin v Carr*[21] the applicant owned a racehorse which took part in a race organised by the Australian Jockey Club. After the horse had not performed very well a steward's inquiry was held. The inquiry resulted in the decision that the owner of the horse had to be disqualified from the club because he was in breach of the club's racing rules. The owner had not been heard in the original inquiry. He appealed against the decision to a committee of the club which dismissed his appeal. The appellant took further legal action against his disqualification in the Supreme Court of New South Wales. His main argument was that the original inquiry had deprived him of a fair hearing. Consequently, the club had acted in breach of natural justice. The action was dismissed by the court and brought before the Privy Council. The Privy Council dismissed the appeal on the grounds that the breach of natural justice had been cured by the hearing in front of the committee of the club. The court held, though, "that no clear and absolute rule can be laid down on the question whether defects in natural justice appearing at an original hearing, whether administrative or quasi judicial, can be "cured" through appeal proceedings". The reason for the absence of such a rule lies in the diversity of the factual situations of all these cases in which this issue arises. In his speech Lord Wilberforce points to two groups of cases. Cases relating to social clubs, on the one hand, allow the conclusion that the lack of a hearing is cured by a consequent hearing in an appeal.[22] On the other hand, there are cases where the defect in the first hearing cannot be cured by a subsequent hearing as stated by Megarry J in *Leary v National Union of Vehicle Builders*:[23]

"If the rules and the law combine to give the member the right to a fair trial and the right of appeal, why should he be told that he ought to be satisfied with an unjust trial and a fair appeal? As a general rule, I hold that a failure of natural justice in the trial body cannot be cured by a sufficiency of natural justice in an appellate body".

---

19 De Smith, S.A., supra n. 5, 475–504.

20 De Smith, S.A., supra n. 5, 490.

21 [1980] AC 574.

22 As examples, the following cases are stated: *De Verteuil v Knaggs* [1918] AC 557 at 563; *Posluns v Toronto Stock Exchange and Gardiner* (1965) 53 DLR (2d) 193; *Re Clark and Ontario Securities Commission* (1966) 56 DLR (2d) 585; *Re Chromex Nickel Mines Ltd* (1970) 16 DLR (3d) 273.

23 [1971] Ch 34.

Lord Wilberforce agreed that the latter principle might apply in trade union cases, for instance, where appeals might not be impartial enough to carry out hearings as fair as at the first level. However, he argued that "it is for the court ... having regard to the course of proceedings, to decide whether, at the end of the day, there has been a fair result, reached by fair methods, such as the parties should fairly be taken to have accepted when they joined the association". Lord Wilberforce's principles not only apply to sporting bodies, but also to administrative bodies exercising statutory powers.

2. The duty to act fairly

The principle that powers of administrative character which intefer with rights position must be exercised fairly has been revived since the 1960's.[24] The principle is being used in many different situations with different definitions.[25] In the case of *McInnes v Onslow-Fane*[26] it was advanced as a duty to act honestly and without bias. Until today the principle remains relevance. In *R v National Lottery Commission, ex p Camelot Group plc*,[27] the Queen's Bench Division of the High Court decided in October 2000 that the National Lottery Commission acted in breach of its duty to act fairly in the bidding process for the award of the new licence to run the National Lottery. The National Lottery is run by granting a seven-year licence to the company which is most successful in the bidding process. This process is organised by the National Lottery Commission. The licence of the then operator of the National Lottery, Camelot Group plc, was to expire on 30 September 2001 and therefore the Commission set up the bidding process and received two bids, one from Camelot and one from the People's Lottery (TPL). By August 2000, the Commission reached the decision that it had found neither of the two bidders to have met the statutory criteria for granting a licence under the National Lottery Act 1993. However, it decided that it would negotiate exclusively with TPL for one month so that TPL could improve its bid. The case was concerned with the issue of fairness, i.e. whether it was fair to exclude Camelot from any possibility further to allay the Commission's concerns regarding its bid. The court held that the exercise of the powers under the National Lottery Act 1993 was subject to the rules of procedural fairness. The court cited Lord Bridge's decision in *Lloyd v McMahon*[28] in which he held:

> "When a statute has conferred on any body the power to make decisions affecting individuals, the courts will not only require the procedure prescribed by the statute to be followed, but will readily imply so much and no more to be introduced by way of additional procedural safeguards as will ensure the attainment of fairness".

---

24 *Re H.K. (An infant)* [1967] 2 QB 617.

25 Wade, H.W.R., Forsyth, C.F., *Administrative Law*, 8th edition, 2000.

26 [1978] 1 WLR 1520.

27 *The Times*, 12 October 2000.

28 [1987] AC 625.

The court held that "the Commission's decision to negotiate exclusively with TPL was, in all the circumstances, so unfair as to amount to an abuse of power". They further added that the decision not to allow Camelot the same opportunity as TPL was alternatively *Wednesbury* unreasonableness: "... to deny the same opportunity to Camelot fell outside the range of decisions open to a reasonable and properly informed decision maker". The court also made clear that the claimant did not have to show that without the unfairness a different decision would have been reached. Unfairness by itself should be enough. However, the court retains a discretion to refuse a remedy if the unfairness would have made no difference:[29] "it is ... common ground that, at the very least, considerable caution is required before the court concludes that a breach of procedural fairness has not affected the substantive result".[30] The decision in *Camelot* has introduced the new ground of review of fairness which has also inspired the judges in the subsequent decision of *Interbrew SA & another v The Competition Commission & The Secretary for State for Trade and Industry*.[31]

3. The duty to give reasons

English law still does not fully recognise a general duty to give reasons for administrative decision makers. As mentioned in the Tribunal and Inquiries Act 1992, tribunals and ministers are under a duty to give reasons. The absence of a general duty to give reasons in English law has been discussed intensely.[32] There are clear advantages in requiring the authorities to state reasons for their decisions. Amongst these are the elimination of extraneous considerations, the encouragement of a careful examination of the relevant issues, the consistency in decision making and guidance to others on the body's likely decision-making process in the future.[33] The JUSTICE/All Souls Report[34] contained the comment that "no single factor has inhibited the development of English administrative law as seriously as

[29] (2001) *New Law Journal*, 15 June 902.

[30] *R v National Lottery Commission, ex p Camelot plc* [2001] All ER (D) 1205 per Richards J.

[31] [2001] All ER (D) 305.

[32] Richardson, G., "The Duty to Give Reasons: Potential and Practice" (1986) *Public Law* 473; Thomas, R., "Reason-Giving in English and European Community Administrative Law" (1997) *European Public Law* 213; Birkinshaw, P., *Freedom of Information* ,2nd edn, 1996, 287–316; Craig, P. "The Common Law, Reasons and Administrative Justice" (1994) *CLJ*; Fordham, M., "Reasons – the Third Dimension" (1998) *JR* 158; Sir Patrick Neill QC, "The Duty to Give Reasons: The Openness of Decision-Making" in Forsyth and Hare, *The Golden Metwand and the Crooked Cord*, 1998; Andrew Le Sueur, "Taking the Soft Option? The Duty to Give Reasons in the Draft Freedom of Information Bill" (1999) *Public Law* 419; Holt, M., "Revisiting the Justice/All Souls Report" (2000) *Judicial Review* 56.

[33] De Smith S. A., *Judicial Review of Administrative Action*, 1995, 459.

[34] Administrative Justice: Some Necessary Reforms, 1988.

the absence of any general duty to give reasons".[35] However, since the decision in *Padfield v Minister of Agriculture, Fisheries and Food* in 1968 the courts have slowly developed the duty to give reasons. Even if this still does not amount to a general duty to give reasons, the number of cases in which the courts have argued that it would not be fair to deny reasons is increasing. The attitude that fairness requires the giving of reasons is based on the idea that it is important for the parties "to enable [them] to know the issues to which [the court] addressed its mind and that it acted lawfully".[36]

The case of *R v Civil Service Appeal Board, ex p Cunningham* was concerned with the dismissal of a 45-year-old prison officer after he allegedly assaulted a prisoner. He won his appeal to the Civil Service Appeal Board, which then assessed the amount of compensation for unfair dismissal at £6,500. The board did not state the reasons for its decision. The applicant applied for judicial review because the amount was considerably lower than an industrial tribunal would have assessed. The case could not have been heard in front of an industrial tribunal. The House of Lords held that "the board was required to give reasons for the way in which it had reached the award made to the applicant and in the absence of such reasons the award, when compared to awards made by industrial tribunals in comparable circumstances, was so low as to be *prima facie* irrational".

The decision in *Doody v Secretary of State for the Home Department*[37] further developed the duty to give reasons. "It is true to say that the decision in *Doody* may well be influenced by considerations of the ECHR. Nonetheless it is a striking vindication of the duty to give reasons for adverse decisions where necessary as a distinct feature of administrative justice".[38] The applicants were four prisoners who served a mandatory life sentence of imprisonment for murder. The question was whether they were entitled to be given reasons for the recommendation of the Lord Chief Justice and the trial judge to the Home Secretary with regard to the length of the remaining prison sentence. The House of Lords held "that the law does not at present recognise a general duty to give reasons for an administrative decision. Nevertheless, it is equally beyond question that such a duty may in appropriate circumstances be implied ..."[39] The House of Lords therefore stated clearly that a prisoner is entitled not only to know the number of years constituting the penal element of the recommendation, but also the reasons for this decision. The prisoner cannot rationalise his objections to the penal element without knowing how it was rationalised by the judges themselves. These cases fall into the category of cases where the nature of the process itself requires reasons on the basis of fairness. Here, the personal liberty of prisoners was at stake. Rather than establishing a general duty to give reasons in the form of legislation, English law

35 Paragraph 3.119, recalling a comment made by the JUSTICE Committee report of 1971.

36 *R v Civil Service Appeal Board, ex p Cunningham* [1991] 4 All ER 320.

37 [1994] 1 AC 531.

38 Jowell, J. and Birkinshaw, P. in Schwarze, J., *Administrative Law Under European Influence*, 1996, English report.

39 [1994] 1 AC 531 at 564.

prefers a pragmatic style and approaches the issue with the question of whether "the refusal to give reasons was fair".[40]

Another category of cases identified by Sedley J in the case of *Institute of Dental Surgery* are those cases in which there is "something peculiar or aberrant in the decision itself which in fairness calls for reasons to be given".[41] The case concerned an application for judicial review of a decision which rated a dental school lower than expected resulting in a reduction of the funds the school was entitled to receive. The court however held that the applicant was not entitled to be given reasons for the decision because it was of a purely academic nature. This decision has been criticised because it is important to know the reasons for a decision of that nature in order to improve certain areas within the department, be it the quality of the research output or other factors.[42] The Privy Council's decision in *Stefan v GMC*[43] reaffirmed that there is no general duty to give reasons. However, the House of Lords stated that the absence of such a general duty was now the exception rather than the norm. They added that the Human Rights Act 1998 might lead to a review of this area with regard to the compatibility under Art. 6(1) of the Convention.

The establishment of a general duty to give reasons has been recommended by the House of Commons Select Committee on Public Administration in its report on the Freedom of Information Draft Bill.[44] However, the Freedom of Information Act 2000 did not quite follow that route and adopted a so-called soft law option: "it envisages a web of quasi legislation".[45] The Freedom of Information Act 2000 requires every public authority to adopt and maintain a scheme which relates to the publication of information, a so-called publication scheme;[46] further, "in adopting or reviewing a publication scheme, a public authority shall have regard to the public interest – in the publication or reasons for decisions made by the authority".[47] The adoption of such publication schemes has been criticised because it might result in "diversity when certainty and clarity are needed".[48]

---

40 Thomas, R., "Reason-Giving in English and European Community Administrative Law" (1997) *European Public Law* 213 [215].

41 *R v Higher Education Funding Council, ex p Institute of Dental Surgery* [1994] 1 All ER 651.

42 Sir Patrick Neill, "The Duty to Give Reasons" in Forsyth and Hare, *The Golden Metwand and the Crooked Cord*, 1998, 183.

43 [1999] 1 WLR 1293.

44 HC 570, 1998–99, para 50.

45 Le Sueur, A., "Taking the Soft Option? The Duty to Give Reasons in the Draft Freedom of Information Bill" (1999) *Public Law* 419.

46 Clause 19(1)(a).

47 Clause 19(3)(b).

48 Le Sueur, A., supra n. 45, 423.

4. Legal consequences of procedural errors

Despite the fact that the right to a hearing has become an important part of procedural protection, its non-observance does not automatically lead to the invalidity of the decision. As outlined above there are a number of exceptions to the right to a hearing. The consequences of a breach of a statutory right to a hearing will depend on whether the right is directory or mandatory.[49] The courts have dealt with the argument that no prejudice has been caused to the applicant because the flawed decision would inevitably have been the same. It is not for the courts to substitute their opinion for that of the authority constituted by law to decide the matters in question. Further:

"Natural justice is not always or entirely about the facts or substance of fairness. It has also something to do with the appearance of fairness. In the hallowed phrase, "justice must not only be done, it must also be seen to be done". These cases support the view that the fundamental principle at stake is that public confidence in the fairness of adjudication or hearing procedures may be undermined if decisions are allowed to stand despite the absence of what a reasonable observer might regard as an adequate hearing, rather than that injustice lies only in holding an individual bound by a decision whose substantive reliability is cast in doubt by the existence of procedural irregularities".[50]

5. Germany's Law on Administrative Procedure (*Verwaltungsverfahrensgesetz*) 1976

Today the law on administrative procedure is a substantial part of the modern *Rechtsstaat*. However, the codified Law on Administrative Procedure is relatively young. Only since 1976 has it been contained in codified rules of administrative procedure (*Verwaltungsverfahrensgesetz*). They are designed primarily to protect the individual's position in securing and obtaining his or her rights against the authorities and to provide the citizen with access to the procedural safeguards contained in the law and to make the law more transparent.[51] It is important to point out that the main general principles have been developed through case law and academic writing. The codification of these principles, which was mainly designed to unify the laws on administrative procedure which were in operation across Germany, is the culmination of a development which reaches back to the seventeenth century when first attempts to codify the principles of administrative law were made.

The desire to codify some of the principles of good administration can be traced back to Veit Ludwig von Seckendorf who published his *Teutschen Fürsten-Stat* as

49 Cane, P., *An Introduction to Administrative Law*, 1996, 192.

50 De Smith, S.A., *Judicial Review of Administrative Action*, 1995, 500.

51 Schlegelberger, cited in Kopp, *Verfassungsrecht und Verwaltungsverfahrensrecht*, 1971, 264. *The Law on Administrative Procedure and Administrative Court Procedure* is available in paperback for the cost of less than £3 and available in any good bookshop.

early as 1656.[52] He was concerned with the fast and correct exercise of public power and required the legislator to enact proper laws to maintain order. One of the most important public lawyers of the eighteeenth century, Johann Heinrich Gottlob von Justi, published his work *Grundsätze der Policey-Wissenschaft* in 1759.[53] He used the terms "administration" and "police" synonymously and demanded legislation for the administration which would enhance its strength and power. Around 100 years later in 1866, Lorenz von Stein required a codification of administrative laws. However, he was of the view that it was impossible to codify the entire body of administrative law. With the emergence of a constitutional state in the nineteenth century, for the first time requests for simplicity and effectiveness of the administration had to yield to the idea of protecting the individual against unlawful exercise of power through the authorities. This trend to protect the individual against administrative intrusion continued until the time of the Weimar constitution and was rediscovered and strongly emphasised after the Second World War. Accordingly, the *Badische Verfahrensordnung* from 1884[54] and the *Preußische Gesetz über die allgemeine Landesverwaltung* from 1883[55] contained provisions for access to files, evidence and procedures. A landmark in the development of the German Law on Administrative Procedure was the Austrian Federal Law on Administrative Procedure 1925. The Thüringen and Württemberg *Länder* were the first to adopt Acts on Administrative Procedure as early as 1926. Clearly, there is a parallel to the procedures applied in reaching judicial decisions. However, the main problem which the legislator faced in the process of codification of administrative procedures was that the rules of the adjudicative process could not be transferred exclusively to administrative procedures. This was due to the fact that the authority is not a neutral third party, but it is involved in the process of decision making and its decision has direct consequences for its own interests. As a result of these difficulties, the Law on Administrative Procedure contains elements of procedural law as well as purely substantive law. For instance, the concept of the administrative act is contained in the Law on Administrative Procedure (Art. 35).[56] The main aims of the codification have been the unification of the variety of rules applied in different parts of the country (due to its federal structure), the rationalisation of the administration and the *Entlastung* of the legislator by a unified law.[57] The lively discussions in the 1960s in academic writing regarding the process of codification illustrate how difficult it was to reach consensus in these questions. In deciding which issues should be included in a code on administrative procedure, the guiding example was the Administrative Court Procedure Act 1960 and other laws on court procedure. Accordingly, provisions

---

52 Frankfurt/Main, 1656 cited in Schmitt-Lermann, H., "Der Musterentwurf eines Verwaltungsverfahrensgesetzes" (1964) *JZ* 402.
53 Göttingen, 2nd edn, 1759 cited in Schmitt-Lermann, ibid.
54 *GVBl* 385.
55 GS, 192.
56 Badura, P., in Erichsen, H.-U., *Allgemeines Verwaltungsrecht*, 1988, 376.
57 Maurer, H., *Allgemeines Verwaltungsrecht*, 1999, 96.

had to be made, for instance, regarding the parties to a process, fact finding, the right to a hearing and access to files.[58]

6. The right to a hearing

The right to a hearing as contained in the modern Law on Administrative Procedure is a reflection of the general principles of judicial procedures. A constitutional right to a hearing is also contained in the Basic Law as a direct response to the disregard of individual rights during the Third Reich. Accordingly, Art. 103(3) of the Basic Law states: "in the courts everyone shall be entitled to a hearing in accordance with the law". However, Art. 103 only applies to judicial procedures and the right to a hearing in an administrative procedure does not enjoy constitutional status.[59] However, it is accepted generally that the right to a hearing is based on the constitution, whether on Art. 1 and the *Rechtstaatsprinzip* or on the analogous application of Art. 103 is not quite clear.[60]

Article 28 of the Law on Administrative Procedure states:[61]

"The hearing of parties

(1) Before an administrative act may be adopted which interferes with the rights of a party involved, that person must be given the opportunity of expressing his opinion on the facts relevant to the decision.

(2) A hearing need not be given where it is not required by the circumstances of the individual case, in particular where:

1. an immediate decision appears necessary on the grounds of danger if there is a delay or danger to the public interest;
2. a hearing would endanger the observance of a time limit crucial to the decision;
3. it is not intended to depart in any manner, which would be detrimental to a party from the factual statements, which he has made in a petition or a declaration;
4. the authority wishes to adopt a general disposition, large numbers of similar administrative acts, or administrative acts using automatic equipment;
5. measures are to be taken by way of administrative enforcement.

(3) A hearing shall not take place where it would conflict with a compelling public interest".

The right to a hearing is restricted to such cases in which the administrative act interferes with the rights of the party involved. The Federal Administrative Court held that a right to a hearing is only available if the administrative act alters the legal position of the party in a negative way, i.e. reduces or takes away an existing legal status.[62] However, the exact meaning of this statement has been discussed widely. On the one hand, it is argued in legal writing that the right to a hearing only covers those situations in which a genuinely unfavourable decision is made. This does not include the refusal of a benefit. On the other hand, other decisions

---

58 In Schmitt-Lermann, H., supra n. 53, 404.

59 Schwarze, J., *European Administrative Law*, 2006, 1256.

60 Maurer, H., *Allgemeines Verwaltungsrecht*, 1999, para 19 Rn 20.

61 Translation by Schwarze, J., *European Administrative Law*, 2006, 1256 [1257].

62 BVerwGE 66, 184.

such as the refusal of a licence or a benefit require a hearing as well because they are equally burdensome for the applicant.[63]

Further, a variety of exceptions as contained in Art. 28 paras 2 and 3 of the Law on Administrative Procedure apply. In particular, cases of urgency fall under this exception because danger might result from a delay or time limits would elapse. A hearing may also be denied if it contradicts with the public interest, for example, in case of danger to national security. As a result the scope of the right to a hearing is not very broad and the provisions dealing with the curing of defects within the administrative procedure which have been amended in 1996, as will be discussed further below, reduce the relevance of the right to a hearing in German administrative procedure.

7. The duty to give reasons

The duty to give reasons is a significant requirement for the procedural legality of an administrative act.[64] According to Art. 39 of the Law on Administrative Procedure:

"(1) A written administrative act or an act confirmed in writing must contain written reasons. In the reasons important factual and legal grounds, which the authority has taken into consideration in arriving at its decision, have to be communicated. Reasons for discretionary decisions should also exhibit the viewpoints on which the authority has exercised its discretion".

The latter provision regarding discretionary decisions has been criticised for allowing the authorities too much discretion. According to its critics, administrative bodies should be obliged to issue reasons for discretionary decisions, in particular, because the administrative body itself can only name those reasons. The main aim of the duty to give reasons is to enable the authority to assess its own reasoning. The giving of reasons forces the authority to assess the factual and legal requirements of the administrative act carefully. Further, it enables the citizen to review the decision and decide whether or not to appeal against it. Finally, the giving of reasons facilitates the work of the appeal body or the courts in judicial review proceedings because the reasons for the decision are more transparent.[65] The duty to give reasons has to be seen in close connection with the right to a hearing and the constitutional guarantee to access to justice as contained in Art. 19(4) of the Basic Law.[66] Exceptions from the general duty to give reasons are contained in Art. 39 Sect. 2:

"Reasons are not required

1. To the extent the authority conforms to an application or follows a declaration and the administrative act does not affect the rights of a third party.

---

63 Maurer, H., supra n. 60, para 19, Rn 20; Schwarze, supra n. 59, 1259.

64 Schwarze, J., supra n. 59, 1386.

65 Maurer, H., supra n. 60, para 10, 13.

66 Badura, P. in Erichsen, H.-U., *Allgemeines Verwaltungsrecht*, 1988, 418.

2. To the extent the opinion of the authority on the factual or legal position is already known or is easily discernible even without written reasons given to whom the administrative act is addressed or who is affected by it.
3. If the authority takes similar administrative acts in large numbers or with the help of automatic equipment and in the circumstances of the particular case reasons are not expected.
4. If this is contained in a legal provision.
5. If a general order is publicly notified".

8. Legal consequences of procedural errors

Despite the fact that the right to a hearing and the general duty to give reasons are codified provisions and have gained fundamental importance in the administrative procedure, the legal consequences of a lack of an opportunity to be heard or the omission of reasons may not necessarily lead to the illegality of the administrative act. The Law on Administrative Procedure provides for very detailed provisions on how to treat a procedurally flawed decision.

Generally, a procedural flaw in an administrative act may lead to different legal consequences. These legal consequences of procedural errors in the administrative process are governed by Arts. 44 to 46 of the Law on Administrative Procedure. Depending on its nature, a procedural flaw in the administrative process may lead to different legal consequences. An administrative act may either be annulled (Art. 44), its procedural flaws may be cured (Art. 45) or a procedural flaw may be held to be irrelevant (Art. 46). In serious cases as described in Art. 44, the administrative act is null and void:

"Nullity of administrative act
(1) An administrative act is null and void to the extent it suffers from an especially grave defect and the defect is evident on the appreciation of the surrounding circumstances.
(2) Without prejudice to the provisions of clause (1) an administrative act is void
1. If it is expressed in writing but does not disclose the authority that has taken it;
2. If under the law it can only be taken by the delivery of a document but its form is not satisfied;
3. If it is taken by an authority outside its competence as laid down in Sect. 3(1) no. 1 without being authorised to do so;
4. If for factual reasons nobody can perform it;
5. If it requires the commission of an illegal act which creates liability for punishment or a fine;
6. If it violates the principle of good morals.
(3) An administrative act is not void merely because
1. The provisions about territorial competence have not been observed except in case of clause (2) no. 3;
2. A person excluded under Sect. 20(1) nos. 2 to 6 has participated;
3. A committee required by law to participate in the taking of an administrative act has not passed the decision prescribed for the taking of an administrative act or did not have the quorum;
4. Any other authority required by law to participate has failed to do so".

The principle that less serious procedural flaws may be cured at a later stage is contained in Art. 45 Curing of Defects of Procedure and Form:

"(1) Setting aside the cases in which an administrative act is void according to Art. 44, a violation of the provisions relating to form or procedure is inconsequential if:
1. An application required for the taking of an administrative act is made after the act;
2. The required statement of reasons is given after the act was issued;
3. The required hearing to a participant is given after the act was issued;
4. The decision of a committee whose participation in the taking of the administrative act is required has considered it afterwards;
5. The required participation of another authority takes place afterwards".

According to no 2, the lack of reasons for an administrative act may be cured by providing for reasons at a later stage. The lack of a hearing may also be cured by allowing the applicant to be heard after the issue of the act. The crucial question is, however, until what time a procedural error may be cured. Article 45 used to provide for a time limit at the end of the pre-trial procedure.

Article 45(2) (old version):

"Actions under Sect. (1) nos. 2 to 5 may only be taken before the conclusion of the pre-trial procedure (*Vorverfahren*) and in case no such pre-trial procedure takes place before the filing of a suit in an Administrative Court".

However, the reforms of the Law on Administrative Procedure in 1996 now provide for the opportunity to cure procedural errors as late as until the end of the court trial in the final instance.

Article 45(2) (new version):

"Action under Sect. (1) can be taken until the end of a court trial in the final instance".

Accordingly the administration is now permitted to cure a procedurally flawed administrative act which might otherwise be rendered illegal and transform it into a legal one. The purpose of the extended opportunity for the administration to transform illegal acts into legal ones is the ideal of an accelerated court procedure.[67] The extended option of curing of procedural flaws aims to reduce the number of applications for judicial review in the same matter. This occurred in cases where the courts quashed decisions on procedural grounds and the applicants subsequently applied for judicial review in the same matter on different grounds. The main changes therefore concern the timing for the curing of procedural effects. In summarising the above, until 1996, procedural flaws could be remedied by the relevant authority until the end of the administrative proceedings as long as the administration was in charge.[68] According to the new Art. 45 Sect. 2, administrative authorities may now transform an illegal administrative act into a legal one at the end of the administrative court trial in the final instance and reasons for an administrative decision may be given as late as at the court trial stage. This provi-

67 *Deutscher Bundestag*, Drucksache 13/3993 of 6 March 1996, p. 1; 13/1433 of 18 May 1995, p. 1.

68 Hatje, A., "Die Heilung formell rechtswidriger Verwaltungsakte im Prozeß als Mittel der Verfahrensbeschleunigung" (1997) *DÖV* 477.

sion has been controversial as it jeopardises the purpose of reason giving which, *inter alia*, can be described as providing the authority with an opportunity to review its own decision. It may also indicate the authority did not investigate the facts of the case properly.[69]

A similar development has taken place with regard to the curing of flaws in the consideration process in the context of discretionary decisions. The reasons required by Art. 39 should show the considerations which led to the discretionary decision. Until the reforms of 1996 a defect in the consideration process led to the incurable illegality of an administrative act once the court trial had started.[70] However, according to the new Art. 114 sentence 2 of the Law on Administrative Court Procedure[71] considerations for discretionary decisions may now be completed up until the end of the court trial. This new provision is concerned with the curing of a substantive flaw in the consideration process, however, it appears in close connection to the issue of curing of the lack of giving reasons. Lack of reasons as described above is, however, concerned with a procedural flaw. Article 114 deals with decisions for which reasons have been given, however, the reasons are insufficient and are supplemented at the trial stage. The new provision is closely related to the previous jurisprudence of the Federal Administrative Court which has established three criteria subject to which a flawed discretionary decision may be cured in the court proceedings.[72] The principle is based on the consequences flowing from the inquisitorial principle according to which the court has to take into account all evidence that is offered.[73]

However, there are exceptions to the general rule which are as follows: reasons may not be supplemented if they lead to a change in the nature of the decision, if the supplemented reasons change the procedural position of the applicant in the court proceedings and if it concerns a decision to be taken by a collegiate which cannot be reproduced at trial stage.[74] However, a recent decision by the Federal Administrative Court has clarified some of the uncertainties concerning the scope of the supplementation of the considerations. Considerations concerning the exercise of discretionary powers may be supplemented, but not fully exchanged.[75]

In order to enable the administrative authorities to cure procedural flaws within the court proceedings, changes had to be made to the Law on Administrative Courts as well. Accordingly, under Art. 94 sentence 2, the court may now stay the proceedings so that the administrative authority may remedy the procedural flaws. These legislative changes to the *Verwaltungsverfahrensgesetz* illustrate the tendency to minimise the legal consequences that follow from the violation of procedural requirements. This opening of the court proceedings for the purpose of curing defects which occurred within the administrative procedure has been criticised

---

69 Hufen, F., *Verwaltungsprozessrecht*, ,3rd edn, 1998, 448.

70 Article 113(1) Law on Administrative Court Procedure.

71 New version after the 1996 reform.

72 More recently *BVerwGE* 105, 55; (1998) *NJW* 2233.

73 Hufen, F., supra n. 69, 449.

74 Hufen, F., supra n. 69, 450.

75 BVerwGE 106, 351; Schenke R.P., "Das Nachschieben von Ermessenserwägungen – BVerwGE 106" (2000) *JuS* 231 [233].

by the judiciary in particular because it conflicts with the right to a fair trial as it places the authorities in a more favourable position.[76] Secondly, it is argued that the new provisions violate the right to be heard by an unbiased judge as provided for in Art. 97 of the Basic Law. This principle could be violated by the fact that the judge may stay the proceedings so that the authority may have the opportunity to cure the procedural error.

Finally, some procedural errors cannot be cured or simply have not been cured. However, another provision in the Law on Administrative Procedure provides that they may not even require curing if no other decision could have been taken in the matter. Originally, this provision only concerned non-discretionary decisions.

Article 46 (old version):

> "Annulment of an administrative act which is not void according to the provision in Art. 44 cannot be sought if the flaw only relates to either the procedure, the formal aspects or the local administrative competence if no other decision could have been taken in the matter".

Article 46 Consequences of Defects of Procedure and Form (new version):

> "Annulment of an administrative act which is not void according to the provision in Art. 44 cannot be sought if the flaw only relates to either the procedure, the formal aspects or the local administrative competence if it is obvious that the breach had no influence on the decision on its merits".

The reforms in 1996 have not been uncontroversial. It has been argued that the extensive curing of procedural flaws within the court procedure is in stark contrast to the association of the administrative process with the protection of human rights under the Basic Law.[77] However, this might be a contradiction, but the German tradition shows that procedural guarantees are worthless if the decision of the authority is wrong in substance. Most importantly, therefore, is that the decision in itself is correct and does not breach the human rights standards as set out in the Basic Law.[78]

The relevance of procedural errors is therefore decreasing in Germany. This might raise the question in the future whether that part of German administrative procedure law is still in accordance with the Basic Law and European standards. Hatje argues that the new provision amounts to a violation of the constitutional principle of effective judicial protection in Art. 19 IV of the Basic Law.[79] The curing of procedural errors might soon result in a reaction by the European Court of Justice, which will require a duty to give reasons in connection with the indirect administration of Community law.[80] Germany traditionally takes a liberal approach regarding the application of strict procedural rules. This is mainly due to the fact that, as illustrated in the previous chapter, the intensity of judicial review is greater than in English law. The scope of review is restricted to legal norms

---

76 Hatje, A., supra n. 68, 477.

77 Maurer, H., supra n. 60, para 10, 43.

78 Maurer, H., supra n. 60, para 19, 9/10.

79 Hatje, A., supra n. 68, 477, 481.

80 Classen, C.D., *Die Europäisierung der Verwaltungsgerichtsbarkeit,* 1995, 174 who refers to EuGH, Slg. 1987, 4097 [4117], Rs 222/86 – Heylens.

which create subjective rights for the individual (Art. 113(1) and (5) Law on Administrative Court Procedure). Consequently procedural errors do not automatically give rise to a claim. The administrative procedure only has a serving function and therefore the main emphasis is on the substantial decision.[81] The emphasis on substantive review in Germany is deeply rooted in German legal tradition and expressed in the inquisitorial procedure applied by the Administrative Courts.

9. Evaluation

Both administrative law systems recognise the right to a fair hearing. The provisions on administrative procedure play an important role in safeguarding individual protection. Therefore the emphasis is laid on the subjective legal protection of the citizen against administrative action. In contrast, the French and Italian administrative legal systems emphasise a more objective purpose of procedural safeguards with a variety of provisions dealing with the consultation of other authorities or organs in the administrative decision-making process.[82] Both in England and Germany, the rules on procedure for administrative decision making have been modelled on the court procedures which had been operating before the emergence of administrative law procedures. This historical development of administrative procedure as a reflection of the principles of the court procedure in each country explains the different approaches. The comparison shows that both systems have developed the right to a hearing. In England, it is contained in the rules of natural justice which originated in the seventeenth century and which have undergone phases of revival and decline and which, since the 1960s, constitute an important part of administrative justice in England. In Germany, the right to a hearing does not have quite as far-reaching historical roots, but has been clearly formulated by the German Administrative Courts during the Weimar Republic and have been revived after the Second World War. With the codification of the Law on Administrative Procedure in 1976, it has found statutory recognition in the general principles of administrative law procedure as well as in special statutes.

In both legal systems the denial of a right to a hearing constitutes a ground for review. Both systems contain a variety of exceptions to the right to a hearing in the form of case law or as codified exceptions contained in Art. 28 of the Law on Administrative Procedure. Further, the notion that defective decisions can be cured in subsequent appeal procedures is equally an issue in English decisions and it is a codified and recently modernised principle in German law. The national reports have shown that English judges are increasingly "willing to accept that an appeal has "cured" a defective decision".[83] Further, the case of *Cheall v Association of Professional, Executive, Clerical and Computer Staff*[84] illustrates that in

[81] Ibid 122.

[82] Schmidt-Assmann, E., "Das Verwaltungsverfahren und seine Folgen" (1993) *European Review of Public Law* 99.

[83] De Smith, S.A., *Judicial Review of Administrative Action*, 1995, 490.

[84] [1983] QB 126.

cases where the decision maker exercises no discretion, the defect in the decision, i.e. the denial of a hearing, may be irrelevant if it has made no difference to the result. However, English courts are not as rigorous as German courts in applying these principles.

The German Code of Administrative Procedure, ironically, displays an increasing devaluation of procedural guarantees within the administrative procedures. The right to a hearing and the duty to give reasons are still important features of the decision-making process. However, flawed decisions can now be cured up until the end of judicial review proceedings. Therefore, in Germany, court proceedings often replace the administrative decision-making process. Administrative judges are bound to proceed according to the inquisitorial principle. Accordingly, the judge is under a duty to undertake investigations in his own right and his investigation is not limited to submissions by the parties. The judge can allow the authorities a period of up to three months to cure defects in its decision-making process. This approach reflects an attitude which is at the cost of a strong position of the public authorities. This is due to the fact that German courts insist that there is only one correct application of the law which is expressed by the inquisitorial procedure applied by the Administrative Courts and leads to a far more searching substantive review of the case. In particular in cases where the authorities had no discretion, the German courts apply the rule that a procedural defect will have no consequences "if no other decision could have been taken in the matter".[85] This rule has now also been extended to discretionary decisions in the reformed version of Art. 46.

In English law, the right to a hearing as part of the rules to natural justice is "in essence a skeletal version of the elaborate rules of judicial procedure to be found in their fullest form in the Rules of the Supreme Court".[86] Accordingly, the adversarial system is concerned with allowing the parties to present their case and their "version of the truth and leave it to an impartial third party to decide which version more nearly approximates to the truth".[87] As a consequence under the adversarial procedure, the issue of fact finding is a matter for the parties. The English tradition of adversarial adjudication is described well by Pollock and Maitland:

"The behaviour, which is expected of a judge in different ages and by different systems of law, seems to fluctuate between two poles. At one of these the model is the conduct of the man of science who is making researches in his laboratory and will use all appropriate methods for the solution of problems and the discovery of the truth. At the other stands the umpire of our English games who is there not in order that he may invent tests for the powers of the two sides, but merely to see that the rules of the game are observed. It is towards the second of these ideals that our English medieval procedure is strongly inclined. We are

85 Article 46 Law on Administrative Procedure; see Nolte, G., "General Principles of German and European Administrative Law – A Comparison in Historical Perspective" (1994) *Modern Law Review* 191.

86 Cane, P., *An Introduction to Administrative Law*, 1996, 163.

87 Ibid.

so often reminded of the cricket match. The judges sit in court not in order that they may discover the truth, but in order that they may answer the question "how's that?""[88]

II. Comparative cases

1. The right to a hearing

a) Legal effects of denial of a hearing in English courts

English courts are equally concerned with the question of how likely is it that a hearing would have changed the final outcome of a case. It is submitted as:

"Any remedy would be pointless because it would not benefit the applicant who has already received all that he would obtain by way of relief, the applicant has not suffered any real prejudice, the decision would have been no different if the decision maker had followed the precepts of natural justice".[89]

However, this type of question takes the courts beyond the question of whether a decision was taken in a procedurally proper manner. It touches upon issues of substance and the courts have not dealt with that question as easily as the German courts: "where, *ex hypothesis*, the adjudicatory body has failed to observe natural justice, its protestations that a hearing would have made no difference must in principle be viewed with scepticism".[90]

The court decision on this issue reveals three types of answers to the question of whether a hearing would have made a difference to the outcome of a case. First, the courts have denied the existence of the principle of *audi alteram partem* or fairness altogether if they found it unlikely that a hearing would have made a difference as in *Cinnamond v British Airports Authority*.[91] This case was concerned with six car hire drivers who were refused entry to Heathrow airport. They all had offended the byelaws for loitering and offering services to passengers and had not paid the fees which were imposed upon them. The authority had failed to give them an opportunity to be heard before giving them notice of the prohibition order. Lord Denning held that because of their misconduct they had no legitimate expectation to a hearing. Brandon LJ held that "... it seems to me that no prejudice was suffered by the minicab drivers as a result of not being given that opportunity". Lord Denning's speech suggests that they had no right to a hearing because they had no legitimate expectation, whereas Brandon LJ's speech reveals a slightly different position. He expresses the argument that a hearing would have not made a difference to the plaintiff's position: "... no one can complain of not

88 Pollock, F. and Maitland, F.W., *The History of English Law Before the Time of Edward I*, 1898, 670–671 cited in Allison, J.W.F., *A Continental Distinction in the Common Law, A Historical and Comparative Perspective on English Public Law*, 2000, 216.

89 De Smith, S.A., *Judicial Review of Administrative Action*, 1995, 498.

90 Bailey, Jones & Mowbray, *Cases and Materials on Administrative Law*, 1997, 441.

91 [1980] 1 WLR 582.

being given an opportunity to make representations if such an opportunity would have availed him of nothing".

Secondly, the courts have exercised their discretion in awarding a remedy when they considered it unlikely that the hearing would have made a difference. In *Glynn v Keele University*[92] the Vice-Chancellor of the University of Keele took disciplinary action against the plaintiff who had sunbathed naked on the university campus. He imposed a fine on the student and excluded him from residence in any university-owned accommodation on campus for the whole of the academic year 1970/71. The plaintiff was not granted a hearing before this decision was reached. The plaintiff does not dispute the fact that he had taken part in the incident, but sought an injunction against the university. The court held that the Vice-Chancellor had acted in a quasi judicial function and had therefore been in breach of the rules of natural justice when denying the plaintiff a right to a hearing. However, the court decided to exercise its discretion by not granting an injunction. The judge considered the situation if a hearing would have been afforded to the plaintiff:

"So the position would have been that if the Vice-Chancellor had accorded him a hearing before making his decision, all that he, or anyone on his behalf, could have done would have been to put forward some general plea by way of mitigation. I do not disregard the importance of such a plea in an appropriate case, but I do not think the mere fact that he was deprived of throwing himself on the mercy of the Vice-Chancellor in that particular way is sufficient to justify setting aside a decision which was intrinsically a perfectly proper one".

Thirdly, in some cases the courts have interpreted the concept of fairness to answer the question whether the decision was fair and reasonable as indirectly stated in *Chief Constable of North Wales Police v Evans*.[93] This case was concerned with an order by the Chief Constable of North Wales Police which required the plaintiff to resign or be dismissed. Inaccurate rumours concerning the private life of Constable Evans led to this order. However, Constable Evans was not explained the background of that decision and was not given the opportunity of a fair hearing. In his speech, Lord Bridge of Harwich agreed that there had been a breach of natural justice. However, he clearly dissented from the findings of the Court of Appeal which stated that:

"Not only must [the probationer constable] be given a fair hearing, but the decision itself must be fair and reasonable. If that statement of the law passed into authority without comment, it would in my opinion transform, and wrongly transform, the remedy of judicial review. Judicial review, as the words imply, is not an appeal from a decision, but a review of the manner in which the decision was made".[94]

Lord Hailsham of St Marylebome LC held that "it is not intended to take away from those authorities the powers and discretions properly vested in them by law

---

92 [1971] 1 WLR 487.

93 [1982] 1 WLR 1155.

94 Ibid at 1160–1161, 1174–1175.

and to substitute the courts as the bodies making the decisions. It is intended to see that the relevant authorities use their powers in a proper manner".

b) Legal effects of denial of a hearing - Germany

This case concerns the application of Art. 46 of the Law on Administrative Procedure according to which a procedural error may be regarded as irrelevant.

In 1984 a powerstation known as *Buschhaus II* in northern Germany received permission to commence its operation. The planning process regarding this powerstation had started in 1978 when a local public inquiry was held. In *Buschhaus II (Powerstation)*[95] the plaintiffs, a one-year-old child and its father who lived nearby, appealed against the permission for the powerstation to go into operation. They submitted, *inter alia*, that they were not allowed a hearing before the powerstation was granted permission to operate. The law governing the running of powerstations is the *Bundesimmissionsschutzgesetz* (Federal Protection Law Against Emissions). According to Sect. 10 para 1 sentence 2 of this law, the authorities were under a duty to enable the general public to inspect the plans as early as 1978. Accordingly, the public should have had the opportunity to inspect the plans during normal office hours. However, the planning authority failed to comply with this requirement because the plans were only accessible for inspection at restricted times. Because of this procedural error the *Bundesimmissionsschutzgesetz* provided for another hearing before the powerstation would commence its operations in 1984. However, the public was denied the right to a hearing. The plans revealed that any emission was minimal and that no danger to health would be made. The court held that the initial inquiry was procedurally flawed because access to the plans was restricted to short periods during the week. It further held that the denial of a right to a hearing before the start of operation of the powerstation was a second procedural defect in the planning process. Nevertheless, the court held that a hearing would have made no difference to the decision on its merits. According to Art. 46 of the Law on Administrative Procedure, the annulment of an administrative act which is not void according to the provision in Art. 44 cannot be sought if the flaw only relates to either the procedure, its formal aspects or local administrative competence if it is obvious that the breach had no influence on the decision on its merits. The court held that the right to a hearing is important because the running of a powerstation encroaches upon the basic rights of the applicants. However, procedural rights of that kind are only complementing the protection of basic rights. Procedural safeguards, however, become meaningless if a violation of substantive basic rights is clearly not the case. The court further held that the authorities could have made no other decision because they had no discretion in deciding whether to grant permission for the powerstation to operate.

---

95 BverwG, *DVBl* 1983, 271.

c) Evaluation

The cases have illustrated that, like German courts, English courts too are sometimes concerned with the question which effect a defect in the procedure has for the outcome of a case. However, unlike the German courts, they refuse to concern themselves with matters of substance. The English approach is a careful disguise for answering a question which is too concerned with issues of substance and which might amount to a second guessing of the original decision. As illustrated, they either deny the applicability of the rules of natural justice or exercise their discretionary powers to refuse a remedy. As a result, English courts reach similar decisions with different means. It is, however, not always clear how the courts identify the cases in which they refuse relief.[96]

2. The duty to give reasons

a) Deficient reasons made good in course of proceedings - England

The following case illustrates well that English courts take procedural requirements quite seriously. As discussed above, no general duty to give reasons exists in common law. However, statutes may require that decision makers explicitly state reasons for their decisions. Section 64 of the Housing Act 1985 requires that reasons should be given at the same time as the decision is communicated. In *R v Westminster City Council, ex p Ermakov*[97] the applicant, a national of the Republic of Uzbekistan, applied to the respondent council to provide housing for himself and his family on the ground that they were homeless. The applicant's statement contained detailed information for their wish to live in the UK after their relatives had made their lives in Greece, where they last resided in their own house, unbearable by persecuting them and threatening their lives. Subject to its powers under the Housing Act 1985, the local council had to ascertain whether the applicant had become homeless intentionally. Further, the local council was under a statutory duty to provide reasons for a decision made in this matter. However, the council was not successful in gaining information about the applicant's situation in Greece as it did not receive any reply to its letters to those in Greece who could corroborate the applicant's statement. The council then decided that the applicant had become homeless intentionally and notified him of his reasons. The reasons given were that the council was not satisfied that the applicant had experienced harassment and that it was therefore reasonable for him and his family to remain in Greece. The applicant sought judicial review on the grounds that the council had failed to carry out proper inquiries, that it wrongfully assumed that the lack of response meant that the homelessness was caused intentionally, that the applicant had not been formally heard and that the council failed to assess whether the applicant suffered from harassment. The heart of the problem in this case was the fact that the council's employee who was in charge at the time swore an affidavit

---

96 De Smith, S.A., *Judicial Review of Administrative Action*, 1995, 499.
97 Ibid.

which contained the true reasons for his decision: Accordingly, he had turned down the applicant because he accepted the applicant's statement to be true, but nevertheless decided that it would have been reasonable for him and his family to continue to occupy the accommodation in Greece.

The Court of Appeal decided that it would in appropriate cases admit evidence to "elucidate or exceptionally correct or add to the reasons given by a housing authority", but that "it would be very cautious about doing so".[98] The case shows how serious the court is about the fulfilment of the statutory requirement of the duty to give reasons. It is of the opinion that admitting the affidavit containing in its view wholly different reasons "nullifies the very objects and advantages underlying the requirement to provide reasons".[99] The court referred to authoritative case law such as *R v Croydon London Borough, ex p Graham*[100] and reached the conclusion that insufficient reasons lead to the unlawfulness of the decision and that the court should be "circumspect about allowing material gaps to be filled by affidavit evidence".

The introduction of the true reasons was also turned down "for good policy reasons". The court held that "to permit wholesale amendment or reversal of the stated reasons is inimical to the purpose of reasons giving [i.e. the information of parties why they have won or lost]", it further "encourages a sloppy approach by the decision maker" and "gives rise to potential practical difficulties". Concerning the latter point, the court referred to the problem of applications for cross-examination and discovery, "both of which are, while permissible in judicial review proceedings, generally regarded as inappropriate".[101]

b) Deficient reasons made good in course of proceedings - Germany

The *Extradition* case (BverwGE *NVwZ* 1999, 425) is very important because, for the first time, the Federal Administrative Court dealt with the new provision in Art. 114 sentence 2 of the Law on Administrative Procedure which provides an opportunity for an administrative authority to amend its considerations in a discretionary decision as late as during the court proceedings.

The applicant was an asylum seeker of Kurdish origin. Between 1992 and 1994 he committed several crimes in Germany in connection with activities in support of the PKK. In 1994 the authorities ordered him to leave the country. In exercising its discretion, the authority failed to consider the exception in Art. 55 of the Law on Asylum (*Ausländergesetz*). Accordingly, an alien subject may remain in the country if there are factual or legal reasons which make the order to leave the country impossible. Nevertheless, the authority supplemented its considerations in the Administrative Court proceedings and came to the same conclusion. The court held that according to Art. 114 of the Law on Administrative Procedure the court may complete its reasoning until the end of the court trial. It emphasised that the

98 *R v Westminster City Council, ex p Ermakov* [1996] 2 All ER 302.

99 Ibid at 310.

100 (1993) 26 HLR 286.

101 *R v Westminster City Council, ex p Ermakov* [1996] 2 All ER 316 (3).

provision confirms what had been accepted in the jurisprudence of the Federal Administrative Court for many years. Accordingly, the reasons may be supplemented if the delayed reasons existed at the time of the decision, the decision has not changed in its nature and if the applicant's procedural position is not affected.[102] The court made clear that Art. 114 merely permits the supplementation of the reasons and not a complete change of reasons. In this case the court held that the authority was permitted to supplement its decision, however, that the decision reached was unlawful because the applicant had a right to remain in the country according to the exceptions stated in Art. 55 of the Law on Asylum.

c) Evaluation

The cases illustrate well that both jurisdictions might have come to the same result in the case of *Ermakov*. Even though German law is more accepting of the idea that flaws in the reasoning process may be cured within the court process, there are limitations to this approach. Nevertheless, the starting positions are different. In Germany, a lack of a discretionary decision in the consideration process, which is displayed in the provided reasons, may be cured as late as at trial. The latest reforms of the Law on Administrative Court Procedure have incorporated this jurisprudence of the highest Administrative Court into Art. 114 sentence 2 allowing the curing of defects in the reasoning of discretionary decisions until the end of the judicial review trial. The arguments brought forward for this approach emphasise the inquisitorial role of the court in considering all factual and legal issues underlying the decision and this may include the assessment of additional reasons given by the authority. The general rule that deficient reasons may be cured, however, is subject to restrictions. Accordingly, considerations may not be completely exchanged. Therefore, even the German courts might have reached the conclusion in the case of *Ermakov* that the delayed reasons could not have been brought into the proceedings.

The English case has shown that there is no general principle which allows the curing of procedural flaws such as deficient reason giving. However, there is case law mentioned which equally allows the delayed giving of reasons in court if no reasons had been given at all.[103] Secondly, the courts are cautious to permit evidence which may elucidate or correct or add to the reasons in cases where there is a statutory duty to give reasons. Further, a statement of principle was cited that "the idea that material gaps in the reasons can always be supplemented *ex post facto* by affidavit or otherwise ought not to be encouraged". The court in *Ermakov* rejected the argument that the correction of the reasons was a merely technical matter. Therefore it appears that in English law the completion of reasons is only permitted in limited circumstances, whereas the position in Germany is marked by an approach which generally permits the curing of deficient reasoning safe under particular circumstances. The caution exercised by the English courts can be explained by the will to fulfil Parliament's intention which is reflected in the Hous-

[102] BVerwGE 3 C47.81 – Buchholz 418.02 Tierärzte Nr 2.

[103] *R v Swansea City Council, ex p John* (1982) 9 HLR 55.

ing Act. Section 64 requires a decision and at the same time reasons. Highly interesting are the policy arguments advanced by the English court which have equally been raised by critics of the new German provisions, i.e. that allowing delayed reasons runs counter to the purpose of reason giving and leads to a sloppy approach by decision makers.[104] German critics even fear an increased case load in the Administrative Courts because of an increase in badly prepared decisions.[105] The final argument that hearings would be made longer and more expensive has also been raised by critics of the German provisions. Nevertheless, arguments in favour of the new provision have been based on the duty of the court under the inquisitorial procedure to take into account this type of evidence, whereas in the English courts the admission of affidavit evidence is a matter for the judge's discretion.

In conclusion, the position taken by the English courts favours a stronger role to be played for administrative authorities: The court held that the authority should not just be left with the mechanical or formal function to perform; rather it should reconsider the decision properly. In Germany, on the other hand, administrative decisions are increasingly shifted to the Administrative Courts. Whether this will lead to an acceleration of court proceedings as intended by the new legislation is more than doubtful.

III. European influences

1. English administrative law and Art. 6(1) of the European Convention on Human Rights

The discussion above has been concerned with the protection of procedural rights at common law. However, the Human Rights Act 1998 has brought home the dimension of the protection of rights under the European Convention on Human Rights. English courts are now under a duty to interpret legislation in the light of Convention rights. According to Sect. 2 of the Human Rights Act, national courts must take into account the jurisprudence of the institutions in Strasbourg, even though they are not bound by it. Amongst these is the case law on Art. 6(1) of the Convention.

Article 6 of the European Convention on Human Rights guarantees the right to the fair administration of justice. It is a broad article and has many facets. English law has been influenced by its guarantees and its impact on English law has been described as "revolutionary".[106] Some of its ramifications on the position of the

104 Bonk H.J., "Strukturelle Änderungen des Verwaltungsverfahrens durch das Genehmigungsverfahrens-Beschleunigungsgesetz" (1997) *NVwZ* 324.

105 Goller, B., Schmid, A., "Reform of the German Administrative Courts Act" (1998) *European Public Law* 31 [36].

106 Satvinder Singh Juss, "Constitutionalising Rights without a Constitution: The British Experience under Art. 6 of the Human Rights Act 1998", 27 *Statute Law Review* 29 [60].

Lord Chancellor have been discussed in Chapter Two. Some famous case law on restricted access to the courts will be discussed in Chapter Five. In the following section, the independence from the executive to ensure a fair decision-making process and access to legal assistance in English courts will be addressed.

Article 6(1) of the European Convention on Human Rights was at stake in the recent case of *R v Secretary of State for the Environment, Transport and the Regions, ex p Alconbury Developments Ltd.*[107] In this case the Divisional Court had held that where the Secretary of State calls in a planning application for his own determination, if he decides a planning appeal himself or if he confirms his own highway or compulsory purchase order, a breach of Art. 6(1) of the European Convention on Human Rights occurs. The complaint was based on the fact that the Secretary of State in that function did not act as an independent and impartial tribunal. Accordingly, the Divisional Court granted a declaration of incompatibility under Sect. 4 of the Human Rights Act 1998. However, the House of Lords reversed the decision and held that the availability of judicial review was sufficient to comply with Art. 6(1) of the Convention. The main question in *Alconbury* was whether the Secretary of State's power to appoint planning inspectors and judge cases himself is inconsistent with the concept of an independent tribunal as specified in Art. 6(1) of the European Convention on Human Rights. The Queen's Bench Division was of the view that it was not. The next issue was whether the inherent supervisory jurisdiction of the UK's superior courts was sufficient to satisfy the provisions of Art. 6(1) and therefore able to "save the process". The procedural protections granted by Art. 6(1) do not have to apply at every stage in the decision-making process, but must be present at the final stage. In *Albert v Belgium* the European Court of Human Rights had held that:

"The Convention calls for one of the following two systems: either the jurisdictional organs themselves comply with the requirements of Art. 6(1) or they do not so comply, but are subject to control by a judicial body which has full jurisdiction and does provide the guarantees of Art. 6(1)".[108]

The Queen's Bench Division was of the view that judicial review was too restricted to procedural issues that they were not enough to "save" the process. Surprisingly, the House of Lords did not agree. The House of Lords' decision interpreted the European jurisprudence on Art. 6 and judicial review as drawing a line between decisions of policy and decisions of a quasi judicial nature. In the former, no full jurisdiction was required. Lord Hoffmann held that:

"There is nothing to suggest that, in finding the primary facts and in drawing conclusions and inferences from those facts, an inspector acts anything other than independently, in the sense that he is in no sense connected with the parties to the dispute or subject to their influence or control; his findings and conclusions are based exclusively on the evidence and submissions before him."

The House of Lords agreed that in matters of policy the Secretary of State was not independent, but that he did not have to be. He clarified that judges should not interfer with matters of policy: "the 1998 Act was no doubt intended to strengthen

[107] [2001] UKHL 23

[108] *Albert v Belgium* (1983) 5 EHRR 533 at 542.

terfer with matters of policy: "the 1998 Act was no doubt intended to strengthen the rule of law, but not to inaugurate the rule of lawyers".

One could argue that this decision was a politically expedient one as a declaration of incompatibility would have had massive consequences on the entire planning law system. Nevertheless, the House of Lords' decision marks a more subtle development in human rights jurisprudence. *Alconbury* illustrates the view of the House of Lords as to the scope of the existing principles of judicial review. Lord Nolan held that judicial review could include the review of questions of fact. Lord Slynn's view on the application of the principle of proportionality was:

> "I consider that even without reference to the Human Rights Act the time has come to recognise that this principle [of proportionality] is part of English administrative law, not only when judges are dealing with Community acts but also when they are dealing with acts subject to domestic law. Trying to keep the *Wednesbury* principle and proportionality in separate compartments seems to me to be unnecessary and confusing".

In the case of *Runa Begum v Tower Hamlets London Borough Council*[109] the House of Lords expanded its reasoning in *Alconbury* to a situation in which the fact-finding process, rather that the decision of policy matters, was at stake. Accordingly, it was held that judicial review would be sufficient to comply with the requirements under Art. 6 of the Convention. The European Court of Human Rights has not ruled on this issue yet.[110]

In *Steel and Morris v UK*[111] the Strasbourg court held that because of the complexity of the case the applicants should have been afforded Legal Aid in order to ensure a fair trial. This case, better known as the *McLibel* case, concerned a libel action by McDonalds against two campaigners. Matters which raise issues of a procedural nature in England may well be treated as questions of substantive constitutional relevance in Germany. Here, a case concerned with the denial of Legal Aid by a lower court in accordance with previous jurisprudence was recently decided by the Federal Constitutional Court.[112] Interestingly, the constitutional claim was not based on due process rights, but on the right to equal treatment enshrined in Art. 3 I and the *Rechtsstaat* principle in Art. 20 III of the Basic Law. The case was concerned with the Legal Aid application of two asylum seekers which had been denied by the Administrative Court on the basis that the claim would have little prospect of success. However, the Federal Constitutional Court ruled that the legal question at stake was complex and that therefore the applicants had a right to clarification by the higher court. However, compared to a claimant in a better financial position, they would be at a disadvantage if Legal Aid was not granted. This in the court's view amounted to a violation of the right to equality and the principle of the *Rechtsstaat*.

---

109 [2003] UKHL 5.

110 Cooper, J., "Procedural Due Process, Human Rights and the Added Value of the Right to a Fair Trial" (2006) *Judicial Review* 78 [88].

111 (2005) 41 EHRR 22.

112 2 BvR 626/06, 14 June 2006.

2. German administrative law and Art. 6(1) of the European Convention on Human Rights

The procedures available in the European Court of Human Rights have comparatively little importance in Germany. Germany does not have to defend itself as much as for instance the United Kingdom because human rights are enforced by way of proceedings in the *Bundesverfassungsgericht.* The European Court of Human Rights is only the competent court if national procedures, including those of the *Bundesverfassungsgericht,* are exhausted. Having said that, however, in case these national procedures are not sufficient because, in particular, of their length, recourse to the European Court of Human Rights is open.[113] Article 6(1) of the Convention has therefore been continuously invoked against the Federal Republic of Germany. There are no cases in the field of tortious liability in which the court has ruled that Germany was in violation of Art. 6(1). However, both in civil and administrative law matters, German courts have been held liable for a violation of Art. 6(1) of the ECHR.

In *König v Federal Republic of Germany*[114] Germany was sentenced for the first time for overlong proceedings before an Administrative Court. The applicant was Dr Eberhard König, a German doctor. In 1967 his authorisation to run a clinic was withdrawn at the request of the Regional Medical Society. It was alleged that he was unreliable regarding the management of the clinic and that he lacked the diligence and knowledge to run a clinic. On 9 November 1967 König appealed against the decision of the authorities to reject his objection. The Frankfurt Administrative Court dismissed the appeal ten years later on 22 June 1977. At the date of the judgment of the European Court of Human Rights in 1978, the Hessen Administrative Court of Appeal had not yet ruled on the appeal from the Frankfurt Administrative Court. In addition König's authorisation to practice was withdrawn on 12 May 1971 because König was held to be unfit to practice medicine. In 1978 the Hessen Administrative Court of Appeal dismissed the appeal which had been lodged against the judgment of the Frankfurt Administrative Court in 1971 (seven years later). In his application lodged with the Commission on 3 July 1973 Dr König claimed that the length of the proceedings before the Frankfurt court had exceeded the "reasonable time" referred to in Art. 6(1) of the Convention. The European Court of Human Rights found that the length of the proceedings was due to the conduct of the court and not a result of Dr König's behaviour. As a result it held that in both cases the "reasonable time" had been exceeded and that this violated Art. 6(1) of the Convention.[115]

This groundbreaking decision extended the procedural protection of Art. 6(1). Accordingly everyone is entitled to a fair hearing "in the determination of his civil rights and obligations" to the jurisdiction of Administrative Courts in Germany. Not least as a result of this judgment, reforms regarding the acceleration of Administrative Court proceedings were initiated.

---

113 Ossenbühl, F., *Staatshaftungsrecht*, 1998, 529.

114 (1998) 5 BHRC 293.

115 Vincent Berger, *Case Law of the ECHR*, 1991, 96.

3. The European Court of Justice and German administrative procedure law

It is doubtful whether the developments in German administrative law regarding the reduction of legal consequences of procedural errors is going to be compatible with European standards when it comes to the indirect administration of European Community law.[116] The radical rectification of procedural errors has been described as in contrast to the standards set up by the European Court of Justice.[117] So far no direct conflict between the case law of the European Court of Justice and the German Administrative Courts on the issue of procedural errors and their legal treatment exists. However, it is only a question of time until a case will be decided applying the reformed rules on procedural errors in the context of indirect administration of European law. In particular those areas of European law, such as the law on the environment, which have added an increasing body of procedural safeguards to existing national law will serve as potential battlefields between Germany's relaxed attitude towards procedural irregularities and the European principle of effective judicial protection of individuals. The Act on the Implementation of Council Directive of 27 June 1985 on the Assessment of the Effects of Certain Public and Private Projects on the Environment (85/337/EEC), the Environmental Impact Assessment Act (*Gesetz über die Umweltverträglichkeitsprüfung*[118]), serves the purpose of ensuring that for a variety of projects, among them power-stations, refineries and shipyards to name just a few, effective preventative environmental protection is guaranteed on the basis of uniform principles. The so-called environmental impact assessment represents an integral part of procedures applied by the authorities when deciding upon the approval of projects. An important feature of the environmental assessment is the involvement of the public.[119] However, according to the case law of the *Bundesverwaltungsgericht* procedural errors are only relevant if the correct application of the procedure would have made a difference to the decision on its merits or if it was possible that the decision would have been a different one had the error not occurred. Therefore it has been questioned whether the German provisions on curing procedural errors can only be applied restrictively on procedural provisions in a Community law context such as the Environmental Impact Assessment Act. The European Court of Justice has made it clear that the application of national procedural law should not render it practically impossible to carry out the obligations of Community law provisions. It is therefore important to examine the position of the European Court of Justice itself with regard to the consequences of procedural irregularities.

---

116 Hufen, F., *Fehler im Verwaltungsverfahren*, 1998, 360.

117 Hatje, A., "Die Heilung formell rechtswidriger Verwlatungsakte" (1997) *DÖV* 477 [480]; Classen, C. D., *Die Europäisierung der Verwaltungsgerichtsbarkeit*, 1995, 174.

118 12 February 1990, *Bundesgesetzblatt* 1990 I p. 205, as last amended 17 December 1993, *Bundesgesetzblatt* 1993 I p. 2734.

119 Article 2 Sect. 1 of the Act.

In the case of *UNECTEF v Georges Heylens and others*[120] the European Court of Justice illustrated the importance of reason giving for the protection of fundamental freedoms. Georges Heylens was a Belgian football trainer with qualifications subject to Belgian law. He was employed as a football trainer of a French team in Lille. The French Ministry of Sport refused to recognise his trainer's diploma as being equivalent to the French diploma. The Ministry of Sport did not give any reasons for the refusal. The European Court of Justice held that:

"Where in a member state access to an occupation as an employed person is dependent upon the possession of a national diploma or a foreign diploma recognised as equivalent thereto, the principle of the free movement of workers laid down in Art. 48 of the Treaty requires that it must be possible for a decision refusing to recognise the equivalence of a diploma granted to a worker who is a national of another member state by the member state to be made the subject of judicial proceedings in which its legality under Community law can be reviewed, and for the person concerned to ascertain the reasons for the decision".

The case of *Heylens* has been mentioned by German commentators who criticise the recent reforms of the Law on Administrative Procedure and Law on Administrative Court Procedure. Hufen doubts that procedural errors in the context of implemented secondary EC legislation may be considered as irrelevant subject to the new Art. 46 of the Law on Administrative Procedure.[121] Hatje emphasises the importance of the duty to give reasons as a general principle of European law.[122] The European Court of Justice has frequently stated that errors in procedures which are required under Community law are always relevant. In the case of *British Aerospace plc and Rover Group Holdings plc v Commission*[123] it was decided that a decision by which the Commission finds that aid granted by a member state to an undertaking is illegal because it was in breach of a previous decision authorising aid to the same undertaking subject to certain conditions and by which it orders reimbursement of the aid must be annulled where it has been adopted without the procedure laid down by Art. 93(2) second subparagraph being followed. The omitted procedure would have given the parties concerned the opportunity to submit their comments. The court did not allow the curing of this omission within the court procedures, but annulled the decision. With regard to the German legislation allowing the curing of procedural defects in the court procedures, the jurisprudence of the European Court of Justice sets boundaries which will have to complied with.[124]

In case C-353/01 P, Mr Mattila brought an appeal under Art. 49 of the EC Statute of the Court of Justice against the judgment of the Court of First Instance of 12

[120] Case 222/86.

[121] Hufen, F., *Fehler im Verwaltungsverfahren*, 1998, 360.

[122] Hatje, A., "Die Heilung formell rechtswidriger Verwaltungsakte im Prozess als Mittel der Verfahrensbeschleunigung" (1997) *DÖV* 477 [484].

[123] Case C-294/90, European Court reports 1992 p. I-00493.

[124] Classen, D., "Strukturunterschiede zwischen deutschem und europäischem Verwaltungsrecht, Konflikt oder Bereicherung?" (1995) *NJW* 2457 [2459] with further references; Nolte, G., "General Principles of German and European Administrative Law" (1994) 57 *Modern Law Review* 191 [198].

July 2001 in Case T-204/99 *Mattila v Council and Commission* [2001] ECR II-2265 (the contested judgment). In this case it had dismissed his application seeking the annulment of the decisions of the Commission of the European Communities and the Council of the European Union of 5 and 12 July 1999 respectively refusing to grant him access to certain documents (the contested decisions). Amongst other pleas, the claimant argued that the decision refusing him access to the documents had not been provided with sufficient reasons. The reasons were supplied in court for the first time. The court found that on this ground alone the claim was well founded. It referred to the opinion of the Advocate General:

"Permitting the Council and the Commission to communicate to the appellant the reasons for the refusal to grant partial access to a document for the first time before the Community courts would render redundant the procedural guarantees expressly laid down in Decisions 93/731 and 94/90 and seriously affect the appellant's rights which require that, except in exceptional cases, any decision adversely affecting a person must state the reasons on which it is based, in order to provide the person concerned with details sufficient to allow him to ascertain whether the decision is well founded or whether it is vitiated by an error which will allow its legality to be contested (see, in particular, Case 195/80 *Michel v Parliament* [1981] ECR 2861, para 22)".[125]

Even though this case was not concerned with German provisions, it is evident that procedural protection plays a greater role at Community level than currently in German administrative law.

IV. Conclusion

Judicial review of the administrative procedure in both jurisdictions is increasingly subjected to standards set by European jurisprudence. In England, the planning process has been subject to scrutiny under human rights jurisprudence. Even though no declaration of incompatibility was made, the more subtle outcome of *Alconbury* is the definition of judicial review principles in planning cases as including the principle of proportionality. However, the result of the case remains that the English planning system remains unchanged so far. In Germany, the new legislation concerning the curing of administrative defects within court proceedings is likely to be in conflict with the jurisprudence of the European Court of Justice in cases of procedural errors which occur in the course of indirect administration of Community law. European case law concerning the application of the new rules in Germany can be expected. Ironically, though the reforms are partly due to earlier case law by the European Court of Human Rights regarding the overlength of German Administrative Court proceedings, which in the case of König were held to be in contravention to Art. 6(1) of the European Convention on Human Rights.

In both legal systems the denial of a right to a hearing constitutes a ground for review. Both systems contain a variety of exceptions to the right to a hearing in

[125] Case C 353/01 P, no. 32.

the form of case law or as codified exceptions contained in Art. 28 of the Law on Administrative Procedure. Further, the notion that defective decisions can be cured in subsequent appeal procedures is equally an issue in English decisions and it is a codified and recently modernised principle in German law. The National Reports have shown that English judges are increasingly "willing to accept that an appeal has "cured" a defective decision".[126] Further, the case of *Cheall v Association of Professional, Executive, Clerical and Computer Staff*[127] illustrates that in cases where the decision maker exercises no discretion, the defect in the decision, i.e. the denial of a hearing, may be irrelevant if it has made no difference to the result.

However, English courts are not as ruthless as German courts in applying these principles. The German Code of Administrative Procedure ironically displays an increasing loss of status of the procedural safeguards within the administrative procedure. For the purpose of procedural efficiency, the right to a hearing and the duty to give reasons within the administrative process have lost some of their meaning. Since 1996, it is codified law that procedural flaws concerning both rights can be cured before the end of judicial review proceedings within the trial. Further, the courts apply a test according to which the lack of a hearing is irrelevant if it would not have influenced the administrative decision in its substance.[128]

The reasons for the different approach are to be found in the history of the Administrative Courts and the development of the *Rechtsstaat*. This leading principle automatically sets the limits to a reduction of judicial protection. The German judicial review process is marked by the attitude that only the courts can reach the correct answer. The German tradition of finding justice is unlike the English tradition not based on an adversarial battle of two parties and procedural fairness, but on the belief that there is only one correct answer to a legal question. As a consequence, administrative procedure law does not enjoy the same status as in the common law system, it merely has an ancillary or facilitative function. This attitude has found legislative expression in the new reforms of the Law on Administrative Court Procedure which allows the extensive curing of procedural defects within the court proceedings. As shown in Chapter Two, the strong position of the administrative courts in reviewing decisions by the administration has its roots in the nineteenth century when they emerged as a reaction to the parliamentary failure of the 1848 revolution. However, in the absence of a strong constitutional tradition and the protection of individual rights, the courts were mainly concerned with the review of *ultra vires* acts and the administration enjoyed comparably wide discretionary powers.

The concept of the *Rechtsstaat* originally merely embraced the requirements "that the state must act within the framework of the law and that the law must be precise, calculable and enforceable".[129] This formal concept of the *Rechtsstaat* did not contain the protection of higher values such as fundamental rights or basic

[126] De Smith, S.A., *Judicial Review of Administrative Action*, 1995, 490.
[127] [1983] QB 126.
[128] Article 46 Law on Administrative Procedure.
[129] Nolte, G., supra n. 124, 200.

principles of justice. The concept of the formal *Rechtsstaat* was based on the ideas of legal positivism which believed in the approach that "law is law" and not concerned with value-oriented legal thinking. The extreme change that occurred in German legal thinking after the Second World War, i.e. the transformation from legal positivism to a more natural law approach, is a clear answer to the abuses suffered by individuals under the Nazi regime. The emergence of the "substantive" *Rechtsstaat* after the Second World War transformed German jurisprudence fundamentally.

Clearly, an important tool in deciding whether the correct decision has been made is the power of the courts to investigate the facts of the case fully. Unlike the judicial review procedures in England, which are concerned with a supervisory role, the German courts carry out a full investigation into the underlying facts of the decision. The courts have been empowered by the legislature with the power to "advise" authorities within the court procedures to correct flawed decisions with the result that decisions which are flawed by the lack of a hearing or by insufficient reason giving may be cured and turned into legal acts.

The Administrative Courts which are bound by the constitution and by the empowering statute to enforce the substantive *Rechtsstaat* with its searching review for "the truth" and the protection of individual rights operate at the cost of an independent executive. As seen in the previous chapter, public authorities enjoy little areas within their discretion or their margin of appreciation and the protection of individual rights justifies an intense review of discretionary decisions. As seen by recent reforms of the Law on Administrative Procedure, the role of procedural safeguards has been further minimised to a "serving function". Procedural safeguards such as the right to a hearing and the duty to give reasons, which have been ironically codified, play such a minor role now within the pre-trial phase that the purpose of the so-called *Beschleunigungsgesetze* (laws to accelerate court procedures) have been questioned. The courts now act as advisors to the authorities and pre-trial procedural safeguards are exercised during the court proceedings. This shift towards overloading the courts with issues stemming from the decision-making process has been widely criticised in academic writing. The speeding up of the court procedures is partly due to pressure from decisions such as *König* where it was held that the German Administrative Court's seven-year trial was in contravention of Art. 6(1) of the European Convention on Human Rights.

By comparison, the developments in English law are less obvious. The judicial review remedies are granted at the discretion of the courts. In *Camelot*, for example, the court retained discretion to refuse relief if it were satisfied that the unfairness made no difference. It takes no reform of empowering statutes to allow courts to "cure" procedural defects in decisions. Further, they can "create" wider concepts such as that of "fairness". The concept of fairness as used in the *Camelot* case appears to blur the difference between the formal and substantive rights position of applicants. Accordingly, the Commission's decision only to negotiate with the competitor in the bidding process for the running of the National Lottery "constituted a lack of evenhandness" which required "the most compelling justification". The concept of fairness fills a gap left by the ground of review of procedural impropriety as Camelot could not expect to be negotiated with if the bidding process resulted in no party winning. Fairness therefore contains an element of equality of the parties which is more founded in a substantive rights position. The concept of fairness in its vagueness therefore acts as a smoke screen for the courts' discretion to cure procedural defects as well as for the courts to protect more substantive rights positions. In that respect, English courts act much more independently and they can exercise discretion whereas the German courts are bound by their commitment to respect the Basic Law and act on the basis of the Law on Administrative Court Procedure.

Further, English administrative law, in its own way and with the new powers given under the Human Rights Act 1998, will develop a much more constitutionalised judicial review. Jeffrey Jowell expresses doubts as to whether the courts will engage in a merit review of cases.[130] It is difficult though to imagine the protection of individual rights by courts who are unwilling to review cases more closely on their merits. It will have to remain a slow process, on a case-to-case basis. The increasing importance courts ascribe to the duty to give reasons illustrates a development which will enable the courts to review cases more closely.

In conclusion, German courts are less likely to quash a decision for procedural flaws such as the lack of a hearing or insufficient reasons. German courts play an important role in advising authorities if the reasons for their decisions were insufficient. German courts are traditionally more concerned with the substantive correctness of the decision. Most procedural errors can be cured at trial. The leading argument for the reform of the Law on Administrative Court Procedure was the duty of the courts under the inquisitorial procedure to take account of all kinds of new submissions. However, this generous attitude might cause conflicts in the European law context. In England, procedural errors are more likely to lead to the quashing of a decision. The courts have traditionally not had the power to review substantive rights, but were merely concerned with a legality review. However, a slow constitutionalisation and Europeanisation of the British style is leading to a more intensive review of administrative decisions. At the same time procedural safeguards contained in Art. 6 of the European Convention will gradually add to the further elaboration of principles of procedural protection in English administrative law. Here it is interesting to note that some questions as to a fair trial are regarded as procedural in the UK, whereas they translate into substantive rights questions in Germany.[131]

---

[130] Jowell, J., "Beyond the Rule of Law: Towards Constitutional Judicial Review" (2000) *Public Law* 671 [683].

[131] See *Steel and Morris v UK* (2005) 41 EHRR 22 and 2 BvR 626/06, 14 June 2006.

Chapter Five Governmental liability

I. Introduction

In the previous chapters we have seen how both countries have developed a system of judicial review of administrative action. Despite the differences that have been identified the review of administrative discretionary powers and administrative procedures controls the legality of administrative action and provides protection for the individual. However, judicial review alone cannot provide satisfactory redress where damage to the individual has already occurred. Therefore this chapter is concerned with an immensely important area, that of the tortious liability of public authorities for unlawful action. The title already suggests that both in England and Germany principles of tort law apply to the acts of public bodies. This chapter analyses a highly complex area of law which illustrates how private and public law remedies merge into one another. Both systems are in need of reform and have been particularly exposed to European influences which might support a desirable systematisation.

Both the English and German legal systems provide for a legal basis for compensation for the unlawful action of public bodies. An interesting observation made in comparison with the position in English law is that despite a few legal foundations in German statute law or constitutional provisions both legal systems have to rely mainly on case law and the development of principles by the courts.[1] Therefore this area of law lends itself in particular to the comparison of cases.

1. Governmental liability in English courts

The English law of liability is in a state of flux. This section will assess the liability of public authorities in tort. Further, the impact of the human rights jurisprudence and developments under the Human Rights Act 1998 as well as the case law of the European Court of Justice.

A claimant in a damage action will have to show that the facts of his/her case fit into one of the existing private law heads of tort. Generally speaking the heads of tortious liability derived from civil law apply to public authorities in the same way as they apply to private citizens. The same remedies as the liability of private persons generally speaking rule English law on governmental liability. The private law remedy in different heads of tort is equally applicable to public as well as to

---

1 Ossenbühl, F., *Staatshaftungsrecht* ,1998, 3.

private bodies. In England the liability of public authorities is ruled by a constitutional principle which has best been described by Dicey in his *Introduction to the Study of the Constitution*:

"When we speak of "the rule of law" as a characteristic of our country, not only that with us no man is above the law, but (what is a different thing) that here every man, whatever his rank or condition, is subject to the ordinary law of the realm and amenable to the jurisdiction of the ordinary tribunals ... With us every official, from the Prime Minister down to a constable or a collector of taxes, is under the same responsibility for every act done without legal justification as any other citizen".[2]

He was talking of personal liability. Dicey made no mention, however, of the extensive immunities and privileges which the Crown enjoyed in his lifetime.[3] The rule of law provides nonetheless an important foundation of governmental liability in that one can generally say:

"That there is a basic principle in English law concerning the liability of public bodies that rules of private law liability apply to the activities of bodies and officials exercising public functions in the same way and to the same extent as they apply to the activities of private citizens, unless some good reason can be found why they should not".[4]

"The basic premise is that an *ultra vires* act *per se* will not give rise to damages liability. For the plaintiff to succeed the claim must be capable of being fitted into one the recognised causes of action which exist".[5] The major ones are negligence, to some extent nuisance, breach of statutory duty and misfeasance in public office. However, to succeed in any of such claims the plaintiff has to overcome a variety of hurdles which have been developed by the courts in order to avoid a flood of cases trying to establish liability in damages.

a) Negligence

Probably the most pervasive head of tort is that of negligence, either in breaching a duty which was directly imposed on the authorities or by way of vicarious liability. The focal point of attention when establishing a claim in negligence is the existence of a duty of care. The negligence action is "in terms of legal history, of comparatively recent birth and it remains in its adolescence. It lacks many of the characteristics of a mature system of law, most notably a settled conceptual apparatus and a set of reasonably clear boundaries".[6]

The action in negligence is comparatively young and its modern basis was established in the famous case of *Donoghue v Stevenson*.[7] In this case the claimant had gone to a cafe with a friend. This friend bought the applicant a tumbler with

---

2 Dicey, A.V., *Introduction to the Law of the Constitution*, 1927, 189.

3 Hogg, P.W., *Liability of the Crown* ,2nd edn, 1989, 3.

4 Cane, P., *An Introduction to Administrative Law*, 1996, 233.

5 Craig, P., "The Domestic Liability of Public Authorities in Damages" in Tridimas, T., *New Directions in European Public Law* ,1998, 83.

6 Mullis, A., Oliphant, K., *Torts* ,3rd edn, 1999, 11.

7 [1932] AC 562.

ice cream, over which the owner of the cafe poured some ginger beer. In the ginger beer were the remains of a decomposed snail. The question was whether, in the absence of any contractual relationship, the manufacturer of the beer owed a duty of care to the final consumer. The case was decided in the claimant's favour and established the self-contained tort of negligence. Lord Atkin tried to find "some general conception of relation giving rise to a duty of care" and found it in the neighbour principle which has become "one of the most quoted passages in the law of tort".[8] *Donoghue* clearly established the duty of manufacturers not to cause physical injury to the consumers of their products. However, the neighbour principle did not necessarily determine the way in which other duties in other areas of activity existed. Lord Macmillan, though, said in *Donoghue* that "the categories of negligence are never closed".[9]

Particularly the concept of duty of care caused problems and later cases further defined its scope. In the case of *Anns v Merton LBC*[10] the plaintiffs alleged that the council had been negligent in the inspection of foundations causing cracks in their flats. The council argued that it had no duty to consider whether it should inspect or not. The House of Lords, however, held that the council owed a duty of care in respect of purely economic loss. In *Anns* a distinction was drawn between those actions which in the exercise of a statutory power are of a policy nature and those actions which implement settled policies and are therefore described as operational. In this case, the issue was considered to be of operational character, i.e. the implementation of a settled policy. The House of Lords held that "it can be safely said that the more "operational" a power or duty may be, the easier it is to superimpose upon it a common law duty of care". Lord Wilberforce in *Anns* further laid down a two-stage test for the establishment of a duty of care. The first step was that of proximity:

> "... One has to ask whether, as between the alleged wrongdoer and the person who has suffered damage, there is a sufficient relationship of proximity or neighbourhood such that, in the reasonable contemplation of the former, carelessness on his part may be likely to cause damage to the latter, in which case a *prima facie* duty of care arises".

Secondly, issues of public policy are to be considered which might result in a denial of the award of damages.

Anns was criticised for being too lenient a test for the establishment of liability and the decision in *Caparo Industries v Dickmann*[11] added to the two-step test. The plaintiffs owned shares in Fidelity plc and bought further shares relying on incorrect accounts for the year 1984. The House of Lords held that the defendant auditors owed no duty to the plaintiffs. According to the decision in *Caparo* the defendant ought to have foreseen the injury (foreseeability), a proximity between the plaintiff and the defendant has to be shown (the authority's function is to protect specific individuals) and the imposition of a duty of care has to be fair, just and reasonable.

8 Hedley, S., *Tort* ,1998, 19.
9 Ibid 619.
10 [1978] AC 728.
11 [1990] 2 AC 605.

In *Murphy v Brentwood*[12] the plaintiff also discovered cracks in the foundations of his semi-detached house and he found out that the foundations were defective and lead to subsidence despite the fact that the local authority had inspected them. The owner of the house was forced to sell it for £35,000 less than the value in a structurally sound condition. The decision in this case overruled aspects of the *Anns* case. Here, the House of Lords held that in such cases no general principle of liability should apply. It held that the law should develop incrementally by analogy with established situations of liability. It was held that if the likely damage were personal injury then it would be easy to establish a duty of care. However, economic losses such as the loss in this case are only recoverable if they flow from breach of a relevant contractual duty. No such contractual relationship existed between the owner of the building and the authority. Lord Bridge of Harwich further held that there was no relationship of proximity either which in the absence of a contractual duty would lead to the imposition of a duty of care.

Particularly difficult is the establishment of a duty of care in cases where damages are sought because a public body did not exercise its public power. Such a situation occurred in *Stovin v Wise*.[13] The plaintiff suffered injuries when his motorcycle collided with a car which was driven by the defendant. This accident occurred at a junction where the view was restricted because of an earth bank on railway land. The plaintiff sued the council in damages because it had omitted to remove the earth bank which had impaired the plaintiff's vision. The council knew that the junction was dangerous and had tried to get the owner of the land to remove the bank of earth. However, the owner did not respond and the council did not follow up the issue further. The question that arose was whether there was a duty of care imposed on the public authority which was founded on the existence of a statutory power to safeguard people against injury. In determining this question the court held that "the fact that Parliament has conferred a discretion must be some indication that the policy of the act conferring the power was not to create a right to compensation". The minimum preconditions that were set out in *Stovin* for the establishment of a duty of care were that it would have been irrational not to have exercised the power. It was held that the question of whether anything should be done about the junction was at all times firmly within the area of the council's discretion. Secondly, the applicant could not rely on the doctrine of general reliance. This doctrine was developed in a previous case and contains the thought that "a statutory power could never generate a common law duty of care unless the public authority had created an expectation that the power would be used and the plaintiff had suffered damage from reliance on that expectation".[14] Here, however, there was no reliance by anyone that the junction would be improved. The court held that the requirements of the doctrine of general reliance applied because the applicant was treated exactly the same way as any other road user. Finally, the court held that in holding the authorities liable in a case like this would lead to the

12 [1990] 2 All ER 908.
13 [1996] 3 All ER 801.
14 *Sutherland Shire Council v Heyman*, 157 CLR 424 [483].

spending of scarce resources and that the insurance of the applicants provides for compensation.

The case of *Gorringe v Claderdale Metropolitan Borough Council*[15] confirmed that the liability for omissions remains restricted. Lord Hoffmann made this clear: "speaking for myself, I find it difficult to imagine a case in which a common law duty can be founded simply upon the failure (however irrational) to provide some benefit which a public authority has power (or a public law duty) to provide".[16]

However, under certain circumstances authorities might be liable even for the act of third parties where there is an element of control involved in the relationship between the tortfeasor and the authorities as in *Home Office v Dorset Yacht Co Ltd.*[17] This case concerned a claim in negligence of a yacht owner who suffered damage after seven borstal boys had escaped from a training exercise whilst the officers in charge were asleep. The Home Office was held liable for the omissions of its officers because reasonable care should have been taken to avoid omissions which could have been foreseen and were likely to injure neighbours. In *Dorset Yacht* Lord Reid said that the action of a third party "must have been something very likely to happen if it is not to be regarded as a *novus actus interveniens* breaking the chain of causation". In this case it was extremely likely that the borstal boys would try to escape and as they were on an island it was foreseeable that they would use a boat. In addition to the condition of foreseeability it was held in *Dorset Yacht* that the officers were in charge of holding the borstal boys in custody and therefore were under a special duty to prevent harm to the general public which might be suffered in the course of the boys' escape from the officers' control.

Guidance concerning the content of the law of tortious liability was given by Lord Browne-Wilkinson's judgment in *X*[18] which "contains a wealth of analysis and exposition of the rules governing the tort liability of public authorities".[19] In *X* five actions were brought, two of which were based on claims for damages alleging mistakes in the exercise of powers and duties in relation to the protection of children from abuse and three actions concerned powers and duties with regard to children with educational needs. All but two of the education cases were unsuccessful. The first of the "abuse" cases dealt with the complaint by children who were allegedly ill-treated and neglected by their parents and that the authority should have taken steps to take them into care (*Bedfordshire* case). The second case (*Newham* case) was concerned with a complaint against the decision to take the child of applicant 1 into care, a decision based on the suspicion of child abuse by the mother's boyfriend. The decision was reached after inadequate inquiries by a child psychiatrist and a social worker and turned out to be wrong as it was based on the misinterpretation of the child's remarks concerning the name of the abuser.

15 [2004] UKHL 15.

16 Paragraph 32, cited in Stephen Bailey, "Public Authority Liability in Negligence: the Continued Search for Coherence", *Legal Studies*, vol. 26 no. 2, June 2006, 155 [173].

17 [1970] AC 1004.

18 *X (minors) v Bedfordshire County Council* [1995] 2 AC 633.

19 Cane, P., "Suing Public Authorities in Tort" (1996) *LQR* 13.

In the *Bedfordshire* and *Newham* cases a duty of care was denied and the requirements for such a duty were laid out in detail: This minefield of conditions for the establishment of a duty of care appears to be complicated and is at the centre of most recent decisions. The applicants in the *Newham* case appealed to the European Court of Human Rights which delivered a decision on 10 May 2001.[20] This decision will be dealt with at a later stage.

In *W v Essex County Council*[21] the plaintiffs, a couple and their natural children, held the defendants, Essex County Council and one of its social workers, liable in damages for having given them a child into their foster care who sexually abused their children. They had especially asked for a child without a record of sexual abuse. However, a 15-year-old boy was placed with them who abused the children. All the children suffered physical abuse and were psychologically badly affected by this as a consequence. After the parents had found out about the abuse they also were psychologically badly affected. The plaintiffs sued the county council in damages for failure to inform them and for positive misinformation, for misfeasance in public office and breach of contract.

The Court of Appeal supported the decision by the court of first instance to strike out the claims of the plaintiffs for misfeasance in public office, breach of contract and the claim of the parents in negligence. These claims failed because the psychological harm of the parents was caused by learning of the abuse and not by witnessing the abuse. However, the claims in negligence by the natural children were allowed to proceed to trial. The Court of Appeal held that it was arguable that a social worker who places a child into foster care is under a duty of care to provide the potential parents with such information that a reasonable social worker should provide. This lead to the personal liability of the social worker and the vicarious liability of the county council. It was held that the duty of care owed to the children was dependent on the outcome of the fair, just and reasonable test.

The Court of Appeal discussed the policy arguments brought forward in *X v Bedfordshire County Council*[22] to deny a duty of care in respect of a child whose placement in care was under consideration. The Court of Appeal was not unanimous on these issues. Two of the judges held that it was indeed fair, just and reasonable to impose a duty on the social worker because he was not exercising any statutory functions. Stuart-Smith LJ was of the opinion that the arguments brought forward in the *Bedfordshire* case were equally relevant. The policy arguments included the consideration that it would not be fair to scapegoat a single social worker as choosing a child for fostering included the decision of various people. Further he argued that the imposition of a duty of care was incompatible with the social worker's role as mediator between foster children and parents. He further argued that the imposition of liability would encourage the authorities to take a more defensive approach in cases like this and delay the decision-making process. He added that the plaintiffs could have claimed compensation under the Criminal

---

20 *TP and KM v United Kingdom* [2001] 2 FLR 549, [2001] 2 FCR 289, [2001] Fam Law 590, ECHR.

21 [1998] 3 WLR 534.

22 [1995] 2 AC 633.

Injuries Compensation Scheme. Judge LJ held that a duty should only be imposed with regard to the actual knowledge of the authorities and not with regard to the knowledge the authorities should have had. Otherwise such a duty would interfere with the proper exercise of its function.

The requirement of proximity, in particular, has been used in the consequent case of *Phelps v Hillingdon LBC*[23] where it was argued that an educational psychologist was not directly responsible to the plaintiff because she had been primarily employed to advise the local education authority. Here, Stuart-Smith LJ held that:

> "The defendant's psychology service was set up and used by the local education authority to advise it and its other employees on the discharge of its statutory functions in teaching the plaintiff. It is quite different from, for example, a health authority setting up a clinic where people can come to see doctors and nurses for treatment. In such a case there would be a direct relationship of doctor and patient, and an assumption of responsibility to treat him or her".[24]

The requirement of proximity stands for the authority's function to protect specific individuals, but is also seen "as a cover for giving value judgments about the desirable scope of tort liability".[25]

Further barriers to a flood of cases have been set by the requirement that the imposition of a duty of care must be just and reasonable. In *X* the requirement of just and reasonable has been described as consisting of three elements: the compatibility of a duty of care with the statute in question, in case of the exercise of a statutory discretion according to *X*, the question of whether the exercise of that discretion was unreasonable and, thirdly, the question whether non-justiciable issues were raised:

> "The compatibility issue is relevant to deciding whether a statutory functionary can be held to owe a common law duty of care directly to a claimant in respect of the performance of a statutory function (which is not a duty actionable in tort) which involves no exercise of discretion".

The compatibility test is similar to the question whether a statutory duty is actionable in tort. In one of the abuse cases in *X* it was held that the imposition of such a duty "would cut across the whole statutory system set up for the protection of children at risk" and "that civil litigation would be likely to have detrimental effects on the relationship between social worker and client".[26] In *X* Lord Browne-Wilkinson made clear that in the establishment of a tort liability it is essential to distinguish between decisions made at policy level and those made at operational level. This distinction had first been drawn in the case of *Anns v Merton LBC*[27] as mentioned above. Therefore, the establishment of negligence in the course of exercising powers at policy level has since been very difficult. In this case, as held in

23 *Phelps v Hillingdon London Borough Council* [1999] 1 All ER 421.
24 Ibid at 437.
25 Cane, P., *An Introduction to Administrative Law*, 1996, 242.
26 Cane, P., supra n. 19, 15–16.
27 [1978] AC 728.

X, the applicant has to show that the decision at policy level has been made *ultra vires*. Lord Browne-Wilkinson held that *ultra vires* had to be shown satisfying the conditions of *Wednesbury* unreasonableness. Further, a number of non-justiciable decisions were mentioned in *X* such as "matters of social policy", "the determination of general policy" and "the weighing of policy factors".

The decision in *Phelps v Hillingdon LBC*[28] appears to contradict the position taken by Lord Browne-Wilkinson in *X*. Ms Phelps brought an action in damages alleging the negligent failure of an educational psychologist employed by the local authority to diagnose her as suffering from dyslexia. The lower courts found the local authority to be vicariously liable for the psychologist's negligence. Stuart-Smith LJ, however, came to a different conclusion by deciding that there was no such duty of care on the part of the educational psychologist towards the plaintiff. He held that the psychologist was primarily employed to advise the school and the local authority and that there was no personal responsibility for the plaintiff. A number of policy considerations were given to refuse liability:

> "In this case, and no doubt in other such cases, decisions are taken after consideration of the views of many professionals; in this case the CGC, the educational psychologists and teachers both ordinary and remedial. It is likely to be invidious to single out one and make him or her a scapegoat. Yet if all the professionals who had some input to the decisions making and teaching are sued, that obviously circumvents the immunity of the LEA. The question of causation presents enormous difficulties".[29]

These two arguments have been criticised by Hedley asking:

> "Why is the fact that it is hard to establish duty, breach of duty and causation a reason for denying a claim to a plaintiff who has succeeded in doing so? The court's concern that individual employees might be "scapegoated" is also strange, for it is only employees who are demonstrably at fault who have anything to fear".[30]

The case of *Barrett v Enfield*[31] is an important development of the liability of public bodies in negligence. *Barrett* was concerned with the damage action of a plaintiff who had been in the care of the local authority during most of his childhood. He sued the authority in damages for the psychiatric injury caused by the negligence of the authority and its employees whilst he was in their care. The authority had allegedly failed to arrange his adoption and to organise appropriate placements with foster parents and to obtain psychiatric treatment for him. The House of Lords decided that a duty of care should not be ruled out. Lord Hutton supported previous rulings with regard to the issue of justiciability of a matter. Accordingly a negligence action was bound to fail if it touched upon issues which are non-justiciable. In his speech Lord Hutton said that:

---

28 Supra n. 23.

29 Supra n. 23, 442.

30 Hedley, S., "Negligence – Vicarious Liability of Health Authorities – Diagnosis of Dyslexia" (1999) *Cambridge Law Journal* 270 [272].

31 *Barrett v Enfield* [1999] 3 All ER 193 at 197–198.

"... These judgments lead me to the provisional view that the fact that the decision which is challenged was made within the ambit of a statutory discretion and is capable of being described as a policy decision is not in itself a reason why it should be held that no claim for negligence can be brought in respect of it ... It is only where the decision involves the weighing of competing public interests or is dictated by considerations which the courts are not fitted to assess that the courts will hold that the issue is non-justiciable on the ground that the decision was made in the exercise of a statutory discretion".[32]

He further said:

"... I consider that where a plaintiff claims damages for personal injuries which he alleges have been caused by decisions negligently taken in the exercise of a statutory discretion, and provided that the decisions do not involve issues of policy which the courts are ill-equipped to adjudicate upon, it is preferable for the courts to decide the validity of the plaintiff's claim by applying directly the common law concept of negligence than by applying as a preliminary test the public law concept of *Wednesbury* unreasonableness to determine if the decision fell outside the ambit of the statutory discretion".[33]

Barrett has therefore made two important points. A negligence action is not deemed to be unsuccessful only because the authority has acted within the scope of its discretionary power. Secondly, the standard of reasonableness is no longer identical with the concept of reasonableness contained in the *Wednesbury* test. The decision in *Barrett* has therefore lowered the hurdle to overcome for applicants and as a result "it will be increasingly possible to succeed in a damages action even though it might not be possible to challenge the action successfully via judicial review".[34]

In *Gower*[35] another striking out action was decided on an educational malpractice issue. The plaintiff suffered from muscular dystrophy and complained that the school staff had not exercised its educational duty to him in the form of providing him with a computer, etc. The claim that the educational authority could be vicariously liable for its teacher's breach of duty to take reasonable care in the provision of education to the plaintiff was not struck out. This is quite a revolutionary decision, but it also shows clearly that a differentiation between educational psychologists and teachers who are in direct relation to pupils seems to be unjustified.[36]

---

32 Ibid at 220.

33 Ibid at 225.

34 Craig, P. and Fairgrieve, D., "Barrett, Negligence and Discretionary Powers" (1999) *Public Law* 626 [648].

35 *Gower v London Borough of Bromley*, *The Times*, 28 October 1999.

36 Fairgrieve, D. and Andenas, M., "A Tort Remedy for the Untaught? Liability for Educational Malpractice in English and Comparative Law", a paper presented at a Senior Practitioner Seminar, 5 November 1999, Centre of European Law, King's College London.

b) Breach of statutory duty

In his often recited speech in which the principles of tort liability against public bodies were clearly stated, Lord Browne-Wilkinson gave the unanimous judgment of the House of Lords and confirmed that:

"The basic proposition is that in the ordinary case a breach of statutory duty does not, by itself, give rise to a private law cause of action. However, a private law cause of action will arise if it can be shown, as a matter of construction of the statute, that the statutory duty was imposed for the protection of a limited class of the public and that Parliament intended to confer on members of that class a private right of action for breach of the duty".[37]

A further condition usually relied upon to establish a cause of action for breach of statutory duty is that the statute in question provides no remedy for its breach.[38] As in German law, as will be shown, the plaintiff has to establish the particular statute conferred rights and that the plaintiff was among this protected group of people (in German law: *Drittschutz*). The House of Lords did not establish such a right stemming from the Act in question by saying that the Act was not intended for the protection of children, but for the benefit of society as a whole. The establishment of a statutory duty causes the problem of "tracking down that elusive concept – the intention of Parliament".[39] Despite many cases dealing with the issue of breach of statutory duty and academic discussion, the courts do not seem to have found a clear position and this area of law is in particular need of reform.[40] In the field of housing law, for instance, two cases illustrate that judges have become much more reluctant over the years to award damages for breach of statutory duty.

However, the reasoning in more recent cases leaves some questions to be answered. In *Thornton v Kirklees DC*[41] the applicant was without a home and had to sleep in the streets. After his application to the local council for accommodation had failed he filed an action in the County Court for the award of damages and an injunction. The case went to the Court of Appeal and there it was held, allowing the appeal, that the Homeless Persons Act 1977, in the absence of any provision for the enforcement of the duties contained in it, gave rise to a civil action in damages if such duties were not performed properly. *Thornton* gave rise to further cases which dealt with the damages claims resulting from the Homeless Persons Act 1977 which were brought in the County Court. However, in the early 1980s judges began to put a hold on the flood of cases by emphasising that issues relating to the question of whether a statutory duty existed or not such as dealt with in *Thornton* should be brought by judicial review. This new approach was clearly expressed in *O'Reilly v Mackman*[42] and *Cocks v Thanet DC*.[43]

---

37 Bailey, Jones & Mowbray, *Cases and Materials on Administrative Law*, 1997, 714.
38 The Hon. Sir Robert Carnwath (1998) *Public Law* 407.
39 Ibid.
40 Ibid at 422.
41 [1979] QB 626.
42 [1983] 2 AC 237.
43 [1983] 2 AC 286.

c) Vicarious liability

In *X* an important distinction was drawn between the direct liability of public authorities and vicarious liability. This differentiation appears to be difficult to understand. It is important to note that statutory social welfare and education authorities are juridical persons and that they therefore can only carry out their duties through human agents. As a consequence both the direct and vicarious liability stems from the acts of others. Vicarious liability is the liability of an employer for the tortious act of his employee, whereas direct liability is the liability for the act of another, whether tortious or not.[44] Further, the decision in *X* did not out rule the possibility of vicarious liability of public authorities for the acts of its officers, but made clear that if no direct duty of care was established on the side of the authority, no duty of care is to be imposed on the officers because this would circumvent the immunity of public authorities from liability. Unlike the reasoning in the abuse cases, in the education cases in *X* it was held that vicarious liability might be one route to hold the education authorities liable. In the case in which it was alleged that the educational authorities were vicariously liable for the negligent advice given by its psychology service in relation to the applicant's condition of dyslexia, Lord Browne-Wilkinson held that "psychologists hold themselves out as having special skills and they are, in my judgment, like any other professional bound both to possess such skills and to exercise them carefully".[45] The decision in *X* therefore leaves the way open for a successful claim in damages against educational psychologists resulting in their personal liability in tort and the vicarious liability of the authorities.[46]

d) Misfeasance in public office

Misfeasance in public office is the only public law tort remedy. For this cause of action to be successful it must be shown "that the official who is alleged to have inflicted the injury on the plaintiff knew that the action was *ultra vires* or acted for an improper purpose".[47] This tort has been defined as a "deliberate abuse of power causing damage".[48] Only a few cases have been reported in which the tort of misfeasance in public office has been established. A very recent decision is the judgment by the House of Lords in May 2000 in *Three Rivers District Council and others v Governor and Company of the Bank of England.*[49] The plaintiffs deposited funds with a deposit taker, the Bank of Credit and Commerce International SA (BCCI), a Luxembourg corporation, which was licensed by the Bank of England. They lost all their money when BCCI went into liquidation. The plaintiffs al-

44 Cane, P., "Suing Public Authorities in Tort" (1996) *LQR* 1996.

45 *X (minors) v Bedfordshire County Council* [1995] 2 AC 353 at 393.

46 Hedley, S., "Negligence – Vicarious Liability of Health Authorities – Diagnosis of Dyslexia" (1999) *Cambridge Law Journal* 270.

47 Cane, P., *An Introduction to Administrative Law*, 1996, 255.

48 Wade and Forsyth, *Administrative Law*, 1994, 792.

49 *Three Rivers District Council v Bank of England* (No. 3) [2001] UKHL 16, [2003] 1 AC 1.

leged that named senior officials of the Banking Supervision Department of the Bank of England committed the tort of misfeasance in public office. They alleged that that the defendants acted in bad faith when licensing BCCI in 1979 knowing that it was unlawful. They alleged that they were "shutting their eyes to what was happening at BCCI after the licence was granted and that they were failing to take steps to close BCCI when the known facts cried out for action at least by the mid-80s".[50]

The judgment of the House of Lords spelt out clearly the conditions of the tort. The first requirement is that the defendant must be a public officer. The second requirement is the exercise of power as a public officer. The third requirement concerns the state of mind of the defendant which contains two degrees:

> "The case law reveals two different forms of liability for misfeasance in public office. First, there is the case of targetted malice by a public officer, i.e. conduct specifically intended to injure a person or persons. This type of case involves bad faith in the sense of the exercise of public power for an improper or ulterior motive. The second form is where a public officer acts knowing that he has no power to do the act complained of and that the act will probably injure the plaintiff. It involves bad faith inasmuch as the public officer does not have an honest belief that his act is lawful".[51]

Three Rivers was not concerned with targetted malice, but with the second limb of the tort. The disputed issue in this case was whether "recklessness was a sufficient state of mind to ground the tort". It was held that it is sufficient if a state of mind could be demonstrated that amounted to subjective recklessness.[52] Misfeasance in public office remains difficult to prove because of these subjective requirements and a narrow test of damage and remoteness.[53] In *Watkins v Home Office* the House of Lords held recently that the case was only actionable if loss had been caused by the public officer.[54]

e) Crown immunity

A special feature of the liability of public authorities in England is still the position of the Crown. The immunity of the Crown has traditionally been summarised in the maxim "the King can do no wrong". This originally meant that the King was not privileged to commit illegal acts and then in the Middle Ages the maxim had been used to impose liability on the King to give redress to an aggrieved subject.[55] However, in the nineteenth century the courts were engaged in finding remedies for contractual and non-contractual liability of the Crown. With regard to breaches of contract committed by the Crown, liability was established reviving

---

50 Ibid.

51 Ibid.

52 *Three Rivers District Council v Bank of England* (No. 3) [2001] UKHL 16, [2003] 1 AC 1 at 191.

53 Hannett, S., "Misfeasance in Public Office: the Principles" (2005) *Judicial Review* 227 [231].

54 *Watkins v Home Office and others* [2006] UKHL 17 at 27.

55 Hogg, P., W., *Liability of the Crown*, 1998, 6.

the so-called petition of right, an old form of procedure against the Crown.[56] However, the courts interpreted the maxim that "the King can do no wrong" as an exclusion of tort claims from the available procedures against the Crown. As a result the Crown was immune from any liability claims in tort until the reform introduced in 1947.

According to the Crown Proceedings Act 1947 the Crown can be held liable under the rules of tort law. The Crown today is defined as the "executive branch of central government" which includes "ministers of state and the departments for which they are constitutionally responsible". Parliament and the judiciary are not part of the Crown.[57] However, some privileges and immunities remain in connection with acts committed by the Crown. Among these privileges is Sect. 25 of the Act according to which money judgments cannot be executed against the Crown. A further privilege is contained in Sect. 40(2) of the Act which lays down the principle that the Crown may benefit from a statute even if the statute does not mention the Crown as a beneficiary. Further, according to Sect. 2(2), the Crown is not liable for breach of statutory duty unless the duty is also imposed on persons other than the Crown and its officers. It is important to note that the Crown has to be understood as having a corporate nature, which still leaves room for claims against single ministers or officers of the Crown.[58] Similarly, the German law on governmental liability has to be seen within its historical context.

2. Governmental liability in Germany

The German law on the liability of public authorities to compensate an individual for any loss or injury caused is complicated and in need of reform. The different heads of state liability in modern Germany apply the Prussian General Land Law 1794 laying down the legal basis for the "special sacrifice" (*Sonderopfer*) and Art. 14 of the Basic Law which deals with compensation for expropriation, tortious liability in the Civil Code (BGB) dated 1900 and provisions in the Basic Law, i.e. Art. 34 laying down vicarious liability of the state for its servants. There are two main strands of liability which run parallel to each other. These are the tortious liability of public authorities and the compensation of pecuniary and non-pecuniary damage resulting from any lawful or unlawful governmental action which places an unequal burden on the individual. No uniform legal basis exists for these claims. An attempt to codify the different remedies in a single statute (*Staatshaftungsgesetz 1981*) failed after the Federal Constitutional Court held that the federation had no competence to legislate in this area of law.[59] As a result there is a large body of case law on each head of liability.[60] Governmental liability has

---

56 *Thomas v R* [1874] LR 10, QB 31.

57 Cane, P., *An Introduction to Administrative Law*, 1996, 236.

58 Ibid.

59 BVerfGE 61, 149

60 for an excellent account of the case law see Ossenbühl, F., *Staatshaftungsrecht*, 1998.

been described as a "grown chaos" which cannot be tamed by any attempts of systematization.[61]

This chapter does not intend to cover all areas of liability of public authorities in great detail, but will concentrate on the provision of tortious liability as laid down in the Civil Code.

a) Tortious liability according to section 839 of the Civil Code (BGB)[62] in connection with Art. 34 of the Basic Law

Similar to the position in English law the liability of public authorities in Germany is governed by the law of torts contained in Sect. 839 of the Civil Code which is concerned with damages for the breach of an official duty. However, the legal construction of this tort, which is a hybrid between public and private law, has been criticised for a long time. Liability for the wrongdoing of an official is a combined liability between the official and the state. However, the personal liability of the official is transferred to the state according to Art. 34 of the Basic Law (see below).[63]

One similarity is the fact that the tortious liability of public authorities in Germany is equally difficult to grasp and has been described as "incomprehensible" and "badly constructed".[64] This is due to its historical development from a purely private law liability in tort to a constellation in which the state accepts responsibility for the tortious acts of its civil servants. However, it is still not clear whether it can be regarded as a private or public law remedy.[65] Due to its original private nature, the cause of action has to be filed in the civil courts and is outside the jurisdiction of the Administrative Courts. Similar to the position in English law, liability for breach of an official duty is governed by the law of torts which is laid down in the BGB, the Civil Code that was drafted in 1900. Originally, the liability of a civil servant for the breach of an official duty was purely dealt with as a private law matter contained in Sect. 839 of the BGB. Accordingly, the relationship between the state and its officials was considered as being of a purely private law nature. Therefore the official was personally liable for all unlawful acts. This reasoning is still clearly expressed in section 839 BGB:

(1) If an official intentionally or negligently violates an official duty which falls upon him as against a third party, he must compensate the third party for the harm arising therefrom. If the official can only be charged with negligence, a claim can only be made against him if the person suffering harm cannot obtain compensation in another manner.[66]

---

61 Ossenbühl, F., *Staatshaftungsrecht*, 1998, 2.

62 Abbreviation for *Bürgerliches Gesetzbuch* which came into force in 1900.

63 Ossenbühl, F., *Staatshaftungsrecht*, 1998, 2.

64 Ibid at 6.

65 Ibid at 6.

66 This provision imposes liability for the breach of an official duty on the civil servant himself acting on behalf of the state. It is a personal liability of the official. If the requirements of Sect. 839 are met, the official has to compensate any damage, including pure economic loss.

(2) If an official violates his official duty through a decision on a legal issue, he is only responsible for the harm arising therefrom if the violation of duty consists of a criminal act. This provision has no application to a refusal or delay in the exercise of the office which is contrary to a duty.[67]
(3) The duty to compensate does not arise if the person suffering the harm has intentionally or negligently omitted to avert the harm by the use of a legal remedy.[68]

However, the aggrieved citizen was often unable to gain compensation from civil servants. In order to protect the citizen claims were gradually allowed to be made against the state. Therefore the law changed around the second half of the nineteenth century and from 1919 the Weimar constitution contained the provision which is now contained in Art. 34 of the Basic Law:

"Should anyone, in exercising a public office, neglect their duty towards a third party liability shall rest in principle with the state or the public body employing them. In the event of wilful intent or gross negligence, a remedy may be sought against the person concerned. In respect of claims for compensation or remedy, recourse to the ordinary courts shall not be precluded".[69]

Claims for tortious liability of public authorities in Germany are dealt with by the ordinary courts unlike in France where the administrative courts determine these questions. German law on tortious liability remains uncodified and has to be deduced from judicial decisions and legal writings. Reform attempts starting in the 1950s to draft a uniform liability law culminated in the enactment of a Law on State Liability 1981. However, it was invalidated by the Constitutional Court on the ground of lack of competence by the federal Parliament to enact a law in this area which would be applicable to federal as well as land authorities.

To make sure that officials would not misuse the immunity granted to them from personal liability Art. 34 reserves a right of the state to recover damages from the official in question in case the breach of duty was wilful or grossly negligent.

This tort in German law lends itself to a comparison of the breach of a statutory duty in English law. As will be discussed below, the issues particularly concerned with the establishment of a statutory duty bear resemblance with the German model. However, some of the arguments brought forward in the English decisions such as *Stovin v Wise* and *X v Bedfordshire*, which are described as "policy" arguments, appear alien to modern German reasoning. The four policy arguments as identified by Markesinis, Auby, Coester-Waltjen and Deakin[70] are that imposing liability would make bad economic sense, would inhibit public authorities from carrying out their duties, that the courts would be allowed to substitute the authori-

---

67 This is the so-called judge's privilege clause. It limits the liability for judges. A judge is only liable if the breach of his official duty constitutes a criminal act The purpose for the limitation is to maintain the independence of the judiciary.

68 This means that the citizen has to seek judicial review first before claiming compensation.

69 Ordinary courts mean the private law courts as opposed to the Administrative Courts.

70 Markesinis, B.S., Auby, J.B., Coester-Waltjen, D. & Deakin, S.F., *Tortious Liability of Statutory Bodies, A Comparative and Economic Analysis of Five English Cases* ,1999.

ties' decisions by having a "second guess" and that alternative remedies were available.[71] However, a closer look at material stemming from the time when the German Civil Code was drafted reveals that similar arguments were considered.

aa) Persons exercising public office

Tortious liability of the state or public authorities exists for the wrongs of any person exercising a public office irrespective of the fact whether such person is in the employment or service of the state or a public authority. Even if Sect. 839 of the Civil Code speaks of an "official", the courts have always taken a very liberal approach on the matter. There has been a shift to "any person" who is entrusted with a public office. The courts have held that the state cannot escape its liability by handing over a public law duty to a private person. For example, the city authorities, who were under an obligation to provide safety measures on the roads, have been held liable for the negligence of a private contractor who failed to install proper traffic signs on a road under construction due to which the plaintiff suffered an accident resulting in injuries.

bb) Breach of duty

Article 34 of the Basic Law and Sect. 839 of the Civil Code do not contain a catalogue of official duties. Official duties may stem from any legal source. In the courts the requirement of official duty has been interpreted very liberally. Examples are the duty to act lawfully as contained in Art. 20 of the Basic Law and the duty to exercise discretionary powers. The review of discretionary powers was originally limited to extreme cases of arbitrary exercise of the discretion. "The *Reichsgericht* constantly held that the courts should not interfere with discretionary power. The courts could only decide in cases where the public body acted outside the ambit of its discretionary power".[72] However, the control of the exercise of discretionary powers has been extended by the highest court in civil matters (*Bundesgerichtshof*) so that it now includes the failure to exercise discretionary powers, the excessive use of discretionary powers or the incorrect exercise of discretionary powers parallel to the grounds of review of an administrative act:

> "A discretionary decision may thus be reviewed by a court in a public wrong case even if it is within the ambit of discretion. However, the court will not go into the question whether the decision taken by the public body was "right" (*Richtigkeitsprüfung*), but only whether the decision seems plausible (*vertretbar*). The test for plausibility allows far more control than was sanctioned in the past, but it still does not mean that the court is substituting its own judgment for that of the administrative authority".[73]

---

71 Ibid at 62.
72 Ibid at 45.
73 Ibid at 63.

The courts review the erroneous use of discretion (*Ermessensfehlgebrauch*), the excess of the exercise of discretion (*Ermessensüberschreitung*) and the omitted use of discretion (*Ermessensnichtgebrauch*).[74] The landmark case is the decision of the highest court in civil matters in 1979 where it found a breach of an official duty in the course of the exercise of a discretionary power even though the breach did not amount to an obvious level of abuse.[75]

In a case decided by *OLG Hamm*[76] the plaintiffs sued the youth welfare department of the defendant city in damages because they had failed to inform them that the child that they had adopted suffered from early childhood harm. They had expressly wished a child without mental disabilities. However, the youth welfare department placed a little boy aged two with them who was going to have special needs. The youth welfare department possessed information in a medical report stating that the boy had progressed only slowly in his development and had only reached the mental age of an eight-month-old baby when he was already two years old. However, they had failed to link these deficiencies to potential brain damage. The plaintiffs claimed damages for loss of earnings and the material damage incurred by a child with special needs. The *Landgericht* (District Court) granted the claim, but the *Oberlandesgericht* (Court of Appeal) dismissed the defendant's appeal. It held that the youth welfare department was in breach of its official duty according to Sect. 839 of the Civil Code in connection with Art. 34 of the Basic Law. It should have informed the parents that the child's development was unusually slow. No statutory duty exists regarding the duty to inform parents about the health of the child in an adoption process, however, the youth welfare department is under an obligation to undertake all necessary inquiries whilst preparing the adoption. This includes the gathering of information regarding the state of health of the child. This official duty was owed to the parents.

cc) Duty towards a third party

Both Sect. 839 of the Civil Code and Art. 34 of the Basic Law require that the official duty must be owed to *a third party*. Whether a person is a third party in that sense depends on whether the object of the duty is directly to safeguard the interests of that person. If for instance a policeman remains inactive while a theft is being committed, he is in breach of his official duty towards the owner because his power to interfere is conferred on him not merely in the interest of the general public, but at the same time in the interest of each single individual. In each case it has to be seen whether according to the object and the legal provisions of the official task the affected interests should have been protected. Three conditions have to be met in order to establish a duty towards a third party. First, the official duty must be capable of protecting individuals, secondly, the plaintiff has to belong to the protected group of people and, thirdly, the damage must be included in the

---

74 Ossenbühl, F., *Staatshaftungsrecht*, 1998, 46.

75 BGHZ 74, 156.

76 *VersR* 1994, 677.

protective effect of the duty.[77] The establishment of such a duty owed to a third party is extremely difficult. The determination of which duties are capable of protecting third party effects is left to the courts. The decision on this issue is crucial for the success or failure of an action. The fact that Sect. 839 of the Civil Code does not enumerate official duties which confer rights on individuals illustrates that the courts are given some leeway as to how to interpret the concept of duty.

3. Evaluation

Both English and German law provide a legal basis for compensation for unlawful acts of public bodies. This is a principle which is based on the rule of law and the *Rechtsstaatsprinzip* respectively. For A.V. Dicey the rule of law meant "equality before the law",[78] by which he meant the equal subjection of all, including officials, to the ordinary law administered by the ordinary courts.[79] Accordingly, the same rules of tortious liability apply, in principle, against private citizens and public bodies. The German *Rechtsstaatsprinzip* as contained in Art. 20 III of the Basic Law similarly subjects all acts of public bodies to review by the courts. In that respect public bodies in Germany do not receive any treatment different from private citizens. However, in Germany there exists a much more distinct division between public and private law courts dating back to the nineteenth century. The protection of the citizen against unlawful acts of public bodies is at the centre of the *Rechtsstaatsprinzip*. A clear constitutional basis for that can be found in Art. 19 IV of the Basic Law. Generally speaking, all public law disputes fall within the jurisdiction of the Administrative Courts. The liability of public bodies is governed in both legal systems by the law of torts. In Germany, however, due to the historical development of the liability of public bodies, this cause of action has a hybrid nature. The transfer of personal liability contained in the much older provision in Sect. 839 of the Civil Code onto the state as provided for by Art. 34 of the Basic Law is primarily designed for the protection of the aggrieved citizen. It is aimed to provide an efficient judicial protection for the individual and therefore an expression of one of the core principles of the *Rechtsstaat*.

In determining liability both systems apply the requirement of a duty for the official body. In English law the tort of negligence requires the establishment of a duty of care to be imposed on the public body. Within the tort of breach of statutory duty the statute in question has to be imposed for the "protection of a limited class of the public and that Parliament intended to confer on members of that class a private right of action for breach of the duty". German law equally requires that the duty imposed on the official be designed for the protection of a limited class of people. In determining the meaning of this concept of duty the legal systems apply rather vague tests such as the *Caparo* test or the test relating to the protective purpose of the official duty in German law. Both the concept of duty in English tort

77 Ossenbühl, F., supra n. 74, 58.

78 Dicey, A.V., *The Law of the Constitution*, 1885, 202–203.

79 Turpin, C., *British Government and the Constitution*, 1999, 68.

law and the concept of the protective purpose play a pivotal role in each liability case. As a consequence in both legal systems the limitations imposed on the concept of duty operate as a means to reduce the amount of cases won. Despite the fact that German tort law provides for a statutory provision dealing with the liability of public bodies this provision does not contain a catalogue of official duties. Therefore the interpretation of the meaning of official duty as contained in Sect. 839 of the Civil Code has to be established by the courts. Similar to English law, German law contains groups of established duties in certain areas of public administration such as the duty of school teachers, building authorities and the state prosecution office, to name just a few. However, as seen in the social services cases, in contrast to English courts in negating the existence of a duty of care German courts tend not to resort to policy arguments of the kind used by English judges such as the floodgate arguments, the diversion of scarce resources and others.

II. Comparative cases - governmental liability and Human Rights

1. Governmental liability for breaches of Human rights in the UK

a) The English law of negligence under European influence[80]

The claimants in *X v Bedfordshire County Council* brought their cases to the European Court of Human Rights. The restrictive approach to liability in negligence has come increasingly under the influence of an emerging human rights culture in the United Kingdom and which, for some time, has occupied practitioners and academics alike.[81] Since the widely criticised ruling of the European Court of Human Rights in the *Osman*[82] case in 1999, two judgments have been handed down by that court in the cases of *Z v UK* and *TP and KM v UK*[83] in May 2001 which distance themselves from parts of the *Osman* ruling. These decisions have

80 This section formed part of an article published by the author in (2002) *European Public Law* 25.

81 Bowen, A.J., "A Terrible Misunderstanding? Osman v UK and the Law of Negligence" (2001) *Scots Law Times* 59; Carnwath, R.,"Welfare Services – Liabilities in Tort After the Human Rights Act" (2001) *Public Law* 210; Craig, P. and Fairgrieve, D., "Barrett, Negligence and Discretionary Powers" (1999) *Public Law* 626; English, R.,"The Decline and Fall of Osman" (2001) *New Law Journal* 973; Gearty, C.A., "Unravelling Osman" (2001) *Modern Law Review* 159; Giliker, P., "Osman and Police Immunity in the English Law of Torts" (2000) *Legal Studies* 372; Monti, G., "Osman v UK – Transforming English Negligence Law into French Administrative Law?" (1999) *International and Comparative Law Quarterly* 757; Markesinis, B.S., *Tortious Liability of Statutory Bodies, A Comparative and Economic Analysis of Five English Cases* 1999.

82 *Osman v United Kingdom* (1998) 29 EHRR 245.

83 *TP and KM v United Kingdom* [2001] 2 FLR 549, [2001] 2 FCR 289, [2001] Fam Law 590, ECHR.

already been held to admit to a "misunderstanding" of the English law of negligence as displayed in the *Osman* case.[84] As a consequence, *Osman* has been "bid farewell" and "consigned to the bin of judicial mistakes".[85] This section assesses the case law of the European Court of Human Rights and its impact on the future development of the liability of statutory bodies in the UK. It argues that the recent decisions of the European Court of Human Rights are mainly in line with its previous reasoning with the exception of its attitude towards striking out procedures. They reinforce a narrow reading of *Osman* and indicate a willingness of the European Court of Human Rights to review its understanding of English procedural law. The ruling in *Z v UK* was mainly concerned with the compliance of the rules of negligence with Art. 6(1) of the European Convention on Human Rights than in the decision in *TP and KM v UK*. However, the latter decision gives important guidance to the way in which the Human Rights Act will give applicants a right to claim for the violation of their rights.

A focal point of this section is the decision by the House of Lords in *Barrett v Enfield*[86] in 1999 which under the influence of the court's ruling in *Osman* set a trend towards a more careful consideration of policy arguments on the basis of facts established at full trial rather than on the basis of hypothetical facts.

aa) The ruling of the European Court of Human Rights in Osman v UK[87]

The case of *Osman v UK*[88] concerned a teacher who was obsessed with one of his pupils, Osman. This obsession eventually ended in the death of the pupil's father and the wounding of Osman. The police had failed to prevent this disastrous outcome and the family brought an action in negligence against the police force. The Court of Appeal decided that the claim should be struck out finding that it was not fair, just and reasonable to impose a duty of care on the police in respect of their handling of criminal investigations. The Court of Appeal based its decision on the case of *Hill*,[89] which had established a public policy exclusion of negligence actions against the police for the investigation and suppression of crime. The policy arguments in *Hill* were set out as follows: a negligence action would lead to the diversion of scarce resources, the police would exercise their functions in a defensive frame of mind and the conduct of such an investigation involves the exercise of discretion which "would not be regarded by the courts as appropriate to be called into question".[90]

The European Court of Human Rights saw in the application of this rule an infringement of Art. 6(1) of the European Convention on Human Rights which pro-

---

84 Bowen, A.J., "A Terrible Misunderstanding? *Osman v UK* and the Law of Negligence" (2001) *Scots Law Times* 59.

85 English, R., "The Decline and Fall of *Osman*" (2001) *New Law Journal* 973 [974].

86 [1999] 3 All ER 193.

87 (1998) 5 BHRC 293.

88 (1998) 5 BHRC 293.

89 *Hill v Chief Constable of West Yorkshire* [1989] AC 53.

90 Ibid at 63.

vides that "in the determination of his civil rights and obligations ... everyone is entitled to a hearing ... by [a] ... tribunal ..."

The European Court of Human Rights held that Art. 6(1) was applicable because the Osmans:

"Must be taken to have had a right, derived from the law of negligence, to seek an adjudication on the admissibility and merits of an arguable claim that they were in a relationship of proximity to the police, that the harm caused was foreseeable and that in the circumstances it was fair, just and reasonable not to apply the exclusionary rule outlined in the *Hill* case".[91]

The European Court of Human Rights held that the denial of the Court of Appeal to award damages to the Osmans by way of striking out their claim on the basis of the *Hill* rule did not comply with Art. 6(1) for two connected reasons.

First, it submitted that the right under Art. 6 is not absolute and may be subject to restrictions. However, "a limitation will not be compatible with Art. 6(1) if it does not pursue a legitimate aim and if there is not a reasonable relationship of proportionality between the means employed and the aim sought to be achieved".[92] The European Court of Human Rights therefore required that any limitation on the right to damages should be decided in each case afresh, in other words by weighing the counter arguments of the applicant against the policy arguments of the defendant. Otherwise, as in this case the lack of weighing up of competing interests amounted to a blanket immunity. Secondly, the European Court of Human Rights was of the opinion that the striking out action deprived the applicant of the right of access to a court because they could not argue their case on its merits.

The main criticism against *Osman* as expressed extra-judicially by Lord Hoffmann and others was that the ECHR was using Art. 6(1) to decide on the content of a person's civil rights and obligations, rather than upholding the right of access to a court.[93] This apparent judicial activism and over-interpretation of Art. 6 is rooted in the fundamental difference between the continental law approach and the common law. *Osman* is "difficult to understand" as Lord Browne-Wilkinson admitted in *Barrett* because the European Court of Human Rights applied an approach to the English law of negligence which is alien to the common law. The Strasbourg court's reasoning appears less strange from a continental law perspective.

In German law, for instance, the right to damages against public authorities is codified in provisions contained in the Civil Code (Sect. 839)[94] and the constitu-

---

91 *Osman v United Kingdom* (1998) 29 EHRR 245 at para 139.

92 Ibid at para 147.

93 Lord Hoffmann, "Human Rights and the House of Lords" (1999) *Modern Law Review* 159; Bowen, "A Terrible Misunderstanding? *Osman v UK* and the Law of Negligence" (2001) *Scots Law Times* 59.

94 Section 839 para 1 Civil Code: "if an official intentionally or negligently violates the official duty which falls upon him as against a third party, he must compensate the third party for the harm arising therefrom. If the official can only be charged with negli-

tion (Art. 34 Basic Law).[95] This provision on the liability of public authorities is part of the so-called substantive law of rights rather than purely remedial law. It belongs "rather to the rights and not to the remedies side of the matter".[96] English law still displays a much more remedial conception of law as expressed by Maitland's quote that "the forms of action we have buried, but they still rule us from their graves".[97] The English remedial conception is characterised by a fact-oriented approach[98] which as, for instance, in the *Hill* case led to the setting of a precedent which denies the availability of a remedy under specific factual constellations. In English law "it is a prerequisite to there being any liability in negligence at all that as a matter of policy it is fair, just and reasonable in those circumstances to impose liability in negligence".[99] The defendant in *Osman* submitted in the Court of Appeal that the facts in the present case were indistinguishable from those in *Hill* so far as public policy was concerned.[100] In German law, however, the action would automatically be connected to the potential violation of a civil servant's duty arising out of a protective norm or other relationship. In the absence of the principle of precedent, which could rule out the existence of an action, a case would proceed to a full trial and the court will examine whether a civil servant was subject to a duty of care in the particular case. The difficulties which were experienced by English judges in understanding the ruling in *Osman* were partly due to this conceptual difference. As will be shown below, the case of *Osman* marks the beginning of a dialogue between the European Court of Human Rights and the House of Lords on the understanding of the law of negligence of public bodies in the United Kingdom and its compatibility with Art. 6(1) of the European Convention on Human Rights.

bb) Impact of the ruling in Osman on subsequent decisions

As mentioned earlier, the decision of the House of Lords in the case of *Barrett v Enfield*[101] is an important development of the liability of public bodies in negligence. *Barrett* was concerned with an action in damages by a plaintiff who had been in the care of the local authority during most of his childhood. He sued the authority in damages for the psychiatric injury caused by the negligence of the authority and its employees whilst he was in their care. The authority had allegedly

gence, a claim can only be made against him if the person suffering harm cannot obtain compensation in another manner".

95 Article 34 (first sentence) Basic Law: "should anybody, in exercising a public office, neglect their duty towards a third party liability shall rest in principle with the state or the public body employing them".

96 Ruffert, M., "Rights and Remedies in European Community Law: A Comparative View" (1997) *Common Market Law Review* 307 [332].

97 Maitland, F.W., *The Forms of Action at Common Law: A Course of Lectures* (Cambridge University Press, 1948) 2.

98 Allison, J.F., *A Continental Distinction in the Common Law*, 2000, 127.

99 *Barrett v Enfield* [1999] 3 All ER 193.

100 *Osman v Ferguson* [1993] 4 All ER 344, CA.

101 *Barrett v Enfield* [1999] 3 All ER 193.

failed to arrange his adoption and to organise appropriate placements with foster parents and to obtain psychiatric treatment for him. The House of Lords decided that a duty of care should not be ruled out. With regard to the effects of the decision in *Osman* Lord Browne-Wilkinson's speech is highly important. He admitted that he found "the decision of the Strasbourg court extremely difficult to understand".[102] His following summary of the reasoning of the European Court of Human Rights and its application to the English law of negligence is an enlightening illustration of the difficult task of doing justice to the rights and the remedies approach.

First, unlike the understanding of the European Court of Human Rights in *Osman* in English law "it is a prerequisite to there being any liability in negligence at all that as a matter of policy it is fair, just and reasonable in those circumstances to impose liability in negligence".[103]

Secondly, "the decision as to whether it is fair, just and reasonable to impose a liability in negligence on a particular class of would-be defendants depends on weighing in the balance the total detriment to the public interest in all cases from holding such class liable in negligence as against the total loss to all would-be plaintiffs if they are not to have a cause of action in respect of the loss they have individually suffered".[104]

Thirdly, this question whether the imposition of such a duty is just, fair and reasonable is a question of law and once a decision had been taken for a particular case "that decision will apply to all future cases of the same kind. The decision does not depend on weighing the balance between the extent of the damage to the plaintiff and the damage to the public in each particular case".[105]

Despite his criticism of the ruling in *Osman*, the decision in *Barrett* has set a new trend in negligence cases against public bodies.[106] *Osman*'s influence on the decision in *Barrett* was clearly expressed by Lord Browne-Wilkinson's statement that "in the present very unsatisfactory state of affairs, and bearing in mind that under the Human Rights Act 1998 Art. 6 will shortly become part of English law, in such cases as these it is difficult to say that it is a clear and obvious case calling for striking out".[107] Further, the House of Lords refused some of the often-raised policy considerations such as "the existence of other avenues of complaint"[108] ruling out a right of action and the argument that the imposition of a duty of care would lead to a defensive attitude of statutory bodies: "if the conduct in question is of a kind which can be measured against the standards of the reasonable man, placed as the defendant was, then I do not see why the law in the public interest should not require those standards to be observed".[109] The case was allowed to

---

102 Ibid at 198d.

103 Ibid at 199e.

104 Ibid at 199f–g.

105 Ibid at 199h–j.

106 Craig P., and Fairgrieve, D., "Barrett, Negligence and Discretionary Powers" (1999) *Public Law* 626 [631].

107 *Barrett v Enfield* [1999] 3 All ER 193 at 200a.

108 Ibid at 228h.

109 Ibid at 228f.

proceed to trial. This trend was followed in subsequent decisions such as *W and others v Essex County Council*[110] and *Phelps v Hillingdon Borough Council*.[111] The facts of the former case have been dealt with before. *Phelps* was concerned, *inter alia*, with the common law claims in negligence of four applicants against the local authorities concerning the misdiagnosis of dyslexia or the failure to provide educational support for children with learning difficulties or special needs. The House of Lords allowed all but one appeal. In the second case, where the authorities failed to provide educational support for the severely dyslexic applicant, Lord Clyde referred to the decision in *Osman* which required the proportionate weighing of competing policy considerations. He was not convinced that there were any policy considerations strong enough to exclude the liability of the local authority.[112]

In conclusion *Osman* has set a trend towards a more cautious use of striking out actions. The requirement in *Osman* that policy considerations should be weighed carefully with competing interests of the applicants has led to a slow erosion of the public policy immunities previously enjoyed by welfare services.

cc) The ruling of the European Court of Human Rights in Z v UK

The case of *Z* concerned the claim of four siblings in damages for personal injury arising out of a breach of statutory duty and negligence by Bedfordshire County Council in failing to protect them from parental abuse.[113] The children were so hungry that they had to steal food, they were locked in their bedrooms and had to sleep in soiled bedding. The mother could not cope and stated that she would batter them if they were not taken into care. However, it took the authority's social services unit several years before care orders were made.

Z is of particular interest because the European Court of Human Rights' surprising admission that with regard to a violation of Art. 6(1) "its reasoning in the *Osman* judgment was based on an understanding of the law of negligence which has to be reviewed in the light of the clarifications subsequently made by the domestic court and notably the House of Lords ..."[114] Unlike the European Commission of Human Rights, the European Court of Human Rights found that Art. 6 was not violated.[115]

When looking at this decision in some more detail it becomes evident that the Strasbourg court is only partly willing to review its previous reasoning in *Osman*. The decision in *Z* contains three main points.

---

110 [2000] 2 WLR 601.

111 [2000] 3 WLR 776.

112 [2000] 3 WLR 776 at 809. Breaches of a statutory duty under the Education Acts 1944 and 1981 were not actionable.

113 The House of Lords decision was cited as *X v Bedfordshire County Council* [1995] 2 AC 633.

114 *Z v United Kingdom* Application no. 29392/95 (10 May 2001, ECHR) para 100.

115 See the "Report of the European Commission of Human Rights" dated 10 September 1999.

First, the European Court of Human Rights has shown that it still regards Art. 6 as applicable in cases in which applicants assert that English courts deprive them of their right to a court in holding that it was not just, fair and reasonable to impose a duty of care on a statutory body. The European Court of Human Rights is still convinced that Art. 6(1) is applicable because the applicants whose actions were struck on the basis that no cause of action existed were denied access to court. In that respect the question of whether Art. 6(1) is applicable at all in these type of cases is still not clearly answered. The European Court of Human Rights held that "the government's submission that there was no arguable (civil) "right" for the purpose of Art. 6 once the House of Lords had ruled that no duty of care arose has relevance rather to any claims which were lodged or pursued subsequently by other plaintiffs".[116] This is a circular argument because such subsequent plaintiffs would according to the European Court of Human Rights be faced with an immunity which again would be in violation of Art. 6(1). The European Court of Human Rights is not willing to accept that under the English law of negligence there is no cause of action in negligence if it is not fair, just and reasonable to impose a duty of care on the defendant. As a result, English law after *Z* will still have to comply with the original findings in *Osman* regarding the applicability of Art. 6.

Secondly, the European Court of Human Rights still requires a balancing of competing policy considerations in each case to determine whether it was just, fair and reasonable to impose a duty of care. In *Z* it was satisfied that such a balancing of interests had taken place. In that respect the court upheld its ruling in *Osman* according to which a "proportionate immunity"[117] of the defendant, i.e. one which resulted from the proper balancing of competing policy considerations, would be in compliance with Art. 6. The court is not generally criticising the use of policy considerations, but it is opposed to a practice as displayed in *Osman* where the Court of Appeal failed to take competing considerations into account and applied the *Hill* rule in a way which amounted to a blanket immunity for the police.

Finally, the European Court of Human Rights has clearly reviewed its reasoning in *Osman* by acknowledging that the striking out procedure complied with the requirements under Art. 6: the applicants' claims:

> "Were properly and fairly examined in light of the applicable domestic legal principles concerning the tort of negligence. Once the House of Lords had ruled on the arguable legal issues, the applicants could no longer claim any entitlement under Art. 6(1) to obtain any hearing concerning the facts. As pointed out above, such a hearing would have served no purpose, unless a duty of care in negligence had been held to exist in their case".[118]

---

116 *Z v United Kingdom* Application no. 29392/95 (10 May 2001, ECHR) para 89.

117 Giliker, P., "Osman and Police Immunity in the English Law of Torts" (2000) *Legal Studies* 372 [378].

118 *Z v United Kingdom* Application no. 29392/95 (10 May 2001, ECHR) para 100.

dd) Impact of the decision in Z v UK on the law of negligence

The question now remains: what likely effect is the decision in *Z v UK* going to have on the future direction of the courts in negligence cases against public bodies?

The application of a blanket immunity such as the constraint under the *Hill* rule would amount to a violation of Art. 6. Therefore *Z* does not place the courts in a pre-*Osman* situation and even if it did it has been doubted whether the "trend set by *Barrett* would be reversed, i.e. less resistance by English courts to allowing an action to proceed in negligence".[119]

The Strasbourg court's main revision of its understanding of the "law of negligence" concerns the practice of striking out actions. It is now satisfied that competing interests can be properly and fairly discussed in interlocutory hearings. However, it is interesting to note that in *Barrett* Lord Browne-Wilkinson expressed unease with the practice of striking out actions even before he proceeded to discuss Art. 6. He referred to his speech in *X v Bedfordshire County Council* and explained that it was important that the development of the law of negligence of public bodies "should be on the basis of actual facts found at trial not on hypothetical facts assumed (possibly wrongly) to be true for the purpose of the strike out".[120] The decision in *Z* is therefore unlikely to reverse the more recent approach by the House of Lords to allow cases to proceed to a full trial.

Having said that, the Court of Appeal has delivered a judgment in April 2000 in the case of *S v Gloucestershire County Council; L v Tower Hamlets London Borough Council and another*[121] which might have an influence on the approach taken by other courts in cases of this kind. This case concerned the claim against the local authority in negligence resulting from sexual abuse suffered in foster care. The case is of some importance as it deals with the new Civil Procedure Rules which were referred to in previous chapters. They now govern civil procedure in rule 24.2(a)(i)[122] which contains powers of "summary disposal" to be distinguished from rule 3.4(2)(a) derived from former RSC Order 18 rule 19 concerning striking out.[123] The main difference between these rules is of a technical nature in as much as there is "no longer an embargo on the court receiving evidence"[124] under rule 24.2(a)(i). In *S v Gloucestershire County Council; L v Tower Hamlets London Borough Council and another* the Court of Appeal dealt with the question of com-

---

119 English, R., "The Decline and Fall of *Osman*" (2001) *New Law Journal* 973 [974].

120 *Barrett v Enfield* [1999] 3 All ER 193 at 197f.

121 [2000] 3 All ER 346.

122 Rule 24.2: "the court may give summary judgment against a claimant … on the whole of a claim or on a particular issue if – (a) it considers that – (I) that claimant has no real prospect of succeeding on the claim or issue … (b) there is no other reason why the case or issue should be disposed of at a trial".

123 Rule 3.4: "… (2) The court may strike out a statement of case if it appears to the court – (a) that the statement of case discloses no reasonable grounds for bringing or defending the claim …"

124 "The Right to a Fair Hearing and Summary Disposal" (2000) *Civil Justice Quarterly* 341.

patibility with Art. 6 in some detail. It explained that under the old rules according to which *Barrett* was decided, no evidence was admissible on an application and that the decision to strike out was made under the assumption of hypothetical facts. Accordingly the House of Lords felt that it was safer to allow a full trial in order to avoid the applicant's complaint in Strasbourg. The new rule 24.2(a)(i) now allows for cases to be disposed of on the whole or in part "if the court considers that the claimant has no real prospect of succeeding on the claim or issue and there is no other reason why the case or issue should be disposed of at a trial".[125] In applying the new rule and thereby deciding the cases in the light of *Barrett* "by reference to the actual facts and not to hypothetical facts"[126] the court allowed the first appeal because the court was not persuaded that it had no real prospect of success and dismissed the second case as it showed no real prospect of success.

Another English case concerned with child abuse reached Strasbourg. The case was based on the facts of the "*Newham* case" which was decided by the House of Lords in 1995 and reported as *M v Newham County Council* as described above. In *TP and KM v UK*[127] the applicants, mother and daughter, alleged that the daughter had been wrongly taken into care and separated from the mother. They further alleged that they were refused access to court or an effective remedy for the violation of their rights in the United Kingdom.

In 1983 the first applicant was 17 years old and gave birth to a daughter. In the time between 1984 and 1987 the London Borough of Newham suspected that the first applicant's boyfriend sexually abused the second applicant. In an interview, which was recorded on videotape, the daughter told the child psychiatrist and a social worker that a man called X had abused her. The first applicant's then boyfriend was called X. The first applicant was also interviewed and told that X had abused the daughter. After the interview, however, the video containing the daughter's interview was not disclosed to the first applicant. The first applicant then asked her daughter whether X had abused her. The daughter denied this. However, the psychiatrist and the social worker interpreted this as an attempt by the first applicant to influence the daughter. They decided to take the child into care immediately. About a year later the first applicant and her solicitor were shown the video and it was clarified that the daughter had not identified the applicant's boyfriend, but someone else who had been made to leave the household at an earlier stage. The House of Lords held that there was no breach of a statutory duty because the Child Care Act 1980 was not designed "to establish an administrative system designed to promote the social welfare of the community". Further, the court held that the local authority and the health authority were not vicariously liable for the psychiatrist and the social worker because they owed no duty of care to the applicants. There was no proximity between the applicants, the psychiatrist and the social worker because they are employed in order to advise the council

[125] *S v Gloucestershire County Council; L v Tower Hamlets London Borough Council and another* [2000] 3 All ER 346 at 372.

[126] Ibid at 373.

[127] *TP and KM v United Kingdom* [2001] 2 FLR 549, [2001] 2 FCR 289, [2001] Fam Law 590, ECHR.

and it would not be just and reasonable to impose such a duty. The European Court of Human Rights found a violation of Arts. 8 and 13 and no violation of Art. 6 of the European Convention on Human Rights. The court found a failure to respect the family life of the applicants in the fact that the local authority failed to provide access to the information which it held in form of the video recording of the daughter's interview. Knowledge of the content of that tape would have enabled the applicant to get involved in the decision-making process concerning the care of her daughter. The court held that this was a failure of the authority to respect the applicants' family life protected under Art. 8 of the Convention. Further, the court held that there was no violation of Art. 6 of the Convention.

In conclusion, the decision in *Osman* has undoubtedly influenced the reasoning of English courts with regard to allowing cases to proceed to full trial and to give a more thorough consideration to policy arguments. The case of *Barrett*, in particular, has set a trend towards a more critical analysis of policy considerations. *Z* is unlikely to reverse that trend. *Z* has clarified that in clear cases striking out actions in which policy considerations are balanced against each other (proportional immunity) are not in violation of Art. 6 of the European Convention on Human Rights. After *Z* a more rigorous balancing of policy considerations is necessary to comply with Convention rights.

However, the novelty in *Z* is that cases might not have to proceed to full trial incurring the costs as illustrated in *Barrett*. *Z* does not require factual evidence to be heard at a full trial. However, as stated by Lord Browne-Wilkinson *in X (minors) v Bedfordshire County Council* and *Barrett*, there are good reasons for allowing a case to proceed to examine factual evidence rather than simply striking out. He made it clear that the law of liability of public bodies, which is a developing area of law, should be based on actual facts found at trial. In his view it might even reduce misunderstandings and a "proliferation of claims" if the facts are clearly proven.[128] This trend towards a more careful weighing of policy considerations on the basis of the actual facts rather than hypothetical ones seems unlikely to change in the light of the new Civil Procedure Rules. Rule 24.2 provides a good compromise between the interests of the defendants in keeping the costs of proceedings low and the new approach of a more thorough balancing of policy considerations on the basis of the actual facts. The subject of liability of public bodies has, in the author's view, benefited from the lively exchange of jurisprudence from judges in the common law and judges applying the Convention. Finally, it is worth noting that in *Z* the plaintiffs succeeded in their claim under Art. 3 and in the absence of a remedy provided by the domestic law there was a further breach of Art. 13. The plaintiffs in *TP and KM* were successful in establishing breaches of Arts. 8 and 13. As well as suing local authorities in negligence, applicants in these type of cases (occurring after 2 October 2000)[129] will in future be able to claim breaches of Arts. 3 and 8 of the Convention under Sects. 7 and 8 of the Human Rights Act 1998.

---

[128] *Barrett v Enfield* [1999] 3 All ER 193 at 198.

[129] Section 22(4) Human Rights Act 1998.

The decision in *Z v UK* had been celebrated as a retreat from *Osman v UK*. However, the more recent decision in *JD v East Berkshire NHS Trust*[130] illustrates that indeed a slightly more careful approach towards granting "blanket immunities" seems to have take root in English law.

The case was concerned with the diagnosis of child abuse carried out by the children's parents. The House of Lords held that it would not be fair, just and reasonable to impose a common law duty of care on the doctors. However, it did not grant a "blanket immunity" for doctors: Lord Nicholls held:

"This should be the general rule, where the relationship between doctor and parent is confined to the fact that the parent is father or mother of the doctor's patient. There may, exceptionally, be circumstances where this is not so. Different considerations may apply then. But there is nothing of this sort in any of these three cases. The fact that a parent took the unexceptional step of initiating recourse to medical advice is not a special circumstance for this purpose. Nor is the fact that the parent took the child to a general practitioner or to a hospital to see a consultant."[131]Further, the court held that doctors owed a common law duty of care towards the children.

Lord Bingham dissented and by referring to French and German law emphasized that a shift towards a discussion of the breach element would be preferable to striking out a claim and that this would not bear the risk of a flood of litigation:

"I would for my part regard that shift as welcome, since the concept of duty has proved itself a somewhat blunt instrument for dividing claims which ought reasonably to lead to recovery from claims which ought not. But I should make it plain that if breach rather than duty were to be the touchstone of recovery, no breach could be proved without showing a very clear departure from ordinary standards of skill and care. It should be no easier to succeed here than in France or Germany."[132]

There will be more cases, no doubt, waiting to be decided. This area of law remains complex and unpredictable. A new avenue for claimants is the pecuniar remedy provided by section 8 of the Human Rights Act 1998. To date there have only been few damages cases under the Act.

b) Damages for breaches of the Human Rights Act 1998

Section 8 of the Human Rights Act 1998 provides for the award of damages for breaches of Convention rights:

"(1) In relation to any act (or proposed act) of a public authority which the court finds is (or would be) unlawful, it may grant such relief or remedy ... within its powers as it considers just and appropriate.

(2) But damages may be awarded only by a court which has the power to award damages, or to order the payment of compensation in civil proceedings.

---

130 [2005] UKHL 23.

131 [2005] UKHL 23, 91.

132 [2005] UKHL 23, 49.

(3) No award of damages is to be made unless, taking account of all the circumstances of the case, including

(a) any other relief or remedy granted, or order made, in relation to the act in question (by that or any other court), and

(b) the consequences of any decision (of that or any other court) in respect of that act,

the court is satisfied that the award is necessary to afford just satisfaction to the person in whose favour it is made.

(4) In determining whether to award damages, or the amount of an award, the court must take account of the principles applied by the European Court of Human Rights in relation to the award of compensation under Art. 41 of the Convention".

The principles as to the award of damages under the Human Rights Act have taken shape over the last few years.[133] Granting damages under the Human Rights Act is within the discretion of the court and compensation is only awarded if "necessary". The courts are empowered to award damages under the Act, but are under no duty to do so. Further, English courts should take principles developed by the European Court of Human Rights into account so that damages are equivalent to those awarded by the Strasbourg court. The courts are therefore encouraged to take account of European principles, but are under no duty to do so[134] as opposed to the requirements under European Community law.[135] Gradually, more decisions in this area of law are shedding light on how the courts apply Sect. 8 of the Human Rights Act. The report by the Law Commission in 2000 had illustrated in detail how difficult it would be for the courts to detract coherent guidelines from the patchy jurisprudence of the Strasbourg court.[136] Currently, the two most important rulings are the decision by the Court of Appeal in *Anufrijeva* and the decision by the House of Lords in *Greenfield.*[137] The claimants in *Anufrijeva*[138] submitted that their accommodation was insufficient and that there had been delays in the administration of their application. They claimed a violation of Art. 8 of the Convention entitling them to the award of damages under Sect. 8 of the Act. The applications were unsuccessful. Lord Woolf established important guidelines in this case: the claimant should so far as is possible be reinstated to the position as if his rights under the Act had not been violated, the European Court of Human Rights does not pay out compensation for the violation of procedural errors and that the seriousness of the case has to be taken into account. The case of *Greenfield* concerned the claim of a prisoner who had been subject to disciplinary proceedings resulting in additional days' imprisonment. He claimed that the procedure had been carried

---

133 Clayton, R., "Damages After Greenfield: Where Are We Now?", *Judicial Review* 2006, 230, 230.

134 Clayton, R., "Damage Limitation: The Courts and the Human Rights Act Damages" (2005) *Public Law* S. 429, 430.

135 EuGH, Verb. Rs. C-6 und 9/90, Slg. 1991, I-5357 – *Francovich und Bonifaci/Italien*; Verb. Rs. C-46 und 48/93, Slg. 1996, I-1029 – *Brasserie du Pecheur und R/Secretary of State for Transport, ex p Factortame* [1996] QB 404.

136 Law Commission Report no. 266, "Damages Under the Human Rights Act", Cm 4853 (2000).

137 *R v Secretary of State for the Home Department, ex p Greenfield* [2005] UKHL 14.

138 [2003] EWCA Civ 1406, [2004] QB 1124.

out in breach of Art. 6. The issue to resolve for the House of Lords was the question of damages under the Human Rights Act. Lord Bingham held that it was important to treat the jurisprudence of the ECHR as guidance and that a finding of a breach of a Convention right is generally sufficient affording just satisfaction in itself.[139] The award of damages should be the exception and the Human Rights Act is not a tort statute. [140] Awards under the Human Rights Act should reflect the modest approach of the European Court of Human Rights. [141] . There have only been a few cases after *Greenfield*.[142] It has been suggested that the limits on the award of damages under the Human Rights Act "may also have implications for the development of common law causes of action."[143] This development could lead to claimants achieving "a more effective remedy if they seek Francovich damages in cases where they have both an HRA claim and a European Union claim."[144] As we shall see below, the award of damages under the head of member state liability has been less problematic in the UK.

2. Child abuse claims in Germany[145]

In Germany, failures by youth authorities to the detriment of children are equally posing complex legal issues. A few cases have put local youth authorities and the work of social workers into the spotlight and led to criminal convictions and/or tort claims against the authority.[146] The subject has been widely discussed in the media and articles mainly written by legal practitioners and the dilemma of the social workers in fulfilling their difficult task between supporting the unity of the family and the protection of the individual child has become evident.[147] The work

139 *R v Secretary of State for the Home Department, ex p Greenfield* [2005] UKHL 14. para. 2.6.

140 *R v Secretary of State for the Home Department, ex p Greenfield* [2005] UKHL 14. para 19

141 *R v Secretary of State for the Home Department, ex p Greenfield* [2005] UKHL 14. para 17.

142 *R (Wilkinson) v IRC* [2005] UKHL 30; *R (Anthony) v Parole Board* [2005] EWHC; *Van Colle v Chief Constable of Hertfordshire* [2006] EWCH 360 (damages were awarded for breaches of Art 2 and 8).

143 Clayton, R., "Damages After Greenfield: Where Are We Now?", *Judicial Review* 2006, 230, 230, 235.

144 Clayton, R., "Damages After Greenfield: Where Are We Now?", *Judicial Review* 2006, 230, 237.

145 This section is based on a publication by the author in Fairgrieve, D. and Green, S., *Tortious Liability of Public Bodies in a Comparative Perspective*, 2004.

146 The case of "Jenny", LG Stuttgart, 17.9.1999, 1 (15) KLs 114 Js 26273/96 and OLG Oldenburg, 2.09.1996, ZfJ 1997, 95; BGH 21.10.2004 III ZR 254/03; BGH 23.2.2006 III ZR 164/05.

147 Friedrichsen, Gisela, "Musste Jenny sterben?", *Der Spiegel*, 39/1999; Bringewat, Peter, "Kommunale Jugendhilfe und strafrechtliche Garantenhaftung (1998) *Neue Juristische Wochenschrift* 944; Lehman, Karl-Heinz, Helfen ohne Risiko Justiz contra Sozialarbeit, Referat anlässlich der Fachtagung des DBSH Landesverbandes Niedersachsen am

of local youth authorities has also been the subject of numerous petitions by individuals or initiatives to the members of the *Länder* and the federal Parliament and the *Kinderkommission* of the *Bundestag*. Among other complaints, the petitions are concerned with the supervision of children in care and the lack of co-operation with the biological family concerning the return of the child[148] similar to the factual circumstances in *Barrett v Enfield London Borough Council*.[149] The more serious cases have been subject to criminal prosecution which have led to the sentencing of youth workers in 1999.[150]

Local youth authorities have only very rarely been sued for negligence.

The decision by the European Court of Human Rights in *Z v UK*[151] did not receive much attention in Germany.

The basic right of children in care to a hearing by the relevant youth authority (Art. 1, 2 I and II 1 Basic Law) and the tortious liability of the latter was addressed in a more recent decision by the BGH.[152] The case concerned the abuse of three young children in foster care, one of whom tragically died of starvation. Both lower courts, the *Landgericht* and the *Oberlandesgericht*, agreed that the youth authority had failed to comply with its statutory duties. According to the SGB VIII (*Kinder und Jugendhilfegesetz*), the youth authority was under a duty to acknowledge its own responsibility for the case, assess the foster family and observe the right of the children to be heard and to participate in their own fate. This constitutionally protected basic right of the child outweighed the right to the protection of the autonomy of the foster family (Art. 6 Basic Law).[153] All three courts agreed on the award of relatively modest compensation amounting to €25,000. The decision emphasises the right of the child to participate in its own fate. Nevertheless, it was criticised for simplifying complex questions of causation in the context of childcare and medical issues.[154] The BGH found that the youth authority failed to accept responsibility for the claimant who had moved into its jurisdiction. This was held to be a breach of the duty under Sect. 37, 3, 1 of the SGB VIII, according to which the youth authority has to inspect the conditions in which foster children are brought up. Instead the authorities had exchanged correspondence between 1994 and 1997 during which time the claimant and two other foster children suffered severe malnutrition which led to the death of a third foster child.

1.6.2000 in der KFH; Nolte, Susanne, "Elternrecht, Rechte des Kindes und Kinderschutz bei Kindesmisshandlung Gegenpole im Spannungsfeld", *Kindesmisshandlung und – Vernachlässigung*, December 2001, 77.

148 Wiesner, Reinhard, Problemaufriss zum Thema "Kontrolle/Arbeit der Jugendämter", Tagesdokumentation "Kindeswohl" – Dilemma und Praxis der Jugendämter – epd-Dokumentation Nr. 6/97 vom 3 Febr. 1997, p. 70 http://www.pappa.com/ja/ wies_ ja.htm.

149 [1999] 3 All ER 193.

150 LG Stuttgart, 17.9.1999, 1 (15) KLs 114 Js 26273/96.

151 *Z v United Kingdom* [2001] 2 FLR 612.

152 See Hinrichs, K., *Evangelische Jugendhilfe* (2004).

153 BGH III ZR 254/03, pp. 15–16.

154 See Meysen, T., (2003) *NJW* 3369 [3372, 3373].

In case *III ZR* (164/05, 23 February 2006) the BGH decided, however, that the youth authority will not be liable for any harm suffered by the foster child in the care of the fostering parents if they had been selected carefully and in accordance with the provisions governing fostering.

a) Section 839 BGB in connection with Art. 34 Basic Law

aa) Duty of care owed to a third party

Both Sect. 839 of the BGB and Art. 34 of the Basic Law require that the official duty must be owed to *a third party*. Whether a person is a third party in that sense depends on whether the object of the duty is directly to safeguard the interests of that person. If, for instance, a policeman remains inactive while a theft is being committed, he is in breach of his official duty towards the owner because his power to interfere is conferred on individuals and illustrates that the courts are given some leeway as to how to interpret the concept of duty. In the context of child care cases the establishment of such a duty is clearly to be found in the KJHG (*Kinder und Jugendhilfegesetz* or SGB VIII). The duty to intervene in cases in which a child is at risk of injury by its parents is contained in Sect. 2 of the KJHG. The official duties of the youth authorities are enumerated here and contain the provision of educational assistance and other services and the taking of young children into care if necessary (see Sect. 42 KJHG). Potential cases in negligence against public bodies would not fail at this early stage. There is little doubt that the local youth authority is under a duty to protect the welfare of children as soon as the authority obtains knowledge of the neglect.

However, some of the arguments brought forward in the English decision in *X v Bedfordshire County Council*, which are described as "policy" arguments, appear alien to modern German reasoning. Among the policy arguments in *X v Bedfordshire County Council* were those that imposing liability would make bad economic sense, that it would inhibit public authorities to carry out their duties, that the courts would be allowed to substitute the authorities' decisions by having a "second guess" and that alternative remedies were available. However, a closer look into material stemming from the time when the German Civil Code was drafted in 1900 reveals that similar arguments were considered. However, a study has been carried out and revealed that the expenses for state liability cases amounted to only 0.015 per cent of the total budget. It was discussed whether imposing liability would make civil servants act too cautiously. However, it was agreed that that would be better than allowing careless behaviour on the part of civil servants. Further, discretionary decisions may be reviewed and give rise to liability.[155]

---

155 For an excellent discussion of these points, see Markesinis, B.S., Auby, J.B., Coester-Waltjen, D. & Deakin, S.F., *Tortious Liability of Statutory Bodies, A Comparative and Economic Analysis of Five English Cases,* 1999.

bb) Fault

Liability is only imposed on the official if he or she has wilfully or negligently breached an official duty. However, it has been shown that the element of fault does not constitute a particular problem in the establishment of a claim in negligence against public bodies.

cc) Causation

The breach of the duty owed towards the plaintiff has to have caused the damage. This condition of liability may cause difficulties in cases where the authorities have a choice between different forms of action. In providing assistance to parents under the KJHG such as educational assistance, family therapy and other supplementary services or the taking of children into care, the authorities exercise a certain amount of discretion. A causal link between the breach of the duty of care and the damage can only be established if the lawful exercise of the duty of care would have avoided the damage with the highest probability.[156] In this context, it is crucial to identify how the authority in acting lawfully would have decided the case. If the authority was exercising discretion it would be impossible to predict how the authority would have decided. The causal link can only be established in cases where there was only one correct form of the exercise of discretion (*Ermessensreduzierung auf Null*) or where it is absolutely clear how the discretion should have been exercised lawfully and that this exercise would have avoided the damage. In the case of *Barrett* it might have been difficult to establish what the only correct exercise of the authorities' discretion would have been.

Having outlined the difficulties in obtaining compensation under the provisions for official liability an excursion into the constitutional framework of child care laws and the availability of primary legal protection in the form of judicial review of administrative decisions will follow.

b) The constitutional framework for the law governing childcare

The law governing the relationship between the state, parents and their children is contained in different statutes such as the BGB (Civil Code) and the KJHG (a special law for the help of children and youths, also called the SGB VIII) and can only be understood in the context of the constitutional protection of the family as guaranteed in Art. 6 of the Basic Law which reads:

"(1) Marriage and family shall enjoy the special protection of the state.

(2) The care and upbringing of children are a natural right of parents and a duty primarily incumbent on them. It is the responsibility of the community to ensure that they perform this duty.

(3) Children may not be separated from their families against the will of their parents or guardians save in accordance with a law in cases where they fail in their duty or there is a danger of the children being seriously neglected for other reasons".

---

156 BGH VersR 1983, 1031.

When the Basic Law was drafted in 1949 in the light of Germany's history the main purpose of a written catalogue of rights was to protect the individual against infringements by the state (*Abwehrrechte gegen den Staat*). Accordingly, the constitution protects the unity of the family against state intervention. Art. 6 para 1 Basic Law is equally an example for a Basic right which guarantees a duty of the state to provide protection for the family (*staatliche Schutzpflicht*). The child is considered to be part of the family. The care for and the bringing up of children is considered to be the right and the duty of the parents. The state is under a duty to act as a guardian (*Wächterfunktion*) which can be enforced by local youth authorities or in extreme cases by the courts. Accordingly, the law for the help of children and youths states that the care and the education of children is the natural right and duty of the parents.[157]

c) Judicial review of administrative decisions in childcare cases

The law provides for the power of the local youth authority to take children who are at serious risk into care.[158] However, for the protection of the unity of the family the law for the help of children and youths provides for measures of help such as the counselling of the parents and special living arrangements such as boarding. According to Sect. 27 of this law it is the parents who hold the right to help in the caring for their children. The law was not intended to provide children with a right to receive help, but contains the right of parents to receive help in the upbringing of their children if needed. The protection of the parents' rights to receive such help is enforceable in the German Administrative Courts. There is a wealth of cases concerned with judicial review of the decisions of youth authorities in granting or refusing such help.[159] Therefore the primary protection of these interests in Germany is very strong. This is due to the constitutional mandate in Art. 19 IV of the Basic Law which provides for judicial control of administrative decisions. In other words, families who are not coping very well may request help in the upbringing of their children. If such help is refused by the youth authority, the decisions can be reviewed by the Administrative Courts.

To illustrate this point I have chosen a recent decision by the highest Administrative Court in Rheinland-Pfalz in Koblenz.[160] The applicants were the parents of a boy aged 15 who suffered from serious behavioural problems which were partly due to the mother's depression and the lack of time of the father to look after his son. As the parents had difficulties in coping with the child and in order to prevent further social neglect of the child they applied for the placement of the child in a care institution. The local youth authority, however, refused the request and offered help in the home in the form of a supervisor to aid and support the family (*Erziehungsbeistand*). The parents applied for judicial review of the decision, but

157 Paragraph 1(2) KJHG.

158 Paragraph 42 KJHG.

159 See Hinrichs, K., Selbstbeschaffung im Jugendhilferecht – Zur Aktualität fürsorgerechtlicher Grundsätze in der Jugendhilfe, 2002.

160 OVG Koblenz, 11.05.2000 – 12 A 12335/99.OVG.

were unsuccessful with their claim. The Administrative Court held that decisions concerning the review of pedagogic considerations were not fully reviewable as the decision maker had a margin of evaluation (*Beurteilungsspielraum*). Nevertheless the decision could be reviewed with regard to whether the decision maker had taken irrelevant considerations into account and whether the decision was necessary and suitable. In applying these tests the court held that the decision had been lawful.

This decision illustrates that in the light of the constitutional protection of the family one of the main aims of child protection laws is the provision of help for parents in the upbringing of their children. The person entitled to these benefits is the parent and decisions by the youth authorities are subject to review by the Administrative Courts. The intensity of review applied by the Administrative Courts varies between different courts and is highly controversial.[161] Nevertheless, the case was aimed at illustrating that primary legal protection (often in speedy procedures) is of great importance in Germany. Negligence claims are secondary which is clearly stated in Sect. 839 III of the BGB. Accordingly, a negligence claim is excluded if the applicant has not exhausted other judicial remedies such as judicial review of the original decision. A hypothetical claim in negligence for damage caused by this decision would be bound to fail as the decision by the Administrative Court would be followed by the court dealing with the tortious claim.[162] The wealth of judicial review cases involving childcare illustrates that the decisions of authorities concerning the provision of help in the upbringing of children are subject to judicial scrutiny. Many cases are concerned with the payment for services carried out by independent providers which parents have chosen and for which they request financial support from the youth authorities. Further, it has been suggested that individual citizens appear to know their rights, even though they may not be aware of the statutory basis for their claims.[163]

Nevertheless, there are situations in which help under the childcare laws has not been requested and the youth authorities failed to intervene in time to prevent tragic outcomes. In these cases there are no parents to sue local authorities. Here we need to look at the legal position of the child. The case of *Jenny*[164] illustrates that children may find themselves in a legal vacuum between parental rights and the unity of the family structure and the reluctance of youth authorities and the courts to separate them from their family for their own safety. Such care orders can only be made if the safety of a child is seriously at risk. According to Sect. 1666a of the BGB the provision of help inside the family structure has to preside over the separation of family and child. The youth worker in the case of *Jenny* should have informed his colleague in southern Germany, where the mother and

161 See Hinrichs, K., Selbstbeschaffung im Jugendhilferecht – Zur Aktualität fürsorgerechtlicher Grundsätze in der Jugendhilfe, 2002.

162 BGHZ 9, 129, 132; BGH NVwZ 1984, 333; BGHZ 118, 235, 255 = *NJW* 1992, 2218.

163 See Hinrichs, K., Selbstbeschaffung im Jugendhilferecht – Zur Aktualität fürsorgerechtlicher Grundsätze in der Jugendhilfe, 2002.

164 Jenny, three, was found dead after having been abused and battered by her mother. The case was known to the local youth authorities. The case led to the criminal conviction of one social youth worker: LG Stuttgart, 17.9.1999, 1 (15) KLs 114 Js 26273/96.

child had moved, of the special circumstances of the case. He was sentenced for being negligent in omitting this vital piece of information. The problem raised by this case was that children at risk often change their residence which is intended by the parents to shake off observation by the youth authorities. This has the effect that in the absence of a national register for abused children, children in these situations often fall through the net of childcare protection.[165]

Finally, due to the conservative mode of the family unit as protected in Art. 6 of the Basic Law children are not legally entitled to childcare measures themselves. The right to receive such help is primarily linked to the parental right. However, children from these deprived families are often not confident enough to sue youth authorities, the cases are not lucrative enough to be taken up by solicitors and the concept of the guardian *ad litem* is only just developing to improve the position of abused children in court proceedings. So far there are no guidelines for the legal representation of children.[166] Only a few years ago the introduction of the concept of a guardian *ad litem* (*Verfahrenspfleger*), an independent representative of the child's rights, was introduced into Sect. 50 of the FGG (*Gesetz über die freiwillige Gerichtsbarkeit*). Despite comparative research into the function of the guardian *ad litem* before the provision was drafted, the role of the guardian *ad litem* has to be improved.[167] Often they are not independent enough to support a child's case in negligence against an authority.[168]

In conclusion, reasons for the relatively few negligence claims in child abuse cases in Germany are due to the emphasis on the primary legal protection against decisions of youth authorities concerning the welfare of children. Due to the constitutional protection of the family unit in Art. 6 of the Basic Law child welfare provisions in the BGB and SGB VIII are primarily concerned with the support of the parents in the upbringing of their children. They are entitled to measures of help as enumerated in the KJHG and these rights are enforceable in the Administrative Courts. Article 19 IV of the Basic Law guarantees the judicial review of such decisions. Accordingly, a wealth of case law concerned with child welfare matters can be found. Further, the law of tortious liability against public bodies is a secondary legal remedy which is clearly excluded if legal remedies to prevent the damage have not been used.

In technical legal terms a claim in negligence would not fail at the early stage of the establishment of a duty of care. Such a duty towards children could be derived from the KJHG which puts youth authorities under an official duty to support the welfare of children. However, the requirement of causality could cause difficulties if the authority had discretion in exercising its powers. A claim could fail unless it can be shown that the authority was under a duty to perform its dis-

165 Nolte, S., "Elternrecht, Rechte des Kindes und Kinderschutz bei Kindesmisshandlung: Gegenpole im Spannungsfeld", *Kindesmisshandlung und Vernachlässigung*, December 2001, 77.

166 Marquardt, C., Sexuell missbrauchte Kinder im Gerichtsverfahren ,1999, 150.

167 Salgo, L., *Der Anwalt des Kindes*, 1993.

168 Nolte, S., "Elternrecht, Rechte des Kindes und Kinderschutz bei Kindesmisshandlung Gegenpole im Spannungsfeld", *Kindesmisshandlung und Vernachlässigung*, 2001, 77 [85].

cretion in a particular way (*Ermessensreduzierung auf Null*). As seen above, if a case overcomes these hurdles the award of damages remains on the low side.

The legal position of children, however, is comparatively weak in this relationship between parental rights and the intervention of the state. For practical reasons they may fall through the net of social support and legal protection. This is both due to the fact that there is little control over children being moved from one jurisdiction to the next and due to the emphasis in the law on the preservation of the family unit. A legal vacuum is further created by the lack of individual children's rights. The introduction of a *Verfahrenspfleger* in 1998, modelled on the British guardian *ad litem*, is a step in the right direction.

d) The violation of basic rights and compensation

Case *III ZR* (361/03, 4 November 2004) concerned the claim of a prisoner complaining about the conditions of imprisonment. For two days he had to share a small cell with three other prisoners and very basic sanitary facilities which provided little privacy. He claimed compensation of at least €200 on the basis of Art. 34 of the Basic Law in connection with Sect. 839 of the BGB. The *Landgericht* decided in the claimant's favour, but the *Oberlandesgericht* and BGH dismissed the claim.

Similar to the *Greenfield* case the issue was the question of compensation for a breach of a basic right, here Art. 1, the protection of human dignity. The BGH drew parallels to its jurisprudence on compensation in cases of violations of the right to privacy and held that in this case the violation of the claimant's right to privacy was not severe enough to justify monetary compensation.

The result is correct. However, the reasoning of the court has been criticised for not distinguishing clearly enough between private and public law.[169] Unlike Lord Bingham in *Greenfield*, the BGH treated the claim like one in private law according to the rules that apply to private law relationships. These are quite restrictive since Sect. 253 of the BGB contains a prohibition to compensate for immaterial damage. Only in exceptional cases has the BGH awarded compensation. The BGH failed to draw a clear line between between the jurisprudence established for the protection of the right to privacy (*Persönlichkeitsrechtsschutz*) in purely private law and the protection of Art. 1 of the Basic Law (human dignity) in a case involving the actions of a public authority. Lord Bingham, on the other hand, made it clear in *Greenfield* that the Human Rights Act is not a "tort statute and that its objectives were different and broader; a finding of a violation is an important vindication of the right asserted".[170]

---

169 Unterreitmeier, J., "Grundrechtsverletzung und Geldentschädigung – kein zwingendes Junktim?" (2005) *DVBl* 1235.

170 [2005] UKHL 14 at 19.

3. Evaluation

From the cases it is noticeable that the German judgments are free from any policy arguments whereas the English judgments contain arguments based on policy considerations such as the following.

One common argument is the fear that an increase in liability would lead to a more defensive approach of public authorities in their work. Further, the argument is often raised that many decision-making processes involve more than one person and that it would amount to scapegoating to hold a single person responsible for damage. Another policy argument is that of "floodgates", which refers to the fear of public bodies that an increase of claims in negligence could lead to a great reduction of available means of public bodies. Further it is argued that alternative forms of protection exist which make it unnecessary to file a claim in damages against the authorities.[171]

Policy arguments of that kind are not mentioned in German judgments. However, they have played a role, in particular, at the time when the German Civil Code was drafted which dates back to 1900.[172] The argument regarding the fear that claims in negligence could inhibit the exercise of public powers was of particular concern to the drafters of the Code. However, it was decided that the inhibitions of public servants were better than any "careless or less diligent behaviour on the part of civil servants".[173] The economic argument concerning the expenditure of scarce economic resources has also been mentioned in Germany, but had little impact on the legislature and court decisions; it is noteworthy that German awards in damages are much lower than in England.[174]

Striking out actions are not unknown as such in Germany. The equivalent is the *Prozeßurteil*, a judgment being given if the claim is unsubstantiated (*unschlüssig*). This is the case if the alleged (hypothetical) facts do not sufficiently substantiate a claim or cause of action. However, in *Osman*, the hypothetical facts would have been sufficient to say that under German law there is a possibility that the Osmans would win the case if the proportionality test is decided in their favour. At the heart of the problem is the difficulty of conciliating the principle of precedence with the European model of proportionality. Lord Browne-Wilkinson in the case of *Barrett v Enfield* has identified the problem with the application of the *Osman* judgment to English law:[175]

"In English law, questions of public policy and the question whether it is fair, just and reasonable to impose liability in negligence are decided as questions of law. Once the decision is taken that, say, company auditors though liable to shareholders for negligent auditing are not liable to those proposing to invest in the company, that decision will apply to all future cases of the same kind. The decision does not depend on weighing the balance between the extent of the damage to the plaintiff and the damage to the public in each particular case".

---

171 See *Stovin v Wise* [1963] 3 WLR 388.

172 Markesinis, B.,S., supra n. 67, 58.

173 Ibid.

174 Ibid at 61.

175 *Barrett v Enfield London Borough Council* [1999] 3 All ER 193 at 199.

Striking out actions in Germany would not apply blanket immunities in the way it was done in *Osman* referring to a previous judgment (*Hill*). The courts examine whether hypothetically a cause of action is given (*Schlüssigkeitsprüfung*) and review the case in more detail if this is the case. They might then still come to the conclusion that the plaintiff's action is unsuccessful (*Begündetheitsprüfung*). Each case is decided afresh. The different approach by the German courts clearly illustrates the gap between the legal cultures. German courts apply the facts in each case to the given rule, here the rules on tortious liability of civil servants as set out in the Civil Code and the Basic Law. In contrast the English system of precedence does not require the courts to decide each case on its merits if a precedent exists which determines the outcome of a case. Therefore no such list of cases to be struck out as can be found in the *Supreme Court Practice*[176] can be found in any German commentary. A further result of these different approaches is that groups of cases such as the "abuse" or "education" cases cannot easily be identified in German law. However, in determining the duty of an official the German statute contains no specific catalogue of such duties. In that respect a considerable amount of groups of cases can be found in German commentaries.

In their extensive use of policy arguments English courts reveal that the functioning of public bodies and economic considerations are still more important than the protection of an individual's rights. However, English public law is developing rapidly now and is an exciting area of law because of the changes it undergoes. These changes are mainly due to the influences of external sources of decision making such as the European Court of Human Rights and the European Court of Justice. The rule of law in its traditional interpretation by Dicey clearly states that English law does not contain a positive catalogue of human rights. However, with the introduction of the Human Rights Act 1998 this statement has lost its relevance. The Act confers new grounds of review on individuals and introduces a new form of compensation for human rights violations as will be shown below. The decision in *Osman* has already had an impact on the development of tortious liability of public bodies to the extent that courts will in future be more careful in striking out actions.

A comparison of the tortious liability of public bodies has to be seen in the light of the historical developments and the constitutional backgrounds in which the liability has developed in both countries. The historical and constitutional background in both systems provides an explanation for the differences in the approaches. Both systems vary in their deeper philosophical approach to awarding damages in liability cases against public bodies. The English justification process is marked by a very policy-oriented reasoning containing elements such as economic considerations, floodgate arguments and the concern that liability might inhibit the performance of public functions. The German concept of state liability is characterised by three main considerations: "the need to control statutory bodies, their willingness to do this by using all possible means at their disposal including

176 *The Supreme Court Practice* ,1991, vol. 1, part 1.

the courts, a complete contempt for the argument that such control would make the civil servant in question reluctant to act".[177]

At the bottom of these differences lies a different attitude in each country with regard to the definition of the state and the relationship between state and citizen. Further, the concepts of parliamentary and constitutional sovereignty in England and Germany respectively serve to explain the differing roles of the courts in reviewing unlawful action of public bodies and awarding damages. English law does not recognise the concept of the state, which might explain the absence of a clearly defined position for applicants in damages claims who are faced with judgments based on policy considerations. Rather, "the tendency to identify the notion of sovereignty with a particular institution or organ has persisted in Britain".[178] The term state "denotes a form of political order that emerged in Europe between the thirteenth and the late eighteenth or early nineteenth century as a result of specific conditions and impulses in European history".[179] It is not possible to give one precise definition of *lo stato, l'État, der Staat* or the state as it meant different things in different countries, at different times subject to a variety of theories.[180] Thomas Starkey has used the word "state" in England as early as 1538 and is still a term attached to positions such as "Secretary of State". The idea of the state as "territorial phenomenon" is fully recognised in Britain.[181] However, Britain does not attach a much greater meaning to the concept of the state than that. This is due to the fact that historically England chose a quite distinct path compared to its European neighbour "states" in the development of the concept. In brief this is due to the impressive "continuity of its political development from its medieval roots". Unlike Germany, which once was divided into more than 150 splinter states, Britain did not have to struggle for unity. On the contrary, as early as the tenth century unity had been achieved and the Crown had a strong position. Secondly, the well-organised legal profession had developed into a close-knit society of legal experts centred in the Inns of Court in London and "an evolutionary judge-made common law served as an instrument of unification".[182] Comparably the German legal profession was not centralised and the law was a rather confused combination of German customary law which differed from state to state. As a result the principles and concepts of Roman law, which were studied with enthusiasm by German medieval scholars in search of a unified body of law for Germany, did not find the same reception in England. On the continent therefore the concept of state was developed mainly through the scholarship of academic lawyers who traditionally had a more leading role in the development of the law:

---

177 Markesinis, B.S., Auby, J.B., Coester-Waltjen, D. & Deakin, S.F., Tortious Liability of Statutory Bodies, A Comparative and Economic Analysis of Five English Cases, 1999, 114.

178 Dyson, K.H.F., *The State Tradition in Western Europe* ,1980, 115.

179 Böckenförde, E.W., *State, Society and Liberty,* 1991, 26.

180 See supra nn. 167 and 168.

181 Dyson, supra n. 178, 38.

182 Ibid at 42.

"Legal scholars sought to provide a doctrine, a body of concepts that were based on elaborate technical distinctions and would enable lawyers and judges to act with promptness and precision, clarify the deliberations of the law maker, and bring unity, coherence and order into the legal system. In particular the German Civil Code, drafted in 1896, is a good example of how much influence academic lawyers had in making the *Rechtsstaat* of the law".[183]

The development of the concept of the state preceded the development of the *Rechtsstaat* as it is contained in today's Basic Law. The first roots of the *Rechtsstaat* can be found in the liberal movement in the nineteenth century. The *Rechtsstaatsprinzip* in its modern version is contained in the German Basic Law and embraces the principle of the separation of powers and the protection of the individual in the courts, in particular, the protection of the individual against governmental action as laid down in Arts. 19(4) and 20(3) of the Basic Law. This constitutional background provides the setting in which the tortious liability of public bodies is embedded.

The *Rechtsstaats* principle is not equivalent to the rule of law. In summary, the rule of law is traditionally concerned with three elements which are equality before the law in the sense that there is no room in English law for a separate system of administrative courts, the absence of wide discretionary powers and the absence of a written catalogue of rights in a single document. Dicey's original conception of the rule of law, however, is outdated with respect to the element of equality considering the developments of a body of English public law.

Allison[184] argues that the public–private law distinction as known in France is a clear example that the establishment of a system of public law containing rules on governmental liability is facilitated by the clear institutional distinction between public and private law courts. This might be a reasonable conclusion following a comparison of English and French law. However, it can be contended that it is not necessarily the institutional distinction between private and public law in terms of a system of separate courts which strengthens the development of the law of governmental liability. The comparison with the German system has shown that it is the principle of the *Rechtsstaat* which defines the relationship between citizen and state.

The differences between the English and German system of tortious liability for unlawful governmental action are not as evident as compared to the French system. In contrast to the French system, both the English and German rules on tortious liability have developed the concept of duty of care in a restrictive way. Both in England and Germany the tortious liability of public bodies is to be enforced in private law courts. Even the German reforms on state liability do not intend to transfer the jurisdiction over state liability cases to the Administrative Courts. Rather, it is suggested to combine the proceedings of review of unlawful action and damages in the same court, be it a finance court, a social court or a private law court. The comparisons of English and German law in this field have revealed different attitudes of the court with regard to the position of the individual and the

[183] Ibid at 112.

[184] Allison, A.W.F.,, *A Continental Distinction in the Common Law*, 2000.

position of the public body. In Germany this is clearly marked by a philosophy of protection against the state and facilitating access to damages as a clear expression of the *Rechtsstaat*. The modern German *Rechtsstaat*, however, which is the result of a development over the last 200 years, contains a number of elements such as the guarantee of human rights, the division of power, judicial independence, the protection against executive acts "and a system of compensation with justly acquired rights in the event of state interference or misconduct, the result being a state based on the principles of proportionality, justice and legal certainty".[185] The protection of human rights as a main part of the *Rechtsstaat* principle clearly indicates that in Germany the constitution is supreme. This has led to the development of a "rights based culture" which also reflects upon the approach that is taken when holding public bodies liable for unlawful action. The policy arguments applied by English courts in liability cases on the contrary reflect an attitude which is not so much concerned with individual positions, but rather the public interest.

Despite these conceptual differences in constitutional history and concepts, current developments in English law might bring the German and English positions taken by judges in damages cases closer to each other. Interestingly, English courts appear to have been more geneours in awarding compensation for breaches of Community law. The next section will assess the case law in this area of law.

III. Comparative cases - member state liability in German and English courts[186]

The criteria for determining the extent of reparation in the realisation of the *Francovich* remedy for breaches of Community law are set by national courts, provided that national rules for the evaluation of damages comply with the familiar principles of equivalence and effectiveness. However, entrusting national legal systems with this task bears risking "national reflexes of legislators and judges in the member states".[187] It has been stated that "the application of national law bears the risk of diverging decisions" in this area of law[188] and that the diversity of legal cultures and legal mentalities sets limitations to a uniform approach.[189] Van Gerven argues that "there are indeed considerable differences in style between the European legal systems".[190] This section assesses to what extent the common law system differs from a codified system in the application of the *Francovich* principle

185 Kirchhof, P., Kommers, D.P., Germany and its Basic Law: Past, Present, and Future: a German-American Symposium ,1993, 23.

186 This section is based on a talk presented at the University of Utrecht in May 2005.

187 van Gerven, W., "The Emergence of a Common European Law in the Area of Tort Law: the EU Contribution" in Fairgrieve, D., Andenas, M., Bell, John, *Tort Liability of Public Authorities in Comparative Perspective*, 2002, 125 [128].

188 Wurmnest, W., Grundzüge eines europäischen Haftungsrechts, 2003, 55.

189 Van Gerven, W., "Bringing (Private) Laws Closer to Each Other at European Level", January 2005, www.law.kuleuven.ac.be/ccle/staff_pub.php, p. 4.

190 Ibid.

and to what extent this results in divergence. Therefore the contribution concentrates on a comparison of the English and German law of state liability.

Pierre Larouche discusses potential difficulties in the tackling of divergence through harmonisation. He states that the legal system can treat the "harmonised" area as a form of foreign body (*Fremdkörper*) and seek to isolate it.[191] This isolation of a harmonised area of law may lead to odd results where national and EU law are applied alongside each other. In an attempt to sanction the European Court of Justice and the principle of member state liability it has been argued that "there is a temporarily more successful option, that of inaction at national level".[192]

For the purpose of this section one can only take a snapshot at the case law in a limited area of law and a limited number of jurisdictions to date, here English and German law. Since the rulings in *Factortame* and *Brasserie*, between 1996 and 2006 there has only been a modest number of decisions in England[193] or Germany.[194] The reputation of the German Federal High Court (BGH, *Bundesgerichshof*) with regard to the application of member state liability had been shaped by its ruling following the European Court of Justice judgment in *Brasserie du Pecheur*. The court held that no liability had arisen as the prohibition on the designation "Bier", which was a sufficiently serious breach, had not caused damage. In respect of this provision no proceedings had been taken by the German authorities.[195]

---

[191] Larouche, P. and Chirico, F., Conceptual Divergence, Functionalism and the Economics of Convergence, Contribution for Binding Unity/Diverging (December 2005), TILEC Discussion Paper No. 2005-027, available at SSRN: http://ssrn.com/abstract=869763.

[192] Talberg, J., "Supranational Influence in EU Enforcement: the ECJ and the Principle of State Liability", *Journal of European Public Policy*, 7:1 March 2000, 104-21 [117].

[193] *Bowden v South West Water and another* [1998] 3 CMLR 330; *R v Ministry of Agriculture, Fisheries and Food, ex p Lay and Gage* [1998] COD 387; *Boyd Line Management Services Ltd v Ministry of Agriculture, Fisheries and Food, Times*, 19 May 1999; *R v Department of Social Security, ex p Scullion* [1999] 3 CMLR; COD 345–426; *Matra Communication SAS v Home Office* [1999] 1 CMLR 1454; *Nabadda and others v City of Westminster and others* [2001] 3 CMLR 39; *HJ Banks & Co Ltd v The Coal Authority, The Secretary of State* [2002] CMLR 54; *Betws Anthracite Ltd v DSK Anthrazit Ibbenburen GmbH* [2004] 1 CMLR 12; *Bavarian Lager v Department of Trade and Industry* [2002] UK Competition Law Reports 160; *Phonographic Performance Ltd v Department of Trade and Industry and another* [2004] 3 CMLR 31; *Alderson* [2004] 1 All ER 1148.

[194] LG Bonn 6 September 1999 1 O 221/98 ZIP 1999, 1592; LG Bonn 16 April 1999, Az: 1 O 186/98; LG Bonn 25 October 1999, Az: 1 O 173/98; OLG Köln 15 July 1997; OLG Köln 26 November 1998, Az 7 U 55/96; OLG Köln 25 May 2000 Az: U 178/99; LG Hamburg 6 August 1999, Az: 303 O 48/99; OLG Karlsruhe 15 April 1999, Az: 12 U 273/98; LG Berlin 9 April 2001, Az: 230650/00; BGH 14 December 2000, Az: III ZR 151/99; BGH 9 October 2003, Az: III ZR 342/02; BGH 28 October 2004, Az: III ZR 294/03; BGH 2 December 2004, Az: III ZR 151/99; BGH 20 January 2005, Az: III ZR 48/01.

[195] BGHZ 134, 30; [1997] 1 CMLR 971; BGH 24 November 2005 – III ZR 4/05; for a case comment in English, see Deards, E., "*Brasserie du Pecheur*: Snatching Defeat From the Jaws of Victory" (1997) *EURLR* 22 (6), 620.

In the assessment of the approaches taken by English and German courts in evaluating member states' discretion as an element within the condition of "sufficiently serious breach" I assess the nature of the remedy. The European Court of Justice has left it to the domestic legal systems to accommodate the application of the *Francovich* liability within their existing legal framework. The choices that are made by domestic courts may have an effect on the effectiveness of the remedy. The task of detecting divergence, assessing its consequences and desirability is therefore an interesting venture.

1. The nature of the remedy in domestic law – Germany

Since the *Francovich* decision was handed down there has been significant discussion among German academic commentators over the nature of the new remedy for breaches of Community law. The majority view follows the highest court in civil matters (BGH) in asserting that member state liability is a *sui generis* remedy. It is argued that it is a Community law remedy which is separate from other national remedies for governmental liability.[196] The codified national law (Art. 34 Basic Law in connection with Sect. 839 BGB) is perceived as inappropriate to accommodate the Community law remedy and that a separation is therefore more progressive to apply it as a new remedy in national law.[197] On the other hand, it is argued that the legal basis for the remedy is purely based on national law.[198] These

---

196 Saenger, I., „Staatshaftung wegen Verletzung europäischen Gemeinschaftrechts, JuS 1997, 865 (869); Detterbeck, S., Staatshaftung für die Missachtung von EG-Recht, VerwArch 85 (1994), 159 (185); Hatje. A., Die Haftung der Mitgliedstaaten bei Verstößen des Gesetzgebers gegen europäisches Gemeinschaftsrecht, EuR 1997. 297 (303); Ossenbühl, F., in: „Staatshaftung zwischen Europarecht und nationalem Recht", Festschrift für Everling, Band II, 1995, 1031, (1037); von Dannwitz, T., „Die gemeinschaftsrechtliche Staatshaftung der Mitgliedstaaten", DVBl 1997, 1 (6); Hidien, W., *Die gemeinschaftsrechtliche Staatshaftung der EU-Mitgliedstaaten*, 1999, 37 f.

197 Fischer, H.G., „Die gemeinschaftsrechtliche Staatshaftung", *JA* 2000, 348 (352).

198 Herdegen, M., Rensmann, T., „Die neuen Konturen der gemeinschaftsrechtlichen Staatshaftung", *ZHR* 161 (1997), 522 (551); Streinz, R., ‚Staatshaftung für Verletzungen primären Gemeinschaftsrechts durch die Bundesrepublik Deutschland", EuZW 1993, 599 (599); Maurer, H., "Staatshaftung im europäischen Kontext", *Festschrift für Karlheinz Boujong*, 591, 1996 591 (597); Jarass, , Hans D., „Haftung für die Verletzung von EU-Recht durch nationale Organe und Amtsträger", NJW 1994, 881 (882); Ehlers, D., „Die Weiterentwicklung des Staatshaftungsrechts durch das europäische Gemeinschaftsrecht" JZ 1996, 776 (778); Nettesheim, M., „Gemeinschaftsrechtliche Vorgaben für das deutsche Staatshaftungsrecht", DÖV 1992, 999 (1000);; Henrichs, C., Haftung der EG-Mitgliedstaaten für Verletzung von Gemeinschaftsrecht, 1995, 140; Geiger, J., „Die Entwicklung des europäischen Staatshaftungsrechts", DVBl 1993, 465 (471); Wittkowski, R.,„ Der "MP Travel Line"- Konkurs im Lichte der Francovich-Rechtsprechung des EuGH, NVwZ 1994, S. 326 ff. ; Kopp, S., „Staatshaftung wegen Verletzung von Gemeinschaftsrecht", DÖV 1994, 201 (205); Classen, D., „Anmerkung zum Urteil des BGH vom 14.12.2000", JZ 2001, 458 (459).

differences in approach are sometimes perceived as of merely academic interest.[199] However, this section aims to show that the separation of national tort law from a European remedy fails to achieve this Europeanisation of German tort law in this area which may in some cases lead to a degree of undesirable divergence in the application of the European remedy.[200]

One decision which illustrates this point well was taken by the BGH (*BGHZ* 156, 153).[201] The case was concerned with damage which occurred due to the levy of inspection fees of meat products. Even though the fees had actually been incurred during the inspection, they were higher than the basic rate stipulated in Directive 85/37/EEC and the corresponding Council decision. The German Law on Hygiene of Meat (*Fleischhygienegesetz*) had stipulated that it was within the competence of the federal states to pass legislation for the levy of higher fees for inspections under certain circumstances. However, no such law had been passed in the case in question. The claimant had to take out a loan to finance the fees and claims he had suffered a loss of DM85,000. He claimed that the levy was in breach of domestic and EU law. The claimant was successful in the lower and higher civil courts, but failed in the *Bundesgerichtshof.*

a) Rights under Community law and duty towards a third party in German law

In *BGHZ* 146, 153 the court based its reasoning on two separate heads of tort and denied a claim in damages for both remedies. First, it argued that the separate head of member state liability is not fulfilled as the Directive and the Council decision in themselves were not designed to confer a right on to the individual. According to the Directive, the federal states were entitled to deviate from the basic rates through legislation. On the other hand, it denied the existence of individual rights under the Community remedy because the claimant had no right to expect lower fees. This approach is questionable because the BGH ignores the decision by the European Court of Justice, which held that the decision of the Council (Art. 2 I 88/408/EEC) could be relied on by individuals wishing to challenge higher fees.[202] Therefore, due to the lack of a breach of a Community right, the claim based on *Francovich* failed.

Section 839 of the Civil Code and Art. 34 of the Basic Law require that the official duty must be owed to *a third party*. Whether a person is a third party in that sense depends on whether the object of the duty is directly to safeguard the interests of that person. If for instance a policeman remains inactive while a theft is being committed, he is in breach of his official duty towards the owner because his power to interfere is conferred on him not merely in the interest of the general

---

[199] Wolff, H.J., Bachof, O., Stober, R., *Verwaltungsrecht* Band 2, 6. Aufl., 2000, 581.

[200] See Wurmnest, W., *Grundzüge eines europäischen Haftungsrechts*, 2002, 55; Schoch, F., Staatshaftung wegen Verstoßes gegen Europäisches Gemeinschaftsrecht (Jura, 2002) 837 [840].

[201] Az: III ZR 151/99 14 December 2000.

[202] ECJ 1992, 5567.

public, but at the same time in the interest of each single individual. In each case it has to be seen whether according to the object and the legal provisions of the official task the affected interests should have been protected. Three conditions have to be met in order to establish a duty towards a third party. First, the official duty must be capable of protecting individuals, secondly, the plaintiff has to belong to the protected group of people and, thirdly, the damage must be included in the protective effect of the duty.[203] The establishment of such a duty owed to a third party is extremely difficult. The determination of which duties are capable of protecting third party effects is left to the courts. The decision on this issue is crucial for the success or failure of an action. The fact that Sect. 839 of the Civil Code does not enumerate official duties which confer rights on individuals illustrates that the courts are given some leeway as to how to interpret the concept of duty.

The highest German court in civil matters (BGH) did not modify the German governmental liability remedy to comply with the conditions set out by the European Court of Justice. Rather, it opted for an "artificial" separation of member states' liability and a second review under the stricter purely domestic conditions of Art. 34 of the Basic Law in connection with Sect. 839 of the Civil Code.

In applying the German law of tort, the court came to the conclusion that the duty towards a third party according to Sect. 839 of the Civil Code was violated. The domestic tort provision in German law therefore proved to be easier to establish. This divergence between the application of the *Francovich* criteria and a claim under domestic law is concerning. In *BGHZ* 146, 153 the court had no difficulty in holding that such a duty was owed toward the claimants. It is not clear at all how the BGH reached this decision. It denied the applicant the right in the context of the Community remedy, but held that in the context of the domestic remedy, a duty was owed for the protection of a third party.

b) The fault requirement in German law

Unlike the condition of "sufficiently serious breach", the German head of tort requires that the official be at fault whilst in breach of his or her official duty. Article 34 of the Basic Law and Sect. 839 of the Civil Code do not contain a catalogue of official duties. Official duties may stem from any legal source. In the courts the requirement of official duty has been interpreted very liberally. Examples are the duty to act lawfully as contained in Art. 20 of the Basic Law and the duty to exercise discretionary powers. The review of discretionary powers was originally limited to extreme cases of arbitrary exercise of the discretion. "The *Reichsgericht* constantly held that the courts should not interfere with discretionary power. The courts could only decide in cases where the public body acted outside the ambit of its discretionary power".[204] However, the control of the exercise of discretionary powers has been extended by the highest court in civil matters so that it now includes the failure to exercise discretionary powers, excessive use of discretionary

203 Ossenbühl, F., supra n. 74, 58.

204 Ibid at 45.

powers or incorrect exercise of discretionary powers parallel to the grounds of review in the review of an administrative act:

"A discretionary decision may thus be reviewed by a court in a public wrong case even if it is within the ambit of discretion. However, the court will not go into the question whether the decision taken by the public body was "right" (*Richtigkeitsprüfung*) but only whether the decision seems plausible (*vertretbar*). The test for plausibility allows far more control than was sanctioned in the past, but it still does not mean that the court is substituting its own judgment for that of the administrative authority".[205]

The courts review the erroneous use of discretion (*Ermessensfehlgebrauch*), excessive use of the exercise of discretion (*Ermessensüberschreitung*) and the omission of the use of discretion (*Ermessensnichtgebrauch*).[206] The landmark case is the decision of the BGH in 1979 where it found a breach of an official duty in the course of the exercise of a discretionary power even though the breach did not amount to an obvious level of abuse.[207] There is a clear trend towards a quasi strict governmental liability.[208] In this light the decision of the BGH appears even more artificial and unconvincing.

c) Europeanisation of the German law of governmental liability

The dualistic concept of governmental liability, i.e. the separation of the European remedy from the application of the domestic head of tort, led in this case to the denial of liability due to the application of the fault principle, a condition which features in a much weaker form within the condition of "sufficiently serious breach".[209] It is not clear at all how the BGH came to the conclusion that the applicant had no rights position under Community law standards so that the claim failed at an early stage. On the other hand, the court was willing to proceed with the claim under purely German law and held that an official duty was owed to the claimant. However, the fault requirement under German law was the stumbling block. The BGH therefore reduced the scope of protection under European law, which may not be in line with the principle of equivalence. The European Court repeatedly held that the protection of European rights if left to national law should not be less favourable than the protection of purely domestic rights.

The arguments for a Europeanisation of the national remedy rather than the artificial separation of national and European law are threefold. First, the lack of legislative competence in the field of governmental liability does not permit the creation of an entirely new legal remedy in the sense of a legal basis. Secondly, the European Court of Justice was entitled to give guidance on how to modify ex-

---

205 Ibid at 63.

206 Ossenbühl, F., *Staatshaftungsrecht*, 1998, 46.

207 BGHZ 74, 156.

208 See Brüggemeier, G., "From Individual Tort for Civil Servants to Quasi-Strict Liability of the State: Governmental or State Liability in Germany" in Fairgrieve, D., Andenas, M., Bell, J., *Tort Liability of Public Authorities in Comparative Perspective*, 2002, 571.

209 Schoch, F., Staatshaftung wegen Verstoßes gegen Europäisches Gemeinschaftsrecht ((2002) *Jura*, 837 [840].

isting national governmental tort law. Thirdly, the principle of indirect administration of Community law requires the application of national law. Accordingly, modified national law is applicable to breaches of Community law through national authorities.[210] It has been argued that the BGH merely pays lip service to the Community law remedy and then denies the claim on the basis that the provision that was allegedly breached gave no rise to individual rights. At the same time the BGH rules, however, that there existed an official duty which also protected the interests of the claimant under German law. The second head of tort, a purely domestic remedy, here Art. 34 in connection with Sect. 839 of the Civil Code, was also unsuccessful due to the application of the condition of fault under the German provisions. Therefore, the claim finally fails under the German law provision due to lack of fault. This is the requirement which is clearly not included in the jurisprudence of the European Court of Justice. Lorz describes this tendency of the German court as ascribing an increasingly inferior function.[211] Further, the BGH declined to refer the question as to whether the claimant had a protected right under EC law to the European Court of Justice, which can be seen as a violation of the principle of lawful judge under Art. 101 I 2 of the Basic Law.[212]

The avoidance of founding a claim on member state liability can also be witnessed in English courts. In the case of *Nabadda*[213] the claimants, Swedish students in the UK, sued for damages because they had been denied a full grant from a local authority towards their education. The claimants founded their claim on the entitlement to damages under the Race Relations Act 1976 and argued that it should be disapplied in part as it contravened Community law. The claim was not based on the European court's case law on member state liability to avoid the condition of sufficiently serious breach, which in this case was harder to prove.[214] However, this case differs from the approach the BGH took. The applicants were of course under no obligation to base their claim on *Francovich* principles if another legal basis would be more likely to produce a liability. However, their claim was unsuccessful.

The German court's approach has not changed so far. In another case in December 2004, the BGH held that the Federal Republic of Germany was not liable due to the domestic provision concerning the competences of national authorities. It held that the *See-Berufsgenossenschaft* was liable under German law. The liability under the European remedy was not assessed in full. Again, it applied a rigid separation between European law and domestic law.[215]

Consequences of this approach are not easily verified. However, in *BGHZ* 146, 153 a more convincing result could have been found at an earlier stage. Instead, the claimant remained largely unsuccessful. The case was finally settled in Octo-

---

210 Ibid.

211 Lorz, A., Anmerkung, *JR* 2001, 413 [415].

212 Schoch, F., Staatshaftung wegen Verstoßes gegen Europäisches Gemeinschaftsrecht (2002) *Jura*, 837 [841].

213 *Nabadda and others v City of Westminster and others* [2001] 3 CMLR 39.

214 *Nabadda and others v City of Westminster and others* [2001] 3 CMLR 39, para 8.

215 2 December 2004 III ZR 358/03.

ber 2004 with the claimant agreeing to pay €35,000 to the defendant authority after having gone back and forward through several instances.[216]

2. The nature of the remedy in domestic law – United Kingdom

It is now well established in English case law that the liability for breach of Community law is to be understood as a breach of statutory duty. This had also been considered in the *Factortame (No 5)* decision.[217] Lord Hobhouse relied on previous case law, i.e. *Garden Cottage Foods*[218] and *Bourgoin v MAFF*[219] and held that the duty was imposed by way of the European Communities Act 1972. The recent decision in *Phonographic Performance Ltd v Department of Trade and Industry and another* [220] which was concerned with the alleged incorrect transposition of the Rental Rights and Related Copyrights and Related Rights in the Information Society Directive (2001/29) confirms this. The court made important statements as to the nature of the claim. It held that a claim in damages for breach of Community law "gives rise to a correlative right in one who has suffered such damages" and that such a "right is not discretionary".[221] The Crown had argued that the cause of action is *sui generis* resulting in a public law claim which "ought to be pursued in a public law claim" in proceedings for judicial review. Such a procedure "will enable the court to exercise control over the claims and the periods for which they may be pursued". The Crown argued that in this case the court should strike out the claim as an abuse of process. The court held that this interpretation of the nature of the claim would be "to subject the rights of an individual to a discretion and a time limit much more restrictive than those normally appropriate to a private law claim for breach of statutory duty and would itself constitute a breach of Community law".[222] Despite the fact that the courts have ruled that the European remedy should be considered as a breach of statutory duty it is still not clear whether the term is used in a wide non-technical sense or whether the traditional tort was referred to. More recently it has been argued that "the Euro tort is simply to be classified as a tort in domestic proceedings and the repeated references to breach of statutory duty are a redundancy".[223] The creation of torts such as the Euro tort as a breach of statutory duty has been described as "obscure".[224] There is little academic discussion on the precise meaning of the breach of statutory duty in

[216] 145 I B 1397/05 OLG Karlsruhe, 7 October 2004.

[217] [1998] 1 CMLR 1353.

[218] [1984] AC 130.

[219] [1986] QB 716.

[220] [2004] 3 CMLR 31.

[221] [2004] 3 CMLR 31, para 47.

[222] [2004] 3 CMLR 31, para 50.

[223] Stanton, K.M., "New Forms of the Tort of Breach of Statutory Duty" (2004) *LQR* 324 [329].

[224] Ibid at 340.

this context.[225] It is not irrelevant though. With a view to the discovery of pure economic loss the distinction is crucial: the traditional breach of statutory duty allows such a recovery more liberally, the tort of negligence does not.[226] A separation of domestic law and a free standing cause of action in Community law as seen in German cases do not feature in the English decisions. In conclusion, the more flexible British approach may be more prepared to accommodate the European remedy in its domestic system of torts and provide an effective protection of Community law rights.

3. The condition of "sufficiently serious breach" in German and English decisions

Since the European Court of Justice has ruled that it is within the members states' courts competence to apply the criterion of a "sufficiently serious breach" to establish member state liability, domestic courts are at times left to take difficult policy decisions as to the application of this criterion. The European Court of Justice clarified that the condition was met if "there was a manifest and grave disregard by the member state of its discretion".

Despite this clarification of the condition, there is a potential for divergent approaches in the member state courts on the interpretation of "discretion" and how it should be reviewed. Discretion in this context is not to be understood in the strict technical and complex sense as developed in German administrative law.[227] Discretion is to be understood in a wider sense than that, including margins of appreciation by the deciding bodies, which may not be based on legislative provisions granting such discretion. The precision and clarity of a rule breached becomes a guiding tool. However, despite this guidance provided for by the European Court of Justice and academic commentators, references to the European Court of Justice on this issue provide evidence for the uncertainty over the application of the condition in both member states.[228] This section will show that even within the member states the courts have taken different views on the application of the criterion of a "sufficiently serious" breach. Further, the interlocking of member state liability and domestic tort remedies against public authorities for potential breaches of Community law appears to vary across the two member states. This grey zone may lead to divergence in the approaches of member states. This section will therefore also provide a comparison of the principles of state liability for breaches of domestic law in the exercise of discretion in the two jurisdictions. An assessment of decisions taken by all member state courts would be an even

225 See, however, Craig, P.,"The Domestic Liability of Public Authorities in Damages, Lessons from the European Community"; Hoskins, M., "The Rebirth of the Innominate Tort", Chapters 6 and 7 in Beatson, J., and Tridimas, T., *New Directions in European Public Law*, 1998.

226 Ibid at 341.

227 Ossenbühl, F., *Staatshaftungsrecht*, 1998, 507.

228 See, for instance, *Evans v Secretary of State for the Environment, Transport and the Regions* [2004] 1 CMLR 47 and *Mau* [2004] 1 CMLR 34.

more interesting though difficult undertaking. However, many cases in lower courts are not reported and the linguistic limitations hinder such a project.[229]

As is well known according to the case law of the court, a breach is sufficiently serious where, in the exercise of its legislative powers, an institution or a member state has manifestly and gravely disregarded the limits on the exercise of its powers:

"The factors which the competent court may take into account include the clarity and precision of the rule breached, the measure of discretion left by that rule to the national or Community authorities, whether the infringement and the damage caused was intentional or involuntary, whether any error of law was excusable or inexcusable, the fact that the position taken by a Community institution may have contributed towards the omission and the adoption or retention of national measures or practices contrary to Community law".[230]

Establishing that the breach is serious requires the application of a test which is concerned with "discretion, good faith, reasonableness and the behaviour of related actors, namely the Commission and other member states".[231] The court further decided that "where the member state or the institution in question has only considerably reduced, or even no, discretion the mere infringement of Community law may be sufficient to establish the existence of a sufficiently serious breach".[232] In other words, the *Brasserie* criteria apply in discretion and non-discretion cases alike.[233] Hilson points out that there is a "strange circularity to such an approach".[234]

According to the case law this enquiry is one for the national member states' courts. The European Court of Justice has shown a less interventionist approach in more recent decisions. It has taken commentators by surprise that the Court of Justice has not provided any further guidance on the seriousness of the breach.[235] The reason for this may have been the interconnection with domestic law. The court made it clear that:

"The discretion ... is that enjoyed by the member state concerned. Its existence and its scope are determined by reference to Community law and not by reference to national law. The discretion which may be conferred by national law on the official or the institution responsible for the breach of Community law is therefore irrelevant in this respect".[236]

---

229 Barav, A., "State Liability in Damages for Breach of Community Law in the National Courts" in Heukels, T., McDonnell, A., *The Action for Damages in Community Law*, 1997, 363 [376].

230 Joined cases C-46/93 and C-48/93 *Brasserie du Pecheur and R v Secretary of State for Transport, ex p Factortame* [1996] ECR I-1029, [1996] QB 404, para 56.

231 Tridimas, T., "Liability for Breaches of Community Law, Growing Up or Mellowing Down?" 150 in Fairgrieve, D., Andenas, M., Bell, J., *Tort Liability of Public Authorities in Comparative Perspective*, 2002.

232 Case C-352/98, *Laboratoires Pharmaceutiques Bergaderm and Goupil v Commission* [2000] ECR I-5291, para 44.

233 See *Larsy v INASTI* [2001] ECR I-5063.

234 Hilson, C., "The Role of Discretion in EC Law on Non-Contractual Liability", *Common Market Law Review*, vol. 42, Issue 3, 677 [681].

235 Ibid.

236 Case C-424/97 *Haim* [2000] ECR I-5123, para 40.

A decision by the Berlin *Landgericht* in April 2001 has been cause for concern over the application of the requirement of a sufficiently serious breach.[237] This decision reflects insecurity in applying member state liability. The decision concerned the incorrect transposition of Directives 68/151/EEC and 78/660/EEC into Sect. 335 of the German Commercial Code (*Handelsgesetzbuch* 1985) on the co-ordination of safeguards which, for the protection of the interests of members and others, are required by member states of companies within the meaning of the second paragraph of Art. 58 of the Treaty with a view to making such safeguards equivalent throughout the Community. The facts of the case are complicated. The claimant sought disclosure of the balance sheet and profit and loss account of the defendant, a limited company (*B-GmbH*), in the course of proceedings related to the return of property under the German property claims law (*Vermögensgesetz*). Reunification of East and West Germany has created the possibility to file restitution or compensation claims for property in Germany expropriated by the Nazi government during the Second World War and by the East German government after 1949. The claimants argued that Sect. 335 of the German Commercial Code incorrectly transposed Art. 6 of the first directive which requires member states to provide for appropriate penalties in the case of a failure to disclose the balance sheet and profit and loss account as required by Art. 2(1)(f).

The German court decided that the failure to interpret the directive correctly was based on an excusable error and therefore not sufficiently serious. Interesting is the reasoning of the court with regard to the discretion left to the Federal Republic in incorporating the directive.

Very early decisions by the ECJ pointed towards a wider interpretation of the first directive, i.e. that everyone should be entitled to view the annual accounts.[238]

In 1998 the European Court of Justice decided that the Federal Republic of Germany had failed to fulfil its obligations under the EC Treaty and those directives by failing to provide for appropriate penalties in cases where companies limited by shares fail to disclose their annual accounts, as prescribed in particular by Directive 68/151/EEC. Only 10–15 per cent of all companies disclosed profit sheets (based on 1991 data) illustrating that the penalties imposed were unsuitable for achieving the purpose of the directive.[239]

The German government argued that "because of the very large number of small and medium-sized limited liability companies, it would be disproportionate to the purpose of the system defined in Art. 54(3)(g) of the Treaty to take legal action against them". However, as stated in C 191/95, the court referred to previous rulings and held "that a member state may not plead internal circumstance in order to justify a failure to comply with obligations and time limits resulting from rules of Community law".[240]

---

237 Az: 23 0 650/00.

238 *Haaga* case 32/74; *Ubbink Isolatie* case 136/87.

239 Leible, S., "Haftung der Bundesrepublik wegen nicht ordnungsgemässer Umsetzung der Publizitätsrichtlinie durch para 335 a HGB" (2001) *EWS* 563.

240 *Commission v Federal Republic of Germany* C-191/95.

The German court held that the incorrect implementation of a directive does not in itself amount to a sufficiently serious breach. It held that the member state enjoyed a certain amount of discretion in implementing the directive and could therefore only be held liable in damages if the legislation is entirely erroneous and unsuitable to fulfil the aim of the directive. Nevertheless, it has been argued that the Federal Republic of Germany exercised its discretion erroneously in that it chose an insufficient sanction.[241] The court was criticised for its insecurity in dealing with EC law matters.[242] The Berlin *Landgericht* interpreted the guidance given as to the interpretation of the directive in a very wide manner. It held that the principle of subsidiarity had allowed such a wide interpretation of the directive. At the time of the drafting of the directive in question,[243] however, the principle of subsidiarity had not been incorporated into the EC Treaty.[244] Further, the judgment of the European Court of Justice in *Daihatsu* had set out clear guidelines. Therefore, it is questionable how the *Landgericht* reached the decision that the Federal Republic of Germany acted in good faith.

In *R v Department of Social Security, ex p Scullion*[245] decided just three months before the House of Lords gave its ruling in *Factortame (No 5)*, the High Court took a textbook approach to the application of the guiding principles of the European Court of Justice and held that the government was liable for the incorrect transposition of Directive 97/7 on the progressive implementation of the principle of equal treatment for men and women in matters of social security. The High Court assessed various factors and took a "basket or global approach".[246] First, the government failed to seek legal advice as to whether discrimination in the different qualifying ages for ICA was within the scope of Art. 7(1) of the directive. The clarity of the directive to be transposed was considered. Article 7(1) of the directive gave member states discretion, but its scope was unclear. However, a number of previous judgments had clarified the position. Discrimination in retirement ages could not be justified in the interests of financial equilibrium since ICA was a non-contributory benefit. The government had acted deliberately, however, the fact that the directive was unclear did not mean that its breach was not sufficiently serious. The High Court held further that where legislative discretion was conferred on member states, a restrictive approach to liability was to be applied. However, the discretion in Art. 7(1) was conferred for the purpose of determining pensionable age and once that was achieved it conferred no broad discretion in relation to other benefits:

---

241 Hirte, H., "LG Berlin: Keine Haftung der Bundesrepublik für Schaden wegen unrichtiger Umsetzung der EG Bilanzrichtline", rws-verlag.de.

242 Leible, S., "Haftung der Bundesrepublik wegen nicht ordnungsgemäßer Umsetzung der Publizitätsrichtlinie durch para 335 a HGB" (2001) *EWS* 563.

243 68/151/EC.

244 Thietz-Bartram, J., *Der Betrieb*, Heft 5, 1.2.2002, 258 [260].

245 [1999] 3 CMLR 798.

246 [1999] 3 CMLR 798, 42.

"Whilst the mere breach of Community law will not be enough to fix the state with liability, the mere fact that the state is able to advance an arguable case in litigation does not mean that the breach is not "sufficiently serious". Given the lack of precision in many directives it will not be too difficult for a government to construct some argument in favour of a particular interpretation".[247]

The breach of the directive was held to have been sufficiently serious. The judgment had great financial implications because of the number of persons concerned.[248]

In England the most important precedent with regard to the condition of sufficiently serious breach in this context is the case of *Factortame (No 5)*.[249] Lord Clyde held on 28 October 1999 that "no single factor is necessarily decisive". He identified eight factors which were of influence to the European Court of Justice and which should guide national courts in their decisions:

"The importance of the principle which has been breached; the clarity and precision of the rule breached; the degree of excusability of an error of law; the existence of any relevant judgment on the point; the state of mind of the infringer, and in particular whether the infringer was acting intentionally or involuntarily; the behaviour of the infringer after it has become evident that an infringement has occurred may also be of importance; the identity of the persons affected by the breach; and the position (if any) taken by one of the Community institutions in the matters".[250]

Of particular interest is that behaviour after the act which gives rise to the claim of damages could be a factor in the decision-making process. He further held that "no single factor is necessarily decisive, but one factor by itself might, particularly where there was little or nothing to put onto the scales on the other side, be sufficient to justify the conclusion of liability".[251] "This indicates a broad and equitable approach".[252]

EC law has been described as "a fertile source of ideas regarding the liability of public bodies ..." The jurisprudence of the ECJ is being considered as "far more sophisticated than that found in England" and a considerable influence on domestic English law is being expected.[253] Lord Hoffmann's statement in the same case indicates a rather different approach in EC law matters from those concerned with purely domestic law: "I do not think that the United Kingdom ... can say that the losses caused by the legislation should lie where they fell. Justice requires that the wrong should be made good".[254]

---

247 [1999] 3 CMLR 798, 64.

248 XVIIth Report on Monitoring the Application of Community Law COM (2000) 92 final, 23 June 2000 http://europa.eu.int/comm/secretariat_general/sgb/infringements/report99_en.htm.

249 *R v Secretary of State for Transport, ex p Factortame* (No. 5) [2000] 1 AC 524.

250 Ibid at 554.

251 Ibid at 554.

252 "Monetary Remedies in Public Law – A Discussion Paper"; Public Law Team, Law Commission, 11 October 2004; www.lawcom.gov.uk.

253 Ibid at 49.

254 *R v Secretary of State for Transport, ex p Factortame* (No. 5) [2000] 1 AC 524 at 548.

Quite differently, Lord Hoffmann stated the position in English law in the case of *Stovin v Wise*, a case which concerned the alleged negligence of a public authority in omitting road works to improve the visibility at a crossroads:

"The trend of [English] authorities [on negligence] has been to discourage the assumption that anyone who suffers loss is *prima facie* entitled to compensation from a person (preferably insured or a public authority) whose act or omission can be said to have caused it. The default position is that he is not".[255]

The British approach to the sufficiently serious breach condition is close to the decisions of the European Court of Justice.[256] This is also evident in the case of *R v Ministry of Agriculture, Fisheries and Food, ex p Lay and Gage*[257] where the Court of Appeal applied all *Brasserie du Pecheur* and *British Telecommunications* factors. Regulation 1078/77 established a scheme whereby a farmer could enter into a non-marketing agreement with another member state in which he undertook for a given period and in return for a premium not to dispose of either milk or milk products from his land, nor to allow any land comprising his property to be used for milk production. In *Gage v Gage*[258] the European Court of Justice had established that the national legislation was in breach of Community law. The question in *Lay and Gage* was whether the breach had been sufficiently serious. The Court of Appeal considered all the factors in *Brasserie du Pecheur* as relevant in determining the extent to which any given breach of Community law is sufficiently serious in so far as they arise on the facts of any given case and denied a claim for damages. "The defendant acted bona fides, and made an excusable mistake as to the interpretation of a legislative provision, which was not clear or precise".[259]

The case of *Boyd Line Management Services Ltd v Ministry of Agriculture, Fisheries and Food*[260] concerned the quota of British fisherman in the Norwegian Sea. The claimant, Boyd Line Management, sued the Ministry of Agriculture, Fisheries and Food in damages because it could not use up all its allocated quota after the EC had declared that the total quota for this region had been exhausted. In assessing whether the alleged breach was sufficiently serious the Court of Appeal considered the case of *Dillenkofer* carefully, but denied the claim.

In *HJ Banks & Co Ltd v The Coal Authority, The Secretary of State*[261] Tuckey J also takes a broad approach and suggested that the courts should take "a robust approach to claims for damages of this kind" and denied that the breach in question was sufficiently serious.

---

255 [1996] AC 923 at 949 referred to in "Monetary Remedies in Public Law – A Discussion Paper"; Public Law Team, Law Commission, 11 October 2004; www.lawcom.gov.uk.

256 Merris, A., "Eurotorts and Unicorns" in Fairgrieve, D., Andeans, M., Bell, J., *Tort Liability of Public Authorities in Comparative Perspective*, 2002, 121.

257 [1998] Crown Office Digest 387.

258 [1997] ECR I-5543.

259 [1998] Crown Office Digest 387 [390].

260 14 October 1998, CA, unreported Westlaw; [1999] EuLR 44.

261 [2002] 2 CMLR 54; *Coal Authority v HJ Banks* [1997] EuLR 610 at 622, QB.

In conclusion, there appears to be more ease in English courts in achieving an integration of the *Francovich* remedy than in German courts.[262] In a more pragmatic case by case approach English courts have successfully embedded the *Francovich* remedy into English law. Harlow remarks that "the UK appears to be an exception to the reluctance noted in the text [referring to the decision by the German Federal High Court in *Brasserie du Pecheur*] embracing the liability principle enthusiastically and dutifully applying it in the *Factortame* case".[263] The political reaction was somewhat different. The UK government issued a White Paper on the 1996 IGC and proposed appeals procedures against judgments of the European Court of Justice. The late 1990s were marked by concern about the increase of judicial review cases and the fact that "national courts might emulate the judicial activism of the two European courts, fuelled by the fact that British judges were happy to admit that European jurisprudence had pushed forward the boundaries of domestic judicial inverventionism".[264] Resistance to European integration was felt at a political level rather than on a judicial level. Membership within the European Union strengthened the role of the judiciary.

Divergence in the approaches to the Europeanisation of existing tort law regimes for official wrongs is not necessarily surprising in a complex area of law that touches upon both private and public law. Pierre Larouche's theory of "path-dependency" may be a helpful tool in attempting to explain the different approaches by English and German judges. Accordingly, legal systems evolve in different directions because their reactions to problems are dependent on different sets of information. Legal systems diverge as "tipping" in the network or path-dependency determines their priorities almost irreversibly.[265]

The integration of member state liability into British law has to be seen in the wider context of the changing role of the British judiciary since the 1960s and the extension of judicial review into many domains of executive activity. In the EU context, despite early assurances that the judges were merely interpreting British legislation, from the early 1970s the courts were getting involved into more than "business as usual".[266] It has been argued that the courts have started to develop "their own principles of constitutionalism".[267] In the context of the *Factortame* decision it has been argued that "the courts are simply putting into effect or "catching up with" a widespread political consensus about the particular constitutional rights and principles they elaborate".[268] Further, constitutional reform through leg-

---

262 See also Harlow, C., *Tort Law*, 2005, 65.

263 Ibid.

264 Nicol, D., *EC Membership and the Judicialisation of British Politics*, 2001, 221.

265 Larouche, P. and Chirico, F., Conceptual Divergence, Functionalism and the Economics of Convergence, Contribution for Binding Unity/Diverging (December 2005), TILEC Discussion Paper No. 2005-027, available at SSRN: http://ssrn.com/abstract=869763.

266 Stevens, R., "Judicial Independence in England, A Loss of Innocence" in Russell, P. H. and O'Brien, D., *Judicial Independence in the Age of Democracy: Critical Perspectives from Around the World,* 2001, 169.

267 Oliver, D., *Constitutional Reform*, 2002, 102.

268 Ibid.

islation confirmed "the process of the constitutionalisation of government that was initiated by the courts independently of these reforms".[269] The motivation of their Lordships with regard to the development of the principle of parliamentary sovereignty in *Factortame* has been described as an "essentially secondary and reflective constitution-developing role".[270]. When "New Labour" came into power in 1997 it initiated legislative reform of the House of Lords, devolution for Scotland and Wales and the incorporation of the European Convention on Human Rights into English law. Much to the regret of the government today these legislative reforms entailed an increase in judicial power.

The willingness to embrace the new remedy on the part of the British judiciary may therefore well be based on the changes in the constitutional relationship between the judiciary and the other powers in the state and an awareness of the need to make changes in the area of tort claims against public bodies.

The German position, on the other hand, is marked by a more reluctant attitude. The case examples have shown that the BGH does not favour a Europeanised version of the codifed tort liability, possibly leaving this to the legislature. The cases show that German judgments are less closely phrased to the rulings of the European Court of Justice. It has even been argued that the EU tort claim in the BGH decision of 14 December 2000 was treated less favourably than the claim under domestic law. The BGH avoids an adaptation of the German tort provisions in fear of thereby introducing liability for legislative wrongs into German national law.[271]

In German courts there is an element of uncertainty or reluctance in the application of the remedy at present. In terms of legal consequences, the German approach reflects a position of stagnation at domestic legislative level. The example of two German cases has illustrated that the uniform application of the right to reparation for breaches of Community law may be compromised by national reflexes, an element of renationalisation or purely inaction on behalf of the national judiciary. Among the German judiciary different approaches to the translation of the principle into domestic law reflect a degree of uncertainty. In 2004 the FDP (Liberal Party) addressed the question of reforming the principles of governmental liability in a parliamentary question. Some of the MPs argued that the system is mainly based on case law and that the process of modernisation is taking place on a case by case basis. They were interested in how other European member states deal with it, whether legislation was needed to tackle this increasingly complex area of law and whether national remedies are comparable to the protection required under Community law.[272]

The highest German court, in particular, has chosen a path which does not lead to a Europeanisation of German tort law. The artificial separation of German governmental liability and the European remedy has led to a decision in December 2000 as we have seen which is unconvincing in its arguments. The claim failed due to the high threshold of the fault requirement under German law – the condi-

---

269 Ibid at 103.

270 Nicol, D., *EC Membership and the Judicialisation of British Politics*, 2001, 195.

271 Säuberlich, B.-P., *Legislatives Unrecht und EU-Amtshaftungsanspruch*, 2005, 105.

272 Deutscher Bundestag, Kleine Anfrage, Drucksache 15/3859, 29.09.2004.

tion that the European Court of Justice clearly avoided within its conditions for member state liability. If like some one advocates a *ius commune* of administrative or tort law throughout Europe one could be concerned about a renationalisation of the remedy from the German point of view. In this case the BGH treated Community law less favourably than the similar national law in contravention of the principle of equivalence or non-discrimination.[273] Interestingly, there is a more recent decision by the Köln OLG[274] which embraces a more open approach to the integration of the ECJ state liability case law. The issue at stake was whether the applicant's claim for compensation was prescribed. The court allowed the case to proceed for revision to the BGH and a decision is eagerly expected. There may be the need for more clarification of the position of the European Court of Justice on how member states should accommodate the remedy in their national legal systems.

The decision by the Berlin *Landgericht* has clearly shown that legal mechanisms are subservient to political or economic considerations. The claim in damages was decided in line with previous political considerations by the German government. The flexibility of the criterion "sufficiently serious breach" clearly permits policy considerations to enter into the decision-making process. This makes it difficult to establish a principle of "full reparation" or a uniform "Community remedy" as was acknowledged by the European Court of Justice itself.[275]

The European Court of Justice should, however, not permit the avoidance of the application of the European remedy altogether. Other ways of tackling divergence have been suggested by Himsworth, including the denial that there is a problem with divergence, reform of the preliminary reference procedure, a Community-wide code (of administrative law in his contribution), a natural alignment of state practices or the establishment of Community courts in a federal style.[276]

The author's view is that with time and younger generations of lawyers trained in different jurisdictions some changes will occur naturally. The reform of the German provisions as proposed (again) by the FDP may have to be delayed a little longer in Germany's new political climate.

4. Causation in member state liability

In both the English and German law of torts the plaintiff has to establish that the damage suffered was caused by the injurious action of the tortfeasor. This comparison of the question of causation in both jurisdictions is important with respect to the case law of the European Court of Justice on member state liability. In *Brasserie du Pecheur* and *Factortame* the European Court of Justice held that "as

[273] Van Gerven, W., "Of Rights, Remedies and Procedures" (2000) *CMLR* 501 [504].

[274] *Oberlandsgericht* Köln, decision of 2 June 2005, 7U 29/04, available at www.olg-koeln.nrw.de.

[275] Advocate-General Mischo in *Francovich* (para 80 of the Opinion); Advocate-General Tesauro in *Brasserie* (para 111 of the Opinion); Advocate-General Cosmas in *Bonifaci* (paras 63 and 103–6 of the Opinion).

[276] Himsworth, C., *Convergence and Divergence in European Public Law* (2002, 99 [109].

for the third condition [i.e. causal link] it is for the national courts to determine whether there is a direct causal link between the breach of the obligation borne by the state and the damage sustained by the injured party".[277] By leaving the establishment of a causal link to the member states' jurisdictions the court ensured that this condition falls within the area of national procedural autonomy. However, whether the rules relating to the establishment of a causal link between the injurious action and the damage can be classified as a substantive or procedural matter is not clear. The court gave no guidance to national courts as to how this condition is to be defined. The court referred to its own case law on Art. 288 (ex 215) only with regard to the conditions of breach of a rule and the sufficiently serious fault. Accordingly, the conditions have to be similar to the general common principles of the member states. "The result is that much room is left to the national courts to define the conditions further, which does not help to ensure the uniform application of Community law throughout the member states, a principle which the court has repeatedly said is a fundamental requirement of Community law".[278] The lack of guidance by the European Court of Justice on the issue of causation may result in the loss of a remedy altogether as has been suggested to be the case in English law.[279] It has also been stated that "it is not correct ... to leave the definition of these essential conditions (damage and causation) entirely to the national legal orders because this would amount to a *de facto* "de-harmonisation" or "renationalisation" of the Community law principle of state liability".[280] The decision of the English Court of Appeal in *R v Secretary of State for the Home Department, ex p John Gallagher*[281] illustrates this well as will be shown below. In that case the court held that despite the fact that the Home Secretary had committed a sufficiently serious breach of Community law the breach was not causal for the harm suffered by Mr Gallagher. The issue of causation in the law of torts committed by public authorities in the different member states has so far hardly been compared.[282] This comparison will show that the differences between the English and the German approach are of a subtle nature, but that they might lead to different results in dealing with similar cases.

In both the English and German law of torts the question of causation is analysed in two stages. The terminology used mirrors the traditional approaches in

277 *Brasserie du Pecheur and Factortame*, joined Cases C-46/93 and 48/93 [1996] ECR I-1029, para 65.

278 Van Gerven in Tridimas, T., Beatson, J., *New Directions in European Public Law*, 1997, 39.

279 Smith, F. and Woods, L., "Causation in Francovich: The Neglected Problem" (1997) *International and Comparative Law Quarterly* 925.

280 Van Gerven, W., "A Common European Law in the Area of Tort Law", in Fairgrieve, D., Andenas, M, Bell, J., *Tort Liability of Public Authorities in comparative perspective*, 2002, 125 [128].

281 [1996] 2 CMLR 951.

282 See Markesinis, B.S., *Comparative Introduction to the German Law of Tort*, 1986; Van Gerven, W., "Bridging the Unbridgeable: Community and National Tort Laws after Francovich and Brasserie" (1996) *International and Comparative Law Quarterly* 507; Hart and Honoré, *Causation in the Law*, 1959, 403.

each legal system. In English law the first stage of the causal inquiry is referred to as "factual causation", "cause in fact" or "but for cause". "This "but for test" consists of posing the question: would the loss have been sustained *but for* the relevant act or omission by the defendant?"[283] Similarly, the German law of torts has adopted the so-called *Äquivalenztheorie* or *conditio sine qua non* formula, which is the equivalence to the "but for test".[284] The more theoretical approach of German legal thinking is illustrated by the efforts to determine how the defendant's conduct (or the event complained of) will be deemed to be or not to be a *conditio sine qua non* of the plaintiff's harm. The so-called elimination theory operates as follows:

> "If one attempts wholly to eliminate in thought the alleged author (of the act) from the sum of events in question and it then appears that nevertheless the sequence of intermediate causes remains the same, it is clear that the act and its consequences cannot be referred to him ... but if it appears that, once the person in question is eliminated in thought from the scene, the consequences cannot come about, or that they can come about only in a completely different way, then one is fully justified in attributing the consequences to him and explaining it as the effect of his activity".[285]

The English approach might be less theoretical as Lord Reid remarked in *McGhee v National Coal Board*:[286] "the legal concept of causation is not based on logic or philosophy", but on "the practical way in which the ordinary man's mind works in the everyday affairs of life". However, English judges reach similar conclusions. There seems to be some truth in the criticism by the French that "if causation did not exist as a subject it would have to be invented so that German lawyers would have something to exercise their minds".[287] Interestingly, in contrast to the theoretical approach of German scholars with the condition of causation, the German courts have shown that "the solution should, in the end, be one dictated by common sense and equity".[288]

The second stage in the causal inquiry is the one that causes more difficulties in both jurisdictions. In English law this is often described as the test of foreseeability or remoteness. "At this second stage the courts make an assessment of whether the link between the conduct and the ensuing loss was sufficiently close. To put it differently, judges decide which of the conditions of the plaintiff's harm should also be regarded in a legal sense to be its causes".[289] Both English and German courts are faced with questions such as liability for damage which would have occurred in any case whether or not a breach of duty could be established (in Ger-

---

283 Deakin & Markesinis, *The Law of Torts*, 1998, 174.

284 Markesinis in Deakin & Markesinis, *The Law of Torts*, 1998, 176 also refers to the "*conditio sine qua non* of the loss, that is to say an event without which the harm would not have happened".

285 Markesinis, B.S., *Comparative Introduction to the German Law of Tort*, 1986, 64.

286 [1972] 3 All ER 1008.

287 Markesinis, B.S., *Comparative Introduction to the German Law of Tort*, 1986, 63.

288 Ibid; see BGHZ 3, 267; BGHZ 30, 154, 157.

289 Deakin, S.F., & Markesinis, B.S., *The Law of Torts*, 1998, 174.

man law: *rechtmäßiges Alternativverhalten*). The following cases deal with that problem in particular.

In *Barnett v Chelsea & Kensington Hospital Management Committee*[290] the plaintiff's husband went to the casualty department of the defendant's hospital suffering from what subsequently proved to be arsenic poisoning. The casualty officer, without examining him, told the plaintiff's husband to consult his own GP. A few hours later the man died and his widow sued the hospital in negligence. Her claim was unsuccessful because the casualty officer's negligence was not shown to have caused the man's death. In its judgment the court applied the but for test which:

"Demands, then, a hypothetical inquiry into what would have happened if the defendant had acted without fault. This entails consideration not only of how the defendant should have acted but also of how the plaintiff would have reacted to the defendant's hypothetical conduct. To be taken into account are both purely physical reactions, e.g. how the plaintiff would have responded to proper medical treatment, and reactions reflecting the plaintiff's deliberate choice".[291]

The court also addressed the question of the burden of proof:

"It remains to consider whether it is shown that the deceased's death was caused by that negligence or whether, as the defendants have said, the deceased must have died in any event. In his concluding submission Mr Paine submitted that the casualty officer should have examined the deceased and had he done so he would have caused tests to be made which would have indicated the treatment required and that, since the defendants were at fault in these respects, therefore the onus of proof passed to the defendants to show that the appropriate treatment would have failed, and authorities were cited to me. I find myself unable to accept that argument, and I am of the view that the onus of proof remains upon the plaintiff ..."

a) R v Secretary of State for the Home Department, ex p Gallagher

In the Court of Appeal's decision of 10 June 1996 in *R v Secretary of State for the Home Department, ex p Gallagher*[292] the issue of causation in member state liability led to the failure of the claim against the UK. Gallagher, an Irish national, was arrested in the UK under the protection of the Prevention of Terrorism Act 1989 on the grounds that he had been involved in acts of terrorism. The Secretary of State made an expulsion order against Gallagher, which Gallagher then challenged in court. Mr Gallagher was entitled under the 1989 Act to make representations and to be interviewed by a person nominated by the Secretary of State and the Secretary of State was obliged to reconsider his decisions after receiving those representations and the report of the interview. On a preliminary ruling, the European Court of Justice held that, in passing the 1989 Act, the UK had failed to give full effect to Art. 9(1) of Directive 64/221 which required that the Secretary of State should not have made any expulsion order until *after* receiving the report of

290 [1968] 1 All ER 1068.
291 Mullis, A., *Torts*, 1997, 108.
292 [1996] 2 CMLR 951.

the person appointed to interview Gallagher. The directive gave effect to the fundamental freedom of movement of workers. Gallagher amended his claim to include an action for damages for breach of Community law:

"... Turning to the issue of causation it appeared that the Secretary of State had approached the matter afresh after receiving the interviewer's report, and there was nothing to suggest that the Secretary of State would have reached a different decision if the correct procedure had been followed. Causation ... is an issue to be decided on the balance of probabilities. The plaintiff must show on the balance of probabilities that the injury for which he seeks compensation was caused by the unlawful conduct of which he complains. Mr Gallagher has established a breach of Community law, but he cannot show that the breach probably caused him to be excluded from the UK when he would not otherwise have been excluded".[293]

In other words, if the Secretary of State had acted without being in breach of the procedural rules would not have changed anything, the expulsion would have taken place anyway. Cane describes this question as "hypothetical" or "counterfactual": "what would have happened if D (the defendant) had acted non-tortiously rather than tortiously?"[294] Gallagher argued further:

"That while he may have been excluded anyway if the correct procedure had been followed, he would have had a better chance of securing a favourable result if he had been able to be interviewed before the Secretary of State had made a decision, and that he was entitled to be compensated for the chance which he had lost of securing a better result".[295]

However, Gallagher failed to prove a causal connection between the breach of the directive and the alleged damage.

b) Germany – breach of procedural provisions and causation

In December 1982 the plaintiff was admitted to a psychiatric hospital on the basis of a compulsory admission based on a court decision.[296] Attached to the court decision was a medical report which contained details concerning the mental health of the plaintiff. The plaintiff was diagnosed as suffering from paranoia and that he posed a threat to himself and others. The report was signed by the plaintiff's GP and the doctor officially assigned to him by the court. The official doctor had signed the report after several telephone conversations with the GP, however, he had not examined the plaintiff himself.

The Law on Mental Health Patients (*PsychKG ND*) governs compulsory admission to psychiatric hospitals. According to Art. 10 ff. of that law the official doctor is required to ensure that temporary compulsory admissions are legal. He was required to examine the plaintiff himself. The plaintiff claimed the act violated his

293 Ibid at 965.

294 Cane, P., *The Anatomy of Tort Law* ,1997, 173.

295 [1996] 2 CMLR 951 at 963, 964.

296 OLG Oldenburg VersR 91, 306, translation of the case in Markesinis, B.S., *Tortious Liability of Statutory Bodies, A Comparative and Economic Analysis of Five English Cases* ,1999, 144.

constitutional rights in Arts. 2 and 104 of the Basic Law. Article 2 of the Basic Law reads:

"(1) Everybody has the right to self-fulfilment in so far as they do not violate the rights of others or offend against the constitutional order or morality. Everybody has the right to life and physical integrity. These rights may not be encroached upon save pursuant to a law".

Article 104 of the Basic Law reads:

"(1) Individual liberty may be restricted only pursuant to a formal law and only in the manner it prescribes".

The defendants argued that even if the official doctor had carried out an examination as required under the Law on Mental Health Patients the plaintiff would have been admitted to a psychiatric hospital under a compulsory admission. Therefore he was not entitled to damages according to Sect. 839 of the Civil Code in connection with Art. 34 of the Basic Law.

The court held that the plaintiff was entitled to damages amounting to DM5000 for having been submitted to the institution in the absence of a medical report by the official doctor. It held that the defendant's argument could not stand because the violation of the Law on Mental Health Patients is of such gravity that this defence is not permitted. The court laid down that the protective purpose of the law is only to allow the limitation of one's personal freedom according to narrow requirements such as the omitted medical examination. This law is directly based on the constitutional protection guaranteed in Arts. 2 and 104 of the Basic Law and therefore of such importance that the violation of procedural rules like the ones in this case is sufficient in itself to lead to the liability of the authorities. The hypothetical consideration that the plaintiff would have been submitted anyway even if the procedures had been followed correctly is therefore irrelevant and not sufficient as a defence for the defendant authority.

These cases illustrate well that the English and German law of torts is concerned with exactly the same question: what would have happened if the defendant had acted lawfully? The defendant can use the concept of the counter-factual situation (*rechtmäßiges Alternativverhalten*) as a defence, but in contrast to the defendant in English courts clearly has to carry the burden of proof. Principally, the counter-factual situation is relevant in deciding whether the non-tortious action would have avoided the injury. Cases are straightforward if the defendant's action was negligent. Here, the defendant can successfully defend himself against the claim by showing that the injury would also have occurred had he acted non-tortiously.

There are, however, restrictions to the defence of the defendant in arguing that the injury would also have occurred had he acted non-tortiously. It appears, however, that restrictions of that kind cannot be found in English law. In some cases the defendant acted with full intention. In these cases it is controversial whether the defendant may later defend himself by saying the injury would have occurred anyway. On the one hand, it is argued that the law of tort is not designed to punish the defendant for having breached a duty as such. This should be the domain of criminal law. On the other hand, the argument is brought forward that someone who has wilfully chosen to act in a tortious way may not be permitted the defence of the counter-factual situation (*rechtmäßiges Alternativverhalten*). The *Bundesgerichtshof* (the highest court in civil matters) applies a theory which is described as the middle path between these views and which is generally followed by lower courts. This is the theory of the protective purpose of the norm (*Schutzzweck der Norm*). Accordingly, the question is asked whether the norm which has been breached was designed to prevent the tortious injury as such. The protective purpose of the norm which was breached may hold the defendant liable even if the injury had occurred if the norm had not been breached. This may be the case if major procedural requirements are not fulfilled such as in the case of a psychiatric patient who was admitted to a psychiatric ward in violation of procedural requirements. The defendant could not successfully challenge the claim by arguing that the patient would have been admitted to a psychiatric ward anyway even if the procedural requirements had been complied with.[297] Here, the German court argued that the protective purpose of the procedural rules is of such importance that their breach leads to liability regardless of whether or not the compliance with the rules would have led to the same result. Similarly, it was held that the theory of the protective purpose of the norm is rather vague and it has been cynically remarked that the *Bundesgerichtshof* favours this formula in order to decide each case flexibly.[298]

The other restriction applies to cases in which the counter-factual situation involves the exercise of discretion. In the case decided by the *Bundesgerichtshof* a public body was sued for having made a decision despite the fact that it was not the competent authority to make that decision. The authority defended its position by claiming that the competent authority in exercising its discretionary powers would possibly have reached the same decision. The *Bundesgerichtshof* held that the plaintiff was entitled to damages because the defendant could not show that the competent authority would certainly have decided identically.[299] Accordingly a plaintiff was held to be unsuccessful with his claim against a public body after it was shown that in the absence of discretionary powers the competent authority would have reached exactly the same decision.[300]

When assessing the decision of the Court of Appeal in *Gallagher*[301] in the light of the principles under German law, three main differences can be observed.

The first point concerns the burden of proof which under the provisions in English law is laid upon the plaintiff. *Gallagher* failed because he could not show that he would not have been expelled from the UK had the procedural requirements according to Directive 64/221 been complied with. In German law it would have been the defendant's defence to show that the same result would have been reached had the procedural requirements been met. In the German case above the

297 Oldenburg VersR 91, 306.

298 Ruessman, H., http://ruessmann.jura.uni-sb.de/bvr99/Vorlesung/kausalitaet-der-pflichtwidrigkeit.htm.

299 BGH NJW 59, 1316.

300 BGH NJW 71, 239.

301 [1996] 2 CMLR 951.

authorities argued that the plaintiff would have been submitted even if the doctor had examined him himself. In this case it might have been easy for the Home Secretary to show that he would have reached the same decision, but there might be cases in which it is harder for the defendant to discharge the burden of proof and therefore German law in comparison to English law facilitates the position of the plaintiff.

The second point concerns the restrictions to the defence with regard to the exercise of discretionary powers. In *Gallagher* the court had to decide whether the Secretary of State would have reached the same decision if he had considered the report and the representation before issuing the expulsion order. This involved the exercise of discretionary powers. Both English and German courts should, however, avoid second guessing as to how a discretionary power is or would have been exercised:

"It is trite law that judicial review (in English courts) is not concerned with the merits of administrative decisions and the court should ordinarily avoid substituting its own opinion for that of the public body as to how precisely a discretion should be exercised. Probability (in establishing causation) will be defined by, among other facts, the degree of discretion possessed by the decision maker".[302]

The European Court of Justice held that the case of *Gallagher* was comparable to the situation in *British Telecommunications* where the UK had discretionary powers in transposing the directive. Therefore the stricter conditions established in *Brasserie*, i.e. the demonstration that the UK violation of Community law was sufficiently serious, applied.[303]

Finally, the theory of the protective purpose of the law which has been breached which is applied by the *Bundesgerichtshof* might lead to a different decision from that of the Court of Appeal. Accordingly it has to be assessed whether the norm which was breached was specifically designed to avoid the damage.[304] The norm breached was Council Directive 64/221 which:

"Sets out to co-ordinate all measures relating to entry and deportation from their territory and issue or renewal of residence permits which member states can adopt on grounds of public policy, security, and health, in relation to the employed, the self-employed, recipients of services, and the families of each".[305]

In *Gallagher* Art. 9 was at stake which contains "procedural rights which must be provided for a person against whom one of the grounds is being invoked".[306] Article 9(1) reads:

"Where there is no right of appeal to a court of law, or where such appeal may be only in respect the legal validity of the decision, or where the appeal cannot have suspensory effect, a decision ... ordering the expulsion of the holder of a residence permit from the territory shall not be taken by the administrative authority, save in cases of urgency, until an opinion

302 De Smith, S.A., *Judicial Review of Administative Action*, 1995, 19-033.
303 [1996] 2 CMLR 951 at 952.
304 von Caemmerer, E., *Das Problem der überholenden Kausalität* (1962) 30ff.
305 Craig, P. and de Burca, G., *EU Law*, 1998, 786.
306 Ibid at 796.

has been obtained from a competent authority of the host country before which the person concerned enjoys such rights of the defence and of assistance or representation as the domestic law of that country provides for".

The procedural rights contained in Art. 9 are very important as they safeguard that the derogations from the fundamental freedoms contained in the Treaty such as the free movement of workers, freedom of establishment and free movement of services are given a narrow scope.[307] Gallagher's damage consisted of the lost chance of securing a better result which he forfeited by not being interviewed before the issue of the expulsion order. When defining the purpose of Art. 9(1) of the directive the European Court held in its previous decision in *R v Secretary of State for the Home Department, ex p Gallagher*:[308]

"That the competent authority ... must follow a procedure enabling the person concerned effectively to present his defence. As the court has already held, the purpose of the intervention of the competent authority referred to in Art. 9(1) is to enable an exhaustive examination of all the facts and circumstances, including the expediency of the proposed measure, to be carried out *before* the decision is finally taken. The court has also ruled that save in cases of urgency, the administrative authority may not take its decision until an opinion has been obtained from the competent authority".[309]

This provision is designed to prevent cases being decided hastily, save in cases of urgency, without taking all facts and circumstances into account. Therefore the damage Gallagher suffered which consisted of the lost chance of obtaining a better result was to be prevented by the provision itself. Therefore one could argue that the breach of the directive caused the damage the plaintiff suffered regardless of the fact that the Home Secretary would have reached the same decision anyway. The Home Secretary's defence that the expulsion would have taken place anyway might have been unsuccessful in a German court.

The case of *Gallagher* is also problematic because it contains a "three party" situation and despite the fact that the United Kingdom was at fault by incorrectly transposing Directive 64/221 into domestic law the state was not held liable. The *Bundesgerichtshof* decided differently in a state liability case containing a three party situation.[310] A State Secretary in Germany required subordinate administrative departments to implement measures for which no legal basis existed. A legal basis could only have been enacted in conjunction with Parliament. The plaintiff was successful with his claim in damages against the State Secretary even though a legal basis could have been enacted easily as all legal requirements for the enactment were fulfilled and the measures would then have been lawful. The State Secretary, however, could not use this as a defence because the legal basis could only have been enacted in conjunction with Parliament. In these cases the rule of law outweighs the hypothetical argument that the measures would have been implemented in the same way because all requirements for the enactment of the legal basis existed at the time. In *Gallagher* the legal basis, the Prevention of Terrorism

307 Ibid at 786.

308 [1996] 2 CMLR 951.

309 [1995] ECR I-4253, [1996] 1 CMLR 557 at 573.

310 BGHZ 63, 319.

Act 1989, was held to be in breach of Community law and required alteration by the UK Parliament. According to the principles in German law it could therefore be argued that it was not within the State Secretary's power to change the legislation and therefore he could not bring the defence of the counter-factual situation.

Applying the principles of causality developed in the German law of state liability to the case of *Gallagher* has shown some important differences. The rules on the burden of proof under German law for situations like the one in *Gallagher* are more in the plaintiff's favour. However, as mentioned earlier, the theory of the protective purpose of the norm (*Schutzzwecklehre*) is vague and was deliberately chosen by the *Bundesgerichtshof* to maintain room for policy decisions.

These cases have shown some parallels in how English and German courts deal with the issue of causation. In both the English and German law of torts the question of causation is analysed in two stages. This "bifurcation" of analysis is a striking similarity. The "but for test" in English law is equivalent to the German *Äquivalenztheorie* or *conditio sine qua non* formula. However, the second stage in the inquiry into the causality of the tortious action shows that both systems face similar issues such as the question of alternative lawful conduct or in other words the question whether a damage would have occurred regardless of the breach of duty. Both systems recognise this concept which results in the negation of a sufficient causal link between the breach and the damage. However, the strong human rights culture in modern Germany has led to a limitation of that concept in cases where the rule that was breached, i.e. a procedural rule, was designed to protect human rights such as the right to personal liberty as shown above in the Law on Mental Health Patients. The decision in *Gallagher* illustrates that no such limitations to this concept are known, not even when important procedural rules are clearly breached.

These potential differences in reaching decisions in state liability cases by applying purely domestic principles of causation do not support the idea of a uniform legal protection of individuals within the European Union. This lack of uniformity in the enforcement procedures for Community law rights through the member states' legal systems is a major problem.[311] In the absence of Community legislation which lays down rules for the protection of Community rights in the national courts the European Court of Justice might continue to define a "set of uniform principles which the national rules on remedies must satisfy where Community rights are in issue".[312]

Some more guidance by the European Court of Justice for the establishment of principles common to all member states is desirable. However, it is not clear to what extent the European Court of Justice is prepared to take further steps in the elaboration of the remedy of member state liability. There appears to be "a retreat from the more interventionist stance the European Court of Justice took in some cases in the 1980s and 1990s". One reason is seen in the "more detailed enumeration of the Community's powers in the TEU, at least in the immediate aftermath of Maastricht, have made the court less willing than previously to compensate for the

---

311 Arnull, A., *The European Union and its Court of Justice* ,1999, 151.

312 Ibid.

shortcomings of the legislature".[313] However, it remains the European Court of Justice's task to ensure that national procedural rules do not make the enforcement of Community law rights impossible or excessively difficult. Therefore the further development of the remedy of member state liability through the European Court of Justice also depends on the questions which are referred to it via national courts.

IV. Conclusion

On reflection on these national angles in governmental liability it is notable that this area of law is equally complex and in itself incoherent in both countries. Both systems feature a combination of private and public law remedies which are based on historical legal concepts not always easily adaptable to change. In the absence of clear legislative guidance the courts are mandated to adapt to changes brought about by membership within the European Union and in the case of England by the increasing significance of human rights protection. Inevitably this comparison was marked by problems of categorisation. The chosen topics reflected by way of highlights show current developments in each member state.

Public policy considerations, the restrictive role of the courts and the developing human rights culture in England which have led to a wealth of governmental liability case law are not a topic of great relevance in Germany. However, the chapter has shown that similar problems exist in Germany, but that the solutions are not found in the law of tort. Germany's approach to governmental liability, despite its shortcomings, is a reflection of the principle of the *Rechtsstaat*.[314] The *Rechtsstaatsprinzip* in its modern version is contained in the Basic Law and embraces the principle of the separation of powers, the protection of the individual in the courts, in particular the protection of the individual against governmental action as laid down in Arts. 19(4), 20(3) and 34 of the Basic Law by way of judicial review, and governmental liability. This constitutional background provides the setting in which the tortious liability of public bodies is embedded. An example of this deep-seated approach to human rights protection is the theory of the protective norm as illustrated. Accordingly, the rules of causation cannot override its significance if an alternative action would have been legal. However, despite the novelty of the role for English judges under the Human Rights Act 1998 the analysis has shown that experience in dealing with constitutional matters in Germany does not always lead to transparent decisions. Governmental liability in Germany is an area of law which requires more systematic structuring, possibly new legislation. Lord Bingham's analysis in *Greenfield* is of great clarity in distinguishing tort claims from claims for breaches of Convention rights, something that the decision by the Federal Constitutional Court in the prisoner case lacks.

---

313 Ibid at 188.

314 Ossenbühl, F., *Staatshaftungsrecht* ,5th edn, 1998, 6.

Within the EU context an interesting juxtaposition of approaches is notable. As we have seen the British approach in *Factortame* differs from the more restrictive approach taken in purely domestic cases.[315] The English court's approach in *Factortame* has been described as "enthusiastically" and "dutifully".[316] In England internal changes in the constitutional relationship between the judiciary and the other powers in the state may serve as an explanation for the greater potential to harmonise domestic law with European jurisprudence. The European case law had "pushed forward the boundaries of domestic judicial interventionism".[317] The resistance towards the integration of the *Francovich* remedy and avoidance tactics in German courts is probably based on far less spectacular reasons: a preference for clear legislation in this area of law.

[315] See Lord Hoffman in *R v Secretary of State for Transport, ex parte Factortame (No. 5)* [2000] 1 AC 524 [548] and *Stovin v Wise* [1996] AC 923, 949.

[316] Harlow, C., *Tort Law*, 2005, 65.

[317] Nicol, D., *EC Membership and the Judicialisation of British Politics*, 2001, 221.

Chapter Six Tradition and change

Much detail and evaluation can be found in the previous chapters. In this final chapter I will attempt to draw some broader conclusions will be drawn. The comparative analysis of Germany's and the UK's administrative legal systems has illustrated the complexities of modern administrative law. To understand the reasons for variations between English and German administrative law one has to uncover several layers. An understanding of the historical traditions aids the process of mapping out the future which inevitably involves some degree of change. Administrative law has to be viewed as a product of each nation's historical development and legal mentality. Further, administrative law and in particular the control of administrative action through the courts is concerned with the question of where to draw the line between the power of the judiciary and the decision makers and with the protection of the individual citizen against state action. This ultimately raises questions constitutional in nature. These can be substantive issues, i.e. who should have the final say on complex questions of policy, to what extent should individual rights be upheld by the courts and can public authorities be sued in damages? In addition questions relating to the institutional organisation of the courts and the selection of judges become relevant. Finally, the role of the courts in adjudicating on administrative law questions can no longer be seen in isolation of the jurisprudence of both the European Court of Justice and the European Court of Human Rights. Increasingly, judges in both jurisdictions had to grapple with case law which does not always fit squarely with established practice under national laws. Here, in particular, the British judiciary has been tested and has taken an active role.

As stated in the introduction to this book the English and German administrative legal systems are increasingly faced with the question of how to balance the dynamics of change, brought on by internal or external pressures, with the preserving forces of tradition.

The judges play a pivotal role in this process. They have to work day in day out with questions as to the intensity of review, protection of rights positions or the question whether compensation for unlawful government action is available.

One of the main findings was that the administrative legal traditions in the reviewed countries vary as one operates within a constitutional setting based on law, the other founded on a constitution based on politics. From that flow important consequences for the scope of judicial review and the protection of individuals against state action which I shall explain.

The German judicial review system is based on the principle of full judicial protection against administrative action as laid down in Art. 19 IV of the Basic

Law which constitutes an important part of the German *Rechtsstaat*: "where rights are violated by public authorities the person affected shall have recourse to law. In so far as no other jurisdiction has been established such recourse shall be to the ordinary courts". Critical discussion within court decisions concerning the constitutional role of the courts as one can find in English decisions are less likely to be found in German court decisions. In England the basis of judicial review has been discussed widely and in the absence of a written constitutional principle there are competing models of justification for judicial review. Judicial remedies in English courts are purely discretionary whereas the German constitutional provision provides a constitutionally guaranteed right subject to the fulfilment of standing requirements. The German Basic Law enjoys the status of the highest form of law in Germany. From that important consequences flow. The Basic Law which contains a long catalogue of human rights has had a profound impact on the development of administrative law principles, some of which even pre-date the Basic Law. Article 1 III states: "… the following basic rights shall bind the legislature, the executive and the judiciary as directly enforceable law". Importantly and in contrast to Sect. 19 of the Human Rights Act 1998, according to Art. 20 III, Parliament is bound by the Basic Law. Most famously, the principle of proportionality and legitimate expectation (now codified in great detail in the Law on Administrative Procedure) are directly based on constitutional provisions. The Administrative Courts have translated the right to equality in Art. 3 into an important administrative law principle ensuring the consistency of the exercise of administrative discretion. Due to the requirement to uphold an individual's rights the German model of judicial review is marked by a high degree of intensity of review. The protection of individual rights positions is not always directly based on constitutional rights, but on the notion of subjective rights.At the same time the protection of procedural safeguards has been neglected. This high level of scrutiny in Germany is based on the constitutional legacy, i.e. the distrust of executive power after the experiences during the Nazi dictatorship. There is less doubt as to what the appropriate role of the judges should be. The inquisitorial procedure aids the role of the judge in that he has great input into the process. The constitutional mandates for the legislative, the administration and the Administrative Courts are enforced by the jurisdiction of the Federal Constitutional Court which is exclusively concerned with constitutional law issues, in particular with individual complaints concerning the violation of basic rights. The Federal Constitutional Court's decisions often deal with politically sensitive topics or difficult questions of expertise. However, the court enjoys a high degree of legitimacy which may partly be due to the selection process. Constitutional Court judges are elected and many of the judges are legal academics. The close link to constitutional provisions does not, however, mean that Administrative Courts are mere miniatures of the Constitutional Court. Administrative law exists in its own right, many administrative statutes are designed to fill in wide constitutional provisions and administrative principles such as the principle of proportionality were established long before the Basic Law was drafted.

The traditional role of the courts in England, on the other hand, is less clearly defined. Constitutional reference points are the sovereignty of Parliament and the rule of law. The absence of a written constitution means that human rights protection is not a constitutional mandate that could bind Parliament. Consequently, no court is entitled to overturn parliamentary legislation. The authority of the Human Rights Act 1998, a mere parliamentary statute, is a great deal weaker than the German Basic Law which as we have seen has contributed to a coherent set of administrative law principles.

However, the courts have over several decades gradually expanded their role. Cases such as *Anisminic* and *Factortame* bear witness to the creative approach of the British judiciary in pushing the boundaries and "catching up with constitutional reality". Judges have developed and applied constitutional principles such as the rule of law and have developed principles of judicial review and human rights protection. The principle of proportionality and legitimate expectation have taken root in English administrative law, but will give rise to further refinement on a case by case approach. Even though a more systematic shape of administrative legal protection is taking shape there is still an element of uncertainty as to the exact scope of some of these principles. This active approach of some judges has, however, at times created unease between decision makers and the courts. The Human Rights Act 1998, an Act of Parliament, has also led to decisions which were not welcome by the government. Any further development of the grounds of review beyond a careful and pragmatic approach by the courts might trespass upon the limits of parliamentary sovereignty. In the absence of a written constitution the development of a thorough human rights culture would be unconstitutional in the UK.

Germany's rights-based approach is not without critics. It bears the risks of distorting the wider spectrum within which administrative decisions are being taken. Some commentators fear that the balance too often tilts towards the protection of individual interests. In the context of European law we have seen that the principle of legitimate expectation had to be adapted significantly. This may lead to changes under domestic law as well. In other areas the courts display a rather hesitant approach. The relatively weak protection of procedural safeguards such as reason giving may well not be sufficient within the European context. More recently, the German provision on standing to sue has to be brought into line with European law requirements. In this area of law German courts display uncertainty.[1] The section on member state liability has illustrated the hesitance of the German courts to integrate the *Francovich* remedy into the German law of torts.

The law on governmental liability is equally complex and still incoherent in both countries. Both systems contain a combination of private and public law remedies which are based on historical legal concepts and not always easily adaptable to change. Despite some commonalities in the approaches, the integration of the *Francovich* remedy appears to be met with more resistance in German than in English courts.

---

1 Callies, C., "Feinstaub im Rechtsschutz deutscher Verwaltungsgerichte, Europarechtliche Vorgaben für die Klagebefugnis vor deutschen Gerichten und ihre dogmatische Verarbeitung" (2006) *NVwZ* 1.

An interesting juxtaposition of approaches is notable. The approach of English courts in *Factortame* differs from the more restrictive approach taken in purely domestic cases.[2] The comparison has shown that there appears to be more ease in English courts in achieving an integration of the *Francovich* remedy than in German courts.[3] In a more pragmatic case by case approach English courts have successfully embedded the *Francovich* remedy into English law. Harlow remarks that "the UK appears to be an exception to the reluctance noted in the text [referring to the decision by the German Federal High Court in *Brasserie du Pecheur*] embracing the liability principle enthusiastically and dutifully applying it in the *Factortame* case".[4] However, this approach led to internal tension. The UK government issued a White Paper on the 1996 IGC and proposed appeals procedures against judgments of the European Court of Justice. The late 1990s were marked by concern about the increase of judicial review cases and the fact that "national courts might emulate the judicial activism of the two European courts, fuelled by the fact that British judges were happy to admit that European jurisprudence had pushed forward the boundaries of domestic judicial inverventionism".[5] Resistance to European integration in the 1990s was felt at a political level rather than on a judicial level. In the UK membership within the European Union strengthened the role of the judiciary. Again, it may be internal changes in the constitutional relationship between the judiciary and the other powers in the state that can provide an explanation for the greater potential to harmonise domestic law with European jurisprudence.

In conclusion, it can be carefully suggested though that a trend towards similar levels of judicial protection in the control of administrative action is emerging. Notable is the traditional sophistication of the English judiciary which has demonstrated its capacity to adapt whilst preserving its traditional reference points. The pace of change is, however, slow. Larger constitutional changes are traditionally incremental – this will hinder convergence with a system which has experienced gigantic constitutional changes. However, the pragmatic, court-centred case by case approach in the common law is at times more apt to progress on this basis. It remains a contrast to the more principled approach in its civil law counterpart which is less open to change on a pragmatic basis and at times is hindered by its abstract approach to move on. National variations in style and mentality will carry on to operate alongside each other and will continue to fascinate comparative lawyers.

---

2 See Lord Hoffman in *Factortame* and *Stovin v Wise*.

3 See also Harlow, C., *Tort Law* ,2005, 65.

4 Ibid.

5 Nicol, D., *EC Membership and the Judicialisation of British Politics*, 2001, 221.

Bibliography

Books

Allison, J. W. F., *A continental distinction in the common law* (Oxford: University Press, 2000)

Andenas, M., Fairgrieve, D., *Judicial Review in International Perspective: Volume II* (Kluwer Law International, 2000)

Andenas, M., *English Public Law and the Common Law of Europe* (London: Key Haven Publications plc, 1998)

Arnull, A., *The European Union and its Court of Justice* (Oxford: University Press, 1999)

Arthurs, H.W., *"Without the Law", Administrative Justice and Legal Pluralism in Nineteenth Century England* (Toronto and Buffalo, University of Toronto Press, 1985)

Bailey, S.H, Jones B.L & Mowbray A.R, 3rd edition, *Cases and Materials on Administrative law* (London, Sweet & Maxwell, 1992)

Barnett, H, *Constitutional and Administrative Law*, 4th edition, (London: Cavendish: 2002)

Beaumont P., Lyons, C., Walker, N. *Convergence and Divergence in European Public Law*, (Hart, Oxford, 2002)

Bell, J. , Bradley, W., *Governmental Liability: A comparative study* (United Kingdom National Committee of Comparative Law, 1991)

Berger, V., *Case law of the ECHR*, (Dublin: Round Hall Press, 1991)

Birkinshaw, P., European Public Law, (London: Butterworths, 2003)

Birkinshaw, P., *Freedom of Information*, 3rd edition, (London: Butterworths, 2001)

Birkinshaw, P., *Grievances, Remedies and the State* (London: Sweet & Maxwell, 1994)

Böckenförde, E.W., *State, Society and Liberty* (New York, Oxford: University Press 1991)

Bradley, A.W, Ewing, K.D, *Constitutional and Administrative law* (London: Longman, 1997)

Brinktrine, R., *Verwaltungsermessen in Deutschland und England* (Heidelberg: C.F. Müller 1998)

Cane, P., *Administrative Law*, 4 th edition, (Oxford: Clarendon, 2004)

Cane, P., *The Anatomy of Tort Law* (Oxford: Hart Publishing, 1997)

Canivet, G., Andenas, M., Fairgrieve, D., Independence, Accoutability, and the Judiciary, (BIICL, 2006)

Cappelletti, M., *New Perspectives for a common law of Europe* (Leyden:Sijthoff, 1978)

Cappelletti, M., *The Judicial Process in Comparative Perspective* (Oxford: University Press, 1989)

Classen, C. D., *Die Europäisierung der Verwaltungsgerichtsbarkeit* (Tübingen: J.C.B. Mohr (Paul Siebeck), 1995)

Craig, P. and de Búrca, G., *EU Law*, 3rd edition, (Oxford: University Press, 2003)

Craig, P., *Administrative Law*, 4th edition (London: Sweet & Maxwell, 2003)

David, R., *English Law and French Law: Tagore law lectures* (London: Stevens, 1980)

David, R., International Encyclopedia of Comparative Law, vol. 2, ch 5 (JCB Mohr: Tübingen, 1970)

Davis, K.C., *Discretionary Justice* (Urbana and Chicago: University of Illinois Press 1971)

de Cruz, P., *Comparative Law in a Changing World*, 2nd edition (London: Cavendish Publishers Ltd 1995)

Deakin & Markesinis, B., *The law of Torts* (Oxford: Clarendon Press, 1998)

De Smith , Woolf, Jowell, *Judicial Review of Administrative Action* (London: Sweet & Maxwell 1995)

De Smith, *Principles of Judicial Review* (London: Sweet & Maxwell, 1999)

Devlin, P., *The Judge* (Oxford: University Press, 1979)

Dicey, A.V., *An Introduction to the Study of the Law of the Constitution, Law of the Constitution*, 10th edition (London: Macmillan 1960)

Donson, F., *Civil Liberties and Judicial Review: Can the Common Law Really Protect Rights?* in Leyland, P., & Woods, T., *Administrative Law Facing the Future* (London: Blackstone Press Limited 1997)

Dyson, K.H.F, *The State Tradition in Western Europe: A study of an idea and institution* (Oxford: University Press, 1980)

Ebenroth, C.T., *Verantwortung und Gestaltung, Festschrift für K.H. Boujong*, München: C.H.Beck. 1996)

Erichsen, H.U., Ehlers, D., Allgemeines Verwaltungsrecht, 12 edition, (Berlin: de Gruyter, 2002)

Ellis, E., *The Principle of Proportionality in the Laws of Europe* (Oxford: Hart Publishing, 1999)

Erichsen, H.-U. and Martens, W., *Allgemeines Verwaltungsrecht*, 8th edition (Berlin, New York: Walter de Gruyter, 1988)

Fairgrieve, D., Green, S., *Child abuse tort claims against public bodies*, (Ashgate, 2004)

Fairgrieve, D., Andenas, M., Bell, J., Tort Liability of Public Authorities in comparative perspective, (London: BIICL, 2002)

Fordham, M., and de la Mare, T. in Jowell, J., Cooper, J., *Understanding Human Rights Principles* (Oxford: Hart Publishing, 2001)

Forsyth, C., *Judicial Review and the Constitution* (Oxford University Press, 2000)

Forsyth, C. and Hare, I., *The Golden Metwand and the Crooked Cord* (Oxford University Press, 1998)

Foster, N., *German Legal System and Laws* (London: Blackstone Press Ltd, 1993)

Foulkes, D., *Administrative Law*, 7th edition (London: Butterworths, 1990)

Frotscher, W./Pieroth, B., *Verfassungsgeschichte,* (München: Beck, 1997)

Frowein, J. A., *Die Kontrolldichte bei der gerichtlichen Überprüfung von Handlungen der Verwaltung* (Berlin: Springer, 1993)

Galligan, D. J., *Discretionary Powers* (Oxford: Clarendon Press, 1986)

Gerber, C.F. v., *Grundzüge eines Systems des deutschen Staatsrechts*, (Leipzig, 1865)

Gerstner, S., *Die Drittschutzdogmatik im Spiegel des französischen und britischen Verwaltungsverfahrens* (Berlin: Duncker & Humblot, 1995)

Gordon, R., *Judicial Review and Crown Office Practice* (London: Sweet & Maxwell, 1996)

Harden, I., Lewis, N., *The Noble Lie* (London: Hutchinson, 1988)

Harlow, C., *Tort Law*, (Hart: 2005)

Harlow, C., Convergence and Divergence in European Public Law, (Oxford: Hart, 2002)

Hart H.L.A. and Honoré A.M., *Causation in the Law* (Oxford: Clarendon Press, 1959)

Hedley, S., *Tort*, 1st edition (London: Butterworths, 1998)

Henderson, E., *Foundations of English Administrative Law: Certioari and Mandamus in the Seenteenth Century*(Cambridge, Masachusetts, 1963)

Heukels, T., McDonnell, A., *The Action for Damages in Community Law*, 1997

Hidien, *Die gemeinschaftsrechtliche Staatshaftung der EU-Mitgliedstaaten*, 37 f

Hinrichs, K. , *Selbstbeschaffung im Jugendhilferecht – Zur Aktualität fürsorgerechtlicher Grundsätze in der Jugendhilfe* (Frankfurt: Peter Lang, 2002)

Hogg, P. W., *Liability of the Crown*, 2nd edition (Toronto: Carswell, 1989)

Hufen, F., *Fehler im Verwaltungsverfahren,* 3rd edition, (Baden-Baden: Nomos, 1998)

Hufen, F., *Verwaltungsprozessrecht*, 3rd ed, (München: C.H. Beck Verlag, 1998)

Hunt, M., *Human Rights Law in English Courts* (Oxford: University Press 1997)

Jacobs, H., *Courts, Law and Politics in Comparative Perspective* (Yale University Press, 1996)

Jarass, H. D. , Pieroth, B., *Grundgesetz* (München: C. H. Beck Verlag, 1995)

Jowell, J. and Birkinshaw, P., *Tendencies towards European Standards in national Administrative Law*, in Schwarze, J., *Das Verwaltungsrecht unter europäischem Einfluß: zur Konvergenz der mitgliedstaatlichen Verwaltungsrechtsordnungen in der Europäischen Union* (Baden-Baden: Nomos, 1996)

Jowell, J.,Cooper, J., *Understanding Human Rights Principles* (Oxford: Hart Publishing, 2001)

Justice (corporate author), Neill P., *Administrative Justice: Some Necessary Reform: report of the Committee of the Justice-All Souls review of administrative law in the United Kingdom* (Oxford: Clarendon Press, 1988)

Kahn-Freund, O., in Brown, L., Cappelletti, M., *New Perspectives for the common law of Europe* (Leyden:Sijthoff, 1978)

Kilpatrick, C., *The Future of Remedies in Europe* (Oxford: University Press, 2000)

Kirchhof, P., Kommers, D. P, *Germany and its Basic Law: past, present, and future: a German-American symposium* (Baden-Baden: Nomos, 1993)

Kommers, D. P, *The constitutional jurisprudence of the Federal Republic of Germany*, 2nd edition (Durham, N.C.: Duke University Press, 1997)

Koopman, T., *Courts and Political Institutions, A Comparative Overview*, (Cambridge University Press, 2005)

Kopp, F.O., *VwGO* 10th edition, (München: C.H. Beck Verlag, 1994)

Lacey, M.J. Haakonssen, K. *A Culture of Rights: the Bill of Rights in philosophy, politics, and law – 1791 and 1991*(Cambridge: 1991)

Lamprecht, R., "Vom Mythos der Unabhängigkeit: Über das Dasein und Sosein der deutschen Richter, (Baden-Baden: Nomos, 1995)

Laband, P., *Das Staatsrecht des Deutschen Reiches*, Bd. II, 5th edition, (Tübingen: J.C.B. Mohr, 1911)

Legrand, P., Munday, R., *Comparative Legal Studies: Traditions and Transitions*, (Cambridge University Press, 2006)

Levi, E.H., *An Introduction to Legal Reasoning* (Chicago: University of Chicago Press, 1948)

Leyland, P., Woods, T., *Administrative Law facing the Future,* (London: Blackstone, 1997)

Limbach, J., *Im Namen des Volkes*, (Stuttgart: Deutsche Verlagsanstalt, 1999)

Lord Slynn of Hadley and M.Andenas eds *FIDE XX Congress* London (2002) Vol.1

Maitland, F.W., *The Forms of Action at Common Law: A course of lectures* (Cambridge: University Press, 1948)

Maitland, F.W., *The Constitutional History of England: A Course of Lectures,* (Cambridge: University Press 1926)

Markesinis, B.S., *A comparative Introduction into the German law of tort* (Oxford: Clarendon Press, 1986)

Markesinis, B.S., The Clifford Chance Millenium Lectures The Coming Together of the Coming Law and the Civil Law, (Oxford: Hart Publishing, 2000)

Markesinis B.S., Auby, J.B. , Coester-Waltjen, D., & Deakin, S.F., *Tortious Liability of Statutory Bodies, A Comparative and Economic Analysis of Five English Cases*, (Oxford: Hart Publishing, 1999)

Maurer, H., *Allgemeines Verwaltungsrecht* (München Beck-Verlag, 1999)

Marquardt, C. , *Sexuell missbrauchte Kinder im Gerichtsverfahren* (Münster, 1999)

Mayer, O., *Theorie des französischen Verwaltungsrechts* (Strassburg: K.J.Trübner, 1886)

Mayer, O., Deutsches Verwaltungsrecht, 3rd edition, (München, Leipzig, 1924)

Mény, Y., *Government and Politics in Western Europe* (Oxford: University Press 1993)

Merryman, J. H., *Convergence of Civil Law and Common Law* in Cappelletti, M., *New Perspectives for a common law of Europe* (Leyden: Sijthoff 1978)

Mullis, A., Oliphant, K., *Torts*, 3rd ed., (Basingstoke: Macmillan 1999)

Nicol, D., *EC membership and the Judicialisation of British Politics*, (Oxford: OUP, 2001)

Oeter, S., in Frowein, J. A., (Hrsg.), *Die Kontrolldichte bei der gerichtlichen Überprüfung von Handlungen der Verwaltung*, Max -Planck-Institut für ausl. öffentliches Recht und Völkerrecht (Berlin: Springer 1993)

Oliver, D., *Constitutional Reform in the United Kingdom, 2002* (Oxford: Oxford University Press)

Ossenbühl, F., *Staatshaftungsrecht* (München: C.H. Beck Verlag 1998)

Pollard, D., *Judicial review of prerogative power in the united Kingdom and France,* in Leyland, P. and Woods, T., *Administrative Law facing the Future* (London: Blackstone Press Limited 1997)

Pollard, D., Parpworth, N., Hughes, D. 3rd edition, *Constitutional and Administrative Law* (London: Butterworths, 2001)

Pollock, F. and Maitland, F.W., *The History of English Law before the Time of Edward I*, 2nd edition, (Cambridge: University Press, 1898)

Redeker, K., von Oertzen, H.J., *Verwaltungsgerichtsordnung,* 12th ed., (Stuttgart, Berlin, Köln: Kohlhammer 1997)

Redlich J.and Hirst F.W., *Local Government in England* (Macmillan, London, 1903),

Richter, I., Schuppert, G.F., *Casebook Verwaltungsrecht*, 2nd edition, (München: C.H. Beck Verlag, 1995)

Rudd, G.R., *The English Legal System* (London: Butterworths, 1962)

Russell, *Judicial Independence in the Age of Democracy: Critical Perspectives from around the world,* (University Press of Virginia: 2001)

Ryan, A., "The British, The Americans, and Rights" in Lacey, M.J. Haakonssen, K. *A Culture of Rights: the Bill of Rights in philosophy, politics, and law – 1791 and 1991*(Cambridge: Woodrow Wilson International Center for Scholars and Cambridge University Press, 1991)

Säuberlich, B.-P., *Legislatives Unrecht und EU-Amtshaftungsanspruch*, (Frankfurt: Peter Lang, 2005)

Scharpf, F., *Die politischen Kosten des Rechtsstaats: Eine vergleichende Studie der deutschen und amerikanischen Verwaltungskontrollen*, (Tűbingen: J.C.B. Mohr (Paul Siebeck) 1970)

Seldon Society, *Select cases in the court of King's Bench under Edward I*, Volume III, (London: Bernard Quaritch 1939)

Schmidt-Assmann, E., Das allgemeine Verwaltungsrecht als Ordnungsidee, Grundlagen und Aufgaben der verwaltungsrechtlichen Systembildung, 2. edition, (Heidelberg: Springer 2006)

Schwartz, B., and Wade, H.W.R., *The Legal Control of Government: administrative law in Britain and the United States* (Oxford: Clarendon Press, 1972)

Schwarze, J., *Das Verwaltungsrecht unter europäischem Einfluß: zur Konvergenz der mitgliedstaatlichen Verwaltungsrechtsordnungen in der Europäischen Union* (Baden-Baden: Nomos, 1996)

Schwarze, J., *European Administrative Law* (London: Sweet & Maxwell, 1992)

Schwerdtfeger, G., *Öffentliches Recht in der Fallbearbeitung*, 10th edition, (München: C.H.Beck Verlag, 1993)

Shapiro, M., *Courts, A comparative and political analysis* (Chicago; London: University of Chicago Press, 1981)

Singh, M., *German Administrative Law* (Berlin, Heidelberg, New York, Tokyo: Springer-Verlag, 1985)

Smith, Bailey, S.H. & Gunn, M.J., on the Modern English Legal System, 4th edition, (London: Sweet & Maxwell, 2002)

Snyder, L. L., *The Weimar Republic,* (Princeton (N.J.): Van Nostrand, 1966)

Starck, C., Rechtsvergleichender Generalbericht, in Bullinger M, *Verwaltungsermessen im modernen Staat, Discretionary power in modern administration,* (Baden-Baden: Nomos, 1986)

Stern, K., *Staatsrecht II*, Band II, (München: C.H. Beck Verlag, 1980)

Stevens, I., *Constitutional and Administrative law* (London: Pitman, 1996)

Stevens, R., *The English Judges*, (London: Hart, 2002)

Stolleis, M., *Geschichte des öffentlichen Rechts, Zweiter Band, Staatsrechtslehre und Verwaltungswissenschaft 1800-1914* (München: C.H.Beck 1992)

Storme, M.(ed.), *Approximation of Judiciary Law in the European Union* (The Storme Report) (Dordrecht; London: Kluwer and Martinus Nijhoff, 1994)

Supperstone, M., Goudie, J., *Judicial Review*, (London: 1991)

The Supreme Court Practice Vol 1, part 1 (London: Sweet & Maxwell 1991)

Thomas, R., *Legitimate Expectations and Proportionality in Administrative Law*, (Oxford: Hart Publishing 2000)

Trimidas, T., Beatson J., *New Directions in European Public Law* (Oxford: Hart Publishing 1998)

Tridimas, T. in Kilpatrick, C., Novitz, T., Skidmore, P. (eds.) *The Future of Remedies in Europe*, (Oxford: University Press, 2000)

Turpin, C., *British government and the Constitution* (London, Edinburgh, Dublin: Butterworths 1999)

Van Caenegem, R.C., *The Birth of the English Legal System* (Cambridge: University Press 1973)

van Gerven, W. in Beatson, J., Tridimas, T., *New Directions in European Public Law,* (Oxford: Hart Publishing 1997)

van Gerven, W., *Cases, Materials and text on National, Supranational and International Tort Law, Scope of Protection, Ius Commune casebooks for the common law of Europe* (Oxford: Hart Publishing, 1998)

van Hoecke, M., *Epistemology and Methodology in Comparative Law*, (Oxford: Hart, 2004)

von Minnigerode, L., *Beitrag zur Beantwortung der Frage: Was ist Justiz- und was ist Administrativezache*? (Darmstadt 1835)

Vile, M. J. C. , *Constitutionalism and the Separation of Powers* (Oxford: Clarendon Press 1967)

von Caemmerer, E., *Das Problem der überholenden Kausalität* (1962)

Wade E.C.S. and Forsyth C.F., *Constitutional and Administrative law* (Oxford: Oxford University Press 1994)

Wade, H.W.R., 8th edition, *Administrative Law* (Oxford: University Press 2000)

Wadham, J., Mountfield, H., Edmundson, A., *Blackstone's guide to the Human Rights Act* 1998, (Oxford: Clarendon Press, 2003)

Walker, P.N., *The Courts of Law* (Newton Abbot: David and Charles 1970)

Wolff, H. J., Bachof, O., Stober, R., *Verwaltungsrecht Band 1*, (München: Beck, 1999)

Wolff, H.J., Bachof, O., Stober, R., *Verwaltungsrecht Band 2*, 6. Aufl., (München: Beck, 1999)

Woolf, H., *Protection of the Public: A New Challenge* (London: Stevens and Sons, 1990)

Wurmnest, W., *Grundzüge eines europäischen Haftungsrechts*, (Tübingen: Mohr Siebeck, 2003)

Zweigert/Kötz, *An Introduction to Comparative Law* (Oxford: Clarendon Press, 1992)

Articles

Allison, J., "The Procedural Reason for Judicial Restraint", (1994) *Public Law*, 452

Armbrüster ,"Braucht Europa ein umfassende Privatrechtskdifikation? Vortragsbericht Juristische Gesellschaft zu Berlin", (1998) *JR*,98

Arthurs, H.W., "Rethinking Administrative Law: A Slightly Dicey Business", (1979) *Osgoode Hall Law Journal*, 1

Bailey, S., "Public authority liability in negligence: the continued search for coherence", Legal Studies, Vol 26 No. 2, June 2006, 155

Basedow, J., "Un droit commun des contrats pour le Marché commun", (1998) *RIDC* ,7

Bell, John, "Reflections on continental European Supreme Courts", *Legal Studies,* (2004) *Legal Studies*, Vol 24 Issue 1 and 2, *Constitutional Innovations: the Creation of a Supreme Court for the UK; Domestic, Comparative and International Reflections, A Special Issue* 157

Birkinshaw, P., "European Integration and United Kingdom Constitutional Law", (1997) *European Public Law*, 57

Bloom-Cooper, L., "Lawyers and Public Administrators: Separate and Unequal" (1984) *Public Law*, 215

Bloom-Cooper, L., "The new Face of Judicial Review: Administrative Changes in Order 53", (1982) *Public Law*, 250

Bonk, H.J., "Strukturelle Änderungen des Verwaltungsverfahrens durch das Genehmigungsverfahrens-Beschleunigungsgesetz" (1997) *NVwZ* 324

Bowen, A.J., "A Terrible Misunderstanding? Osman v UK and the Law of Negligence" (2001) *Scots Law Times* 59

Bringewat, P., "Kommunale Jugendhilfe und strafrechtliche Garantenhaftung, *Neue Juristische Wochenschrift*, 1998, 944

Bundell, D., *Ultra Vires* Legitimate Expectations, [2005], JR 147

Cane, P., "Suing Public Authorities in Tort" 91996) *LQR* 13

Caranta, R., "Judicial Protection against member states: A new *Jus Commune* takes shape" (1995) *C.M.L.R.* 703

Carnwath, R., "Welfare Services-liabilities in tort after the Human Rights Act" (2001) *Public Law* 210

Clark, D.S., "The Selection and Accountability of judges in West Germany: Implementation of a Rechtsstaat", *Southern Californian Law Review*, 1988, 1797

Classen, C.D., "Strukturunterschiede zwischen deutschem und europäischem Verwaltungsrecht" (1995) *NJW* 2457

Classen, C. D., „ Anmerkung zum Urteil des BGH vom 14.12.2000, JZ 2001, 458

Clayton, R., Damage Limitation: The Courts and the Human Rights Act Damages, Public Law 2005, S. 429

Clayton, R., "Damages After Greenfield: Where Are We Now?", *Judicial Review* 2006, 230

Coester-Waltjen, D., ZR: "Europäisierung des Privatrechts" (1998) *Jura* 320

Cornford, T., "The new rules of procedure for Judicial Review" (2000) 5 *Web JCLI*

Craig, P., and Fairgrieve, D., "Barrett, Negligence and Discretionary Powers" (1999) *Public Law* 626

Craig, P., Review Article, "Constitutional Analysis, Constitutional Principle and Judicial Review", (2001) *Public Law*, 763

Craig, P., "The Common law, Reasons and Administrative Justice" (1994) *CLJ*

Deards, E., Brasserie du pecheur: Snatching Defeat form the jaws of victory, EURLR, 1997, 22 (6), 620

de Burca, G., "Proportionality and *Wednesbury* Unreasonableness: The Influence of European Legal Concepts on UK Law" (1997) *European Public Law*, 561

Detterbeck, S. „Staatshaftung wegen der Missachtung von EG-Recht", VerwArch 85 (1994), 159

Ehlers, D., „Die Weiterentwicklung des Staatshaftungsrechts durch das europäische Gemeinschaftsrecht", JZ 1996, 776

Ehlers, D., „Die Europäisierung des Verwaltungsprozessrechts", DVBl, 2004

Eilmansberger, T., *Zur Tragfähigkeit der Staatshaftungskonstruktion des EuGH*, Austr. JIL 52 (1997), 63

Elliot, M., Legitimate Expectation, Consistency and Abuse of Power: The Rashid Case [2005] JR 282

Elliott, M "The Demise of Parliamentary Sovereignty? The Implications for Justifying Judicial Review" (1999) *LQR* 115,

English, R., "The decline and fall of Osman" (2001) *New Law Journal* 973

Fluck, P., "Amtspflichtverletzung durch Staatsanwälte" (2001) *NJW* 202

Fischer, „Die gemeinschaftliche Staatshaftung", JA 2000, 348

Forsyth, C., "Of Fig Leaves and Fairy Tales: The Ultra Vires Doctrine, the Sovereignty of Parliament and Judicial Review" [1996] *CLJ* 122;

Fordham, M., "Reasons - the Third Dimension" (1998) *JR* 158

Fordham, M., "Judicial review: the new rules" (2001) *Public Law* 4

Frankenberg, G., "Remarks on the philosophy and politics of pubic law" (1998) *Legal Studies, 177*

Friedrichsen, G., "Musste Jenny sterben?", *Der Spiegel* 39/1999

Fuller, L.L., "Adjudication and the Rule of Law" (1960) 54 *American society for International Law Proceedings* 1

Fuller, L.L., "The Forms and Limits of Adjudication" (1978) 92 *Harvard Law Review* 353

Galligan, D.J., "The Nature and Function of Policies within Discretionary Power" (1976) *Public Law* 332

Gamerith, H., "Das nationale Privatrecht in der Europäischen Union - Harmonisierung durch Schaffung von Gemeinschaftsprivatrecht", (1997) *ÖJZ* 1997 165

Gearty, C. A., "Unravelling Osman" (2001) *Modern Law Review* 159

Geiger, J., „Die Entwicklung eines europäischen Staatshaftungsrechts", DVBl 1993, 465

Giliker, P., "Osman and police immunity in the English law of torts" (2000) *Legal Studies* 372

Goller, B. and Schmid, A., "Reform of the German Administrative Courts Act" (1998) *European Public Law* 31

Götz, V., "Europarechtliche Vorgaben fur das Verwaltungsprozessrecht" (2002) *DVBl* 1

Griffith, J.A.G., "Judicial Decision-Making in Public Law" (1985) *Public Law* 564

Grimm, D., „Nicht den Parteien, sondern der Verfassung dienstbar", *FAZ* 19.02.2000, Nr 42, p. 11

Gross, T., Terrorbekämpfung und Grundrechte, Zur Operationalisierung des Verhältnismäßigkeitsgrundsatzes, *Kritische Justiz*, 2002, 1

Hale, B., "A Supreme court for the United Kingdom?" (2004) *Legal Studies*, Vol 24 Issue 1 and 2, *Constitutional Innovations: the Creation of a Supreme Court for the UK; Domestic, Comparative and International Reflections, A Special Issue*, p.36

Hannett, S., "Misfeasance in Public Office: the Principles" (2005) *Judicial Review*, 227

Hatje, A., „Die Haftung der Mitgliedstaaten bei Verstößen des Gesetzgebers gegen europäisches Gemeinschaftsrecht, EuR 1997, 297

Hatje, A., "Die Heilung formell rechtswidriger Verwaltungsakte im Prozeß als Mittel der Verfahrensbeschleunigung" (1997) *DÖV* 480

Hedley, S., "Negligence - Vicarious liability of health Authorities - Diagnosis of Dyslexia", (1999) *The Cambridge Law Journal* 270

Henrichs, *Haftung der EG-Mitgliedstaaten fur Verletzung von Gemeinschaftsrecht*, 140

Herdegen, M., Rensmann, T., „Die neuen Konturen der gemeinschaftsrechtlichen Staatshaftung", ZHR (1997), 522

Hickman, T.R., "Between Human Rights and the Rule of Law: Indefinite Detention and the Derogation Model of Constitutionalism," (2005) *MLR*, 655 [668]

Hilson, Chris, "The role of discretion in EC law on non-contractual liability", Common Market Law Review, vol 42, Iss. 3, 677

Himsworth, P., "Things fall apart: the Harmonisation of Community Procedural Protection Revisited" (1997) ELRev, 291

Hinrichs, K., *Evangelische Jugendhilfe*, Kolumne Gesetze und Gerichte, 2004

Hirte, H., LG Berlin: Keine Haftung der Bundesrepublik für Schaden wegen unrichtiger Umsetzung der EG Bilanzrichtline, Anmerkung zu LG Berlin, Urt. v. 9.4.2001 – 23 O 650/00, ZIP 2001, 1639

Hoffmann-Riem, W. (Judge at the Federal Constitutional Court), "Two Hundred Years of *Marbury v Madison*: The Struggle for Judicial Review of Constitutional Questions in the United States and Europe", *German Law Journal* http://www/germanlawjournal.com, Vol 5 No. 6 - 1 June 2004, p. 11.

Holt, M., "Revisiting the Justice/All Souls Report" (2000) *Judicial Review* 56

Ipsen, H.P., von Dannwitz, T., "Verwaltungsrechtliches System und Europäische Integration", (1996) *DVBl* 627

Jarass, H.D., „Haftung fur die Verletzung von EU-Recht durch nationale Organe und Amtsträger", NJW 1994, 881

Jayne, E., "Entwurf eines EU-Übereinkommens über das auf außervertragliche Schuldverhältnisse anzuwendende Recht - Tagung der Europäischen Gruppe für Internationales Privatrecht in Den Haag" (1998) *IPRax* 140

Editorial Comment, "On the way to a European consumer sales law?"(1997) 34 *CMLR* 20

Editorial, European private Law between utopia and Early Reality (1997) 4 *MJ* 1

Jayne, E "Entwurf eines EU-Übereinkommens über das auf außervertragliche Schuldverhältnisse anzuwendende Recht - Tagung der Europäischen Gruppe für Internationales privatrecht in Den Haag (998) *IPRax*

Jowell, J., Lester, A., "Beyond Wednesbury: Substantive principles of Administrative Law" (1987) *Public Law* 368

Jowell, J., "Beyond the Rule of Law, Towards Constitutional Judicial Review" (2000) *Public Law* 671

Jowell, J., 'Is Proportionality an Alien Concept?" (1996) *European Public Law* 401

Jowell, J. "Of Vires and Vacuums: The Constitutional Context of Judicial Review" (1999) *Public Law* 448

Koopman, T., "Comparative Law and the Courts" (1996) 45 *International and Comparative Law Quarterly* 545

Kopp, S., „Staatshaftung wegen Verletzung von Gemeinschaftsrecht", DÖV 1994, 201

Lando , O., "European contract law after the year 2000" (1998) 35 *CMLR* 35 821

Le Sueur, A., "Taking the soft option? The duty to give reasons in the draft Freedom of Information Bill" (1999) *Public Law* 419

Legrand, P., "European Legal Systems are not converging" (1996) *ICLQ* 52

Legrand, P., "Against a European Civil Code" (1997) *MLR* 44

Legrand, P., "How to compare" (1996) *Legal Studies*, 1996

Legrand, P., "The Impossibility of "Legal Transplants" (1997) 4 *Maastricht Journal of European and Comparative Law* 111

Lehman, K.-H., "Helfen ohne Risiko Justiz contra Sozialarbeit, Referat anlässlich der Fachtagung des DBSH Landesverbandes Niedersachsen am 1.6.2000 in der KFH

Leible, S., "Haftung der Bundesrepublik wegen nicht ordnungsgemässer Umsetzung der Publizitätsrichtlinie durch para 335 a HGB", EWS 2001, 563

Le Sueur, A., Cornes, R, "The Future of the United Kingdom's Highest Courts", The Constitution Unit, 2001

Lepsius, O., Liberty, Security, and Terrorism: The Legal Position in Germany, 5 German Law Journal No. 5 (1 May 2004) - Special Edition

Lord Hoffmann, "Human Rights and the House of Lords" (1999) *Modern Law Review* 159

Lorz, A., "Anmerkung zum Urteil des BGH v. 14.12.2000", *JR* 2001, 413

Malleson, K.E., "Creating a Judicial Appointments Commission: Which Model Works Best? *Public Law*, 2004, 102

Maurer, H., "Staatshaftung im europäischen Kontext, Festschrift fur Karlheinz Boujong, 591 (1996)

Malleson, K.E, "Modernising the constitution: completing the unfinished business", *Legal Studies*, Vol 24 Issue 1 and 2, *Constitutional Innovations: the Creation of a Supreme Court for the UK; Domestic, Comparative and International Reflections, A Special Issue*

Martin-Ehlers, A., „Grundlagen einer gemeinschaftsrechtlich entwickelten Staatshaftung", EuR 1996, 376

Meysen, T., " Tod in der Pflegefamilie: Verletzung von Kontrollpflichten im Jugendamt", NJW 2003, 3369

Micklitz, H.-W., "Ein einheitliches Kaufrecht für die Verbraucher in der EG?" (1997) *EuZW* 229

Monti, G., "Osman v UK-Transforming English Negligence Law into French Administrative Law?" (1999) *International and Comparative Law Quarterly* 757

Nettesheim, M., „Gemeinschaftsrechtliche Vorgaben für das deutsche Staatshaftungsrecht", DÖV 1992, 999

Nolte, G., "General Principles of German and European Administrative Law – A Comparison in Historical Perspective" (1994) *Modern Law Review* 191

Nolte, G., Rädler, P., "Judicial Review in Germany" (1996) *European Public Law* 26

Nolte , M., Die Anti-Terro-pakete im Lichte des Verfassungsrechts, Deutsches Verwaltungsblatt, 2002, 573

Nolte, S., "Elternrecht, Rechte des Kindes und Kinderschutz bei Kindesmisshandlung Gegenpole im Spannungsfeld", *Kindesmisshandlung und –Vernachlässigung*, December 2001, 77

Oliver, D., "The Human Rights Act and Public/Private Law Divide" (2000) *EHRLR*, 343

Ossenbühl, F., „Staatshaftung zwischen Europarecht und nationalem Recht", Festschrift für Everling, Band II, 1031, Baden-Baden 1995

Plowden, P., and Kerrigan, K., "Judicial Review –a new test?" (2001) *New Law Journal* 1291

Richardson, G., "The duty to give reasons: potential and practice" (1986) *Public Law* 473

Ruffert, M., "Rights and Remedies in European Community Law: A comparative View", (1997) *CMLR* 307

Rusman, H., http://ruessmann.jura.uni-sb.de/bvr99/Vorlesung/kausalitaet-der-pflichtwidrigkeit.htm

Saenger,I., „Staatshaftung wegen Verletzung europaischen Gemeinschaftsrechts", JuS 1997, 865

Samuel, G., "Comparative Law and Jurisprudence" (1998) *International and Comparative Law Quarterly* 817

Schenke R.P, "Das Nachschieben von Ermessenserwägungen –BVerwGE 106" (2000) *JuS* 231

Schmidt-Assmann, E.,"Das Verwaltungsverfahren und seine Folgen" (1993) *European Review of Public Law* 99

Schmitt-Lermann, H., Der Musterentwurf eines Verwaltungsverfahrensgesetzes (1964) *JZ* 402

Schoch, F., Die Europäisierung des verwaltungsgerichtlichen Rechtsschutzes (1997) *DVBl* 289

Schoch, F., Staatshaftung wegen Verstoßes gegen Europäisches Gemeinschaftsrecht, *Jura*, 2002, 837

Schwarze, J., "Konvergenz im Verwaltungsrecht der EU-Mitgliedstaaten" (1996) *DVBl* 881

Schwarze, J., "Europäische Rahmenbedingungen fur die Verwaltungsgerichtsbarkeit", (2000) *NVwZ* 241

Sendler, H., "Über richterliche Kontrolldichte in Deutschland und anderswo" (1994) *NJW* 1511

Sieckmann, J. R., "Beurteilungsspielräume und richterliche Kontrollkompetenzen" (1997) *DVBl*

Sir Thomas Legg, "Brave New World - Supreme Court and judicial appointments", *Legal Studies*, Vol 24 Issue 1 and 2, *Constitutional Innovations: the Creation of a Supreme Court for the UK; Domestic, Comparative and International Reflections, A Special Issue,* 45

Smith, F., and Woods, L., "Causation in Francovich: The neglected problem" (1997) *International and Comparative Law Quarterly,* 925

Stanton, K.M., "New forms of the tort of breach of statutory duty", LQR 2004, 324

Stevens, R., "Reform in haste and repent at leisure", *Legal Studies*, Vol 24 Issue 1 and 2, *Constitutional Innovations: the Creation of a Supreme Court for the UK; Domestic, Comparative and International Reflections, A Special Issue* 1

Streinz, R., ‚Staatshaftung fur Verletzungen primären Gemeinschaftsrechts durch die Bundesrepublik Deutschland", EuZW 1993, 599

Sydow, G., "Die Revolution von 1848/49: Ursprung der modernen Verwaltungsgerichtsbarkeit" (2001) 92 *Verwaltungs Archiv* 389

"The Convergence Debate", Editorial, (1996) *Maastricht Journal of European and Comparative Law* 105

Takahashi, Y., “Discretion in German Administrative Law: Doctrinal Discourse Revisited” (2000) *European Public Law* 69

Talberg, J., Supranational influence in EU enforcement : the ECJ and the principle of state liability, *Journal of European Public Policy* 7:1 March 2000: 104

Teetzmann, H., “Selbstverwaltung der Justiz; Rechtsvergleichender Überblick'', *Deutsche Richterzeitung*, 2003, 44

Thietz-Bartram, J., „Anmerkungen zu LG Berlin, Beschluss v. 9.4.2001 – 23 O 650/00“, Der Betrieb, Heft 5, 1.2.2002, 258

The right to a fair hearing and summary disposal” (2000) *Civil Justice Quarterly* 341

Thomas, R., “Reason-giving in English and European Community Administrative law” (1997) *EPL* 213

Unterreitmeier, J., Grundrechtsverletzung und Geldentschädingung – kein zwingendes Junktim? DVBl, 2005

van den Bergh, R., “Subsidiarity as an Economic Demarcation Principle and the Emergence of European Private Law” (1998) 5 *MJ* 5 129

van Gerven, W., “Bridging the gap between community and national law: towards a principle of homgeneity in the field of legal remedies”, 32 *C.M.L.R.* 679

van Gerven, W., “Bridging the unbridgeable: Community and National Tort Laws after Francovich and Brasserie” (1996) 45 *International and Comparative Law Quarterly* 507

van Gerven, Walter, Bringing (Private) Laws closer to each other at the European level, January 2005, http://www.law.kuleuven.ac.be/ccle/staff_pub.php

van Gerven, Walter, “Of Rights, Remedies and Procedures”, CMLR 2000, 501

von Dannwitz, T., “Die gemeinschaftsrechtliche Staatshaftung der Mitgliedstaaten” (1997) *DVBl* 1

von Dannwitz, T. VerwARchiv 1993, 73

Voßkuhle, A., Sydow, G., “Die demokratische Legitimation des Richters”, *Juristen Zeitung*, 2002, 673

Wade, W. “Human Rights and the Judiciary” [1998] EHRLRev 520

Wahl, R.. “Das Bundesverfassungsgericht im europäischen und internationalen Umfeld“, *Aus Politik und Zeitgeschichte,* B 37 - 38/2001, 45

Ward, I., “The Limits of Comparativism: Lessons from UK-EC Integration” (1995) *Maastricht Journal of European and Comparative Law* 23

Weber-Grellet, H.W., Judge at the BFH (Federal Finance Court), „Eigenständigkeit und Demokratisierung der Justiz“, *Deutsche Richterzeitung*, 2003, 303

Werner, F., “Verwaltungsrecht als konkretisiertes Verfassungsrecht” (1959) *DVBl* 527

Wittkowski, R.,„ Der "MP Travel Line"- Konkurs im Lichte der Francovich- Rechtsprechung des EuGH, NVwZ 1994, S. 326 ff.

Wong, G., “Towards the Nutcracker principle, Reconsidering the objections to proportionality” (2000) *Public Law* 92

Woodhouse, D., “The constitutional and political implications of a UK Supreme Court, ibid (2004) *Legal Studies*, 134.

Woolf, H., “Public Law-Private Law: Why the Divide? A Personal View” (1986) *Public Law* 220

Zöller, V., Liberty Dies by Inches: German Counter-Terrorism Measures and Human Rights, 5 German Law Journal No. 5 (1 May 2004) - Special Edition

Index

FSC
www.fsc.org
MIX
Papier | Fördert
gute Waldnutzung
FSC® C083411

Kolibri 360 GmbH
Ferdinand-Jühlke-Straße 7
99095 Erfurt, Deutschland
produktsicherheit@kolibri360.de